PITT LATIN AMERICAN SERIES **PLAS**

Cuba Under the
Platt Amendment, 1902–1934

Cuba Under
the Platt Amendment
1902–1934

Louis A. Pérez, Jr.

UNIVERSITY OF PITTSBURGH PRESS

Published by the University of Pittsburgh Press, Pittsburgh, Pa. 15260
Copyright © 1986, University of Pittsburgh Press
All rights reserved
Feffer and Simons, Inc., London
Manufactured in the United States of America

LIBRARY OF CONGRESS CATALOGING-IN-PUBLICATION DATA

Pérez, Louis A., 1943–
  Cuba under the Platt Amendment, 1902–1934.

  (Pitt Latin American series)
  Bibliography: p. 387.
  Includes index.
  1. Cuba—Politics and government—1909–1933.
2. Cuba—Foreign relations—United States. 3. United States—Foreign
relations—Cuba. 4. Cuba. Treaties, etc. United States, 1903
May 22. I. Title. II. Title: Platt Amendment. III. Series.
F1787.P416 1986   972.91′062   85-26451
ISBN 0-8229-3533-3

To my father

Contents

Acknowledgments

This book has been in the making for nearly a decade. For much of this time, it persisted as an idea, a way of approaching some understanding of the complexities of the early Cuban Republic. Many of the propositions that follow, hence, have been a long time in the making. In the course of this time, they have benefited by the research of others. They have benefited, too, from the comments and criticisms of friends and colleagues. Thomas P. Dilkes, Nancy A. Hewitt, Robert P. Ingalls, José Keselman, and Steven F. Lawson read portions or all of early drafts of the manuscript at various stages of the writing. They also listened with patience and forebearance over the years to what on occasion, no doubt, appeared as an incomprehensible preoccupation with some obscure rendering of the Platt Amendment. They know more about the Platt Amendment than they want to. They provided gratifying responses to my musings, often in the most unexpected ways, occasionally under the most improbable circumstances. Sometimes they agreed, sometimes they did not. When they read the book they will know that their advice was not heeded every time. I want to assure them, however, that their suggestions were indeed considered each time. We simply disagree. I am grateful for their disagreement, for it forced me to reconsider my arguments and refine my analysis.

During the research for this book I incurred debts to a number of staffs of libraries and archives. They include the personnel at the Archivo Nacional and the Biblioteca National "José Martí" in Havana; the National

Archives and the Library of Congress in Washington, D.C.; the University of Florida Library, Gainesville, Florida; the Historical Society of Pennsylvania, Philadelphia, Pennsylvania; Alderman Library at the University of Virginia, Charlottesville, Virginia; Western Historical Manuscript Collection at the University of Missouri, Columbia, Missouri; the University of South Carolina Library, Columbia, South Carolina; Robert Frost Library at Amherst College, Amherst, Massachusetts; Sterling Memorial Library at Yale University, New Haven, Connecticut; Franklin D. Roosevelt Library, Hyde Park, New York.

I owe an especially large debt of gratitude to the staff of the University of South Florida Library. In the Inter-Library Loan office I continue to rely on Mary Kay Hartung, Florence Jandreau, and Cheryl Ruppert. In the public documents division, Donna Asbell provided unflagging support.

There is also the staff of the Word Processing Center in the College of Social and Behavioral Sciences at the University of South Florida, about whom enough cannot be said. Without their assistance, this book would still be unfinished. During her last months at the Word Processing Center, Robin L. Kester transformed chaotic first drafts into legible chapters. Her helpfulness and enthusiasm have been missed. Cecile L. Pulin saw the book take final form—or more correctly, she put the book into final form, and for this I cannot overstate my appreciation. Peter Selle and Michael G. Copeland were always ready to assist in the resolution of crises and in the meeting of deadlines of all types. They never disappointed. And to Michael, a special thanks for maintaining an office environment of professionalism with informality and efficiency with congeniality.

I am especially sensible of the support I have received over the years from Peggy Cornett. I have been a beneficiary of her steadfastness and constancy. She has meant a great deal to me over the years. Sylvia Wood has brought effervescence to our workplace environment. She has been a wonderfully delightful officemate, a constant source of support and sustenance.

The sabbatical policy of the University of South Florida provided me with a term off. It was during the fall semester of 1984 that I was able to complete the research and much of the writing of the final draft. I acknowledge with gratitude, too, the receipt of a Research and Creative Scholarship Grant from the Division of Sponsored Research at the University of South Florida. I am particularly appreciative of the continuing support and assistance received from Frank Lucarelli and his staff. They provided under difficult circumstances continuity and stability in the Division of Sponsored Research. The American Philosophical Society provided generous support in 1984, permitting me to complete some important aspects of the final research.

I am most appreciative of the continuing support and constant encouragement from Frederick Hetzel and Catherine Marshall at the University of Pittsburgh Press. They have been wonderful collaborators over the years. I am also grateful to Jane Flanders for her editorial efforts in my behalf.

And lastly—but always first: for Amara and Maya, against whom everything else is measured, and thereby placed in its proper perspective: with love.

University of South Florida
Tampa, Florida
October 1985

Introduction

Hegemony began inconspicuously, perhaps even unnoticed—not entirely unlike the fit of absentmindedness that Macaulay attributed to British imperialism. But, in fact, the U.S. imperial enterprise proceeded more like spasms of purposefulness. Empire came easily to the United States. Establishing U.S. mastery over the Western Hemisphere incurred few risks and encountered less resistance. Certainly during the initial phase of economic penetration and political expansion in the Caribbean, the United States enjoyed privileged access to and virtually undisputed preeminence over its resources and markets.

These were the decades in which the United States proclaimed its interests paramount in the circum-Caribbean, interests to which all other nations were to defer. U.S. investments in the region expanded with minimum competition and a maximum guarantee of protection. The "Roosevelt Corollary" proscribed European warships in Caribbean waters. "Dollar diplomacy" preempted European capital from Caribbean economies.

The exercise of hegemony created an auspicious environment for U.S. investment in the region. Capital carried its own set of imperatives. Investors demanded specific conditions, including access to resources, assurances of protection, and guarantees of profits. Capital demanded, too, a docile working class, a passive peasantry, a compliant bourgeoisie, and a subservient political elite.

It was these objectives to which United States policy was given. And nowhere were they in a more advanced state of development than in Cuba. The defense of the U.S. capital stake became a matter of policy priority, a convenient method of both promoting political hegemony abroad and solving economic problems at home.

Both as a means and an end of hegemony, the defense of capital interests served as the cornerstone of U.S. policy. Local obstacles to investment were eliminated as foreign capital insisted upon freedom of transaction. U.S. capital was invested unconditionally, or not at all. The policies of the host country could not be permitted to restrict either the manipulation of power or the margin of profit. To local government was assigned the responsibility for the well-being of foreign property. And when local government itself threatened U.S. interests through pernicious state policy, or when local authorities proved incapable of protecting foreign property against internal disorders, U.S. intervention followed routinely.

This was the idiom of empire, informal but never casual—the assumptions binding a client state to custodial responsibility for the well-being of foreign interests. But the nature of patron-client relations varied, as did the nature of the U.S. capital stake in the region, and not all Caribbean nations were held uniformly to a common standard of performance. The nature of hegemony in Cuba, as well as the exercise of that power, was always in a state of flux, reflecting changes overtaking the political economy of the United States. But just as certain, adaptions corresponded to changes in Cuban society that were themselves the effects of hegemony. Social structures, political institutions, and economic development were profoundly affected by U.S. hegemony, and necessarily induced policy adjustments to new social realities.

The republic was launched in 1902 amid great fanfare, and under singularly inauspicious circumstances. The process of decolonization was arrested and reversed almost at its inception. The United States' armed intervention in 1898 and subsequent military occupation renewed those elements of the old colonial system of potential use to the new imperial design. During these years, occupied Cuba ceded territory for the establishment of a foreign naval station, acquiesced to limitations of national sovereignty, and authorized future U.S. intervention. These were the conditions of independence, forced on Cuba, appended directly into the Constitution of 1901, and negotiated later into the Permanent Treaty of 1903, loosely known as the Platt Amendment.

The military intervention in 1898 obstructed more than a victory of Cuban arms over the colonial government, however. It arrested Cuban efforts to end the colonial system. The imposition of a vast military presence over the next four years gave renewed life to old colonial relationships. Cuba inaugurated the republic with the task of decolonization incomplete and unfinished. Since Washington effectively guaranteed the survival of colonial status quo in the form of the republic and under the guise of order and stability, continuing efforts to complete the nineteenth-century goal of decolonization placed Cubans on a collision course with the United States.

During the following decades, the Platt Amendment served as the principal instrument of hegemony. Immediately through direct rule during the occupation and subsequently through indirect rule under the Platt Amendment, the United States exercised authority over Cuba not unlike sovereignty. The Platt Amendment was an organic document—evolving and changing as circumstances dictated. It opened Cuba to the expansion of U.S. capital and held the republic to its continued defense. It was a pursuit that required increasingly deeper involvement in Cuban internal affairs, and the amendment served this purpose too. Indeed, in the end there was little in the exercise of hegemony that did not find sanction in the Platt Amendment.

These developments had far-reaching consequences. The exercise of hegemony on this scale for such a sustained period distorted the principal institutions of the republic. Economic relationships, social formations, political culture, and in the end, the very character of the state itself acquired definitive character under the conditions created by imperialism.

Beginning first, and especially, with the armed intervention of 1898 and the military occupation of 1899–1902, and followed by the intervention and occupation of 1906–1909, the willingness of the United States to use superior military force against Cuba cast a long shadow over the republic. Never again did it become necessary to resort to full-scale military occupation, for the threat alone was sufficient to induce Cuban compliance to U.S. demands.

Under the auspices of the Platt Amendment, Washington established formal proprietary authority over the Cuban national system. Little escaped the purview of U.S. intervention. Indeed, so thoroughly had the United States penetrated the social order, that in the end nonintervention served the same purpose as intervention.

But just as inevitably, such an exercise of hegemony created internal contradictions and national tensions. They found expression most frequently in political instability, social conflict, and economic dislocation. In the end, U.S. hegemony contributed powerfully to galvanizing the very forces it sought to contain: nationalism and revolution.

Cuba Under the
Platt Amendment, 1902–1934

1.

Everything in
Transition

I

Everywhere there was war: in the eastern mountains, on the central plains, in the western valleys. It was a chilling panorama. The Cubans were in rebellion again, and this time, everywhere. The war was not going well for Spain in 1896, and slowly a presentiment of disaster settled over the loyalist community in Cuba. Many like planter attorney Raimundo Cabrera saw beyond the colonial rebellion and recognized a Cuban revolution. "Without question," Cabrera wrote to a friend in the United States, "this has not been like the Ten Years War—not in its origins, or in its means, or in its expansion, or much less in its social, political, and economic aspects. Cuba today is revolutionary. . . . Everything is undone and in transition."[1]

This allusion to the Ten Years' War (1868–1878) was altogether fitting, for the forces released by the earlier separatist conflict had totally transformed the colonial political economy. Property relations and production modes were in transition. Social formations were in flux. Commercial ties were changing. So were political loyalties. Even the nature of change changed. The Pact of Zanjón (1878) marked more than the end of the war—it announced the passing of an age. For the million and a half inhabitants of the island, life soon returned to normal, but it would never be the same.

The Ten Years' War marked an era of transition in Cuba. By the following decade, the period of adjustment and adaptation was rapidly coming to an end, and the effects were telling. The war had thoroughly disrupted the colonial economy. Planters who operated before the war on marginal profits, those who lacked either the finances or the foresight to modernize their mills, were among the earliest casualties. Of 41 mills operating around Sancti-Spiritus in Las Villas province in 1861, only 3 survived the war. The 49 mills in Trinidad were reduced to sixteen. In Santa Clara, only 39 of 86 survived. The Cienfuegos mills were reduced from 107 to 77. In Güines, almost two-thirds of the 87 mills operating before the war had disappeared by 1877. In some districts of the eastern provinces the collapse of sugar production was all but total. None of the 24 mills in Bayamo and the 18 mills in Manzanillo survived the war. The 64 mills of Holguín were reduced to 4. Of the 100 *ingenios* operating in the district of Santiago de Cuba in 1868, only 30 resumed operations after Zanjón. In Puerto Príncipe, only one of 100 survived the war.[2]

Planters fortunate enough to escape the ravages of the Ten Years' War survived only to discover capital scarce and credit dear. Prevailing rates of interest fluctuated typically between 12 percent and 18 percent—with 30 percent not at all uncommon—and foreclosed any possibility that local credit transactions would contribute significantly to the economic recovery of post-Zanjón Cuba.[3]

The war and the attending decline of Cuban sugar production set the stage for the next series of calamities. The disruption of Cuban sugar led immediately to a decline of local supply and ultimately an increase in international demand. Everywhere in the world sugar growers expanded production to meet new conditions. After Zanjón Cuban planters faced new adversity, this in the form of expanded competition from new producers and expanded production from old competitors. Not since the end of the eighteenth century, when revolution in Saint-Domingue ended French supremacy over sugar production, was the opportunity for rival producers to extend their share of the world market as great as in the 1870s.

They did not hesitate. In the United States, new varieties of cane were introduced in Louisiana, while experimentation with beet sugar in the West and Southwest expanded under the auspices of state and federal government subsidies. In 1876 cane sugar from Hawaii entered the United States duty-free. Production also expanded in Latin America, most notably in Argentina, Peru, and Mexico. The resettlement of displaced Cuban planters in Santo Domingo contributed to an increase of Dominican sugar exports. But it was in Europe that sugar production recorded its most significant advances. European beet production increased markedly, and during the 1880s, France, Austria, and Germany emerged as the principal sources of sugar for the world market. Beet sugar, accounting in 1853 for only 14 percent of the total world production of sugar, had by 1884 come to represent 53 percent of the international supply. Even metropolitan Spain was not immune to the lure of profits from beet sugar. In 1882, two beet factories commenced operations in Granada and Córdoba; another two opened ten years later in Zaragoza and Aranjuez. Spanish beet production increased from 35,000 tons in 1883 to 400,000 in 1895.[4]

And there was more. Even as Cuban planters prepared to resume production after Zanjón, they discovered that they faced more than new sources of competition and loss of old markets. They confronted, too, an increase in local taxes and a precipitous decline in the value of their principal product. A rise in public spending during the 1870s to finance the cost of the war in Cuba and an increase in the circulation of paper money in the 1880s brought on the first in a series of devastating inflationary spirals. After Zanjón, Madrid transferred the war debt directly to producers and consumers in Cuba. At about the same time, the value of sugar collapsed. In 1884, the price of sugar plummeted from eleven cents a pound to an all-time low of eight. The decline of sugar prices and the imposition of a new series of crushing taxes occurred just as planters were adjusting to the transition from slave labor to wage labor. All at once, the Cuban planter class encountered declining prices, increased taxes, mounting debts, and shrinking markets.

Sugar planters everywhere were in crisis. "Out of the twelve or thirteen hundred planters on the island," the U.S. consul in Havana reported early in 1884, "not a dozen are said to be solvent."[5] Only a year earlier, U.S. Vice-Consul David Vickers reported similar conditions in Matanzas province. Heavy taxes assessed against agriculture and livestock, municipal taxes on land, sales taxes, transportation taxes, duties on imported equipment and food—"everything that the people eat comes from abroad," Vickers noted—threatened the planter class with extinction:

> Through want of frugality and foresight and with enormous taxation, added to the competition of other sugar countries, the planter, to meet all demands, has discounted his crops at such ruinous rates of interest, piling mortgage upon mortgage, that to-day he finds himself irrevocably

involved in debts equal to at least one year's excellent crop and in some instances much more. In the event of a poor crop, he would not have enough money either to pay current expenses or even to commence grinding his cane when the harvest beings, and no one to loan it to him.[6]

Many planters resumed postwar production perched on the brink of disaster, heavily in debt and lacking the resources to renovate their mills. In the past, Cubans had worried about producing large harvests as a hedge against disaster. During the 1880s, they produced good crops, but their markets had dwindled and prices had declined, and disaster struck. The combination of rising taxes, increased operating costs, declining prices, and deepening indebtedness forced many planters into bankruptcy. Property changed hands at accelerating speed. As early as 1883, the U.S. consular agent in Cienfuegos reported that all the mills in his jurisdiction had changed ownership at least once as a result of indebtedness and foreclosures.[7]

Crisis in sugar meant calamity for Cuba. By the mid-1880s, all of Cuba was in the throes of depression. Business houses closed and banks collapsed. Seven of the island's largest trading companies failed. Credit dear after Zanjón was almost nonexistent a decade later. In October 1883 the Bank of Santa Catalina closed. In March 1884 the Caja de Ahorros, the most important savings institution in Havana, suspended payments, ostensibly in response to the suicide of the bank's president. "It is more probable," the North American consul in Havana speculated, "that the Director committed suicide because the bank was unable to meet its engagements."[8] Two weeks later the Caja de Ahorros went into liquidation. In the same month, panic runs on the Banco Industrial and the Banco de Comercio forced both institutions to close. Two months later, the Banco Industrial went into liquidation. The Bank of Santa Catalina was closely linked to agricultural interests, and its failure affected principally sugar planters. The Caja de Ahorros served a much broader clientele, and when it failed small depositors of all kinds, including workers, professionals, merchants, civil servants, and shop owners, faced catastrophe.[9] In the first three months of 1884, business failures totaled over $7 million. "The entire population is reduced . . . to blank despondency and universal ruin," the U.S. consul reported in 1884.[10]

Similar conditions prevailed in the provinces. In March 1884 the prestigious house of Rodríguez in Sagua la Grande and its correspondents in Havana, Miyares and Company, failed. The once opulent city of Trinidad was in an advanced state of decay and destitution. Business houses closed and retail shops were abandoned. The vital rail link to Casilda, the port of Trinidad, ceased operation due to the disrepair of the track.[11] From Santiago a New York correspondent reported: "Failures, extra-judicial arrangements, and the liquidation of commercial houses follow each other in rapid succession."[12] Economic collapse was almost total in Matanzas. The surplus of unsold sugar mounted as prices dropped and markets declined. By 1885, the prevailing price of sugar did not suffice even to defray the cost of local production.[13] Some three hundred estates faced imminent ruin. "Firms are going into bankruptcy every day," Consul Vickers reported from Matanzas in July 1884; "Planters are discharging their laborers and threaten—to save themselves further disaster—to abandon their estates; gold fluctuates two and three and sometimes ten points a day; all credits are denied even to the most substantial and men are wondering how and where they will obtain the means to live; and in many cases relatives are doubling up apartment style to save expenses."[14] A month later, conditions had deteriorated further. Wrote Vickers:

> Every day the situation is becoming more and more serious and the condition of the people more and more sad. All credits are being suspended, laborers are unpaid, plantations being abandoned. . . . House owners are receiving little or no rent. In a word the condition of all classes, rich and poor alike, is most lamentable; and what is worse, there is no hope in the future.[15]

These conditions also affected the colonial treasury. Government revenues diminished and public services declined. Sanitation services periodically ceased. Public works programs were suspended. The city of Havana faced a staggering utility bill of $400,000, and a threat from an impatient Spanish-American Light and Power Company in New York to suspend gas for city street lights unless the debt was speedily and satisfactorily settled.[16]

But more than public services were threatened. Public administration itself was in crisis. The salaries of thousands of public officials fell hopelessly in arrears, with little prospect of relief in sight. "Employees of the government and municipalities have received no pay for months," Consul Vickers wrote from Matanzas. "As a sample, this city is in arrears to the Gas company over $95,000—to the schools about eighteen months, the police nine months. Even the public hospital—which collects a tax of

$2—has been obliged to beg bread from the *bodegas*, and door step to door step."[17] In Havana, the capital press reported the plight of public officials obliged to pawn their furniture in one last desperate effort to stave off destitution.[18]

These were desperate times in Cuba—a period of transition announcing a prelude to transformation. Everywhere in Cuba the cost of living increased, even as wages and salaries decreased. The price of food rose. Rents in Havana and its immediate suburbs increased. So did evictions.[19]

Conditions in post-Zanjón Cuba had especially calamitous consequences for the Cuban working class. Where employment existed, it became increasingly common to pay workers in depreciated script.[20] They were the lucky ones, for unemployment in the cities increased as factories, shops, and business houses closed in rapid succession. In Havana alone, some 20,000 workers were without jobs. In 1885, the once thriving Havana naval yard closed, forcing hundreds of workers out of jobs. The decline of cigar imports in the late 1880s and early 1890s played havoc with one of the major labor-intensive sectors of the Cuban economy. The decline was striking:[21]

	Total Cigar Exports	Cigar Exports to the United States
1889	250,467,000	101,698,560
1890	211,823,000	95,105,760
1891	196,644,000	52,115,600

The repercussions were immediate and far-reaching. Cigar production provided employment for over 100,000 people in all phases of agriculture and manufacturing, the vast majority of whom resided in the two western provinces of Pinar del Río and Havana. The factories alone employed some 50,000 workers. As the amount of cigar exports decreased, the number of cigar factory closings increased. By the early 1890s some 35,000 cigar makers were totally without work, with the balance of workers reduced to part-time employment.[22] Thousands of workers were forced to emigrate in search of employment in the expanding cigar centers in Key West, Tampa, Ocala, and Jacksonville.[23]

These were years, too, of deepening distress in the countryside. Peasant families displaced by the war became destitute during the peace. Not all farmers recovered their land after the war. Property titles were lost, records were destroyed, land claims became confused and contested. In those instances where ownership was clear, the destruction of crops and equipment was so complete and the cost of beginning anew so great that all but the most determined were deterred from returning to the land. By the late 1880s, unemployment reached desperate proportions. Thousands of rural workers migrated to the already overcrowded cities in search of jobs, only to join the swollen ranks of the urban unemployed. An urban underclass was created, made up principally of impoverished rural migrants, in which women entered a marginal labor force as domestics and prostitutes and men became beggars, vagrants, and criminals.[24] Against this generally bleak economic landscape, the abolition of slavery was completed. Tens of thousands of former slaves joined Cuban society as free wage laborers at a time of rising unemployment and decreasing wages.

The disarticulation of the Cuban social structures was total. Hard times arrived in Cuba at the precise moment the post-Zanjón generation of creoles sought places for themselves in the colonial economy. But there was little work. The collapse of sugar production had catastrophic results; Cuba was in depression. Between 1862 and 1882, the island lost some two-thirds of the value of the total wealth:[25]

	Agricultural and Urban Property	Industry, Commerce, and the Professions
1862	$ 55,072,545	$ 77,384,649
1877	39,656,717	17,388,125
1882	36,386,685	12,075,467

The contraction of commerce, the collapse of banks, and the closing of factories were only the most visible expressions of desperate conditions. Jobs were few and competition fierce. The Cuban economy could not absorb the growing ranks of the creole petty bourgeoisie. Countless numbers of Cuban professionals, including attorneys, physicians, pharmacists, engineers, educators, and writers, were forced to emigrate, engendering in many a mixture of anguish and anger against the colonial system that failed to accommodate the growing needs of Cubans. A generation of expatriated creoles became socially disenfranchised, economically displaced—and politically disgruntled.

Nor could the state bureaucracy relieve unemployment pressures.

These were hard times in Spain, too, and of political necessity, public administration in Cuba served as a source of relief for economic distress in the metropolis. These were also years of remarkable growth in the Spanish population, which rose from 9.3 million in 1768 to 18.6 million in 1900.[26] Spaniards emigrated to Cuba in vast numbers. Cuba late in the nineteenth century remained very much of what it was early in the sixteenth century: a place where the destitute and dispossessed of Spain could start over. Public office and political appointments in Cuba were little more than colonial extensions of the patronage system in Spain. The rise of one government ministry in Spain announced the arrival of thousands of new office seekers and the departure of countless others, a vast turnover of personnel from which Cubans were largely excluded. Even the appointments of lottery ticket vendors were reserved for retired Spanish military pensioners.[27]

But *peninsulares* monopolized more than public positions. They also dominated private property. Spaniards controlled trade and commerce, banking and finance, industry and manufacturing. They owned and managed the factories and the farms, they were retail shopkeepers and wholesale merchants as well as the moneylenders and land brokers.[28] Spaniards were preponderant in the professions and trades as artisans and apprentices, in the offices as clerks, and in the fields as day laborers. Most of all, they controlled the jobs. And whether by formal contract or informal consensus, Spaniards preferred to hire Spaniards, a private practice that coincided with public policy.[29] Spain actively encouraged immigration to Cuba as a comparatively convenient and cost-effective method through which to reduce the size of a socially unstable population at home and increase the number of loyalists in Cuba's politically unreliable population. It offered, too, a way of maintaining the "racial equilibrium," guaranteeing a white majority in a racially restive colony.[30]

Beginning in 1886, Madrid subsidized the cost of travel for all Spaniards seeking employment in Cuba. And they arrived in shipload after shipload. In the decades after Zanjón, 250,000 Spaniards emigrated to Cuba.[31] And these were different Spaniards. The new immigrants were from the north, mostly from Galicia and Asturias, destitute, often desperate, but strong-willed and determined to make it. They worked hard and long, often for little and always for less. It was a labor market in which Cubans could not compete. *Peninsular* employers extended an avuncular patronage to their countrymen, giving rise among Cubans to the derisive sobriquet of *sobrinismo*, the practice, quite literally, of uncles in Cuba employing nephews from Spain.

Times in post-Zanjón Cuba were difficult for everyone, but for Cubans especially. There seemed to be no place for Cubans in Cuba. For the peasantry as well as members of the professions and the proletariat, Spanish administration was incapable of discharging the central clause of the colonial social contract: the opportunity for livelihood. Cubans seemed in danger of becoming a superfluous population, unemployable and expendable, outcasts in the society they claimed as their own. They faced exclusion and, ultimately, expatriation. And indeed emigration was one dramatic expression of the crisis in colonial Cuba in the late nineteenth century. Cubans "either live as outcasts in the land of their birth," lamented one Cuban emigre, "or they wander, like a people damned, over distant lands, spending their energies in foreign countries." [32] During the last third of the nineteenth century, some 100,000 Cubans of all occupations and professions, of all ages, from all classes and races, emigrated—to Europe, to Latin America, to the United States. [33]

II

No sector of Cuban society escaped the depression unaffected, and even property and privilege offered an insufficient hedge against destitution. Indeed, the disintegration of the Cuban social order began at the top. The Ten Years' War witnessed the dismemberment of the creole bourgeoisie, especially that sector of the eastern planter class that had enrolled in the ill-starred separatist cause. This was a portent of things to come. Planters suspected of separatist sympathies paid dearly for subversive sentiments. Through a series of punitive expropriation decrees, Cuban property was confiscated and subsequently auctioned to finance the war. Cubans lost property estimated at 16 million pesos. [34] The landed elites of Oriente and Camagüey, including the sugar interests of Carlos Manuel de Céspedes, Pedro Figueredo, Francisco Vicente Aguilera, Jaime Santiesteban, as well as cattle interests of Bartolomé Masó, Donato Marmol, Ignacio Agramonte, and Joaquín Morales, failed to survive the combined effects of Spanish expropriations and wartime destruction. [35]

Indeed, the creole bourgeoisie across the island was in crisis. Planters survived the crisis of the 1880s, but only at the cost of their traditional supremacy over production. The price of solvency was displacement and ultimately dependency. Cuba's efforts to recover its former primacy announced the reorganization of the production system and restructuring of property relations. A new stage of capitalist organization was about to transform sugar production, and with it all of Cuba. It would be a recovery from which planters in increasing numbers would be excluded.

Changes in organization and ownership proceeded apace during the late 1880s and early 1890s. Greater efficiency was needed to market sugar profitably under existing conditions of international competition and prevailing world prices. Production strategies shifted from increasing the number of sugar mills to increasing the production capacities of existing *centrales*. New credit, fresh capital, and new ownership, originating principally in the United States, enabled the industry to recover. Improved varieties of cane, innovations in manufacturing techniques, and technological and industrial advances became generally available by the 1880s and enabled producers in Cuba to respond aggressively to new conditions. New machinery to extract maximum sugar from cane and grind the increased volume of harvested cane efficiently was introduced. New vacuum pans and centrifugal equipment were installed to distill and crystallize more sugar from improved strains of cane. In the 1880s the Bessemer steel process made the rapid expansion of railways possible. The effects were immediate, as networks of privately owned railroads contributed to expanding the zones of sugar cultivation and increasing production.

These were fateful developments. The modernization of sugar production was beyond the capital reserves and credit resources of local planters. Many came out of the war indebted and impoverished, and conditions did not improve in peace. The cost of converting to new machinery alone was well over a quarter of a million dollars.[36] Additional expenditures required for the development of railway systems, the expansion of storage facilities, and the acquisition of additional land severely limited Cuban participation in the reorganization.

The shift in production strategies led to sharper divisions between field and factory. Planters unable to meet the growing capital requirements necessary for the revival of sugar production abandoned the industrial end of production altogether and devoted themselves exclusively to agriculture. The prevailing system whereby the grower milled his own cane gave way to a new specialization of operations and ownership; increasingly the mill owner concentrated on the manufacturing of sugar and the farmer *(colono)* tended to the cultivation of cane.

Across the island the Cuban grip over production slipped, announcing the demise of the planter bourgeoisie. These conditions invited foreign capital, first by way of secured loans to planters in distress, and later in the form of direct ownership through foreclosures. Many planters survived, principally as *colonos,* but it was a survival that transformed entirely the character of the creole bourgeoisie. Others did not survive at all. The displacement of the planter bourgeoisie in the area of Cienfuegos was suggestive of the developments occurring everywhere in Cuba. In 1884 E. Atkins and Company foreclosed on the Juan Sarria family estate "Soledad." Atkins subsequently acquired the "Carlota" plantation from the de la Torriente family, the "Caledonia" estate from the heirs of Diego Julián Sánchez, "Guabairo" from Manuel Blanco, "Limones" from the Vilá family, "Brazo" from the Torre family. From the declining Iznaga family Atkins acquired "Vega Vieja" and "Manaca" and obtained a long-term lease on "Algoba." The "Santa Teresa" estate was purchased from Juan Pérez Galdós and "Veguitas" from José Porrua. From the Barrallaza family Atkins secured the "Vacquería" estate and the "San Augustín" estate, formerly owned by the Tomás Terry family. The "Rosario" estate, owned by the Sarrias, was later attached to "Soledad." The Atkins interests also secured long-term leases on several other estates, including "San José," "Viamones," and "San Esteban." During these years, the interests of Perkins and Walsh in New York acquired control of "Constancia," at the time the largest sugar estate in the world. The "Hormiguero" estate, owned by Ponvert family of Boston, expanded its holdings at the expense of the smaller properties of insolvent Cuban planters.[37]

The position of the Cuban planters grew increasingly precarious. The creole bourgeoisie who survived exchanged titles of property for ownership of stocks in U.S. corporations and relinquished positions as landowners for places on corporate boards of directors. They were transformed into administrators and lived off incomes, not rents. Planters would henceforth function as agents of North American capital, instruments of U.S. economic penetration of Cuba, and advocates of U.S. intervention. Their well-being depended increasingly on the success foreign capital enjoyed in extending control over property and production.

The transfer of property, further, was accompanied by a transformation of nationality. Through the latter half of the nineteenth century, planters in growing numbers found it convenient to acquire U.S. citizenship. Naturalization offered a hedge against local instability and a means through which to defend privilege and property. It entitled planters to call for protection from the U.S. government when Spanish colonial authorities demonstrated inefficiency or indifference to the needs of local property interests. Equally important, as U.S. citizens, planters were in a position to request reparation and receive indemnification for property losses stemming from political disorders. A new habit developed in Cuba, a practice to endure into the twentieth century, in which the local bourgeoisie, able to petition the United States in its behalf in disputes with local authority, looked to Washington for the defense of privilege and property. These developments served, further, to internationalize Cuban politics and, in still another fashion, gave the United States entree into the island's internal affairs. In the closing decades of the nineteenth century, as the beleaguered bourgeoisie sought to adjust changing conditions, the transfer of planter nationality placed the object of planter allegiance above national interests and located the sources of planter patronage outside the island.[38]

These developments were products and portents of shifting colonial relationships. In one decade, the Cuban economy revived with U.S. capital and began to rely on U.S. imports and markets. By the late 1880s, 94 percent of Cuban sugar exports found their way to the United States.[39] The center of Cuban political authority was no longer the source of economic security. The colonial political economy would never be the same. The implications of those contradictions passed virtually unnoticed during years of peace and prosperity. For the time being, planters could congratulate themselves on their success in having achieved the best of both worlds.

III

Planters wanted more, however. The Ten Years' War heightened the planters' demands for increased political participation. For the better part of a decade, the island had been subjected to the ravages of two opposing armies, neither of which inspired confidence among planters. Not that the planters were neutral—they were not. They viewed the separatist cause with a mixture of dismay and dread. They opposed independence, fearful that separation from Spain would lead to political instability and social strife, and that both would result in economic ruin.

However, the creole bourgeoisie derived less than complete comfort from the victory of Spanish arms. Colonial administration, at least traditional colonial administration, had few defenders among the Cuban elite.

They needed little reminding that it was the combined follies and failures of Spanish policy that had plunged the island into the abyss of civil strife in the first place. Spain had administered Cuba as an overseas colony, primarily through the *peninsular* officeholding caste, principally for the benefit of *peninsular* needs. In Cuba there had been little significant or sustained political activity. Administration prevailed in the place of politics. If problems were recognized, changes were made for—not by—the island population; attempts to resolve Cuban questions came from above and abroad. Outside of an occasional and short-lived armed protest, a general consensus had supported this arrangement—until the Ten Years' War.

Certainly planters welcomed the end of the colonial insurrection in 1878. But they welcomed more the opportunity to step into the colonial breach and assert leadership over the shattered polity. The moment was right. The Pact of Zanjón served as a summons to the planter class and its local allies. Neither revolution nor reaction seemed capable of resolving colonial grievances. The peace created conditions for a third alternative—reform, not separation from Spain. Not that planters were immune from the appeals of *cubanidad,* and indeed, some believed that it could be fulfilled through an independent nationality. Most, however, believed that it could be best achieved within existing structures of empire.

The creole bourgeoisie had a second purpose in its pursuit of public office. Planters sought political power as a means to promote their economic interests and social status. They recognized the necessity of participating in the formulation of tax policies, currency and fiscal plans, and commercial programs—all of which affected them vitally.

In this sense, the Cuban planter class had arrived at a point similar to the position of the creole petty bourgeoisie. Both demanded wider participation in local government, but more than participation, public positions and political power. The social reality of the two sectors of Cuban creoles determined the course of this pursuit. Planters rich enough to mount a political challenge to Spanish exclusivism over local affairs chose collaboration with colonialism and reformist politics. Members of the creole petty bourgeoisie lacking the resources to compete with Spaniards chose opposition to colonialism and revolutionary politics.

Thus the first political party to organize in Cuba after Zanjón represented planter interests. Established in 1878, the new Liberal (Autonomist) party committed itself to the pursuit of reform within existing colonial relationships. Autonomists rejected outright the means and objectives of armed separatism. They advocated home rule, representation in the Spanish parliament, and free trade. They also endorsed the legitimacy of the colonial regime and the primacy of empire as the central and unchallenged tenets of colonial politics. For Autonomists, reforms were the best guarantee of empire, and empire was the best guarantee against revolution.[40]

In a larger sense, Autonomists, anxious to steer a course between the uninspired policies of Spain and the uncertain prospects of nationhood, pursued power as the means with which to defend property and privilege. This was the creole elite, drawn to colonial politics to obtain colonial reforms as a means to obviate colonial revolution; this was the creole oligarchy, the possessors of the land who placed their considerable wealth and prestige at the service of reformist politics.

But the formation of the Autonomist party did not announce the emergence of a new colonial consensus. Nor did it signal the triumph of planter hegemony. On the contrary, it deepened old divisions in the colony, and created new ones. The resident Spanish population reacted to the new party with revulsion. They were ill disposed to acquiesce to a program of reform that involved granting in peace concessions denied in war. Indeed, for *peninsulares* victory over rebellious Cubans in 1878 signified vindication of Spanish sovereignty, putting to an end any further need to compromise traditional colonial prerogatives. The Autonomist party aroused fear among Spaniards that the extralegal dispute of the previous decade had found a spurious if not sinister legality in postwar Cuba. The party was always suspect, perceived as little more than a legal political fiction behind which lurked the malevolent force of Cuban separatism.

An unequivocal *peninsular* response to autonomism was not long in coming. In late 1878, the conservative reaction to liberal reforms produced the second postwar political party—the Partido Unión Constitucional. Unabashedly pro-Spanish in its sympathies, overwhelmingly *peninsular* in its composition, it attracted to its ranks the most intransigent advocates of *Cuba española:* merchants, manufacturers, industrialists, and financiers—all devoted to the regeneration of Spanish dominance in Cuba.

The challenge to the planter bid for hegemony was not limited to Spaniards. Opposition also originated from Cuban separatists who rejected Autonomist means as much as they repudiated Unión Constitucional ends. Separatists held that reconciliation with Spain on any basis other than independence was unacceptable, and independence had to be won by force. In 1892, the revolutionary movement was transformed into the Cuban Revolutionary party (PRC), pledged to renewed commitment to the liberation of Cuba through armed struggle.[41]

Subsumed into the post-Zanjón political struggle was a conflict of a different sort: competition for power between the planter class—identified with reform and colonialism—and the emerging populist coalition consisting of petty-bourgeois elements, the impoverished gentry, an expatriate proletariat, blacks, and peasants, identified with revolution and independence. Planters adhered to colonialism as a means of political hegemony; separatists aspired to independence as a means of political power—which meant that two obstacles stood in the way of independence: *peninsulares* and planters.

IV

Autonomists enjoyed mixed success in the years following Zanjón. The vaunted prospects for political reform in the 1870s became the vanquished promises of the 1890s. The inauspicious achievements of two decades of political labor strained the faith of even the most devoted Autonomists. *Peninsulares* continued to prevail at the polls and dominated politics. They were preponderant in the Cuban delegation to the Spanish parliament. They were in the majority in colonial government, provincial posts, and municipal administration, as well as in the military and in the clergy. They dominated the administration of justice—they were the presidents of *audiencias*, judges and magistrates, prosecutors and solicitors, court clerks and judicial scribes. Their power in the electorate was well out of proportion to their numbers. Some 80 percent of the *peninsular* population were qualified to vote, compared to only 24 percent of the Cuban population. Electoral rolls favored *peninsulares* and discriminated against Cubans.[42] The town of Güines counted a population of 13,000 inhabitants, 500 of whom were Spaniards. The electoral census included 400 Spaniards and 32 Cubans.

The results were predictable, and surprised no one. The Güines municipal council did not include a single Cuban member. Of the thirty-seven *ayuntamientos* in the province of Havana, Spaniards held a majority in thirty-one. Of the thirty-two aldermen in the Havana *ayuntamiento*, twenty-nine were Spaniards. Three-quarters of all mayors across the island were *peninsulares*.[43] After two decades of political competition and loyal opposition, the Autonomist party had failed to achieve even its mini-

mal goal—that of becoming a power contender. Spaniards clung tenaciously to public administration and political office. It was this intransigence that gave rise first to misgivings within the creole bourgeoisie,
and later to the frightful realization that perhaps Spaniards were determined to retain control at all costs. "Cubans are driven from local
administration as if they resided in a foreign land," complained the Autonomist newspaper *El País* in January 1890. "The policy of the past is
the one that dominates at present—the dismal policy of intransigence
and exclusivism. . . . The *peninsulares* still enjoy the irritating privileges
of the old regime, as well as those obtained by the subversion of the new
one. They have lost nothing; in everything they have gained. The country, on the other hand, finds itself impoverished and mocked."[44]

The planter bid for political leadership in the colony after Zanjón had
failed. Worse than this, it had situated the creole bourgeoisie directly in
the cross fire of the contentious extremes of the colonial polity, a middle
position that earned Autonomists the suspicion of the loyalists and the
scorn of the separatists. It was a position that reflected accurately the
anomalous social reality of the planter class, dependent upon U.S. markets for prosperity but relying on the Spanish military for security. It was
a position, too, of immense vulnerability, one that had neither the support
of the leadership of the colonial body politic nor the following of the colonial body social.

In the post-Zanjón euphoria, planters as a class, possessed of social
status and economic resources, representing principally local landed interests, had challenged the historic *peninsular* monopoly over public
office. They had believed that autonomism would lead at once to collective economic expansion through freer trade arrangements and to individual mobility through the liberalization of colonial politics, and that
both would eliminate the source of future colonial instability.

But the prospects had been overdrawn. Autonomists had not fared well
in colonial politics. Not because, they insisted, they lacked public support
and popular following, but as a result of official intimidation and political
fraud. Suffrage manipulation, ballot stuffing, and certification frauds
were only the most blatant of the abuses routinely practiced by Spanish
authorities in Cuba. Autonomist leaders were harassed; the provincial
Autonomist press was periodically suspended. In 1891, the party withdrew from local elections to protest official indifference to formal charges
of fraud.[45] Three years later the provincial Autonomist committee of Santiago de Cuba dissolved in protest of Spanish policy.

The failure of Autonomist politics signified fundamentally a failure of both the reformist creole bid for political ascendancy and the bourgeois bid for hegemony. After almost two decades, the Cuban planter class had failed to develop enough political strength either to establish itself as a power contender or to protect local property interests. Their faith in the colonial system remained unrequited. The effects of misplaced faith did more than shake Autonomist devotion to the colonial order—an impiety that was, in any case, without immediate consequences. In the end, Autonomists could not abandon colonialism without visiting enormous grief on themselves—and this they were not willing to do. Moreover, by seeking to establish hegemony over the colonial polity within the framework of empire, planters lost the opportunity to pursue dominance over the larger constituency forming around the ideal of nationhood. For Spanish loyalists, planter attempts to reform imperial structures were evidence of subversion, and always suspect; for Cuban separatists, planter attempts at reform were a sign of servility, and always suspect. Worse still, in the mid-1890s the economy was in crisis, and discontent was everywhere on the increase. And a revolution was about to begin.

V

The year 1895 began under the pall of despair and impending depression; the economy faltered and political discontent increased. These were difficult times for Autonomists. Traditional allegiances were shaken. The planter class occupied a nether world where friends and foes appeared to have exchanged identities, a condition complicated by increasingly unrealizable expectations of both protection from Spain and profits from the United States. Planters in the past loyal to Spain now questioned the assumptions of their allegiance and the continued efficacy of colonialism: it was not clear if it was a beneficent Spain that lacked the vitality to control the colonial system or if it was a negligent Spain that lacked the volition to defend colonial subjects. Whatever the source, it bode ill for the property interests and social standing of the creole elite.

These were idle musings, for in 1895 planters were spared the agony of a painful decision. The outbreak of a new separatist war in February forced the disgruntled bourgeoisie to return instinctively to the metropolitan fold. It was again time to choose sides, proclaim faith, and give testimony. Not that the planters' sudden reconciliation with the colonial regime in February 1895 signaled conformity with colonial policies. Rather, the separatist alternative was wholly unacceptable. Whatever doubts may have sapped elite morale, whatever grievances may have weakened elite loyalties, planters were neither so desperate nor so reckless as to confuse the separatist cause with their own. In 1895, planters had nowhere to go but back.

They went back, but not entirely without conditions. Certainly they pronounced their adhesion to Spain. In April 1895, the Autonomist party dutifully issued a manifesto to the nation denouncing the insurrection as "criminal," urging Cubans in arms to seek a peaceful resolution of their grievances.[46] At the same time, however, Autonomists seized the latest colonial crisis to press for reforms. The colonial insurrection, they argued, was the result of Spanish misgovernment. Spain would either have to concede reforms or confront a revolution that would end Spanish rule.[47]

And for a brief moment, it actually seemed as if Autonomist arguments had prevailed. The appointment of Arsenio Martínez Campos as governor general in April 1895 served to renew flagging Autonomist hopes for a negotiated political settlement. No one was committed more to reconciliation through reform than Martínez Campos. It was this well-known commitment that contributed to prolonging Autonomist faith in reform as the salvation of the colony—a fateful prolongation, for as the war expanded, the planter class became increasingly isolated between the embattled extremes of the colonial polity, and vulnerable to attacks from both.

In the spring of 1895, however, reform seemed wholly plausible. The rebellion remained confined to the eastern third of the island, still very much a provincial affair. But reforms would have to originate in Spain, and they would not come easy. In fact, they did not come at all. Spanish authorities refused to concede colonial reforms as long as Cubans remained in arms, and Cubans refused to relinquish their arms for reforms that did not end colonialism.

In the meantime, during the autumn months, the unthinkable occurred: insurgent armies marched into the western valleys. The presence of separatist armies in the west, coincident with preparations for the 1896 harvest, stunned the loyalist community. In ten months, the insurrection had dramatically outgrown its provincial dimensions and reached regions never before disturbed by the armed stirrings of nationalism. By early 1896 insurgent forces operated in every province. The prospects for the 1896 harvest were bleak—and when it was finally completed, even the pessimists were shown to have been overconfident: from a record million-ton crop in 1894, the harvest fell to 225,000 tons in 1896. Not since the

1840s had Cuban sugar production been so low. And in 1897 it dropped to 212,000 tons. The effects were disastrous. Trade and commerce declined, retail sales collapsed, unemployment increased.

The presence of insurgent forces in the west signaled more than the failure of Spanish military policy. In a very real sense, it announced the insolvency of Autonomist politics. Not a few rushed to fix responsibility for Spanish reversals on those officials, principally Martínez Campos, who had subordinated military operations to political solutions. But more than the governor general suffered ignominy. Upon Autonomists generally fell the full weight of *peninsular* ire. The politics of reaction acquired a new appeal and a new urgency. *Peninsular* patience with reform and reformers had expired, and now they demanded a turn at ending the colonial conflict.

In early 1896, public attention turned to Spain's General Valeriano Weyler. A veteran campaigner known for parsimony of language, he outlined his approach: "I believe that war should be answered with war."[48] Indeed, he plunged the island deeply into war—totally, without quarter. Reinforcements increased the size of the Spanish army to 200,000 officers and men. New military units were organized with troops recruited locally. In early 1896, the war expanded as Weyler mounted new operations against Cuban forces in the western provinces. In the same year, Weyler undertook the final measure of his "war with war" policy—a decree ordering the concentration of the rural population in fortified towns.[49]

But there was more to come. Weyler arrived in Cuba with two purposes: first, of course, to end the Cuban conflict by military means. Second, and no less important, to restore the colonial consensus by political methods. Weyler's appointment signaled the ascendancy of the intransigent *peninsular* population, loyalists who had never discerned a substantive difference between autonomism and separatism. Both were perceived as enemies of Spain, distinguished only by the means they employed to subvert metropolitan authority.

Weyler's reputation preceded him, and news of his appointment immediately precipitated a new wave of emigration. In February 1896, in the space of one month, some 1,300 Cubans left for the United States. In the first two months of Weyler's government, another 2,000 families emigrated to Europe.[50]

Cuban misgivings were not unfounded. Under Weyler, Autonomists were all but formally banished from political forums on the island. The rigor with which Weyler pursued separatists in the field was surpassed only by the relentlessness with which he persecuted Autonomists in the cities. Political harassment previously sporadic and local became systematic across the island. Public criticism of government policies was banned. Spanish civil and military authorities everywhere attacked Autonomists at every opportunity. Autonomist political meetings were banned and party newspapers suspended. Party members were arrested, beaten, and routinely subjected to house searches.

This was calculated terrorism directed against the creole elite that claimed hundreds of victims. Waves of arrests resulted in the imprisonment and deportation of thousands of Cubans suspected of insufficient ardor for Spanish policy, the majority of whom were Autonomists. Within days of Weyler's arrival, provincial authorities made some fifty arrests in Pinar del Río. By July, the U.S. consul general reported 720 political prisoners in Havana alone.[51] In the small Matanzas city of Jovellanos, some 600 people fled after a wave of government arrests led to the imprisonment of forty people in two days. Hundreds of Cubans were summarily deported to Spain to serve prison terms in *peninsular* jails. Others were sent to Spain's African penal colonies in Ceuta, Chafarinas, and Fernando Poo. In December 1896, several hundred political prisoners disembarked in Cádiz; this particular group included landowners, businessmen, lawyers, and former provincial public officials.[52] Gilson Willets, an American traveling through Cuba in 1896, noted: "Every ten days or so crowds of handcuffed men are driven through the streets of Havana, which they will never tread again, on their way to the transport ships which will convey them to penal settlements on the African coast. Many of these men represent the elite of Cuban society." In all, Willets estimated, some 10,000 prominent citizens "had been shipped to overseas penal colonies."[53]

For decades Autonomists had struggled against the abuses of colonialism rather than the system itself. By the end of 1896 they were in disarray and despair. Their debut in politics had been inglorious. The island's propertied elite had failed in its quest for political power. More than this, it faced political extinction from the very authorities upon which it had traditionally relied upon for survival. But in 1896, the planter class acquired a new and much more formidable adversary: Cuban separatism.

VI

During the last quarter of the nineteenth century, uprisings in the name of Cuba Libre had become as commonplace as they were ill starred. After the Ten Years' War, the call to arms was heard recurrently across the island. "La Guerra Chiquita" of 1879 was an armed affair of only months. Another rebellion in 1883 ended in disaster. So, too, did one two years later. Another abortive effort in 1892 lasted only days. In 1893, two rebellions were launched within three months of each other, and both failed just as quickly.

But 1895 was different. Certainly one difference was planning. This was a war three years in preparation, and in 1895 Cubans were prepared. It was different, too, because Cubans were organized and united. A broad coalition had formed under the auspices of the PRC, sustained during times of enormous adversity by an indissoluble commitment to a sentiment that by the late nineteenth century had fully assumed the proportions of a revolutionary metaphysics.

But neither preparation nor organization, however vital to the success of Cuban arms, was the decisive difference in 1895. The difference was found in the ideological content of separatist thought and the social origins of separatist leadership. Cuba had changed between the "Grito de Yara" in 1868 and the "Grito de Baire" in 1895, and in the intervening years Cuban grievances no longer came exclusively from the rule of a distant European power. By the late nineteenth century, Spain was neither the principal beneficiary nor the primary benefactor of colonialism. Inequity in Cuba in 1895 had a peculiarly home-grown quality. These internal and social sources of oppression gave armed separatism definitive shape during the 1880s and 1890s. Armed separatism was committed to more than independence. Its vision of a free Cuba had a social imperative.

Not that these notions were entirely new; they had always been vague elements of nineteenth-century separatist politics. What was different in 1895 was the recognition that inequity was not caused principally by Spanish political rule, but was the effect of the Cuban social system, for which the transformation of Cuban society was the only remedy. Cubans continued to speak of independence, but political separatism had expanded into revolutionary populism, committed as much to ending colonial relationships within the colony as to ending colonial connections with Spain.

The political conflict between bourgeois reformism and populist separatism involved more than competition for hegemony. It turned on the social purpose to which political power would be put. For the reformist political party, power offered the means to defend property and protect privilege; for the populist revolutionary party, power promised social justice, economic freedom, and democracy. And it became quickly evident that the creole bourgeoisie was just as much an enemy of Cuba Libre as the *peninsular* officeholder.

The vision of Cuba Libre remained admittedly ambiguous. Cubans spoke more to aspiration than action, promise rather than program. The separatist leadership identified the problems and committed the future republic to their resolution. But these vague commitments established the ideological premises of the separatist cause, the articles of faith around which Cubans gathered to make history. The many sources of Cuban discontent, social, economic, political, racial, historic, converged into a radical movement of enormous force dedicated to the establishment of a new nation and a new society.[54]

It was not only that the social content of separatist ideology was different; a new constituency had come together around Cuba Libre: the politically and socially dispossessed, the economically destitute—Cubans for whom armed struggle offered the means through which to redress historic grievances against the colonial regime and its local defenders. Displaced professionals, impoverished planters, an expatriate proletariat, a dispossessed peasantry, poor blacks and whites in and out of Cuba responded to the summons to arms. The difference between the Ten Years' War and the war of 1895, army chief Máximo Gómez proclaimed, was that the former originated from "the top down, that is why it failed; this one surges from the bottom up, that is why it will triumph."[55] In sharp contrast to the patrician origins of separatist leadership during the Ten Years' War, separatist leaders in 1895 consisted principally of men of modest social origins. Many came from the ranks of the disgruntled and displaced creole petty bourgeoisie, representatives of the liberal professions including José Ramón Villalón and Mario G. Menocal (engineers), Adolfo de Aragón and Leandro González Alcorta (teachers), Fermín Valdés Domínguez, Eusebio Hernández, Emilio Núñez, Pedro E. Betancourt, Leopoldo Figueroa, Joaquín Castillo Duany, Nicolás Alberdi, Eugenio Sánchez Agramonte, Santiago García Cañizares, Francisco Domínguez Roldán, Cosme de la Torriente, Juan Bruno Zayas (physicians), and Rafael Portuondo y Tamayo, Manuel Sanguily, Fernando Freyre de Andrade, Juan Manuel Menocal, Domingo Méndez Capote, Aurelio Hevia, and Severo Pina (attorneys). Many army officers came from working-class backgrounds, such as Antonio Pardo Suárez and Juan Delgado (cigar workers). Others originated from the burgher ranks—shopkeepers, merchants, and traders, men like José Tarafa and Calixto García. Some officers came from formerly comfortable families, once prosperous landowners who had fallen on hard times, victims of confiscation and expropriation: Adolfo Castillo, Salvador Cisneros, Lope Recio Loynaz, Bartolomé Masó, José Lacret Morlot, and Oscar Primelles. Some interrupted their schooling to join the patriotic cause, while others did so immediately upon completion of their studies: Carlos Mendieta, Gerardo Machado, José Miró y Argenter, Rafael Montalvo, and José Miguel Gómez. Many were men of color who occupied command positions in the Liberation Army: Antonio and José Maceo, Alfonso Goulet, Jesús Rabí, Pedro Díaz, Félix Ruen, Flor Crombet, Agustín Cebreco, Quintín Banderas, Juan Vega, Guillermo Moncada, Jesús González Planas, Silverio Sánchez Figueras, Juan Eligio, and Vidal Ducasse. Indeed, some 40 percent of the senior commissioned ranks of the Liberation Army was made up of men of color. Others moved into key positions in the PRC and the provisional government, including Juan Gualberto Gómez, Martín Morúa Delgado, Rafael Serra, Santiago Pérez Zúñiga, Enrique Medín Arango, José León Quesada, and Juan Bonilla.[56] In sum: these were Cubans for whom the old regime was as much a social anathema as it was a political anachronism. They had committed themselves to a movement that promised not only to free them from the old oppression but also to give them a new place in society, a new government they would control, and a new nation to belong to.

VII

The advance of insurgent armies into central and western Cuba in 1896 set the stage for more than a military confrontation with Spanish forces. It announced, too, an assault against the economic sources of bourgeois prominence. The invasion of the west brought insurgent Cubans face to face with the local allies of colonialism. After January 1896, Cubans found themselves in position of toppling the twin pillars of the colonial system: the Spanish army and the Cuban planter class.

Until 1896, the conflict was primarily a struggle between the colony and Spain over competing claims of sovereignty over Cuba. After 1896, the conflict expanded into a struggle between the creole bourgeoisie and the populist coalition over competing claims of hegemony within the colony. The defeat of the politico-military power of Spain required, too, the destruction of the socioeconomic power of the bourgeoisie, the only other power contender in Cuba capable of rivaling the separatist bid for political supremacy. To take power, the social amalgam that had formed around armed separatism used the war of liberation both to expel Spain from Cuba and extinguish the creole bourgeoisie. The revolt was now transformed into revolution, and the enemy was as much the creole as the colonial bureaucrat. The insurrection was now "an economic war," insurgent Colonel Fermín Valdés Domínguez wrote in his diary, "against capital and production."[57]

This was the defined purpose of Cuban arms. As early as July 1895, General Máximo Gómez proclaimed a moratorium on all economic activity—commerce, manufacturing, agriculture, ranching, but most of all sugar production: no planting, no harvesting, no grinding, no marketing. Any estate found in violation of the ban, Gómez vowed, would be destroyed and its owner tried for treason. "All sugar plantations will be destroyed, the standing cane set fire and the factory buildings and railroads destroyed," the decree warned. "Any worker assisting the operation of the sugar factories will be considered an enemy of his country . . . and will be executed."[58]

The Cuban moratorium against sugar production threatened the planter class with ruin. To ignore the insurgents' ban was to risk the destruction of property, and after 1896, with Cuban army units operating fully across the breadth of the island, it was a risk not to be undertaken lightly.[59] But the suspension of production also threatened calamity. Planters had traditionally borrowed against future crops at prevailing world prices, and years of accumulated indebtedness found the planter class operating with little margin for mishap. In those circumstances where planters tottered at the brink of bankruptcy from harvest to harvest, the loss of a single year's crop promised catastrophe.

But there was a deeper meaning to the Cuban method. The suspension of production as a device of war also set the stage for the redistribution of property as a design for peace, and both gave decisive expression to the social content of armed separatism. The question of property relations was of central importance in separatist thought. Cuba Libre committed itself to a nation of small landowners, each farmer to enjoy security derived from direct and independent ownership of land.[60] More than an opportunity to end colonial rule, the war created the occasion to destroy one social class and create another. In a sweeping land reform decree in July 1896, the insurgent leadership committed the revolution to a new regimen of landownership. Exhorting Cuban military forces to "burn and destroy all forms of property" as "rapidly as possible everywhere in Cuba," the army command pledged:

All lands acquired by the Cuban Republic either by conquest or confiscation, except what is employed for governmental purposes, shall be
divided among the defenders of the Cuban Republic against Spain, and
each shall receive a portion corresponding to the services rendered, as
shall be provided by the first Cuban Congress, after Cuban Independence has been recognized by Spain, and this shall be given to each in
addition to cash compensation for all services previously rendered, and
as a special bounty and reward. . . . All lands, money, or property in any
and all forms previously belonging to Spain, to its allies, abettors or sympathizers, or to any person or corporation acting in the interest of Spain
or in any manner disloyal to the Cuban Republic are hereby confiscated,
for the benefit of the Cuban Army and of all the defenders of the Cuban
Republic.[61]

VIII

The Cuban planter class held few illusions after 1896. Spain was
losing the war. In any case, the price of Spanish redemption was slowly
exceeding the cost of the Cuban revolution. Sugar production approached
collapse. Trade and commerce ceased. The reconcentration policy had all
but totally disrupted agriculture. Taxes increased, and prices on basic
foodstuffs soared. After almost two years, planters were suffering as
much at the hands of their Spanish allies as they were from their Cuban
adversaries. On one hand, they faced extinction as a political force by the
policies of reaction directed by Spanish loyalists. On the other, they faced
extinction as a social class by the program of revolution directed by
Cuban separatists.

For the better part of the nineteenth century, the planter class had endured the injustice of colonial rule as the best guarantee against the un-
certainties of self-rule. Whatever liabilities attended colonialism, none,
planters understood correctly, could offset the guarantees of property,
prosperity, and privilege. The creole bourgeoisie preferred security to
change, and was not disposed to risk social predominance for political independence. If in time of war the creole elite looked to Spain to uphold
privilege, in times of peace they looked to the United States to underwrite
prosperity. Under more or less normal conditions, the apparent contradiction of the Cuban political economy in the nineteenth century posed little
difficulty for them, for whatever else planters may have been, they were
pragmatic. Their impatience with Spanish economic policies in 1894 was

eclipsed by their fear of Cuban social revolution in 1895. And after 1896, they did not doubt for a moment that the revolution posed as much threat to their economic interests as it did to the political authority of Spain. Caught between political reaction from above and social revolution from below, the beleaguered bourgeoisie contemplated its impending extinction with deepening desperation. They needed help, and quickly. Planters were now predisposed to sacrifice traditional colonial relationships as the price necessary to prevent the loss of privilege and property. A social class faced revolution and extinction. They were prepared to shed old colonial loyalties for new ones, provided of course they could guarantee their interests.

Planters turned to the nation where they had found markets, and the government to which many had—precisely for such an occasion—pledged allegiance. Convinced that Spanish rule in Cuba was doomed, they sought an alternative regime, one that would protect them from the rising tide of colonial revolution. In June 1896, more than one hundred planters, attorneys, and manufacturers appealed to the United States for intervention and annexation.[62] A year later, as the Cuban insurgent command prepared for final military operations against Spanish armed forces, planters in Cienfuegos petitioned the United States to establish a protectorate over Cuba.[63] From Santiago, the U.S. consul reported a similar mood: "Property holders, without distinction of nationality, and with but few exceptions, strongly desire annexation, having but little hope of a stable government under either of the contending forces."[64]

2.

The Imperial
Transfer

I

The Cuban revolution threatened more than the propriety of colonial rule or property relations. It challenged, too, pretensions of colonial
replacement. For the better part of the nineteenth century, the United
States had pursued the acquisition of Cuba with purposeful resolve, if
only with partial results. The United States had early pronounced its
claim to imperial succession in the Caribbean; acquisition of Cuba was
envisaged always as an act of colonial continuity, legitimately ceded by
Spain to the United States—a legal assumption of sovereignty over a territorial possession presumed incapable of a separate nationhood. But in
ending Spanish sovereignty in 1898, Cubans also endangered the U.S.
claim of sovereignty. That possession of Cuba had eluded U.S. efforts had
neither diminished North American determination nor deterred North
American designs. But the Cuban challenge to Spanish rule had ominous
implications for the seers of union in the United States. In 1898 Cuba
was lost to Spain, and if Washington did not act, it would be lost also to
the United States.

In April 1898 President William McKinley requested of Congress authority to intervene militarily in Cuba. War ostensibly against Spain, but
in fact against Cubans—war, in any case, as an alternative medium of
political exchange, just as Clausewitz posited.

The president's war message provided portents of U.S. policy: no mention of Cuban independence, not a hint of sympathy with Cuba Libre,

nowhere even an allusion to the renunciation of territorial aggrandize-ment—only a request for congressional authorization "to take measures to secure a full and final termination of hostilities between the Govern-ment of Spain and the people of Cuba, and to secure in the island the establishment of a stable government, capable of maintaining order and observing its international obligations." The U.S. purpose in Cuba, McKinley explained, consisted of a "forcible intervention . . . as a neutral to stop the war."[1] "Neutral intervention" offered a means through which to establish, by virtue of military conquest, U.S. claims of sovereignty over Cuba. Forcible intervention, McKinley announced to Congress on April 11, "involves . . . hostile constraint upon both the parties to the con-test."[2] War was directed against both Spaniards and Cubans, the means to establish the grounds upon which to neutralize the two competing claims of sovereignty and establish by superior force of arms a third.

McKinley's message did not pass unchallenged. Administration op-ponents in Congress made repeated attempts to secure recognition of Cuban independence, and by mid-April, McKinley grudgingly accepted a compromise. Congress agreed to forego recognition of independence in exchange for the president's acceptance of a disclaimer. Article 4 of the congressional resolution, the Teller Amendment, specified that the United States "hereby disclaims any disposition of intention to exercise sover-eignty, jurisdiction, or control over said island except for pacification thereof, and asserts its determination, when that is accomplished, to leave the government and control of the island to its people."[3] And the United States proceeded to war.

II

The intervention changed everything. A Cuban war of liberation was transformed into a North American war of conquest. The United States first laid claim to victory, from which so much else would flow. There was design in these developments. The intervention and related events would provide the basis upon which the United States would es-tablish its claim of sovereignty over Cuba. The Cubans seemed to have achieved little in their own behalf, the North Americans concluded. The palpably few decisive battles in the war and the apparent absence of note-worthy insurgent military achievements were attributed immediately to the deficiency of Cuban operations, if not of Cuban character. These im-pressions encouraged the belief that Cubans had accomplished nothing in more than three years of war and that U.S. arms alone determined the outcome.

Minimizing the Cuban role in the defeat of Spain, the United States could play the role of liberator. This was a popular war for a popular cause, and enthusiasm to liberate Cuba led easily, and not unnaturally, to the exaggerated credit that North Americans would take for their part in the defeat of Spain—nothing more sinister than celebration of a popular mission accomplished.

But there was a darker side to these pronouncements. The United States wanted more than credit. That Cubans appeared to have vanished from the campaign altogether served immediately to minimize their participation in final operations against Spain, and ultimately justified excluding Cubans altogether from the peace negotiations. In appropriating credit for the military triumph over Spain, the United States established claim to negotiate peace terms unilaterally; in appropriating responsibility for ending Spanish colonial government, the United States claimed the right to supervise Cuban national government.

So it was that the Cuban war for national liberation became the "Spanish-American War," a name that in more than symbolic terms denied Cuban participation, and announced the next series of developments. This construct legitimized the United States' claim over Cuba as a spoil of victory. The Cuban struggle was portrayed as an effort that by 1898 had stalled, if not altogether failed. The United States completed the task the Cubans had started but were incapable of completing alone. The proposition was established early and advanced vigorously. Cubans were told of their indebtedness to the United States, from whose expenditure of lives, treasury, and resources Cuba had achieved independence from Spain. Cubans were denied more than victory—they were deprived of their claim to sovereignty.

III

The military occupation began on January 1, 1899, and after nearly a century of covetous preoccupation with the island, the United States assumed formal possession of Cuba. But it was not an unqualified possession. Certainly the Teller Amendment obstructed direct fulfillment of the nineteenth-century design—annexation. But the obstacle to permanent acquisition was neither primarily nor principally the congressional resolution. A far more formidable challenge appeared in the form of *independentismo*. Three decades of revolutionary activity between 1868 and 1898 had involved two generations of Cubans in three major wars and had consecrated the cause of independence. It was not a sentiment to be trifled with. The principal challenge to U.S. hegemony lay in the wartime populist coalition. The United States realized that it was necessary to eliminate the Cuban challenge to North American hegemony directly and devitalize a nationalist movement of enormous popular vitality and political vigor.

The *independentista* ideal persisted through the early period of the occupation and never lost its appeal. Much effort was devoted to discrediting both. Cuban motives for independence were suspect, almost as if opposition to the presence of the United States was itself evidence that self-serving if not sinister motives lurked behind separatist strivings. Cubans were not inspired by love of liberty but by the lure of looting. "From the highest officer to the lowliest 'soldier,'" one North American wrote, "they were there for personal gain."[4] The Cuban desire for independence, North Americans concluded, was motivated by a desire to plunder and exact reprisals. One observer reported that Cubans were possessed by the "sole active desire to murder and pillage."[5] "If we are to save Cuba," a New York journalist exhorted, "we must hold it. If we leave it to the Cubans, we give it over to a reign of terror—to the machete and the torch, to insurrection and assassination."[6]

The North Americans drew a number of inferences from this proposition. First, Cubans were not prepared for self-government. Again and again they struck the same theme. The ideological imperative of empire took hold early and deeply. The consensus was striking. Admiral William T. Sampson, a member of the U.S. evacuation commission, insisted that Cubans had no idea of self-government—and "it will take a long time to teach them."[7] Some officials believed Cubans incapable of self-government at any time. "Self-government!" General William R. Shafter protested. "Why those people are no more fit for self-government than gunpowder is for hell."[8] General Samuel B. M. Young concluded after the war that the "insurgents are a lot of degenerates, absolutely devoid of honor or gratitude. They are no more capable of self-government than the savages of Africa."[9] For Major Alexander Brodie, the necessity for a protectorate, or outright annexation, was self-evident: "The Cubans are utterly irresponsible, partly savage, and have no idea of what good government means."[10] A similar note was struck by Major George M. Barbour, the U.S. sanitary commissioner in Santiago de Cuba. The Cubans, he insisted, "are stupid, given to lying and doing all things in the wrong way. . . . Under our supervision, and with firm and honest care for the future, the people of Cuba may become a useful race and a credit to the world; but to attempt to set them afloat as a nation, during this generation, would be a great mistake."[11] General William Ludlow, military governor of Havana, concurred: "The present generation will, in my judgment, have to pass away before the Cubans can form a stable government."[12] In mid-1899, Governor-General John R. Brooke agreed: "These people cannot *now*, or I believe in the immediate future, be entrusted with their own government."[13] In mid-1899 Leonard Wood, as military governor of Santiago, declared, "The mass of the people are ignorant. . . . As yet they are not fit for self-government."[14] One year later, as governor-general of the island, he reiterated his conviction that Cubans were "not ready for self-government." "We are going ahead as fast as we can," he informed the White House, "but we are dealing with a race that has steadily been going down for a hundred years and into which we have to infuse new life, new principles and new methods of doing things."[15]

The attempt to discredit independence was surpassed only by the effort to deprecate its advocates. Only the "ignorant masses," the "unruly rabble," and "trouble makers"—in Wood's words, "the element absolutely without any conception of its responsibilities or duties as citizens"— advocated independence. "The only people who are howling for [self-government] are those whose antecedents and actions demonstrate the impossibility of self-government at present."[16]

The social origins of *independentismo*, and especially the prominence of Afro-Cubans in separatist ranks, raised suspicions of a different sort. "The negroes," one American noted, " who number at least one third, and possibly one half of the population, are said to belong to the party which clamors for independence."[17] Governor General Brooke reported in mid-1899 that "the lower, or negro, element is talking about matters in such way as it places it in opposition to annexation and in favor of independence."[18] In central Cuba, Lieutenant A. P. Berry reported the existence of three general political groupings in Matanzas. The annexationists represented Spaniards, Americans, and "many of the better educated Cubans." A second group, consisting of "the better class" of Cubans, favored a republican form of government under a U.S. protectorate. "The Independents," Berry concluded, "wanting a government republican and democratic in form and entirely independent of the United States, . . . is made up of the turbulent, the ignorant and the negroes and is the largest party."[19]

IV

But the purpose of the intervention was to foreclose more than the rise of a new political force; it was also to forestall the fall of an old social system—the latter if only as a means to the former. The propertied elite greeted U.S. intervention as nothing less than a providential deliverance from expropriation and extinction. And for this they were grateful. But *independentismo* was a spectre that would not go away. The colonial elite recognized the immense vulnerability of their position. They had historically entrusted their fate and fortunes to a colonial government now discredited and defeated—more important, one no longer able to discharge its traditional responsibility for the defense of property and privilege. Certainly the U.S. intervention had the immediate effect of keeping at bay the social forces released by the revolution. But those forces were still there. The survival of the propertied elite depended now on the continued presence of the United States, and they were willing to go a long way to accommodate that presence.

As early as July 1898, a delegation of businessmen in Santiago met with the General William R. Shafter to learn if the United States planned to retain control of Cuba. If not, the merchants indicated, they would liquidate their assets and return to Spain. Shafter wrote to Washington, "I have assured them that I did not believe the United States was going to relinquish [its] hold on Santiago or leave it without a stable and sufficient garrison and suitable government."[20] Several weeks later, a delegation of seven of the most prominent merchants of Santiago asked for assurances of a continuation of U.S. rule before committing millions of dollars to replenishing inventories. "Unless these men are assured of protection," the *New York Tribune* correspondent learned, "they will take no steps in this direction."[21] In Havana, Nicolás Rivero, editor of the conservative daily *Diario de la Marina,* delivered a petition signed by several hundred planters, appealing directly to McKinley for the annexation of Cuba.[22] Another group of property owners appealed to the United States for protection against independence: "The conservative element of Cuba, composed of property owners, holders of mortgages, etc., require to be assured in the most emphatic manner that they have due protection, from whatever

Government that may be established on the island. At present they think themselves on the verge of a precipice and all their hopes of salvation are fixed on the United States."[23] The Marquis de Apezteguía, the head of the *Partido Unión Constitucional,* insisted that in ending Spanish rule, the United States had assumed a "moral duty" to guarantee order and stability in Cuba. And the first and necessary step in this direction was the "destruction beforehand of all insurgent or insurrection elements."[24] "The insurgent independent party (wishing to be rid of American control)," Edwin F. Atkins wrote to McKinley in early 1899, "represent no property interest as a class, and their control of affairs is equally feared by Cuban property-holders, Spaniards, and foreigners."[25]

But the ideal of independence persisted, and the appeal of those Cubans who opposed Spanish rule and defended national sovereignty was irresistible. Most North Americans in Cuba conceded, if only in private, that a majority of Cubans were devoted to the ideal of independence.[26] But numbers alone, they were quick to counter, could not be permitted to determine the fate of Cuba—particularly when the sentiment of the majority was identified with disruption and disorder. That Cubans in large numbers opposed annexation was cause enough to discredit independence sentiment. If there were people who opposed U.S. rule, they were probably led by wicked men, or knew no better. In either case, opposition to the United States from this source served only to confirm the Cubans' incapacity for self-government. Over time, the North Americans insisted, under U.S. protection and patronage, the call for annexation would rise above the clamor for independence. There existed in Cuba a yet unrevealed majority, silent in its preference but steadfast in its desire for annexation. "The real voice of the people of Cuba," Leonard Wood reassured the White House in late 1899, "has not been heard because they have not spoken and, unless I am entirely mistaken, when they do speak there will be many more voices for annexation than there is at present any idea of."[27]

In the meantime, if the United States found no support in the anti-annexation majority, it derived some consolation in the quality of the proannexation minority. The "better classes," the propertied, the educated, the white—those sectors, in short, most deserving of North American solicitude—were desirous of close and permanent ties with the United States. There was, certainly, "much plausibility," correspondent Herbert P. Williams learned during his travels in Cuba, that the large majority of the "half-barbarous rabble in a vote would request us to leave the island." It was "probably true," too, that "the Cubans who want us to go outnumber those who want us to stay." But mere numbers were inconsequential. Conceding that the United States "ought not go into the business of government without the consent of the governed," Williams nevertheless concluded: "The point is that if all, or nearly all, the people whose convictions deserve respect are on one side, mere numbers should not be allowed to decide the matter."[28]

However, as U.S. officials knew only too well, "mere numbers" would indeed decide the matter, and in popular elections, "quantity" would prevail over "quality." The establishment of a Cuban government organized around political competition created an obvious dilemma. An electoral system based on popular suffrage threatened to overwhelm the "better classes," and all but guaranteed the triumph of the representatives of the revolutionary polity. These were considerations very much on the mind of Governor General John R. Brooke in 1899. A stable form of government, he feared, did not seem to be "practicable in the early future." Those who would "naturally be the leaders" had not yet fully developed either the support for electoral supremacy or the skill for political success: "They are few and could not expect to cope in an election with the 'Liberating Army' leaders, who are clamorous for places for which they manifested no capacity during the war, and have demonstrated by their acts since their utter incapacity for any leadership which would benefit the people."[29] A year later, Leonard Wood warned that liberal suffrage posed a "menace to Cuba" and would result in "serious alarm among [the] better classes."[30] There was a feeling of "genuine alarm among the educated classes," Wood explained, "lest the absolutely illiterate element be allowed to dominate the political situation." Such a development "would be fatal to the interests of Cuba and would destroy the standing and influence of our government among all thinking intelligent people in the island. . . . Giving the ballot to this element means a second edition of Haiti and Santo-Domingo in the near future."[31] General William Ludlow agreed. "To give universal suffrage to such a people," he predicted in an address to the New York Chamber of Commerce, "would be to swamp the better class. We might just as well retire and let it drift to Hayti No. 2."[32]

The generally bleak prospects for the electoral success of the elite had direct implications for the United States. A political challenge to the representatives of the "better classes" was no less a threat to U.S. policy, for it was upon bourgeois political ascendancy that North American hopes for hegemony rested. The United States early detected in the shattered ranks of the colonial bourgeoisie its natural allies. Both opposed Cuban independence. Both opposed Cuban government. Policymakers needed supporters, property owners needed security. The United States searched for a substitute for independence, the bourgeoisie sought a substitute for colonialism. The logic of collaboration was compelling and politically opportune. The old colonial elite in need of protection and new colonial rulers in need of allies arrived at an understanding. There was more than bluster to General William R. Shafter's startling pronouncement in late 1898: "As I view it, we have taken Spain's war upon ourselves."[33]

In rescuing the beleaguered bourgeoisie from colonial revolution, the United States obtained the services of a dependent client class, an ally willing to serve as an instrument of hegemony, if only as a means of its own survival. U.S. efforts during the occupation centered on enrolling the propertied elite as the front-line political surrogate in opposition to *independentismo*. This strategy served also to institutionalize U.S. hegemony at the point of maximum effectiveness—from within Cuba. It mattered slightly less if Cuba were independent if that independence was under the auspices of a client political elite whose own social salvation was dependent on U.S. hegemony.

But few believed the propertied elite capable of competing successfully with the separatist representatives under liberal suffrage. *Independentismo* remained an enormously popular sentiment, conferring creditability on any candidate originating from its ranks. The "better classes" could not hope to compete against candidates with *independentista* antecedents unless there were significant suffrage restrictions. One way to foreclose the rise of the "unruly masses" and to enhance the political fortunes of the "better classes" was to prevent the insurgent leadership from mobilizing the vast political force committed to *independentismo*— to exclude the "rabble" from the electorate.

In early 1900 the United States undertook a census of the island before fixing final suffrage requirements for municipal elections scheduled for June. The decision to restrict suffrage had already been made in Washington. Secretary of War Elihu Root predicted confidently that restricted suffrage would exclude the "mass of ignorant and incompetent," promote "a conservative and thoughtful control of Cuba by Cubans," and "avoid the kind of control which leads to perpetual revolutions of Central America and other West India islands." Opposition to restriction, like support of independence, was immediately suspect. "I think it is fair," Root suggested, "that the proposed limitation is approved by the best, and opposed only by the worst or the most thoughtless of the Cuban people."[34] And in this, Root was supported by Wood: "Almost all the educated people are in favor of restricted suffrage."[35]

In Cuba, Wood anticipated opposition to this decision. It was not only that universal manhood suffrage had been centrally important in the separatist program. More immediately, a literacy requirement threatened to disenfranchise the vast majority of army veterans. And even Wood recognized the folly of seeking to exclude from voter rolls the tens of thousands of Cubans who had served the cause of Cuba Libre in arms. Wood originally had proposed a "soldier clause," waiving the literacy requirement for officers and noncommissioned officers.[36] But this, too, he recognized, was still inadequate. In the end, the "soldier clause" was expanded to include all army veterans, as a means of removing, in Wood's words, "the only elements which would be dangerous."[37]

Final suffrage requirements balanced immediate political obligations with long-term policy objectives. Voters for the June 1900 municipal elections were required to be Cuban-born males or sons of Cuban parents born while in temporary residence abroad or Spaniards who had renounced their citizenship. All voting males were to be twenty-one years of age, free of felony conviction, and residents of the municipality in which they intended to vote at least thirty days preceding the first day of registration. In addition, voters were required either to be able to read and write, or to own real or personal property worth $250, or to have served honorably in the Liberation Army prior to July 18, 1898.[38]

The results were telling. By Root's calculations, there were 315,000 Cuban males over the age of twenty-one—188,000 whites and 127,000 blacks—and some 50,000 Spanish males over twenty-one entitled to Cuban citizenship. Two-thirds of all adult Cuban males were excluded from the franchise. Suffrage restrictions reduced the electorate to some 105,000 males and reduced the electorate to some 5 percent of the total population.[39]

But this was still not enough. In the municipal elections of 1900, the National party, representing the revolutionary sector, prevailed. The victorious Cubans were not slow to bring the moral of the elections to the attention of U.S. authorities. "The Cuban National Party," an exultant General Alejandro Rodríguez taunted McKinley, "victorious in the election, salutes the worthy representative of the North American Nation, and confidently awaits an early execution of the Joint Resolution."[40]

The municipal elections dealt a serious setback to U.S. efforts to promote bourgeois political ascendency. Wood had labored diligently in behalf of conservative candidates, seeking to forge the "better classes" into a political coalition capable of competing successfully with the "extreme and revolutionary element." He consulted "all classes," he explained to Root in February 1900, "the Spanish and the conservative elements; property holders as well as foreigners" to promote a conservative consensus. "I am preaching but one policy, and that is for all people to get together and unite for good government."[41] He gave private encouragement to conservative candidates, repeatedly reassuring them of U.S. support while seeking to neutralize the opposition.[42] "Of course," Wood acknowledged, "the usual opposition party will gradually develop, but I shall endeavor to give them as slender a foundation as possible to stand on."[43]

No sooner had the municipal elections passed when preparation for new ballotting for a constituent assembly began. This time Wood participated more actively in behalf of the "better classes." He plunged himself into the thick of late summer politics with the zeal of a candidate himself seeking elected office. In August, he undertook an arduous tour of the island to campaign for the election of the "better classes." He cabled Root on August 13, "I leave tonight for a trip around the east end of the Island for . . . the purpose of telling the leaders of all parties that they must not trifle with this Constitutional Convention and that if they send a lot of political jumping-jacks as delegates they must not expect that their work will be received very seriously."[44] In Santiago de Cuba, Wood publicly appealed for the election of the "best men":

> I beg you as a personal favor to me and the United States Government to sink your political differences and passions and to send men to the convention who are renowned for honor and capacity, so that the convention may mean more than the Cubans even now anticipate. Again, I say send the best men. The work before your representatives is largely legal work. . . . For the present party considerations must be suspended for the sake of the greater end in view. . . . Bear in mind that no constitution which does not provide for a stable government will be accepted by the United States. I wish to avoid making Cuba into a second Haiti.[45]

In Puerto Príncipe, Wood warned Camagüeyans that if Cubans elected delegates who failed to provide for stability and order, the United States would not withdraw its military forces.[46] From Cienfuegos, he could report confidently that the "better class of men [were] coming to the front daily for candidates to the convention."[47] In a final preelection report to the White House, Wood detailed the achievements of his travels around the island. "I have seen most of the prominent men using every effort to have them send the best and ablest men to the Constitutional Convention without consideration to political parties. Some of the men nominated are excellent, others are bad. I hope, however, that the latter will be defeated." Nevertheless, he struck a note of caution and appealed to McKinley to proceed slowly with plans for evacuation "until we see what class are coming to the front for the offices called for under the Constitution."[48] A week before the election, an optimistic Wood predicted that "a very good class of men" appeared "to be coming to the front in most provinces. . . . On the whole, I think we will come out fairly successful."[49]

V

Again the United States was rebuffed. "I regret to inform you," a disheartened Wood wrote Senator Orville H. Platt in December 1900, "that the dominant party in the convention to-day contains probably the worst political element in the Island and they will bear careful watching." He continued:

> The men whom I had hoped to see take leadership have been forced into the background by the absolutely irresponsible and unreliable element. . . . There are a number of excellent men in the Convention; there are also some of the most unprincipled rascals who walk the Island. The only fear in Cuba to-day is not that we shall stay, but that we shall leave too soon. The elements desiring our immediate departure are the men whose only capacity will be demonstrated as a capacity for destroying all hopes for the future.

And he made his point: "I do not mean to say that the people are not capable of good government; but I do mean to say, and emphasize it, that the class to whom we must look for the stable government in Cuba are not as yet sufficiently well represented to give us that security and confidence which we desire."[50]

Wood shared his despair with the Secretary of War Root: "I am disappointed in the composition of the convention." The responsibility of framing a new constitution had fallen to some of the "worst agitators and political radicals in Cuba." Wood questioned again the wisdom of proceeding with plans for evacuation. "None of the more intelligent men claim that the people are yet ready for self-government," Wood wrote plaintively.[51] "In case we withdraw," the convention represented "the

class to whom Cuba would have to be turned over . . . for the highly intelligent Cubans of the land owning, industrial and commercial classes are
not in politics."[52] Two-thirds of the convention delegates were "adventurers pure and simple," not "representatives of Cuba" and "not safe leaders."[53] "These men are all rascal and political adventurers whose object is
to loot the Island."[54] In his desperation he alluded to the unthinkable: repudiation of the Joint Resolution. "You can be assured," he wrote to Root,
"that the real interests and the real people of Cuba will support any reasonable demands, and if the rascals in the Convention who are attempt-
ing to make trouble succeed even to a small extent they will, before the
world, absolve us from any reference to the [Teller] resolution." He reiterated: "I do not contemplate anything of this sort, but it is better to have it
than to destroy the island by surrendering it . . . to the class of people
whom I have always characterized as unprincipled and irresponsible."[55]
In March 1901, Wood was blunt: "To abandon this country to the control
of the element now very largely influencing the Convention . . . would,
in my opinion, destroy all immediate hopes for the future advancement
and development of the Island and its people."[56]

VI

By late 1900 the United States faced the unsettling prospect of
evacuation without having established the internal structures of hegemony. Time was running out, and so were justifications for continued military occupation. An anomalous situation arose. By 1900, the United
States found itself in possession of an island that it could neither fully
retain nor completely release. The restraint against the former was a condition of the intervention; the rationale against the latter was a cause of
the occupation. By 1900, too, the United States confronted the imminent
ascendancy of the very political coalition that the intervention had been
designed to obstruct. If the United States could not establish hegemony
from within, it would impose dominance from without.

The exercise in the democratic process in Cuba served to underscore
for the United States the perils attending independence. By failing to
elect the candidates approved by the United States, Cubans had demonstrated themselves ill suited to the responsibility of self-government.
Cubans could simply not be trusted, U.S. officials contended, to elect the
"best men." Hence some conclusions seemed in order. They lacked political maturity; they were swayed easily by emotions and led readily

by demagogues. Cubans were still not ready for independence and the United States could not release Cuba into the family of nations so palpably ill prepared. One member of the McKinley cabinet asserted bluntly that the United States did not intend to expel Spain only to turn the island "over to the insurgents or to any other particular class or faction." The United States' purpose in Cuba was not to be guided by the political issue of independence but by the moral necessity to establish a "stable government for and by all the people."[57] "When the Spanish-American war was declared," Wood argued, "the United States took a step forward, and assumed a position as protector of the interests of Cuba. It became responsible for the welfare of the people, politically, mentally and morally."[58] President McKinley proclaimed in his 1899 message to Congress,

> This nation has assumed before the world a grave responsibility for the future of good government in Cuba. We have accepted a trust the fulfillment of which calls for the sternest integrity of purpose and the exercise of the highest wisdom. The new Cuba yet to arise from the ashes of the past must be bound to us by ties of singular intimacy and strength if its enduring welfare is to be assured. . . . Our mission, to accomplish when we took up the wager of battle, is not to be fulfilled by turning adrift any loosely framed commonwealth to face the vicissitudes which too often attend weaker states.[59]

The rationale for the continued exercise of U.S. rule required, further, a transformation of the meaning of the Joint Resolution. If the principle of the Teller Amendment could not be purposely repudiated, its premises would be purposefully refuted. It was first necessary to devise a substitute for immediate independence that did not foreclose ultimate annexation—an arrangement that neither defied the purpose of the congressional commitment nor disregarded the policy of the president. Not that Washington abandoned century-long designs on Cuba. Indeed, many in the administration persisted in the belief that annexation remained Cuba's ultimate destiny, if not at the immediate conclusion of the occupation, then as the inevitable culmination of artful policy designs. Annexation was a probability that could be temporarily postponed as long as its possibility was not permanently precluded. "The United States," the Teller Amendment stipulated, "hereby disclaims any disposition or intention to exercise sovereignty, jurisdiction, or control over said island except for pacification thereof." Through this last portentous caveat— "except for pacification thereof"—the administration could pursue a variety of options, all within the letter of the resolution. And quickly "pacification" came to mean something considerably more than merely cessation of hostilities.

Certainly the Joint Resolution had the immediate effect of precluding annexation either as a deliberate outcome of the war with Spain or as a direct outgrowth of the occupation of Cuba. But it is equally untenable to suppose that the United States suddenly renounced nearly a century of national policy, one based on the proposition on the inevitability of the annexation of Cuba, solely as the result of a self-denying clause adopted by, many felt, an overzealous Congress in a moment of fervor. The administration's position was clear: formal annexation was proscribed, but complete independence for Cuba was preposterous. If in early 1899 neither alternative offered the means of reconciling the presidential resolve with the congressional resolution, it was also true that neither the president nor Congress challenged the premises upon which the military occupation rested. Had not the Joint Resolution sanctioned the task of pacification? All agreed on necessity of maintaining U.S. sovereignty, if not permanently then provisionally, from which would emerge the policy justification for the exercise of the substance of sovereignty without the necessity for its structures.

A general consensus soon gained official currency that the requirements of "pacification" specifically involved conditions of stability. But "stability" and "stable government" were many things to many people. "What does 'pacification' mean in that clause?" Senator Orville H. Platt asked rhetorically in mid-1900. "We became responsible for the establishment of a government there, which we would be willing to endorse to the people of the world—a stable government, a government for which we would be willing to be responsible in the eyes of the world."[60] And at another point, Platt observed: "'Pacification' of the 'island' manifestly meant the establishment in that island of a government capable of adequately protecting life, liberty and property."[61] Governor General John R. Brooke also insisted that the United States was determined first to "establish a stable government," and then deliver the island to Cubans.[62]

Once "stability" was incorporated into the meaning of the Joint Resolution, independence itself became a condition the United States claimed authorization to recognize, or restrict, or revoke, as circumstances warranted. These were responsibilities the United States assumed under the provisions of the treaty with Spain, and it became clear that it would not unconditionally transfer these obligations to Cubans as an attribute of sovereignty. Stability, like pacification, however, also underwent repeated ideological transfiguration. When asked during congressional hearings if Cubans should be "entirely independent in the administration of their own local affairs," General James H. Wilson answered unequivocally: "Only so far as they are willing to bind themselves to manage their own affairs, in a way that would be acceptable and agreeable to us."[63]

Stability was more than simply political order. It meant a condition that inspired public confidence and encouraged private capital. The "era of prosperity appears to be at hand," Brooke predicted in late 1899; "all that is needed is to have capital satisfied as to the future conditions, and this being reasonably assured, there can be no doubt but that the fertility of the soil and the industry of the people will work out a happy solution of the problem."[64] Leonard Wood characterized stability wholly as a function of "business confidence." "The people ask me what we mean by stable government in Cuba," he wrote to Elihu Root during his first month as governor general. "I tell them that when money can be borrowed at a reasonable rate of interest and when capital is willing to invest in the island, a condition of stability will have been reached."[65] Wood later wrote to McKinley: "Business is gradually picking up, but capital is still very timid in regard to Cuban investments. When people ask me what I mean by stable government, I tell them 'money at six percent'; this seems to satisfy all classes."[66]

VII

The failure of the propertied elite to win political control required the United States to seek alternative means of hegemony. The "better classes" had shown themselves to be of limited political value. They had fared poorly at the polls, and no amount of U.S. backing, it seemed, was adequate to elevate them to power. In Washington, the administration was coming under increasing political pressure to comply with the Joint Resolution. By early 1901 a new impatience arose. On January 9, Root outlined in some detail his views to Wood. The occupation of Cuba was entering its third year and had become a "burden and annoyance," and expensive, too—estimated at half million dollars a month. It was also a growing political nuisance in Washington. Root conceded: "I am getting pretty tired of having Congress on one hand put us under independence of Cuba resolutions . . . and resolutions of hostile inquiry and criticism, and on the other hand shirk all responsibility." He confessed dread at the prospect of another year with "the Cubans howling at us to do something and the Democratic press abusing us because we do not do something. I think we are in great danger of finding ourselves in a very awkward and untenable position." The administration was prepared, and even anxious, to end the occupation, but not without first securing guarantees necessary to U.S. interests.[67] Root sought to give hegemony legal form, something in the way of binding political relations based on the Monroe Doctrine.[68] "Cubans should consider . . . that in international affairs the existence of a right recognized by international law is of the utmost importance." Root continued:

> We now have by virtue of our occupation of Cuba and the terms under which sovereignty was yielded by Spain, a right to protect her which all foreign nations recognize. It is of great importance to Cuba that that right, resting upon the Treaty of Paris and derived through that treaty from the sovereignty of Spain, should never be terminated but should be continued by a reservation, with the consent of the Cuban people, at the time when the authority which we now exercise is placed in their hands. If we should simply turn the government over to the Cuban Administration, retire from the island, and then turn round to make a treaty with the new government . . . no foreign State would recognize any longer a right on our part to interfere in any quarrel which she might have with Cuba, unless that interference were based upon an assertion of the Monroe Doctrine. But the Monroe Doctrine is not a part of international law and has never been recognized by European nations. How soon some of these nations may feel inclined to test the willingness of the United States to make war in support of her assertion of the doctrine, no one can tell. It would be quite unfortunate for Cuba if it should be tested there.[69]

Two days later, Root outlined to Secretary of State John Hay four provisions he deemed essential to U.S. interests. First, "in transferring the control of Cuba to the Government established under the new constitution the United States reserves and retains the right of intervention for the preservation of Cuban independence and the maintenance of a stable Government adequately protecting life, property and individual liberty." Second, "no Government organized under the constitution shall be deemed to have authority to enter into any treaty or engagement with any foreign power which may tend to impair or interfere with the independence of Cuba." Root also insisted that to perform "such duties as may devolve upon her under the foregoing provisions and for her own defense," the United States "may acquire and hold the title to land, and maintain naval stations at certain specified points." Lastly, "all the acts of the Military Government, and all rights acquired thereunder, shall be valid and be maintained and protected."[70]

These were not new policy formulations. Root acknowledged that his proposals owed some inspiration to England's relations with Egypt— relations that seemed to allow "England to retire and still maintain her moral control."[71] His urgency, however, was new, as well as the means by which Root proposed to fix the terms of political relations. Only eighteen months earlier he had envisioned the question of political relations between Cuba and the United States as properly the subject of future negotiations. "When that government is established," Root asserted in 1899, "the relations which exist between it and the United States will be a matter for free and uncontrolled discussion between the two parties."[72] After 1900, however, Root decided to impose unilaterally on the Cuban constituent assembly the formal terms Cuba's relations to the United States as a part of the "fundamental law of Cuba."[73]

Two considerations contributed to this change of policy. First, ratification of formal treaty relations with Cuba would require a two-thirds vote from the Senate, something by no means guaranteed. The decision to press for binding relations, further, even while the island remained under military occupation, underscored the United States' realization that a free Cuba would not accept limitations on its sovereignty. The original expectation in 1899 that political relations would be the subject of "free and uncontrolled discussion" between both governments rested on the assumption that the United States would be negotiating with representatives of the "better classes" for whom North American hegemony was their source of local ascendancy. Not after 1900, however. The results of local elections raised the real possibility that the republic would pass wholly under the control of the *independentista* coalition, ill disposed to accommodate U.S. needs. It was necessary to use the military occupation as the means to force Cuban acquiescence to U.S. demands. Otherwise, Washington faced the utterly improbable situation of having to negotiate with Cuba on an equal basis the restriction of its own sovereignty. This was the "great danger" to which Root alluded, that would place the United States in "a very awkward and untenable position." The "most obvious meaning" of the Joint Resolution, Root conceded privately in early 1901, called first for the establishment of an independent government in Cuba, followed in the ordinary course of events by the negotiation of a treaty of relations between Cuba and the United States. "Yet," Root hastened to add, "it is plain that such a course would leave the United States in a worse position as to her own interests than she was when Spain held the sovereignty of Cuba and would be an abandonment both of our interests and the safety of Cuba herself." U.S. interests required "constitutional limitations which would never be put into the [Cuban] Constitution except upon our insistence or suggestion." Root continued:

> Congress has thus so tied the hands of the President by its resolution that, unless the Cubans themselves can be induced to do voluntarily whatever we think they ought to do . . . the President must either abandon American interests by a literal compliance with the obvious terms of the resolution or must engage in a controversy with Cubans in which they shelter themselves under the resolution of Congress against the executive, while he has a probably divided country behind him, one part of which is charging him with usurpation and supporting the adverse claims of Cuban extremists.[74]

Senator Platt agreed. To defer the issue of relations until the inauguration of a Cuban government, he warned, risked surrendering "any right to be heard as to what relations shall be," and risked further having to be "contented with nothing at all."[75]

VIII

In late January 1901, Root entrusted a draft of proposed relations to Senator Orville H. Platt. During a meeting of the Republican senators to prepare the final language of the proposed legislation, two additional clauses were attached. One prescribed continuation of sanitary improvements undertaken by the military government. The other prohibited the Cuban government from contracting a debt for which the ordinary public revenues were inadequate. "The danger that the newly liberated people would plunge recklessly in debt was the most serious subject of conversation," Senator William Eaton Chandler later recalled. "The tendency in such cases was adverted to and we all quickly agreed that there must be some provision that Cuba should not run into beyond her means to pay. The danger that in such an event the money would be borrowed in Europe and that in default of payment European powers would threaten to occupy Cuba was comprehended."[76]

In Havana, Wood responded with enthusiasm to the proposed relations. The imposition of binding relations as a condition of evacuation promised to have a salutary effect on the "better classes." Wood had given considerable thought to the inability of what he called the "natural governing class" to assume its proper political role in Cuba. The uncertainty surrounding Cuba's future and, more specifically, the United States' failure to give public expression to future relations with Cuba had sapped elite morale and discouraged the "better classes" from asserting their "natural governing" role on the island. For Wood, the matter of relations was strategically linked to the future of political leadership in Cuba. As Root prepared to submit his proposals for congressional action, Wood urged the administration to take vigorous steps to secure legislative action: "I think Congress should be told very plainly," he counseled in early 1901, "that the men who have been elected to positions of authority in Cuba are in no way competent to protect present interests or develop the future prosperity of the island." He continued:

> The situation is vexatious and annoying, but we should not commit ourselves to actions which, like some of those of '98, will give us cause for regret and annoyance. Let Congress tell these people frankly that we are going to establish a government here if they want it, but that we will not turn the island over until competent men come to the front, men whose ability and character give reasonable guarantee of stability of the coming government. The men on top now are, politically speaking, a danger to the Island and its future.[77]

The relationship between the poor political showing of local elites in Cuba, on one hand, and the lack of a stated U.S. policy on the other seemed self-evident. "Our policy towards Cuba," Wood complained, "has rendered it impossible for business and conservative elements to state frankly what they desire, they fearing to be left in the lurch by our Government's sudden withdrawal." Wood again returned to his enduring concern:

> It must not be forgotten for a moment that the present dominant political elements are not representative of the Cuban people as a whole. In general terms they are a lot of adventurers and to turn the country over to them before a better element has come to the front will be nothing more or less in effect than turning the island over to spoilation. It would be a terrific blow to civilization here. I believe in establishing a government of and by the people of Cuba and a free government, because we have promised it, but I do not believe in surrendering the present Gov-

ernment to the adventurers who are now in the Convention and in many of the municipalities. Let Congress set a definite date of withdrawal provided a suitable government exists and I will make every effort to bring the conservative and representative elements to the front. . . . I have started the new year with a systematic policy of urging and encouraging by all proper means, the conservative element to come forward and interest themselves in the political situation.[78]

"Our best friends," Wood reminded Senator Joseph Benson Foraker, "are the country people, the planters and the commercial classes. Our enemies are the groups of political agitators who want to get their fingers into the treasury and pay themselves their real and fictitious claims." And once again Wood concluded: "No one wants more than I a good and stable government of and by the people here, but we must see that the right class are in office before we can turn the government over."[79] A month later, Wood welcomed the decision to press forward with the proposed relations: "We must find some way of getting the representative people to the front." The "more intelligent, well educated Cuban," Wood noted, privately displeased with the quality of elected officials—continued to be reluctant to offer himself for public office. "It is going to take a little time to bring him out," Wood conceded. However, "with a definite policy announced this class will come forward in self-protection. . . . To go further without giving them time to organize and get rid of the adventurers who are on top simply means to ruin the whole proposition of any Cuban government." Within a year, Wood predicted, with Cuba bound to the United States by formal ties, Washington could end the military government and reduce the North American military presence to several regiments. "What is wanted," he wrote, echoing Root's analogy with Egypt, "is the moral force to hold these people up to their work until the decent element assumes its normal position in the government of the island."[80]

IX

In its essential features, the Platt Amendment addressed the central elements of the United States' hegemonial aspirations in Cuba as shaped in the course of the nineteenth century. Something of a substitute for annexation, it served to transform the substance of Cuban sovereignty into an extension of the U.S. national system. The restrictions imposed on the conduct of foreign relations, specifically the denial of treaty authority and debt restrictions, as well as the prohibition against the cession of national territory, were designed to minimize Cuban international entanglement.[81]

But restraints on Cuban foreign relations did not satisfy all the United States' needs. North American authorities could not contemplate Cuban independence without a presentiment of disaster. Few professed confidence, fewer predicted success. Self-government promised misgovernment, officials warned freely, and the mismanagement of domestic no less than foreign affairs had potentially calamitous repercussions for U.S. interests. If the United States would not permit Cuban sovereignty to be challenged from abroad, it could not allow the solvency of government to be threatened from within. The failure to install the "better classes" in power cast a long shadow over the organization of the republic. If the authority and resources of the United States during the occupation could not contain the potency of the revolutionary ideal, what would follow the evacuation? Elections had underscored the uncertainty if not inefficacy of the democratic process for U.S. interests, and the moral was not lost on U.S. officials. If extenuating circumstances prohibited immediate annexation, political considerations precluded complete independence. The Platt Amendment rested on the central if not fully stated premise that the principal danger to U.S. interests in Cuba originated with Cubans themselves, or at least those Cubans with antecedents in the revolution. Whether in the direction of foreign affairs, or in the management of public funds, or in the conduct of national politics, government by Cubans remained always a dubious proposition. Root was blunt. The proposed relations represented "the extreme limit of this country's indulgence in the matter of the independence of Cuba." Wood's dread had taken hold; the political leadership emerging in Havana did not inspire confidence. "The character of the ruling class," Root acknowledged, "is such that their administration of the affairs of the island will require the restraining influence of the United States government for many years to come, even if it does not eventually become necessary for this government to take direct and absolute control of Cuban affairs."[82] "The welfare of the Cuban people," Senator Albert Beveridge warned, "was still open to attack from another enemy and at their weakest point. That point was within and that enemy themselves. . . . If it is our business to see that the Cubans are not destroyed by any foreign power, is it not our duty to see that they are not destroyed by themselves?"[83] Platt agreed. The United States could not "tolerate such revolutions or disorders upon an island so near our coast, as frequently occur in Southern American republics, more than all, because it stands pledged . . . to maintain quiet and government in Cuba."[84] U.S. policy required "a stable republican government which the United States will assist in maintaining against foreign aggression or domestic disorder," Platt wrote some months later. "We cannot permit disturbances there which threaten the overthrow of the government. We cannot tolerate a condition in which life and property shall be insecure."[85]

Again Root returned to the theme of U.S. responsibilities in Cuba: "The United States has . . . not merely a moral obligation arising from her destruction of Spanish sovereignty in Cuba, and the obligations of the Treaty of Paris, for the establishment of a stable and adequate government in Cuba, but it has a substantial interest in the maintenance of such a government." He continued:

> We are placed in a position where for our own protection we have, by reason of expelling Spain from Cuba, become the guarantors of a stable and orderly government in that Island. . . . It would be a most lame and impotent conclusion if, after all the expenditure of blood and treasure by the people of the United States for the freedom of Cuba, and by the people of Cuba for the same object, we should through the constitution of the new government, by inadvertance or otherwise, be placed in a worse condition in regard to our own vital interests than we were while Spain was in possession, and the people of Cuba should be deprived of that protection and aid from the United States which is necessary to the maintenance of their independence.[86]

"Our obligations to the world at large," Platt similarly argued, "created and assumed by the act of intervention, demand of us that we become responsible both for the character and maintenance of the new government. If duty required us to see to it that Cuba was free, duty equally requires us to see to it that Cuba of the future shall be both peaceful and prosperous. . . . We made ourselves responsible for the establishment and the continuance of good government thereafter. . . . A nation which undertakes to put an end to bad government in a neighboring country must also see that a just and good government follows."[87] It was a theme to which Platt would return. "We became responsible to the people of Cuba, to ourselves, and the world at large," he wrote in 1901, "that a good government should be established and maintained in place of the bad one to which we put an end."[88] And again a year later: "Our obligation did not cease when Spain was driven from Cuba. . . . When we undertook to put an end to bad government in Cuba, we became responsible for the establishment and maintenance as well, of a good government there."[89]

There would be neither compromise with the congressional amendment nor concession to Cuban independence, Washington warned, until Cubans ratified the proposed relations. Root was adamant. "Under the act of Congress they never can have any further government in Cuba, except the intervening Government of the United States, until they have acted." The members of the constituent convention "should have sufficient intelligence to understand that they cannot escape their responsibility except by a refusal to act, which will necessarily require the convening of another Convention which will act." Root warned directly, "No constitution can be put into effect in Cuba, and no government can be elected under it, no electoral law by the Convention can be put into effect, and no election held under it until they have acted upon this question of relations in conformity with this act of Congress." To the point: "There is only one possible way for them to bring about the termination of the military government and make either the constitutional or electoral law effective; that is to do the whole duty they were elected for." Continued resistance to U.S. demands would have dire consequences. "If they continue to exhibit ingratitude and entire lack of appreciation of the expenditure of blood and treasure of the United States to secure their freedom from Spain, the public sentiment of this country will be more unfavorable to them."[90] By early 1901, the meaning of "pacification" had undergone a final transformation. "All that we have asked," Senator Platt explained in a published article, "is that this mutual relation shall be defined and acknowledged coincidentally with the setting up of Cuba's new government. In no other way could a stable government be assured in Cuba, and until such assurance there would be no complete 'pacification' of the island, and no surrender of its control."[91]

X

In Havana, Cubans asked for clarification. Wood discerned that it was Article 3 in particular—"the United States may exercise the right to intervene for the . . . maintenance of a government adequate for the protection of life, property, and individual liberty"—that piqued Cuban sensibilities most. "They are emotional and hysterical," Wood informed Root in February 1901, and appealed for instructions in the face of mounting Cuban resistance to U.S. demands.[92] If there would be no compromise with the implementation of the Platt Amendment, there could be concession in its interpretation. Cuban concern over the meaning of Article 3 could be minimized and resistance to its passage reduced through official reassurances of the intent of U.S. policy. "They chafe somewhat," Wood explained to Root, "under what they consider to be reflections upon their ability to govern themselves, and what they regard as limitation on sovereignty."[93]

Root seized the suggestion, for it provided the opportunity to press for acceptance through discourse rather than force. On March 29, Root instructed Wood to "disabuse the minds of members of the Convention of the idea that the intervention described in the Platt Amendment is synonymous with intermeddling or interference with the affairs of a Cuban Government." The Platt Amendment, Root stressed, sought neither to restrict Cuban independence nor sanction U.S. interference. He continued:

> It gives to the United States no right which she does not already possess and which she would not exercise, but it gives her, for the benefit of Cuba, a standing as between herself and foreign nations in the exercise of that right which may be of immense value in enabling the United States to protect the independence of Cuba.[94]

It was a gesture that had immediate results in Havana. Days later Wood cabled that "everything will go through" if he could "officially" assure the Cubans "that the President and your views of the interpretation and scope of the third clause of the Platt Amendment is as stated in your personal letter of March 29th." A declaration along these lines, Wood predicted, promised to have a most salutary effect in Cuba: "It is most important to do this if possible, for the radical members are using the argument that under the third clause, we can intervene for trifling reasons. An official assurance . . . such as stated in your letter of March 29th will remove this impression and destroy this argument."[95]

Root cabled his response within one day: "You are authorized to state officially that in the view of the president the intervention described in the third clause of the Platt Amendment is not synonymous with intermeddling or interference with the affairs of the Cuban Government."[96]

The Root interpretation of the Platt Amendment calmed Cuban misgivings, and set the stage for direct meetings between members of the convention and representatives of the McKinley administration in Washington. In April, a Cuban commission traveled to the United States to ascertain directly the official interpretation of the Platt Amendment.[97] The commission met with McKinley, conferred with cabinet members, and spoke with ranking legislators on Capitol Hill. From President McKinley

Cubans learned that the "Platt Amendment embraces and combines the measures which in the judgment of the United States are necessary and indispensable for the preservation of the independence of Cuba. This law has no other object. This is its sole purpose." Article 3 served only to give international force to the Monroe Doctrine, thereby enhancing the ability of the United States to defend Cuba against the aggression of European nations. "That clause does not signify intermeddling or intervention in the Government of Cuba," McKinley affirmed categorically. The United States "will intervene in order to prevent foreign attacks against the independence of the Cuban Republic, or when there may exist a true state of anarchy within the Republic."[98] Senator Platt also reassured the commission that the amendment in neither intent nor interpretation threatened Cuban sovereignty. The legislation was drafted specifically to avoid the impression that its adoption "would result in the establishment of a protectorate or suzerainty, or in any way interfere with the independence or sovereignty of Cuba. . . . It seems impossible that any such construction be placed upon that [third] clause." Platt insisted that the "well-defined purpose" of the amendment was to protect the Cuban republic and preserve Cuban independence.[99] During a lengthy meeting with Secretary Root, Domingo Méndez Capote, commission chairman, sought assurances that "intervention will have no reference to the Cuban Government, which will enjoy absolute independence." To which Root responded, "Precisely." Méndez Capote asked for confirmation of the Cuban interpretation that "intervention will only be made possible in the event of a foreign threat either against the Cuban government, or in combination or alliance with the Cubans, or in the absence of any Government in Cuba." And again Root answered, "Precisely." Whereupon he elaborated:

> Intervention will never be exercised against the absolute independence of Cuba, that military intervention on the island will never take the character of occupation; that all the bases of the Platt Amendment which speak of intervention have for their one and only object the maintenance of the independence of Cuba; that the Platt Amendment distinctly limits the rights of the American Government in respect to intervention in Cuba, and that this can take place only in defense of the independence of Cuba, and when it shall have actually been threatened.

Root concluded, "Intervention is incompatible with the existence of a Cuban government" and "would take place only in the event that Cuba should reach a state of anarchy which should signify the absence of any Government, save in the case of intervention against a foreign threat."[100]

The commission returned to Havana in May. Its report stressed the U.S. commitment to a narrow interpretation of Article 3, Root's interpretation of the Platt Amendment. By May, too, it was apparent that the choice before the convention was limited sovereignty or no sovereignty. In early June the convention voted to accept the Platt Amendment as an appendix to the new 1901 constitution.

3.

Heroes Without Homes

I

The military occupation ended on May 20, 1902, with appropriate ceremony and celebration, and with much made of the successful transition from colony to republic. It was not entirely clear, however, that this notion of transition had much relevance to the Cuban social reality. The distinction between old and new was difficult to ascertain. Some things had changed, of course. But much had not, and much of what had not changed was precisely what Cubans had set out to change in 1895. When independence finally arrived in 1902, Cubans discovered that old grievances had assumed new forms.

There were, too, new grievances. Exactly how Cubans were beneficiary to their success remained unclear. In the weeks and months following the peace, across the bleak and devastated countryside, thousands of impoverished veterans wandered aimlessly about, muttering among themselves, "What have we gained by this war?"[1] The Cuban war had been long and ruinous. It succeeded as a means but failed in its ends. Peace was announced by a thunderous anticlimax, for separation from Spain did not signify independence for Cuba or control over the state apparatus. Rather, it precipitated U.S. intervention.

The effects were immediate. The revolutionary polity lost institutional cohesion and ideological unity. The victors had little to show for their hard-won triumph; there was nothing to give the coalition of war an enduring institutional structure in peace. Once in power, the victorious

Cubans should have found themselves strategically placed to consolidate their authority and expand their power. Instead, the revolutionary leadership emerged from the war at the head of a coalition it could not preserve representing a constituency it could not serve. The conclusion of a successful war without gaining control of the state had calamitous consequences and plunged separatism into a crisis from which it never recovered. Blocked by the U.S. intervention from seizing political power, Cubans could not transform the ideology of the colonial revolution into a program of national regeneration.

Vast resources went into efforts by the United States to dissolve the leadership and disperse the following of *independentismo*. At every opportunity, the revolutionary coalition was opposed. No longer could separatism accommodate individual ambitions and collective aspirations. The armed intervention became a military occupation, and in the process the U.S. government—not Cuban separatist agencies—emerged as the source of power, dispenser of resources, and arbiter of the political status of Cuba. When the revolutionary coalition lost its potential to provide advancement, and more, when even affiliation with the separatist amalgam was a liability, separatism lost the allegiance of all but its most intransigent defenders.

The armed intervention of 1898 and the military occupation of 1899–1902 had portentous consequences. The contradictions of colonial society remained unresolved, giving renewed vitality to the historic sources of Cuban discontent. Cubans had been summoned to dramatic action but failed to produce dramatic change. The Platt Amendment complicated matters, for henceforth Cuban attempts to redress the continuing inequities of the colonial system now inevitably involved confrontation with the United States. The real significance of the intervention passed virtually unnoticed. The United States had not only rescued and revived the moribund colonial order, it had also assumed responsibility for its preservation. The republic gave new political form to the socioeconomic infrastructure of the old colony.

Cubans had obtained independence from Spain at a frightful cost. But the conquest of nationhood did not announce the control of nation. In a very real sense, Cubans achieved self-government without self-determination and independence without sovereignty. As a result of the intervention, the state apparatus, including the lawmaking and law-enforcing agencies—legislative bodies, the courts, the armed forces—all the institutions necessary to give Cuban nationality definitive form and to establish the primacy of Cuban interests—came under U.S. control. They were, to be sure, eventually relinquished to Cuban control, but by then the treaty conditions imposed on the exercise of national sovereignty rendered meaningless all but the most cynical definition of independence.

II

Nowhere were these developments more dramatically expressed than in property relations in the early republic. The establishment of U.S. military rule meant that Cubans were without the means to reorder the economy and reorganize property relations to accommodate national interests. The means through which to exact reprisals from loyalists, *peninsular* and creole alike, principally in the form of nationalization of property and seizure of assets, remained beyond the reach of the victorious Cubans. Expropriations would have enabled Cubans to recover lost property, expand control over production, and establish a claim over the economy. Indeed, this was a covenant transacted earlier in the name of Cuba Libre, formally proclaimed in the land reform decree of 1896. The intervention made this impossible. On the contrary, the U.S. presence served to ratify existing property relations and to make a redistribution of property all but impossible. Cubans who had earlier lost property through the punitive Spanish expropriation decrees could not recover their assets through similar measures against their defeated adversaries.[2]

Colonialism ended in Cuba, but colonial property relations persisted substantially intact. Earlier in the century, the independence of Latin America had dislodged the *peninsular* bourgeoisie. Spaniards fled in advance of the liberation armies, hastily divesting themselves of assets, often liquidating property at substantial losses and selling out to local buyers at almost any cost. Those *peninsulares* who remained ultimately shared a similar fate as punitive edicts of expulsion and expropriation in the early republics completed the decolonization process. Throughout Latin America, the end of Spanish political rule served as the prelude to the end of Spanish economic preeminence. *Peninsular* property changed hands and loyalist assets were redistributed to accommodate the material demands of the new republican elite.[3]

Nothing comparable occurred in Cuba. The U.S. presence, first in the form of direct military intervention and later in the threat of intervention posed in the Platt Amendment, guaranteed colonial property relations. The United States actively encouraged the *peninsular* bourgeoisie to remain in Cuba. Even when Spanish property owners did liquidate their assets and returned to Europe, the paucity of local capital and the absence of credit facilities all but totally precluded Cuban acquisition of loyalist property. The principal beneficiary of the *peninsulares'* plight and the divestiture of local property was foreign capital.

Cubans were rapidly falling behind, and increasingly found themselves excluded from participating fully in the society they had sacrificed to create. They found their economic condition deteriorating; foreigners in increasing numbers expanded their control over the national economy. These developments, to be sure, had their origins in the nineteenth century, and even as Cubans plotted to wrest political control they were losing economic control. The process was vastly accelerated in the early twentieth century.

Cuban prospects for security and mobility decreased. Opportunities were few, jobs fewer. Cubans lacked the resources to restore the farms and estates to production, to revive businesses and return to their professions. They lacked capital and the means through which to accumulate it. They were without collateral for credit, without funds to invest, and without the capacity to borrow.

Several factors combined to inhibit national capital formation. The low level of income precluded private savings, and this contributed to the reduced local capital supply. Estimates for national income during the early years of the republic are fragmentary and incomplete. However, as late as 1939, per capita income in Cuba was estimated at less than $100 a year.[4] Nor could the planter bourgeoisie contribute to the capital market, for the war had crippled sugar production, destroyed land and machinery, and plunged planters hopelessly in debt.

Cubans faced insurmountable obstacles in finding a place in the postwar economy. Capital requirements were extraordinarily high. The cost of reconstruction was incalculable. Virtually all machinery and equipment had to be imported over great distances, adding shipping to manufacturing costs. Livestock had to be replaced from abroad. Large inventories were required in the absence of a network of industrial supplies. These needs, in turn, raised the requirement for working capital in addition to fixed capital.

Because many Cubans had given all they had to the cause of independence, their property had been destroyed and production had been stopped during the war. Cubans did not have the resources to expand their control over the economy.

Nothing underscored this development as dramatically as the continued presence of Spaniards in the early republic. *Peninsulares* not only remained in Cuba, they increased their numbers and continued to expand their control over key sectors of the economy. The Spanish population at the end of the war approached some 130,000 out of a total population of 1.6 million. There were vastly more Spanish men (108,000) than Spanish women (22,000), with the largest single number of *peninsulares* concentrated in the province of Havana (62,000) and the majority of these in the capital city (47,000).[5]

The census data of 1899 reveals several striking aspects of the postwar population. The total population of males fifteen years of age and older numbered at some 523,000, 20 percent of whom were white foreign-born. The census categories are somewhat imprecise, but the patterns are nevertheless suggestive. Some 252,000 white males were identified as Cuban (*nativos*). Another 158,000 residents were identified as men of color, without mention of nationality, but presumably largely Afro-Cuban. Similarly, another 113,000 men were identified as white foreigners, also without reference to nationality, but presumably mostly Spaniards. Using the 1899 census categories, the distribution of the male workers fifteen years of age and over reveals a significant Spanish presence in almost every occupational sector, particularly commerce, manufacturing, professional, and personal services:[6]

Male Workers	Agriculture Mining and Fishing	Commerce and Transportation	Industry and Manufacturing	Professional Services	Personal Services
White Cubans	140,569	27,482	33,146	4,675	28,654
Men of color	84,262	7,110	30,570	469	31,867
White foreigners	30,873	41,697	14,263	1,932	21,339

The strategic location of Spaniards in the Cuban economy is set in sharper relief by 1899 census data on specific occupational categories, for which both numbers and nationality are provided. Spaniards clearly prevailed in commerce, retail trade, and industry. More than half the merchants on the island were Spaniards. Of a total 46,851 merchants, 19,644 were Cuban and 23,741 were Spanish. Through the early decades of the republic, Spaniards persisted as a preponderant force in retail commerce. As late as 1927, two-thirds of all general stores (*bodegas*) were foreign-owned, 80 percent of which were owned by Spaniards.[7] *Peninsular* prominence persisted in retail commerce, because Spaniards hired Spaniards, thereby strengthening the Spanish majority in sales positions. Two-thirds of all sales personnel were Spaniards—that is, 9,605 out of a total of 14,533.

This preponderance remained fairly constant during the early years of the republic, and in some instances actually increased slightly. The 1907 census listed some 22,000 Cuban merchants against 24,000 Spaniards.[8] Spanish personnel in sales neared 21,000 while Cubans numbered 10,000.[9] Wrote Irene A. Wright in 1910:

> [The Spaniard] is an important person because he also lends money, and when conditions or events so alarm him that he no longer advances cash or grants credit, his district knows that times are hard. He charges a usurious rate of interest, there being no law against it; he keeps everybody in his debt, and he pockets the profits of their labor. He buys and resells their crops, to his advantage, actually monopolizing what little trade there is in his vicinity. In towns and cities, similarly, the Spanish control, I believe, commerce both wholesale and retail. They are the merchants, large and small, of the country, and constitute the most considerable foreign element of the population. . . . They own, I know, about one fourth of the sugar business. They figure big in the second industry (tobacco). They are wholesale importers in every line, and they are the retailers of merchandise.[10]

Spaniards were also strongly represented in the professions, education, the press, and publishing. The Catholic church remained substantially a Spanish church. The census of 1907 listed 106 Cubans and 202 Spaniards among the clergy. By 1919, the number of Cubans in the clergy had risen to 156 while the *peninsular* priests had increased to 426.[11]

But it was not only Spaniards who occupied strategic points in the Cuban economy. During the latter third of the nineteenth century over 125,000 Chinese had emigrated to Cuba. While this number had diminished considerably by the end of Spanish rule, the Chinese occupied positions in every sector of the Cuban economy, including sugar production, banking, and commerce. The 1899 census identified the Chinese as day laborers (8,033), servants (2,754), merchants (1,923), salespersons (471), peddlers (301), charcoal vendors (287), laundry workers (196), and bricklayers (121).[12] While the 1907 census showed only an increase of 318 in the number of Chinese immigrants arriving in Cuba between 1902 and 1907, some significant changes occurred in the existing Chinese community. The number of merchants increased to 2,059, sales personnel to 968, and laundry workers to 282. A new category appeared in the 1907 census, that of *agricultores,* which included without distinction all farmers and rural workers from sharecroppers to can cutters to *hacendados.* Some 3,813 Chinese were identified as agriculturists. Decreases were registered in the categories of day laborers (816), servants (1,644), charcoal vendors (99), and bricklayers (78).[13]

Joining the Chinese in Cuba, and in many of the same occupations, were immigrants from the Middle East, classified as *turcos.* Between 1902 and 1907, 1,358 Syrians and 689 Lebanese arrived in Cuba. They moved into small retail and sales enterprises, predominating as shopkeepers, street vendors, and peddlers.[14]

III

But if the insurgent petty bourgeoisie could not readily gain entry into the republican economy, the planter bourgeoisie failed to survive at all. Perhaps the single most salient feature of the new republic was the absence of a nationally based dominant class. Cuba entered nationhood with its social order in complete disarray. Disintegration began at the top, and it began early. The war sealed the planters' fate. This was a process so sweeping in scope and enduring in effect as to constitute effectively the overthrow of the dominant social class. The planter bourgeoisie had all but disappeared, and this was arguably one of the principal social consequences of the revolution. The planter elite had chosen reform over revolution and security over sovereignty, and in defending colonialism to the end, they were left without a defense when it fell. They lost prominence, power, and property, but most of all they lost the historic opportunity to lead the nation out of colonialism, and it cost them everything. Leadership over the *independentista* constituency passed on to a new generation of Cubans, men of modest social origins, limited economic resources, and driving political ambitions. By the end of the nineteenth century, the colonial bourgeoisie was everywhere on the defensive and in disarray. Certainly the U.S. intervention saved the bourgeoisie from immediate extinction, but it was not an unconditional redemption.

The toll of Cuban independence reached frightful proportions. The fields were blighted, the pastures were barren, and the fruit trees bare. Agriculture was in desperate crisis in an economy predominantly agricultural. Of the 1,400,000 total acres under cultivation in 1895, only some 900,000 acres returned to production after the war. The rich sugar provinces of Havana and Matanzas were each cultivating fully less than one-half of the area in 1899 than the year before the war.[15] And everywhere the sugar estates were in ruins. Of the 70 sugar mills in Pinar del Río, only 7 survived the war. Of the 166 *centrales* operating in Havana province in 1894, only 20 participated in the 1899 harvest. Of the 434 mills located in Matanzas, only 62 were left. The 332 *centrales* in Las Villas were reduced to 73. In all, of the 1,100 sugar mills registered in Cuba in 1894, only 207 survived the war, and not all these mills contributed either to the 1899/1900 harvest or the 1900/1901 crop.[16]

Everywhere in Cuba, property owners emerged from the war in debt, without either available capital or obtainable credit. The total urban indebtedness of some $100 million represented more than three-quarters of the declared property value of $139 million. A similar situation existed for rural real estate. The value of rural property (*fincas rústicas*) was set at $185 million on which rested a mortgage indebtedness of $107 million.[17]

Even before the war began, the planter class was already in crisis. The lapse of reciprocal trade agreements between the United States and Spain in 1894 found Cuban sugar planters producing record crops at a time of declining markets. The promise of privileged access to U.S. markets in the early 1890s had stimulated the expansion of sugar production and modernization of the mills. But most of all it had encouraged a new round of indebtedness as planters rushed to borrow in response to what appeared to be the unlimited prospects for prosperity offered by U.S. markets.[18] In 1894, the very much overextended sugar planters reached the historic one million ton mark, only to suffer a reduced share of the only market with the capacity to absorb Cuba's expanded production.

The end of reciprocity in 1894 was the first calamity to overtake planters. The second was the 1895 war of liberation. The expansion of the insurrection into the rich sugar zones of the western provinces in 1896 and the insurgents' ban on sugar production announced the demise of the Cuban planter class. At the time of the intervention many planters were hopelessly in debt, and at the brink of ruin. Planters had borrowed at inflated rates of interest, with loans at 20 to 40 percent not at all uncommon. "There are plantations in Cuba today," customs chief Tasker H. Bliss wrote, "which, if they could make a clear profit of 25% could not come anywhere near paying the interest on their mortgage." Continued Bliss:

> Very many [planters] are hopelessly ruined, and were ruined long before the recent insurrection. . . . In former times, and times not long ago, Cuba supplied the largest single crop of sugar in the world. . . . Some planters spent their large profits in reckless extravagance both here and abroad. Other planters squandered money unnecessarily in machinery. . . . And to do this they not only spent the profits of a previous season, but borrowed money at tremendous rates of interest. I know one man in Matanzas Province who borrowed $700,000 at 20% annual interest in order to replace new machinery with other machinery which was just a trifle newer. That man was completely ruined long before the last insurrection. . . . He is a type of a large class of planters in Cuba. . . . These men are all at the wall.[19]

One planter recalled in 1898:

> We well know what the conditions were prior to the war; the enormous debts piled up by abuse of credit and reckless expansion of the centrals; after absorbing all available in the community, they had no recourse to usurers. There are thousands of families ruined and in dire want, whose means have been swallowed up by well-known centrals. There are owners of mortgaged properties all around us who get a good living from them and have not paid a cent of interest in the past three years.[20]

Edwin F. Atkins wrote in April 1901, "I know of some instances where some of them are paying 24 to 36 percent per annum for borrowed money, to carry them along from month to month, and at current prices nothing beyond a living is left them at the end of the crop, while the security to their creditors is constantly diminishing."[21]

Ownership of many encumbered states would have long been transferred if it had not been for repeated prorogation of mortgage regulations between 1896 and 1898. This practice continued during the U.S. occupation, and in April 1899 the military government enacted Military Order No. 46, a provision proclaiming a two-year moratorium on the collection of all debt obligations, "whether or not secured by mortgage on real property."[22]

What planters needed most, however, and quickly and on a vast scale, was financial assistance, immediately to renew production, and ultimately to settle decades of accumulated indebtedness. From the outset of the occupation, Cuban planters turned to the military government for assistance.

U.S. officials understood clearly the problems facing Cuban planters. Testifying before a senate committee at the end of his year as military governor in Cuba, General John R. Brooke recounted:

> The planters after a time appealed to me for some relief in regard to their indebtedness. Most of the planters were in debt. Their properties were under mortgages contracted before or during the war, which began on February 24. Not only were the buildings on the plantations destroyed, but the cane and other crops were burned. The people took refuge in the towns or left the country. They found it necessary to mortgage what they had left, largely in addition to other mortgages which may have existed prior to the war.[23]

But direct aid to planters, either in the form of credit allocations or cash advances, was not part of the United States' design for the postwar reconstruction of Cuba. Brooke reported in October 1899:

> Many requests have been made by the planters and farmers to be assisted in the way of supplying cattle, farm implements, and money. The matter has been most carefully considered and the conclusion reached that aid could not be given in this direction. The limit has been reached in other means of assistance to the verge of encouraging or inducing pauperism, and to destroy the self-respect of the people by this system of paternalism is thought to be a most dangerous implanting of a spirit alien to a free people, and which would, in carrying it out, tend to create trouble by arousing a feeling of jealousy in those who would not receive such aid. . . . The real solution of this question of furnishing means to those who need this kind of aid is through the medium of banks, agricultural or others; through them and through them alone, it is believed, the means now sought from the public treasury should be obtained. . . . This system would not destroy or impair the self-respect of the borrower; he would not be the recipient of charity, but a self-respecting citizen working out his own financial salvation by means of his own labor and brain.[24]

Sufficient capital was available—much of it "lying idle"—Brooke insisted, if "capitalists [were] assured as to the future." Recovery was imminent, Brooke proclaimed in October 1899. "In fact, the era of prosperity appears to be at hand; all that is needed is to have capital satisfied as to the future conditions, and this being reasonably assured, there can be no doubt that the fertility of the soil and the industry of the people will work out a happy solution of the problem."[25]

But good times never arrived—not, at least, for the planter class. Capital remained scarce throughout the early years of the occupation, and not entirely without reason. Even as Brooke predicted imminent prosperity, one Treasury Department official in Cuba concluded that "it would be extremely hazardous to loan money in Cuba on any kind of collateral or property."[26]

Certainly Military Order No. 46 in April 1899 assured a much welcomed continuity with Spanish policy. But this remained substantially a continuation of wartime measures. With the arrival of peace, planters and farmers were anxious to revive the estates and resume production, but lacked resources. Warehouses had been demolished and machinery destroyed. Many private narrow-gauge railroads used for the hauling of cane were in total disrepair. So were locomotives and cane cars. Repair and machine shops had been sacked during the war and vital spare parts had all but disappeared. Some mills survived the war more or less intact, but the cane fields had been destroyed and the workers had dispersed. Without cane, the factories remained idle, and without funds, the fields stood barren.[27]

Not a few landowners shared the discouragement of planter Adolfo Muñoz who in mid-1900 complained of "a feeling of doubt and disappointment" upon the realization that there was "no hope of relief" forthcoming from the military government.[28] Landowners simply could not reconstruct their estates and return to prewar production levels without massive public assistance. Matanzas planter Cristobal Madán, facing some $100,000 worth of damage on his "La Rosa" estate, grew increasingly frustrated and critical of U.S. policy. "On my return to 'La Rosa,'" Madán protested to Governor General Leonard Wood in 1901, "I found that my machinery had been tampered with and pieces of machinery had been carried away, my cattle, horses, mules, in fact, everything moveable had been carried away. It was impossible for me to raise the necessary funds with which to put in working order my estate, and since 1895 I have not ground a single cane, and have had no revenue but from the little cane that grew among the weeds and which I sold to one of my neighbors, investing the proceeds in the preservation of what was left at the estate."[29] Santa Clara planter Francisco Seigle complained in late 1900, "The mortgages represent now more than 100 percent of the wrecked properties and become due next April. They will be foreclosed and the first mortgagees will grab them, leave the other mortgagees and the proprietors with utter ruin for their share." Seigle expressed his gratitude for the prorogation decree of April 1899. "But time has run out," he added, "our condition is worse today. These properties cannot be made productive without capital; capital does not invest in overmortgaged properties and mortgages refuse to come to reasonable terms." [30] This was a position with which Secretary of Agriculture, Commerce, and Industry Perfecto Lacosta agreed. "Up to the present time," he complained only weeks before the expiration of Military Order No. 46, "nothing has been done toward the improvement of our agricultural situation." In one of the strongest criticisms of U.S. policy by a Cuban official, Lacosta protested the lack of "pecuniary resources . . . for the work of the heavy debt with which rural property is burdened, due to the lack of agricultural banks or other institutions of credit which could render immediate assistance on acceptable terms." He called upon the military government "to remove the obstacles" to the establishment of credit sources and to "use every means at its command to foment and favor [agriculture's] most rapid development." [31]

On at least two occasions, attempts to establish local credit institutions met U.S. opposition. In one case, José Antonio Toscano and Celestino de la Torriente proposed establishing a Banco de Crédito y Territorial Hipotecario to facilitate loans to needy planters. The other instance involved the proposal by the civil government of Santa Clara to organize a farmers' loan association (banco pecuario) to promote local agricultural revival. In both instances, the military government rejected the petitions, citing the Foraker Amendment prohibition against the awarding of franchises and concessions for the duration of the occupation. [32]

The United States' appropriation of state revenues, while refusing to sanction public aid, on one hand, and its control of the licensing of banking enterprises, while declining to ratify local franchises, on the other, transformed a difficult situation into an impossible one. The military occupation in effect justified its policies on the grounds that Cuba's future rested on creating in Cuba conditions sufficient, in Brooke's words, to assure "capitalists . . . as to the future." For Wood, no less than his predecessor Brooke, relief of planter distress was part of larger economic considerations. His solution to the problem was giving Cuban products guaranteed access to U.S. markets through preferential tariff discounts.

"There has been considerable thoughtless talk in Cuba about making loans to aid agriculturists," Wood reported. "It is not believed that any such policy is either wise or desirable."

> High rates of interest on money loaned to sugar planters has been due to the low price of sugar and the uncertainty of a profitable marketing of the crop. When the planters and the general public have confidence that the sugar crop can be marketed at a reasonable profit, the principal difficulties of the situation will disappear. For, as the sugar market, so is the condition of business confidence in Cuba. The Island is so rich that her planters can secure capital on easy terms whenever there is reasonable surety of a good market for sugar. . . . What Cuba needs is a liberal degree of reciprocity with the United States, thereby securing a market where her products can be sold at a reasonable profit.[33]

Preferential access to U.S. markets did indeed promise to stimulate revival of sugar production. But for most Cuban planters, privileged entry into the United States offered too little too late. The ratification of the reciprocity treaty in 1903 had far-reaching consequences. It accelerated the transfer of landownership, immediately by way of creating favorable trade conditions permitting Cubans to sell damaged and unproductive estates and ultimately by enhancing the investment value of Cuban land. Nor was this development entirely unintended. Customs chief Tasker H. Bliss predicted correctly in 1902:

> All that reciprocity can do for the [planters] will be that, by an improvement of the general conditions of the country, and by a restoration of confidence, they will be able to sell their mortgaged estates for enough, possibly, to pay their debts. But all these estates must go into the market; they must be acquired by individuals or companies who will consolidate them, and who will work them on a modern basis. But the present owners are ruined, and will stay ruined reciprocity or no reciprocity. . . . The first consequence of reciprocity will be a complete upheaval of the sugar industry in Cuba, with the consolidation of many estates into one, . . . with the consequent reduction in the cost of producing raw sugar, and with the continued administration of the business on the most modern and economical lines.[34]

Almost from the outset of the military occupation, U.S. authorities accepted the dispossession of land and displacement of landowners as inevitable. Indeed, the occupation sealed the fate of many Cuban landowners. "Of all those estates upon which the mills themselves were destroyed," Wood acknowledged in mid-1901, "there is not a single case in which the mill has been reconstructed. The money secured by mortgages on those estates was loaned when the mills were standing; the destruction of the mills has left the estates worth only a fraction of the mortgage. There is no hope of this class of people getting out of the hole."[35] Wood had noted in 1899:

> During the war many of the estates in the interior were abandoned and have become overgrown. Their owners are either dead or in foreign parts or living in towns, too poor to attempt any work tending to reclaim and re-establish their estates, as well as on different portions of the public domain, and have remained in undisputed possession for several years. Their removal will be attended with considerable difficulty and hardship and probably with some considerable disturbance.[36]

In the spring of 1901 the expiration date of Military Order No. 46 neared; very early the military government let it be known that it intended to permit the original decree to lapse. "Any further extension will be a death blow to business confidence," Wood insisted, "and would scare what little money there is in the island, out of it."[37]

The lapse of the April 1899 moratorium provided the occasion for a new decree, establishing a fixed term of four years in which to settle all indebtedness. Military Order No. 139 stipulated in May 1901: "From the 1st of June next, all classes of creditors remain at liberty to take action and enforce the collection of mortgage credits, on all kinds of properties."[38] "Nothing has done more to keep money out of the country and prevent reconstruction than the original stay law," Wood wrote to justify his policy. "It would perhaps have been very hard to have had an immediate foreclosure, but it would have been very salutary." Permitting the decree to lapse promised a "gentle means of bringing the present condition . . . to an end with as little harshness as possible."[39]

Planters did not agree, and protested the provisions of the new law. Santiago Rousseau described himself to Wood as potential "prey" of intriguing creditors. The results of Military Order No. 139, Rousseau warned, would be "disastrous" and signaled "final ruin."[40] The Círculo de Hacendados protested directly to Washington.[41] In Havana, Wood summarily dismissed planter opposition. "The [planter] association," he wrote, "as at present organized and represented, is made up largely of the debtor element, the solvent planters taking no particular part in the transactions. The purpose of the debtor element is to practically repudiate their debts."[42]

The portents were everywhere. Across the island, Cuban planters ceased resisting the inevitable and sold out, often at great losses, to U.S. interests. In the municipality of San José de las Lajas in Havana province, property was selling for one-fifth of its value. "Land is sold at $100 to $200 per *caballería*," complained the mayor, "its real value being $1,000 for first class."[43] The mayor of Gibara reported continued distress and depression: "Agriculture in this municipality is today in the same condition it was on January 1, 1900 owing to the fact that all farms are abandoned for lack of agricultural implements and of oxen and in the few small farms that any cultivation is done it is by hand, producing hardly enough to cover the primary necessities of the farmer."[44] "The lands of this municipality," the mayor of Nueva Paz in Havana province wrote, "represent a taxable income of $236,000, but all are abandoned. Even those which were not completely ruined are in an unproductive state."[45] From Jiguaní came a similar account of distress and despair: "16,000 *caballerías* of this district are devoted to cattle breeding, but these are abandoned because the proprietors of same, excepting a very few, have not the necessary resources to reconstruct them. The agricultural progress is very slow, for the same cause of lack of funds to attend to cultivation."[46]

Three years of armed struggle—disrupting production, destroying property, bringing debt and insolvency—and four years of military occupation sealed the fate of the planter class. The war brought on disaster, and planters initially welcomed the U.S. intervention. But they desired more than an end to hostilities. They were in desperate need of capital to reconstruct the estates and credit to remain solvent. Like the insurgent petty bourgeoisie, the planters were without political power. When the United States seized the state, appropriated the means of policy formulation and enforcement, controlled the collection of revenues and determined the disbursement of public receipts, Cubans lost the only source capable of providing the massive support necessary to save the planters. The moment the United States declined its assistance, the Cuban planter class moved ineluctably toward extinction.

During the occupation public policy served U.S. interests. Under the military government, and continuing through the early years of the republic, U.S. control over sugar expanded. Large-scale acquisition of land accounted for much of U.S. investments. As early as 1899, R. B. Hawley organized the Cuban-American Sugar Company and acquired possession of the 7,000-acre "Tinguaro" estate in Matanzas and the "Merceditas" mill in Pinar del Río, and organized the "Chaparra" sugar mill around 70,000 acres of land in Puerto Padre on the Oriente north coast. Two years later he purchased a sugar refinery in Cardenas. In 1899 a group of North American investors acquired the old Manuel Rionda estate of "Tuinucu" and purchased the 80,000-acre "Francisco" estate in southern Camagüey province. At about this time, the "Constancia" estate in Las Villas passed wholly under U.S. control. The American Sugar Company acquired several damaged estates in Matanzas. In 1901, the Nipe Bay Company, a subsidiary of United Fruit Company acquired title to some 40,000 acres of land also around the region of Puerto Padre and 200,000 acres in Banes on the North Oriente coast. Between 1900 and 1901, the Cuba Company completed the construction of the Cuban Railway through the eastern end of the island, acquiring some 50,000 acres of land for rail stations, construction sites, towns and depots, and a right-of-way 350 miles long. The Cuban Central Railway purchased the "Caracas" estate in Cienfuegos from Tomás Terry. During these years, the Cape Cruz Company acquired the estates of "Aguda Grande," "Limoncito," and "San Celestino," a total of 16,000 acres in the region of Manzanillo. Joseph Rigney, an investment partner with United Fruit, acquired the estates "San Juan" and "San Joaquín" and the damaged *ingenio* "Teresa," all in the region around Manzanillo.[47]

U.S. land speculators and real estate companies also descended on Cuba, acquiring title to vast tracts of land and ownership of countless numbers of estates. Most were similar to the Taco Bay Commercial Land Company. Incorporated in Boston, the syndicate bought vast expanses of land in Oriente. In 1904, the Taco Bay Company purchased the "Juraguá" plantation. Consisting of some 20,000 acres of banana, coconut, and sugar land west of Baracoa, and one of the most successful plantations in Oriente, the "Juraguá" estate had been devastated by the war, and never returned to prewar production levels. Typical of other victims of the insurrection, the owners of "Juraguá" were heavily in debt and lacked the capital to restore the damaged estate to production.[48]

Land companies from the United States multiplied during the early years of the republic and accounted for a large share of foreign purchases. One New York company purchased 180,000 acres along the Cauto River in Oriente. Another syndicate acquired 50,000 acres on Nipe Bay for a winter resort.[49] Illinois Cuban Land Company acquired Paso Estancia, a 10,000-acre tract in central Oriente. The Herradura Land

Company acquired title to some 23,000 acres of land in Pinar del Río. The Cuba Land Company bought up defunct estates in Las Villas, Matanzas, Pinar del Río, and Camagüey. The Carlson Investment Company of Los Angeles acquired 150,000 acres in the region of Nuevitas Bay. Enterprises such as the Potosí Land and Sugar Company, the Buena Vista Fruit Company, the Holguín Fruit Company, the Cuban Land and Steamship Company, the Cuba Colonization Company, the Las Tunas Realty Company, incorporated in Los Angeles, New York, Minneapolis, Chicago, Pittsburgh, Cincinnati, Detroit, Youngstown, Ohio, and Ontario, Canada, bought vast tracts of land.

By 1905, some 13,000 Americans had acquired title to land in Cuba, and these purchases had passed over the $50 million mark. In Camagüey province alone, 7,000 American land titles had an estimated purchase price of $28 million. Some seven-eighths of the land in Sancti Spíritus was owned by Americans, as well as vast tracks of land around Havana, near Cienfuegos, and all along the north coast of Camagüey and Oriente.[50] "Reliable statistics or even a fair estimate of the amount of land owned by Americans," the U.S. minister in Havana observed in 1904, "are extremely difficult to obtain. Estimates range from one third to one fifteenth of the arable land of the island. One thirtieth, however, seems to be the most fair and reasonable figure, but will have to be substituted, of course, by a higher figure as the purchase of land by Americans continues."[51] Two years later, one writer estimated U.S. ownership of land at 4.3 million acres, or 15 percent of the land in Cuba.[52] In sum, an estimated 60 percent of all rural property in Cuba was owned by foreign companies, with another 15 percent controlled by resident Spaniards. Cubans were reduced to ownership of 25 percent of the land.[53] Manuel Rionda used different figures, but arrived at a similar conclusion. "Here," he wrote from Havana in 1909, "Spaniards I dare say own 30/40% of the property—Americans 25/40%. So the Cubans, the real Cubans, do not own much."[54]

IV

Cubans faced exclusion from more than the land. In a capital-starved and credit-hungry economy, they were all but overwhelmed by capital from the outside. Foreign control expanded over all key sectors of the economy, including mining, banking, utilities, and transportation. Foreign capital encountered few obstacles. The creole bourgeoisie was economically shattered, the insurgent petty bourgeoisie was politically debilitated.

U.S. capital seized control of tobacco and the Havana cigar industry. In 1899, the newly organized Havana Commercial Company, under New York promoter H. B. Hollins, acquired twelve cigar factories, one cigarette factory, and scores of tobacco *vegas,* much of this property previously owned by departing Spaniards. Even before the military occupation came to an end, the newly organized Tobacco Trust in the United States had established control of some 90 percent of the export trade of Havana cigars. By 1906, the Tobacco Trust acquired possession of 225,000 acres of tobacco land in Pinar del Río.[55]

Foreign investors established early control over mining. The iron mines of Oriente were almost entirely owned by U.S. capital. During the occupation, the military government issued 218 mining concessions, largely to U.S. investors. The Juraguá Iron Company controlled more than twenty claims around the region of Caney. The Spanish-American Iron Company, a subsidiary of Pennsylvania Steel, obtained claims to Oriente iron mines near Mayarí in the north and Daiquirí in the south. Smaller enterprises included the Sigua Iron Company (Pennsylvania Steel and Bethlehem), Cuban Steel Ore Company (Pennsylvania Steel), and Ponupo Manganese Company (Bethlehem). Copper mines around Cobre were owned by British and U.S. investors.[56]

The early twentieth-century railroad system was dominated almost wholly by foreign capital, principally British with some Spanish and U.S. participation. The United Railways Company, the Western Railway Company, the Matanzas Railway Company, and Marianao Railroad were controlled largely by English investors. The Cárdenas-Júcaro and Matanzas-Sabanilla systems were owned by Spaniards. The Santiago Railroad Company was controlled by the Juraguá Iron Company. The Cuba Railway was owned by the Cuba Company. The Cuban Eastern Railway, the Guatánamo Railroad were controlled by U.S. investors. Similarly with the electric transportation of the island: the Havana Electric Railway Company, a New Jersey corporation, established control of the capital's transportation system during the occupation. The Havana Central, another North American–owned firm, linked the capital to Marianao and Mariel.

Foreign capital also controlled the utility concessions. The Spanish American Light and Power Company of New York provided gas service to major Cuban services. Electricity was controlled by Havana Central and Havana Electric. U.S. contracting companies established branch offices in Havana and competed for government projects. The Havana Subway Company acquired monopoly right to install underground cables and electrical wires. U.S. capital controlled telephone service in the form of the Red Telefónica de La Habana, which ultimately was absorbed by the Cuba Telegraph and Telephone Company, the Cárdenas City Water Works, and the Cárdenas Railway and Terminal Company.

Some three-quarters of the cattle ranches, a value estimated at $30 million, were owned by U.S. interests, principally Lykes Brothers. Sisal farms were owned by International Harvesters and banana lands by United Fruit, Standard Fruit, and DeGeorgio Fruit.[57]

The early banking system was under the control of Spanish capital, with participating English, French, and U.S. interests. The two principal Spanish banks, the Banco Español and the Banco de Comercio, dominated island finances. The Banco Nacional de Cuba and the Banco de La Habana were formed with U.S. capital. North American capital held some $2.5 million in mortgages.[58]

In sum, the Cuban economy was all but totally dominated by foreign capital. Total British investments reached some $60 million, largely in telephones, railways, port works, and sugar. The French share accounted for an estimated $12 million, principally in railroads, banks, and sugar. German investments reached some $4.5 million, divided between factories and utilities.[59] But U.S. capital overwhelmed the local economy. By 1911, the total U.S. capital stake in Cuba passed over the $200 million mark in the following distribution:[60]

Sugar	$50,000,000
Other land	15,000,000
Agriculture	10,000,000
Railway	25,000,000
Mines, mercantile and manufacture	25,000,000
Shipping	5,000,000
Banking	5,000,000
Mortgages and credits	20,000,000
Public utilities	20,000,000
Public debt	30,000,000

The U.S. minister wrote in 1904:

> Some American houses . . . do a great amount of business and enjoy the confidence of the entire community. Among the successful firms of Havana are Knight and Wall, hardware; Charles H. Thrall, electrical supplies; Harris Brothers, office supplies and stationery; the Crown Piano Company; the Singer Sewing Machine Company. . . . Cuban tobacco interests are now for the most part controlled by the Havana To-

bacco Company, an American concern which operates the three largest factories in Havana, besides many smaller factories both in Havana and in the provinces, and owns much tobacco land.

All of the express business done in Havana and most of that done in the Island is controlled by Americans. Americans also control the steamship business between Cuba and the United States, and while there are Norwegians, Danish, German, Spanish, and Cuban lines engaged in the carrying trade, by far the larger part of the business is in the hands of the New York and Cuba Mail Steamship Company, the Peninsular and Occident, the Munson and the South Pacific Lines, all of which are American companies.

In Havana, water, electric, gas lights and the street railway service is for the most part owned by American capital. The English control most of the steam railroads of the Island, but I am informed that American capital has been largely invested in them also. Several companies, as the Cuba Eastern, the Insular, and the Havana and Jaimanitas and others are entirely under American control and management. . . . Americans are also large holders of mining interests which are almost altogether iron and manganese.[61]

Not much had changed by the early 1930s, when Ambassador Harry F. Guggenheim wrote:

The foreign capital in Cuba penetrates the whole economy of the island. The common carrier railroads of Cuba are almost wholly divided between two companies, one American and the other English owned. Practically all of the ships trading with the island are under foreign flags. . . . The cables and wireless are American and English, although the local telegraph service is owned by the Cuban Government. The street railway system is American. The electric light, power and gas works are American. The principal mines are American owned. The sugar industry is roughly 70 percent American, 10 percent Canadian and English, and 20 percent Cuban. In addition, many of the sugar companies are heavily mortgaged to the foreign banks in Cuba.

Aside from a few comparatively small banks which are controlled by Cuban capital, the banks of the island are American and Canadian. They are branches of leading New York, Boston, Montreal, and Toronto institutions which maintain offices being operated by three American banks and about thirty-six by three Canadian banks. . . .

The cultivation of tobacco, an important Cuban product is largely in the hands of Cuban citizens, but Spaniards also play no small part in this industry. The manufacture of tobacco is now chiefly controlled by Cubans and Spaniards, the American companies which dominated the manufacturing branch having transferred most of their operations to the United States in recent years.

Two-thirds of the oil business belongs to American companies and one-third to English companies. An American company operates the only petroleum refinery in Cuba. The packing business is American. Cattle raising is principally Cuban, but there are some American ranchers. Fruit and vegetable farming is mainly Cuban, but there are American farms of importance on the island and on the Isle of Pines. The great majority of the small merchants through the island are Spanish, but there are also many Chinese from the large Chinese colony in Cuba number about thirty thousand.

Seventy percent of the Central Highway was built by an American concern and thirty percent by Cuban contractors. An American contracting firm, long established in Cuba, constructed many of the public buildings, including the Capitol, and most of the larger hotels and office buildings, while an American engineering firm built the principal port works in Havana and other cities.

The two leading hotels and some smaller ones in Havana are American owned, but several of importance are owned by Spaniards, and natives of Spain also operate many of numerous cafes and restaurants. A number of the moving picture theatres are controlled by American companies.[62]

V

The reciprocity treaty of 1903 delivered still another setback to Cuban enterprise and local entrepreneurs. Preferential access to U.S. markets for Cuban agricultural products at once encouraged Cuban dependency on sugar and tobacco and increased foreign control over these vital sectors of the economy. Reciprocity also discouraged economic diversification by promoting the consolidation of land from small units into the latifundia and concentration of ownership from local family to foreign corporation.

The effects of reciprocity were not, however, confined to agriculture. The reduction of Cuban duties, in some instances as high as 40 percent, opened the island to U.S. imports on highly favorable terms. The privileged access granted to U.S. manufacturers created an inauspicious investment climate for Cuban capital. Even before 1903, the dearth of local capital and depressed economic conditions combined to prevent development of new industry. After the reciprocity treaty, prospects for local enterprise diminished further. U.S. goods saturated the Cuban market and hindered local competition. Reciprocity not only deterred new industry, it also had a deleterious effect on existing enterprises. Many could not compete; some cut production, others reduced operations. Business failures increased. One shoe factory in Colón lost the local market to U.S. imports, resulting in the closing of the plant and the dismissal of fifty workers.[63] It was a scene repeated across the island. Seventy-two establishments failed in Pinar del Río, 84 in Havana, 60 in Matanzas, 96 in Santa Clara, 30 in Camagüey, and 15 in Oriente—a total of 357.[64] Reciprocity, lastly, served to consolidate the position of Spanish merchants, who serviced foreign trade without competition from national industry.[65]

VI

The circumstances of war and the conditions of peace also caused havoc within the Cuban working class. For the thousands of urban workers who served the patriot cause in exile as well as the thousands of rural laborers who defended Cuba Libre in arms, the dream of *patria* turned quickly into a nightmare. Both wings of the Cuban proletariat discovered that the transition from colony to republic had also meant a descent into destitution. They left the service of Cuba Libre only to discover themselves displaced from the farms and replaced in the factories, and out of place everywhere else. The problem for workers, however, was not primarily a depressed postwar economy, but competition from cheap labor in the form of immigration.

Outsiders had long rivaled Cubans as wage laborers. At one time the competition had been principally African slaves, followed by contract labor from the Yucatan and later Chinese coolies. Spaniards also displaced Cubans, as did immigrants from the Middle East, Europe, the United States, and Latin America. Immigration depressed local wages and inevitably contributed to driving Cubans from the workplace. The arrival of some 200 Catalan workers to Puerto Príncipe in 1841, on one occasion, forced wages so low that many Cubans accepted work at $6 and $7 a month, approximately one-quarter of the previously prevailing wage.[66]

This trend did not substantially change after 1898. New waves of immigrants continued to augment the ranks of foreign workers in Cuba. Between 1898 and 1901, the total immigration into Cuba reached some 70,000, of whom 55,000 were Spaniards, 2,000 Chinese, and the balance distributed among Europeans, North Americans, and Latin Americans. In 1901 alone 23,000 immigrants arrived in Cuba, consisting of 17,000 Spaniards, 1,000 Chinese, 1,000 Puerto Ricans, and 1,000 North Americans. The work occupation categories included 11,000 laborers, 2,400 mechanics, and 1,500 farmers.[67]

Immigration continued to increase through the early decades of the republic. Between 1902 and 1907, some 155,000 immigrants arrived in Cuba, out of which 98,000 were classified as unskilled. Between 1912 and 1916, another 182,300 immigrants arrived, 85 percent of whom were males and 66 percent illiterate. In total, some 700,000 immigrants arrived in Cuba between 1902 and 1909.[68]

Again, the Spanish arrived in overwhelming numbers. Young, ambitious, driven, and impoverished, Spaniards arrived in Cuba disposed to work hard everywhere, at almost any job, at almost any wage, for almost any number of hours. They were in the main Galicians, Asturians, and Canary Islanders, and they overwhelmed the local labor market. Whereas in much of Latin America the *peninsular* population was expelled after independence, in Cuba the *peninsular* population actually expanded. They arrived in waves: 128,000 between 1902 and 1907, 142,000 between 1908 and 1912, and 116,000 between 1913 and 1916. One-quarter of the 200,000 Spaniards arriving in Cuba between 1912 and 1918 were illiterate. More telling, over 121,000 arrived with less than thirty pesos in their possession.[69]

That Spaniards in great numbers had remained in Cuba after the war, and in large part retained control of manufacture, trade, and commerce, did much to encourage *peninsular* immigration. Ties of kin and culture continued to favor Spanish workers among Spanish employers. But it was also true that foreign employers of all nationalities preferred to hire *peninsulares*. Traveling in Cuba in 1901–1902, Victor S. Clark wrote:

> The Spanish immigrants are reported to be steady, industrious, and regular workers. Some American employers consider them the best unskilled laborers of Europe. They are physically robust and not addicted to many of the vices of laborers of the same class in the United States. They are more docile than the latter, and fully as intelligent for many kinds of service. Unlike the Cuban, they are frugal, seldom gamble, and often allow their savings to accumulate in the hands of their employers. They are not quarrelsome, and do not usually carry concealed weapons.[70]

This view was corroborated by a factory superintendent, who asserted bluntly:

> We employ only Spaniards. They equal in industry and endurance American workingmen and are more regular and steady in their habits. I have had more than twenty years experience in Cuba as factory and plantation manager, and have seldom found native Cubans efficient in occupations requiring physical endurance of manual skill.[71]

"As to labor efficiency," Clark concluded, "all [employers] agree that for manual labor the Spaniard excels the native Cuban. This is true of factory as well as field occupation."[72]

Immigrant workers competed with Cuban labor in all occupations—in the fields and factories, in mines and manufacturing, as artisans and apprentices. Thirty percent of all immigrants remained in Havana, creating a highly congested urban labor market. In Havana Spanish men displaced Cuban women in domestic services.[73] In Oriente, the iron mines employed some 4,000 workers, most of them Spanish. Foreigners filled the jobs created by the expansion of railroad construction during the early 1900s. In 1901, the Cuba Company dispatched agents to Venezuela and Spain for the purpose of "inducing and assisting" 2,000 workers to emigrate to Cuba to work on railroad construction projects.[74] Sixty percent of the 11,000 workers employed by the Central Railway in 1902 were Spaniards. The majority of railroad foremen and engineers were North American and British. Foreigners accounted for more than half of the mercantile work force, sailors and miners and over a fourth of the bakers, tailors, blacksmiths, machinists, and cabinetmakers. Spaniards dominated the carter business. More than two-thirds of all unskilled laborers in Cuba in 1902 were Spaniards.[75] U.S. construction companies contracted North American workers. Bricklayers were hired in the United States. During the occupation, plumbers contracted in the United States organized a local trade union in Havana, and proceeded to exclude Cubans.

Immigration served primarily the interests of foreign capital, outside investors determined to develop Cuban resources and anxious to assure themselves of a plentiful supply of workers at depressed wages without the capacity to organize. This theme was struck early in the occupation. "Foreign labor has been used to some extent at all times," wrote one North American officer in 1900, "both for their example in showing how work should be done and on account of their steadying influence on labor. . . . The Cubans learn early the power of combination and when they believe that their labor is indispensable, strikes are very liable to follow, but if a foreign element is present, which will not unite with them in such movements, besides having the idea instilled in their minds that if they are not satisfied they may go and their places will be filled by foreigners, no trouble is encountered."[76] In 1901, a joint petition of the principal mining interests in Oriente complained to the military government of local labor shortages. In asking for a policy of unlimited immigration, the petitioners explained:

> The activity in road building and other government work, the opening of a large plantation at Banes, the pushing of the railroad work by the Cuba Company, the opening of new mines, and the lesser enterprises which are starting up throughout the province, in addition to the increased activity of the sugar plantations and other established industries, have created a demand for labor altogether unprecedented in this part of the Island and very greatly in excess of the supply.
>
> On account of the severity of the labor in the mines and the fact that the Cubans will not do this class of work, the mining companies are always the first to suffer, and this year, more than ever before, the discrepancy between supply and demand in the labor market is resulting in great detriment and loss to these companies.
>
> In a little more than a month, the Spanish-American Iron Company has lost over 60 percent of its mining force: a similar condition obtains at the mines of the Cuban Steel Ore Company, and the Juragua Iron Company has also been a heavy loser. These companies are willing and anxious to relieve the situation in any way possible. They would gladly import men for the work if there could be any assurance that the men would remain, but experience of many years, during which the Juragua and Spanish-American companies have spent upwards of $60,000 in bringing men to this province, has proven that it is impossible to hold them at the mines. Contracts with this irresponsible class cannot be enforced and the men rapidly spread over the province, only a small benefit accruing to the company in return for its expenditures. . . . To raise the rate of wages would only complicate without relieving the situation.[77]

These patterns continued into the early years of the republic. The national census of 1907 suggests that the condition of Cuban artisans and workers had not materially improved over that of foreign labor. Some 20–30 percent of shoemakers, tailors, bakers, mechanics, machinists, day laborers, carpenters, potters, boilermakers, and masons were non-Cuban. Some 50 percent of sailors, railroad workers, servants, and charcoal vendors, and 96 percent of all miners were foreigners. The numerical distribution included:[78]

	Cuban	Foreign	Total
Day laborers	30,319	11,448	41,767
Servants	8,389	7,445	15,934
Carpenters	16,510	4,910	21,420
Sailors	2,935	3,510	6,446
Masons/bricklayers	9,321	2,840	12,161
Cigarworkers	22,085	2,076	24,161
Mechanics	6,227	1,690	7,917
Miners	71	1,591	1,662
Bakers	4,848	1,313	6,161
Charcoal vendors	1,209	1,302	2,511
Shoemakers	5,551	1,278	6,829
Tailors	3,841	1,254	5,095
Barbers	4,324	687	5,011
Railroad workers	428	520	948
Stonecutters	259	456	715
Machinists	1,067	431	1,498
Boilermakers	606	282	888
Potters	421	134	555
Apprentices	1,104	24	1,130

When foreign capital opened the new cane fields in Oriente province during the 1910s, a new tide of immigrant labor flooded Cuba in the form of cheap contract workers from Haiti and Jamaica: 4,000 arrived in 1915, 12,000 in 1916, 18,000 in 1917, 20,000 in 1918, and 34,000 in 1919.[79]

These conditions gave a distinctive character to the formation of the Cuban working class during the early years of the republic. The struggle to redeem the nation had hardly ended when a new one to recover the national workplace began. Unemployment, underemployment, and depressed wages became the central features of the Cuban labor market. Local unions in Cienfuegos reported one-third of their members without work or working only part-time. In Matanzas, sugar mill mechanics and engineers who previously earned four to five dollars a day during the harvest were working for a dollar a day. Cane cutters who earlier made a dollar a day were working for thirty-six cents a day.[80] Very early the hallmark feature of the republic acquired definitive form: a high cost of living and a low standard of living. Wages remained depressed and prices continued to rise. Between 1904 and 1912, prices on basic foodstuff per commercial unit increased steadily:[81]

	1904	1912
Rice	$ 3.00	$ 4.70
Lard	10.50	17.85
Salt	1.94	2.63
Flour	6.88	7.67
Chickpeas	7.86	8.60
Beans	3.85	4.75
Peas	4.80	5.55
Olive oil	8.00	12.50
Bacon	10.00	13.00
Coffee	20.00	30.00
Potatoes	2.65	3.25
Vermicelli	4.50	5.25

"The cost of living is unusually high," the U.S. minister in Havana acknowledged in 1902, "higher than in New York. Owing to high duties and the fact that almost everything of domestic use, excepting fruits and vegetables, is imported, the prices are dear. Rents are also high, higher than New York City."[82]

VII

These conditions had a pernicious effect on working-class organizations. Labor in the early republic was divided by trade, by nationality, by culture, by geography. Not all, certainly, of the tens of thousands of immigrants who arrived in Cuba during these years remained. Many worked only for a season or the length of a contract and returned home. These conditions created havoc in the Cuban labor movement, hindering early efforts at organizing. Cuban labor, hence, remained disorganized, divided, and in disarray. Even the most wholly Cuban-dominated trade, the cigar workers, where over 90 percent of the labor force was Cuban, was a work force divided against itself, with one sector in Havana in competition with the other in Key West and Tampa.

Spanish laborers, like West Indian contract workers later, worked hard but made comparatively modest contributions to the local economy. The better part of Spanish earnings in Cuba was repatriated to Spain. "Mr. Gruver of the Cuban Central Railway," reported the U.S. military attache in 1903, "told me that eighty percent of the laborers on the road during the construction period were Spaniards, the majority of whom were immigrants secured by agents of the Company in Havana, and that seventy-five percent of their wages or salaries were sent to Spain as drafts." The report continued:

> The same is probably true of the Spaniards working in the mines. The great bulk of the large amount of money recently spent in this Province was accordingly sent out of the Island. The statement was corroborated by Bundy Cole of the Cuban National Bank who told me that he had sold many hundreds of thousands of dollars in drafts on Spain to these Spanish laborers. The same is probably true, in a less degree, of other banks. Many of the signs of prosperity that would naturally follow the expenditure of such a large sum of money are lacking and few are present.[83]

This was a practice followed by all Spaniards. Up through the early 1930s, Spaniards of all classes sent to their families in Spain an estimated $20 million annually.[84] This trend was also a characteristic of West Indian laborers who also repatriated part of the wages to Jamaica and Haiti.[85]

Because so many were seasonal workers, they had little incentive to participate in local trade union politics. Because they were needy and without recourse, and because they were foreign and subject to deportation, many were loath to engage in activities capable of arousing the wrath of local authorities. For all these reasons, and because they were cheap, immigrant laborers were popular among employers. Also for all these reasons they set back the Cuban labor movement almost two decades. Because, finally, foreign capital controlled property and production and trade and commerce, direct attempts by Cuban labor to ameliorate local working conditions necessarily involved confrontation with foreign governments.

These developments created ideal conditions for foreign capital in Cuba. Investors enjoyed unlimited opportunity to buy and sell, to merge and consolidate. They had unobstructed freedom to import cheap immigrant workers in unlimited numbers. Indeed, many capitalists who during the occupation advocated annexation as the best means to protect property within a decade opposed annexation for the same reason. Ten years of antitrust legislation in the United States, together with increasing opposition in Washington to unrestricted immigration, had a chilling effect on capitalists operating in Cuba. "I am not in favor of Cuban annexation to the U.S.," Manuel Rionda wrote to Czarnikow-Rionda headquarters in 1912. "I was for annexation some eight or twelve years ago, but since, I have seen the difficulties in the U.S. with labor—the objection to the importation of foreign labor—[and] the many obstacles in the way of combination of freights and capital."[86]

VIII

These developments had lasting consequences. Cubans would continue to be unable to accumulate local capital and create local credit facilities. That property and production were largely under the control of foreigners meant that capital in the form of dividends and profits went to the United States and Europe. Because vast numbers of workers were foreign meant that wages were repatriated to Spain, Jamaica, and Haiti.

These conditions in the early republic all but totally excluded Cuban participation in agriculture and mining, utilities and transportation, trade and commerce, industry and manufacture, banking and finance. Without the means to aggregate capital, Cubans were without the means to secure control of production and expand ownership over property.

The deteriorating class structure in the early republic reflected accurately the anomaly caused by the disruptions of the late nineteenth century. The planter class had been overturned by a populist coalition made up of an insurgent petty bourgeoisie, workers, and peasants, none of whom possessed the means with which to replace the planters' dominant position. Few Cubans could own property, become merchants and managers, or find jobs as salaried personnel and wage workers. They were undercut by immigration from abroad and overwhelmed by foreign capital. Cubans had succeeded in creating a nation in which they controlled neither property nor production.

It was a devastating disappointment for the patriotic leaders, a disastrous denouement after three decades of patriotic labor. Dedication to Cuba Libre was more than a duty to a cause, it was a faith. Between 1868 and 1898, two generations of Cubans had served the cause. Many had devoted the better part of their adulthood to the pursuit of independence. But the pursuit of *patria* had calamitous consequences: all emerged from the war in various conditions of impoverishment. Some of the creole separatists had plowed personal fortunes into the support of the patriotic cause. Others knowingly exposed their property to expropriation as punishment for their participation in sedition against Spain. Almost all deferred their earnings, depleted their assets, and delayed their educations; they were despoiled of their property and displaced from their professions.

Rather than expressing the economic interest of any one class, the separatist movement itself was expected to produce the opening to mobility and the opportunity for material well-being. Social status and economic security were derivatives of political power—they did not create it. The separatist summons attracted Cubans from all classes, all of whom expected independence to produce a new society. Instead, what Cubans found was that they neither controlled the state nor obtained independence. They were winners who had lost everything. Blocked by the intervention from political ascendancy, Cubans discovered, too, that during the intervening years alternative means of acquiring property and achieving prosperity had diminished considerably. Sources of economic security had slipped beyond the grasp of those who had reached for independence.

These were the years that the separatist amalgam acquired its definitive characteristics, organizing not around the pursuit of property or the expansion of economic power, but around the politics of independence. For members of the creole petty bourgeoisie who had enrolled in the separatist cause, independence was expected to create opportunity. These were Cubans largely of modest social origins, moderate means, and unmet professional aspirations, historically resentful of Spanish monopolization of local administration and insular government. Spain had correctly suspected the subversive undercurrents of the creole clamor for public office, for what Cubans demanded was control of the island: they wanted offices in their country and they wanted all of them. And instead, they received less, so that by the closing decades of the colony, there seemed to be fewer and fewer places for Cubans in Cuba. The economy was not expanding fast enough in sufficiently balanced and diversified form to accommodate the interests of all classes of Cubans.

These circumstances changed the very nature of the separatist polity, and it began early during the U.S. military occupation. Control of public office became an urgent issue, the only available hedge against total impoverishment. Means became ends. After the war, destitute Cubans were preoccupied less with national sovereignty than personal survival. "My family has been with me for a month," General Carlos Roloff lamented in April 1899, "and I have to find work to support it. If I had money, I would pursue any job other than public office; but today I am obligated to find employment."[87] Two months later, General Alejandro Rodríguez wrote in similar despair: "I who have served my country, for which I have sacrificed everything, cannot even have my family at my side for a lack of means to support it; I cannot embark upon any business nor reconstruct my farm for a lack of funds. I see myself perhaps forced to emigrate to search for bread in a strange land, when here there are individuals in high office who were indifferent or hostile to Cuba and always remained on the side of Spain."[88] These were the generals, the senior commanders of the successful war effort, who were in varying conditions of destitution. For the other 50,000 or so officers below general rank and for those without officer grade altogether, life in postwar Cuba was a nightmare. Uncompensated and unthanked veterans became the final casualties of the war for independence.

IX

These were conditions recognized by U.S. authorities early in the occupation, and they had far-reaching political implications. A way had to be found to accommodate the urgent requirement for livelihood among the 50,000 army veterans. Employment for soldiers was the minimum condition for social peace. It was also the minimum requirement of political order and, as the military government understood only too well, the principal means through which to minimize opposition from the only force capable of challenging the U.S. presence. Public administration under Cuban control would have served to solidify the separatist amalgam; under U.S. control, it was used to dissolve it. General J. C. Bates in Santa Clara wrote early in the occupation, "We should give employment to about two thousand Cubans, many of whom are in my opinion very liable to give us serious trouble unless we take care of them."[89] Major John A. Logan agreed: "Unless employed in some manner, many of the Cuban troops will soon be turned loose to find existence as best as they can. That there is not sufficient employment this year in the agricultural districts or in the cities for even fifty percent of them, is evident. How they are to exist is the problem we have to solve."[90] In Pinar del Río, General George W. Davis struck a similar theme:

> They are absolutely destitute and have no property of any kind except a rifle or machete or both, and no means of subsisting. . . . Nor have they any means for procuring the work cattle and farming implements needed in cultivating tobacco. The sugar estates . . . are nearly all destroyed and the owners of these estates cannot give employment.[91]

At the other end of the island, Leonard Wood wrote of creating work as a means "to disintegrate the armed Cuban forces wandering about the mountains."[92]

Pressure was also building within the ranks of the Liberation Army. As the weeks of peace stretched into months of idleness, restlessness among army units across the island increased. Among the earliest political parties formed during the occupation were those organized by army leaders who demanded immediate control of public office.[93] Discontent grew as the military occupation entered its second year. General Julio Sanguily was reported by military intelligence to be "preaching the doctrine that all public offices, without exception, should be given to members of the Cuban Army, threatening, if this is not done, to go to war with the American government."[94] Another intelligence report described the local mood in Santiago in similar terms:

> The soldiers belonging to the rank and file of the Cuban army own or control no property on the island. . . . This condition of the Cuban soldier obtains generally in all of the province. . . . Nearly every officer and petty officer of the Cuban Army has been an applicant for some position under the United States occupation of the Island and that such positions have not been obtained these officers are now engaged in sowing the seeds of discontent by saying that the United States never intended to give the Cubans freedom and independence.[95]

These were stirrings the military government could ill afford to ignore. Almost from the outset, U.S. authorities used funds from public revenues and positions in public administration to provide jobs for army veterans as a way to hasten the dissolution of insurgent army units. "The disbandment of the Cuban forces," Leonard Wood wrote in mid-1899, "can be assigned to only one cause—we have been able to give out enough work at fair pay to break up every organization and scatter many of them among the different working gangs."[96] Across the island, through the course of the occupation, and with great purposefulness, the military government hired veterans. Thousands of ex-soldiers joined the public rolls as day laborers in public works programs: they paved city streets and painted public property. They repaired country roads, renovated public buildings, restored piers and wharves, cleaned streets, collected garbage, and constructed sewers. Thousands of others, principally former officers, occupied positions at all levels of national, provincial, and municipal administration as office clerks, auditors, postmasters and letter carriers, messengers, teachers, policemen, and rural guards.[97] The use of public revenues to create jobs offered employment on a vast scale in conditions where few alternatives existed. That the bulk of these positions passed under the control of the army veterans established among the former soldiers early proprietary rights over public administration, with lasting effects.

4.

The Republic
Inaugurated

I

The military occupation came to an end in May 1902, by which time the United States had made its peace with the separatist polity—or at least one part of it. Elections during the occupation had confirmed the worst fears in Washington, namely, that the tide of *independentista* ascendancy, temporarily stemmed by the intervention, was irreversible. Separatist antecedents gave an advantage to candidates originating from *independentista* ranks, and they could not be denied at the polls.

However, the patriotic coalition consisted always of two competing tendencies. During the best of times, which is to say, during the worst times of the war, both wings of the revolutionary polity preserved the unanimity of purpose necessary to defeat Spain. Peace revealed the extent of the disparity. On one side of the coalition was the populist military sector, largely the officers and enlisted men of the Liberation Army, many of whom were Cubans of color, and almost all men of modest social origins, committed to the most exalted version of *independentismo*. At the other end was the bureaucratic civilian wing, mostly the officials of the expatriate diplomatic corps and the functionaries of the provisional government, most of whom were whites of comfortable social origins, some with Autonomist political antecedents, and not wholly unequivocal in their endorsement of national sovereignty. Certainly there were points of convergence, but in the main these two tendencies delineated the key distinctions between both wings of the separatist polity and the differences that characterized the political parties of the early republic.[1]

These were, in the end, the only real choices available to the United States. Separatism was a force that could be contained only by its own contradictions. It was a belated realization, but one that impelled the United States to seek allies from the most ideologically congenial sector of the most politically potent force in Cuba. For this, the United States turned to the civil representation of Cuba Libre and its titular head, Tomás Estrada Palma. He was the ideal choice. Almost seventy years of age when he became president in 1902, Estrada possessed impeccable separatist credentials. An impoverished planter from Oriente, he had served previously as provisional president during the Ten Years' War. Between 1895 and 1898, he was minister plenipotentiary of the provisional republic and the chief of the PRC. He was, further, unabashed in his pro–United States sympathies, and at one time an advocate of annexation.[2] He supported the intervention in 1898, endorsed the Platt Amendment in 1901, and lobbied for reciprocity in 1902. A converted Quaker and naturalized U.S. citizen, Estrada never wavered in his belief that Cuba's ultimate destiny was political union with the United States.

Estrada Palma prevailed in 1902 as a candidate without a program in a campaign without an opponent. His principal virtue consisted in a lack of affiliation with any political party, towering loftily above partisan passions. His candidacy seemed a fitting way to honor the genteel patriarch of the separatist cause. Estrada had labored faithfully in behalf of Cuba Libre in three wars over four decades. At seventy, Don Tomás inspired reverence not confidence, appreciation not advocacy. And in 1902, a grateful people did not default on their debt of gratitude.

II

These early years gave decisive shape to the social and economic purpose of politics in the republic. The economy continued to flounder. The cost of living in Cuba was high, and rising,[3] and Cubans everywhere were experiencing a decline in their material well-being. Work was still hard to come by. By 1907 more than 525,000 persons were without any work whatsoever.[4] Included among the half million unemployed were some 35,000 veterans, most of whom passed the early years of the republic in conditions between deprivation and destitution.[5] One observer wrote from Santiago in 1903, "The condition of labor is . . . critical, and never before since the end of the Spanish-American War, have so many laborers been without work."[6]

All of which underscored the persisting economic realities of the republic. The economy was not expanding, and what growth did occur was not balanced. Public administration in general, and politics in particular, early acquired a special economic significance. State revenues early became the principal source of economic solvency for the generation of 1895, Cubans who came to define their material well-being in political terms. Public office, patronage appointments, and civil service became ends; politics and electoral competition were the means. The former separatist amalgam assumed definitive form around both.

The public payroll offered economic security. Not infrequently, public office provided higher salaries than comparable positions in business. "The civil service," wrote one traveler to Cuba in 1902, "pays higher salaries for equivalent work than private enterprises. . . . While $1,200 gold ($1,080 American) a year is about the maximum to which a salaried employee of a commercial house in Cuba can aspire, it is but the income of an ordinary clerk in the Government service."[7]

Public administration not only offered higher-paying jobs. Often they were the only jobs. There was a tenor of urgency and, on occasion, ferocity to Cuban public life. Control of public administration was the central unstated issue of national politics. During the first years of the republic, Cuban control over all sectors of public administration expanded quickly. At all levels of government, representatives from the old separatist coalition found a livelihood. Control of elected office meant control of appointments to public positions and access to public funds. Sugar magnate Manuel Rionda noted with some percipience: "Here politics mean personal gain—a government position."[8]

The leadership of political parties emerged intact from the old regimental commands of the Liberation Army, with commanding officers securing key political office and placing in appointive positions former staff and subordinate officers. In municipal government through the office of mayor and on the *ayuntamientos,* at the provincial level through the position of governor and on *consejos provinciales,* and in national administration, through the office of the president, in executive departments of government, in the judiciary, and in the house of representatives and senate, the republican elite found its form and function. As early as 1903, the public payroll had expanded to tens of thousands of public employees, with 8,000 in the city of Havana—a payroll that included public officials from the president to policemen, senators to street cleaners, teachers to tax collectors.[9]

III

There was a noteworthy nonaligned quality to the administration of Estrada Palma. Not that he was not partial in his policies; rather, he was not partisan in his politics. He magnanimously brought into public administration Cubans from almost all political tendencies, without prejudice toward previous political affiliation. Estrada saw his administration as an opportunity to pursue reconciliation and reconstruction. Even as municipal and provincial politics began to polarize around partisan groupings, Estrada strove to maintain balanced representation in the cabinet and throughout the executive departments of his administration.[10]

But events overtook Don Tomás. By the time he neared the end of his term, national politics had become highly partisan. Parties represented an array of special interests, ranging from regions to race, from class to *caudillos*, and almost all with antecedents in one or the other sector of the old separatist coalition. By 1905, in this highly charged partisan atmosphere, a nonpolitical president was an anachronism.[11]

When Estrada Palma contemplated a second term, he needed also to consider affiliation with a political party. Predictably, he chose the Moderates, who had antecedents in the civilian wing of the old separatist coalition. These were the men of the liberal professions who had directed the provisional government, served as functionaries of the provisional republic, worked in the PRC both in and out of Cuba, and represented the cause of Cuba Libre abroad as diplomatic agents.

The decision by Estrada Palma to seek a second term was a fateful one, for it required a sweeping reorganization of his government for palpably political ends. Cabinet positions came wholly under the control of the Moderate party. Rafael Montalvo assumed the portfolio of Public Works. Fernando Freyre de Andrade headed *Gobernación*. Domingo Méndez Capote received the nomination of vice-president. The prospects for patronage were unlimited—spoils that Moderates were eager to receive and indisposed to relinquish.

These early developments signified more than the president's conversion to a new political faith. They were measures preliminary to a vast reorganization of national, provincial, and municipal government. They were, most important, preparations for presidential elections later in 1905 with one objective in view: the defeat of the Liberal party. Led by populist and flamboyant General José Miguel Gómez, the Liberals represented the military wing of the separatist coalition. The party drew its principal support from the former soldiers, workers, and peasants.[12]

The political purges began at the national level, within the executive departments of government. Secretaries Freyre de Andrade of Gobernación and Rafael Montalvo of Public Works purged their departments of all employees not members of the Moderate party. Moderates moved into all positions of national administration, and assumed provincial and municipal offices. The Estrada government displaced the Liberal governor of one province, the Liberal mayors of thirty-two cities and towns, and hundreds of lesser Liberal officeholders. In the predominantly Liberal districts of Pinar del Río, Havana, and Las Villas, the transformation was complete. Members of local school boards were purged to make room for progovernment supporters. Teachers, public clerks, and street cleaners were fired and replaced by Moderates. Moderate judges, police chiefs, and Rural Guard commanders presided over a purge that was as vast as it was thorough.[13] ˙

After 1905, public administration became entirely a function of party affiliation. The U.S. minister reported in April 1905 that Estrada Palma "may be fairly charged with too great partisan activity after following a neutral policy for near three years."[14] Similar developments were reported from towns in the interior, especially those under local Liberal administration. "Fear and apprehension," wrote the U.S. consul in Cienfuegos, "have taken possession of peaceful citizens and hatred for the authorities is hardly concealed. The police force and Rural Guards are used not to preserve order and enforce the law with impartial justice, but as a club to dominate over the opposition."[15] And from Caibarién:

> No time seems to be lost by the Moderate Party to place itself in the best position possible to command any difficult situation. During the week just ended practically the last three employees of the local town government, belonging to the Liberal Party, were dismissed. The Chief of Police was dismissed about two weeks ago for the same reason. The last to be dismissed by the Moderates is the town treasurer. . . . Except for the last mentioned there is not one of the Liberal Party in the public service in this town. This holds good also as to the Post Office and the Customs Service, where complete changes have recently taken place. . . . In Remedios the city employees are practically all Moderates and those who are not will either have to amend their politics or get out.[16]

It was not only that the ruling party had imposed political credentials as the determining qualification for public positions. In September 1905, preliminary elections to select members of local electoral boards resulted in a total moderate sweep. The elections were fraudulent, and there was to be more fraud, for it was the responsibility of local boards to supervise the voter registration and count the ballots in the December general elections. During the subsequent enrollment period, Liberal apprehensions were confirmed: a total of some 432,000 names appeared on the electoral registry, including 150,000 palpably fictitious voters. In September, too, the harassment of opposition candidates increased. Liberal political rallies were disrupted, Liberal candidates were shot at. Events culminated on September 22, when the popular Liberal congressman Enrique Villuendas was assassinated. Several weeks later, the Liberal party announced its decision to withdraw from the December 1 general elections. Undaunted by a Liberal boycott, the government proceeded with elections and on December 2 proclaimed itself the winner of national elections. Not a single Liberal candidate for national, provincial, and municipal office won elective office anywhere.[17]

The magnitude of official fraud, together with the singlemindedness with which the Moderates pursued victory, surprised even those who had come to accept a measure of ballot tampering and voter coercion as normal. But it was not only government abuse that aroused Liberal ire: it was the scope of government misconduct and the utter implausibility of the Moderate electoral preponderance. At the very center of the political dispute was the issue of reelection.

From the inception of the republic, the question of presidential reelection was a source of controversy. In 1901 the constituent assembly approved the principle of the juridicial validity of reelection, but only after hours of acrimonious debate.[18] Opponents' worst fears were realized. In its first application, reelection was identified with government corruption, official coercion, and political violence. Incumbency offered monopoly use of the state apparatus to pursue reelection: the electoral agencies, the courts, and the armed forces. A constitutionally legitimate end came to rely on unconstitutional means.

The passion aroused by the reelection of Estrada Palma in 1905, however, reflected considerably more than an outcry of injured constitutional sensibilities. The forms of conventional electoral competition disguised some urgent nonpolitical issues. At stake was the livelihood of hundreds of political contenders and the many more thousands of dependents and supporters who relied on political patronage and public office for their well-being. The distributive quality of Cuban politics was the mechanism for resource allocation, and the very scarcity of resources required an equitable and periodic sharing of benefits. Monopolization of public office by one party or one faction of a party blocked access to the sinecures of state for others. Because the state served as one of the principal means of economic well-being, elections institutionalized a process among political contenders by which all participants shared access to public administration. Success at the polls offered the victorious candidate, his family and supporters, and the party rank and file control of public revenues. If the incumbent were all but guaranteed a second term, this violated an understood protocol among political contenders. The opposition had little more than the opportunity to participate in—and thereby lend legitimacy to—a ritualized sanction of presidential *imposición*.

In 1905, Moderates had gone beyond reasonable limits. In addition to dismissing thousands of public functionaries in appointed positions, they deposed hundreds of elected officials. The Moderate purge penetrated every aspect of local administration. The prospect of four more years of Moderate rule effectively meant that the removals of 1905 were irreversible. The thousands of veterans appointed to administrative positions during the U.S. occupation and elected in the first years of independence found themselves displaced and again facing destitution. If political means failed to dislodge the incumbents, the opposition would have to resort to military methods to restore parity to the threatened system.

IV

The Liberal response was not long in coming. In August 1906, an attack against a Rural Guard post in Pinar del Río announced the outbreak of insurrection. The soldiers of the old Liberation Army took to the field again, and within weeks all but the cities of the three western provinces had fallen to the insurgents. By the end of August, too, problems of a different sort beset the Estrada government. The expanding insurrection threatened foreign property. In late August, the United States demanded that the Cuban government place "with the greatest energy" in the field "not only enough men to assume active operations against the insurgents, but enough to garrison the towns, keep open the lines of communication, and to protect foreign interests, particularly American lives and property." [19]

A difficult situation had become impossible. Overextended in the field and outmaneuvered in operations, beleaguered government forces strained to avert an outright rout. By the end of August, the Rural Guard could neither guard rural property nor guarantee rural peace. The protection of foreign property suddenly assumed new urgency as the prospect of a protracted conflict raised official concern for the security of the upcoming sugar harvest. General Carlos Asbert, the insurgent chieftain in Havana province, threatened to launch a campaign against property unless the government acceded to Liberal demands.[20] On September 4, U.S. Chargé Jacob Sleeper cabled Washington that the insurgency approached a new phase: "It is persistently reported that unless some peace arrangement is made before the 15th of this month, the rebels will begin burning foreign property."[21]

V

These were portentous developments, but not uncalculated. This was a drama played in good part for the benefit of a North American audience, one designed also to secure audience participation. Moderates had been apparently unconcerned about the consequences of political fraud not only because they controlled the elections, the army, and the courts. Moderates also counted on U.S. support. They did represent, after all, constituted authority, and they were the only authority. And as they understood the terms of the Platt Amendment, the United States was obliged by treaty to assist constituted government in times of internal disorder.

It is not certain that this conviction encouraged government misconduct in 1905. Nor is it certain that it promoted government indifference to Liberal protests. It is certain, however, that once the controversy over ballots became a contest of bullets, once the political dispute erupted into armed conflict, Moderates expected U.S. military support to defeat the insurgents.

But Liberals had a different view. They insisted that under the terms of the Platt Amendment, the United States had committed itself to the maintenance of a government adequate for the protection of life, property, and liberty. Government fraud, Liberals argued, had deprived Cubans of their liberty. Government violence had taken Cuban lives. Under the terms of the Permanent Treaty, these conditions required investigation. And if an appeal to reason failed to secure the United States' attention, an attack against property would not.

VI

In early September 1906 the Cuban government could neither defeat local insurgents nor defend foreign interests. The issue was no longer whether the government possessed the power to protect property but whether it could defend itself. The defense of foreign interests had become at least as important as the defeat of the Liberals. It was not certain that Estrada could do either. It was certain that he could not do both.

On September 8, Estrada Palma appealed for U.S. assistance. Consul Frank Steinhart cabled the White House: "The Secretary of State of Cuba has requested me in the name of President Palma, to ask President Roosevelt to send immediately two vessels—one to Habana, other to Cienfuegos. They must come at once. Government forces unable to quell rebellion. The Government is unable to protect life and property."[22] Four days later, Cuban authorities renewed their request, this time with a new urgency. "Cuban Secretary of State," Steinhart cabled, "delivered to me the following memorandum":

> The rebellion has increased in the provinces of Santa Clara, Havana and Pinar del Rio and the Cuban Government has no elements to contend it, to defend the towns and prevent the rebels from destroying property. President Estrada Palma asks for American intervention and begs that President Roosevelt send to Havana with the greatest secrecy and rapidity two or three thousand men to avoid any catastrophe in the Capital.[23]

On September 13, Estrada issued a third appeal for intervention, admitting bluntly that he had neither the might "to prevent rebels from entering cities and burning property" nor the means to protect North American lives and property in Havana.[24] A day later, the president again repeated the request, this time in the form of a thinly veiled ultimatum. The president, the vice-president, and all the cabinet ministers, Steinhart cabled, threatened to resign unless the United States provided military assistance. The Moderate majority in the congress, further, threatened to block a quorum, thereby foreclosing any possibility of a constitutional resolution of presidential succession. "The consequence," Steinhart warned, "will be absence of legal power and therefore the prevailing state of anarchy will continue unless the Government of the United States will adopt the measures necessary to avoid this danger."[25]

By mid-September the embattled extremes of the Cuban polity had arrived at similar objectives, if for different motives. The leadership of both political parties realized that the Platt Amendment offered a remedy. Liberals, for their part, unable to prevent certain political defeat at the polls, set out purposefully to create the military conditions requiring U.S. intervention. The Moderates, unable to forestall certain military defeat, prepared to create the political conditions requiring intervention. Both believed themselves to be the beneficiaries of intervention.

VII

The fact that the United States was committed by treaty to intervene in case of a Cuban crisis contributed to creating the conditions that the intervention clause was designed to prevent. News of rebellion in Cuba created a policy dilemma in the United States. President Theodore Roosevelt recognized immediately the anomaly of the United States' position. He understood that if Cubans were determined to precipitate intervention, there was little the United States could do but intervene.

These factors filled Roosevelt with indignation. He sensed he was powerless; he understood the degree to which Cubans had created the conditions and controlled the events to which the United States would perforce have to respond. "At the moment," Roosevelt blustered, "I am so angry with that infernal little Cuban republic that I would like to wipe its people off the face of the earth. All we have wanted from them was that they would behave themselves and be prosperous and happy so that we would not have to interfere. And now, lo and behold, they have started an utterly unjustifiable and pointless revolution and may get things into such a snarl that we have no alternative [but] to intervene." [26]

Roosevelt immediately rejected intervention. He exhorted the Cuban government to end the lawlessness by force without compromise. "Tell Palma to use in the most effective fashion," Roosevelt instructed the State Department, "all the resources at his command to quell the revolt." [27] The State Department cabled Havana that no intervention would be contemplated until the Cuban government had "exhausted every effort to put down the insurrection and has made this fact evident to the world." [28]

But Washington recognized, too, that the Cuban government possessed neither the military means nor political support to suppress the revolt or survive the crisis. If Estrada could not dominate the rebellion militarily, he was urged to deal with the rebels politically. Roosevelt urged Cubans to "patch up their differences and live in peace." [29] The United States hoped, Assistant Secretary of State Robert Bacon stressed, that "every effort is being made by the Cuban Government to come to a working agreement which will secure peace with the insurrectos, provided they are unable to hold their own with them in the field." He added: "Until such efforts have been made we are not prepared to consider the question of intervention at all."[30]

Roosevelt contemplated intervention with apprehension. "On the one hand," he mused, "we cannot permanently see Cuba a prey to misrule and anarchy; on the other hand I loathe the thought of assuming any control over the island such as we have over Puerto Rico and the Philippines. We emphatically do not want it; and . . . nothing but direst need could persuade us to take it."[31] "They are not suffering from any real grievances whatsoever," he wrote privately. "Yet they have deliberately plunged the country into civil war, and if they go on will assuredly deprive themselves of their liberty." He hoped to "do some tall thinking in the effort to bring about a condition which shall, if possible, put an end to anarchy without necessitating a reoccupation of the island by our troops."[32] But the prospects of total collapse of constituted government in Havana increased by mid-September. "The situation in the islands seems to be one of impending chaos, with no responsible head," Roosevelt concluded on September 14. "We must act in such a way as to protect American interests by fulfilling American obligations to Cuba." It was apparent, too, that "under the circumstances . . . the ordinary type of diplomatic communication would in this case accomplish no good purpose."[33] Still Roosevelt would not yield on the matter of armed intervention. Instead, he appointed Secretary of War William H. Taft and Assistant Secretary of State Robert Bacon as special representatives to mediate a political settlement in Havana.

VIII

The arrival of Taft and Bacon in Havana immediately had a salutary effect. Hostilities halted, political prisoners were released, and government authorities and Liberal representatives agreed to negotiate, if only by proxy through the U.S. envoys.[34]

But neither the amelioration of political conditions nor the moratorium on military operations offered more than fleeting hope for a negotiated settlement. Taft and Bacon found that conditions in Cuba were desperate. Government forces were everywhere in disarray and near collapse. Havana itself was surrounded by 10,000 insurgent troops. "The Government controls only the coast towns and provincial capitals," Taft cabled Washington, and added portentously: "Anarchy elsewhere."[35]

Taft and Bacon arrived in Cuba with specific objectives: an immediate suspension of armed hostilities, and ultimately a negotiated political settlement. They achieved the former easily enough, but the precise means to the second objective was not immediately evident. Washington initially believed that a negotiated peace involved minimal support of the existing government as means to restore political order, followed by the disbandment of the insurgent forces. And preliminary to both, Taft and Bacon undertook a full inquiry into the developments leading to the rebellion, including examination of Liberal charges, review of the electoral records, and discussions with leaders of both political parties.[36]

The findings of the investigation were startling, and the conclusions inescapable. Government misconduct in the 1905 elections, Taft and Bacon concluded, had discredited the government and had produced discontent everywhere. Some amount of fraud seemed to attend all political contests, they concluded, but the magnitude of irregularities in 1905 and the scale of coercion employed appalled them. The Cuban government "flagrantly and openly used and abused its power to carry elections and in so doing removed many municipal officers in many parts of the island," Taft wrote with indignation. "The open and flagrant way in which it was here done seems to have made a deep impression on the minds of the people, especially because it was accompanied by wholesale removals from office and by levy assessments to the lowest street cleaners."[37] To his wife, Taft acknowledged, "The Government seems to have abused its powers outrageously in the elections and this is a protest against that."[38]

Disappointment with the political performance of the administration did not, however, signify sympathy with armed protest. Taft openly denounced the insurrection and condemned its leaders. But neither could Taft dismiss the validity of Liberal grievances. In the end, Moderates were held responsible for the crisis. And vaguely Taft and Bacon touched upon the powerful undercurrents of the protest: "No such formidable force could have been organized, had there not been some real feeling of injustice and outrage on the part of the less educated poorer classes, who seemed more or less dimly to understand that the victory of the Moderates at the polls was the beginning of the end of power which they might exercise in the government."[39]

Very early the U.S. representatives arrived at two important conclusions. First, the Liberals had achieved far greater military success than had been previously suspected. Insurgent armies were positioned every-where, poised for renewed fighting and prepared confidently for a final offensive against government forces. But, second, if the Liberals were militarily stronger, the Moderates were politically weaker. The Estrada Palma government had less popular support than was earlier believed. "The people of the interior," Taft cabled Washington, "seem to favor the insurgents by a large majority." The government lacks "moral support of large majority of the people, and is without adequate preparation."[40] The government, Taft stressed again days later, lacked "moral support or sym-pathy" everywhere in Cuba except in the province of Matanzas.[41]

These conclusions had far-reaching policy implications. It would have been reasonable to lend armed support to a politically solvent govern-ment, or to provide political backing to a military strong regime. But to support a government that was both politically discredited and militarily debilitated was untenable. "If the present government could maintain it-self or had moral support or following which would be useful in case of intervention," Taft lamented to Roosevelt on September 20, "Bacon and I would be strongly in favor of supporting it as the regular and constitu-tional government because the election was held under the forms of the law and has been acted upon and recognized as valid, but actually the state of affairs is such that we should be fighting the whole Cuban people in effect by intervening to maintain this government."[42] And a day later, Taft cabled: "We cannot maintain Palma Government except by forcible intervention against the whole weight of public opinion in the Island."[43] He concluded, "The truth is that the Cuban government has proven to be nothing but a house of cards."[44]

The extent to which irregularities had compromised Moderates, to-gether with the degree to which coercion had antagonized Liberals, made it impolitic if not impossible to retain the Moderate government as the basis of a negotiated settlement. Within days of their arrival, however, Taft and Bacon had persuaded themselves that Estrada Palma was not privy to the abuses committed in his behalf. This presumption of inno-cence exonerated the president of the misdeeds perpetrated in his name, thereby setting in place the cornerstone of an emerging compromise settlement: the retention of Estrada for a second term. "His continuance in office," Taft argued, "would be valuable to the Island in that everybody accords him honesty, and the property holders and conservatives would be gratified by his continuance. . . . It gives continuity to the Govern-ment and diminishes in some respect the evil of the present situation and of the compromise that must be effected, in that it is a remedying of wrongs by violence and treason to the government. It continues the identity of the government which was established four years ago by the United States."[45] Taft and Bacon made one more leap of faith: "We were of the opinion, from all we could learn, that President Palma would have been elected without any resort to unfair methods which we believe to have been used under the Moderate secretary of government. We deemed it important, in order to maintain the good name of Cuba, and in order to show that a conservative man was retained in power, to have Mr. Palma remain as President. We thought it would preserve the continuity of the Government under the constitution, and perhaps prevent the injury to the credit of the island which a violent or abrupt change in chief executive would be likely to effect."[46]

But presidential continuity as a central condition of a political compromise, Taft and Bacon recognized, meant offering the Liberals some far-reaching concessions in return. Liberal ratification of presidential reelection would not be easily obtained. "It is important if we can keep [Estrada Palma] in office . . . to grant other demands of the insurgents," Taft conceded to his wife.[47]

And, indeed, the compromise proposed by the United States was thorough: annulment of the 1905 congressional elections, the scheduling of new elections under the supervision of a bipartisan commission, resignation of the Moderate cabinet, and the creation of a nonpolitical advisory board. Upon the resignation of Moderate officials, Liberals were to lay down their arms and return to peaceful pursuits under a general amnesty.[48]

Liberals grudgingly accepted the proposed settlement, and making the best of partial success proclaimed complete victory. The Moderates immediately rejected the settlement. The proposal was a betrayal, Estrada protested, a reversal for constitutional administration, a rebuff to constituted authority. The elections were fair, he continued to insist, and he would not accept the purge of his party as the condition of his continuance as president.[49] During a tense meeting at the presidential palace on September 23, Estrada rejected outright the U.S. proposal. "I cannot accept this solution of our difficulties, sir," he protested to Taft. "My honor, the honor of my country, the honor of my advisors, all are at stake. We owe it to our patriotism to stand firm." Sensing the last alternative to armed intervention slipping away, Taft made one more appeal. "Mr. President, there comes a time when patriotism demands a sacrifice—" "Mr.

Secretary," Estrada interrupted, "I do not intend to take any lesson in patriotism from you." Cuban Secretary of State Ramón O'Farrill brought the meeting to an angry end. "Is it for this that you Americans have come here?" O'Farrill demanded. "We could have settled this matter ourselves, put down the revolution unaided. Yet you come here and deal with men in arms against the government."[50]

This ended all reasonable likelihood of a negotiated settlement. The next day Taft and Bacon made one last appeal to Estrada.[51] But Taft sensed that conditions requiring a military intervention were quickly overtaking his efforts to arrange a political settlement. "Palma is proving quite obstinate and makes things difficult," Taft wrote to his wife. "He is honest but is a good deal of an old ass. He doesn't take in the situation."[52] Taft communicated the bad news to Roosevelt bluntly:

> Palma has notified us that he will resign and we are advised that the vice president, all the Cabinet, and all the Congressmen in the Moderate party will resign, leaving nothing of the Government. I think there is nothing to do but to issue a proclamation stating that as the only constituted governent in the island has abdicated it is necessary for you under the Platt Amendment to assume the control of the island and establish a provisional government and name some one as Governor, giving him such powers as may become necessary to preserve law and order, suppress the insurrection and continue the ordinary administration of the government until a more permanent policy may be determined.[53]

Having failed to secure U.S. support, Moderates turned their disappointment into indignation toward the United States. The opposition party had become the party of cooperation; the government party had become the opposition. The proposed compromise, Taft maintained, simply restored political parity in congress while keeping Estrada in possession of the most important branch of government. Not having received all their demands, Taft wrote with some bitterness, "Palma and Moderates will now take their dolls and not play." He continued:

> They are now abusing us and are taking the ground that it was our duty to sustain the government at all hazards and put down the insurrection at all cost. . . . But we did not make and were not responsible for the situation which we found. The government was in a state of collapse, Havana at the mercy of the insurgents, anarchy in the island, and we came here as intermediaries between armed forces to secure peace and prevent a war which circumstances would have rendered disastrous to Cuban interests for a decade. We could only mediate by conferring with

both sides, we could not mediate with the government only, we could not effect a compromise that conformed only to the views of the Government, we must make concessions to the rebels. That is a bad precedent but we did not cause it.[54]

IX

No alternative to intervention remained. For the second time in a decade, the United States intervened militarily to prevent the ascendancy of popular insurgent forces—first the Liberation Army in 1898, and the Liberal party in 1906. The soldiers had been again thwarted.

The 1906 revolt represented more than an armed protest against electoral fraud. It gave powerful expression to the urgency of republican politics. There was much at stake in these proceedings, and because there was so little of anything else, politics was everything: "The great mass of the people are absorbed in politics," the U.S. military attache observed in 1903.[55] This was serious business, at least serious enough to go to war about. Partisan passion was the form assumed by preoccupation with the pursuit of opportunity. Political parties were the means of that pursuit.[56]

Another aspect of the events of 1906 was no less revealing about the developing character of political culture in the early republic. The senior army chieftains of the Liberation Army, now the ranking political caudillos of the Liberal party, were on the march again. Certainly not all military leaders enrolled in the Liberal party, but many—the most popular—did, and none was more popular than José Miguel Gómez. The Liberal victory announced the ascendency of the populist military sector over the civil element. It signaled, too, the overthrow of a government specifically established by the United States as a device to obstruct the rise of the populist forces in the old separatist coalition.[57]

U.S. intervention again thwarted the populists. The second intervention (1906–1909), like the first, resulted in the wholesale displacement of Cubans from the upper reaches of political office. Public administration passed again under the authority of a provisional government organized by the United States. Once more the distribution of resources was controlled by a foreign officialdom.

X

For the United States, the second intervention seemed to reveal the woeful inadequacy of existing policy constructs. The Platt Amendment had failed to prevent conditions of instability. On the contrary, it had directly contributed to creating them. The Platt Amendment gave the government license to pursue electoral fraud, and once the insurrection erupted, Moderates were confident that the United States would assist them to defeat the rebels and underwrite four more years of Moderate rule. Certainly this was a reasonable inference to draw from Elihu Root's pronouncement in 1904: "No such revolutions as have afflicted Central and South America are possible there, because it is known to all men that an attempt to overturn the foundations of that government will be confronted from the overwhelming power of the United States."[58] The United States would have indeed preferred to support constituted authority over the "lawless" element. But so tenuous was the military condition of the government that only the direct deployment of U.S. combat forces could have maintained Estrada Palma in power—something Washington was unwilling to do. The Liberal rebellion tested the United States' commitment to stability: either Washington forced Estrada to make political concessions or it faced a civil war in Cuba. "Had we come in and at once supported the constituted government," Taft reflected privately on the eve of his departure from Cuba, "we should have had a war on our hands in which the American interests would have been the first to suffer and then all would have been involved in one conflagration. Had we not come at all the same thing must have happened and years of destruction would have followed."[59] Cuban power contenders were quick to recognize that U.S. intervention was a continuation of Cuban politics by another means, and very early U.S. policy was subject to manipulation by Cuban leaders.

These developments had important implications for foreign capital in Cuba. The Platt Amendment obliged Cuba as a condition of continued sovereignty to guarantee the security of property. Just as the injunction against revolution served to encourage the revolution, Cuba's obligation to protect foreign property served as an incentive to its opponents to destroy it. Disgruntled political factions seeking to create pressure on the government could not pursue a more effective course than to attack foreign property. "The great trouble is," Taft recognized immediately upon his arrival in Havana, "that unless we assure peace, some $200,000,000 of American property may go up in smoke in less than ten days."[60] A day later, Taft wrote of his hope for a settlement that would "avoid great disaster to business and property interests of the Island."[61]

The Cuban crisis had a sobering effect in the United States. The conviction that the Platt Amendment guaranteed stability and security to foreign capital proved short-lived. The deficiency of the Root interpretation of the Platt Amendment stood in sharp relief. If U.S. intervention was limited specifically to end conditions of chaos, as Root had pledged in 1901, the Platt Amendment offered too little too late. The United States had assumed responsibility for the conduct of government, not only remedying the misconduct of government. To wait for political instability to lead to armed insurrection, to delay until an incumbent government demonstrated an incapacity to end armed protest, exposed foreign property to incalculable danger.

Much of the U.S. effort during the three years of occupation had centered on developing the institutional guarantees of order and stability. A new electoral code and a new population census were prepared. New laws dealt with municipal administration, local election boards, judicial reform, and civil service reorganization.

It became clear, too, that the Cuban government lacked adequate military strength with which to suppress political disorder. The Rural Guard, created during the first intervention, was designed to guarantee order in the interior and protect rural property. But 5,000 Rural Guards organized into some 250 posts and distributed throughout six provinces were inadequate. In 1905, the government's political grasp had exceeded its military reach. The Moderates, in short, lacked the armed forces to back up electoral fraud. Government military weakness had necessitated political concession and had severely limited U.S. options. The "utter military incapacity" of the Estrada government, Roosevelt complained, forced political compromise and, ultimately, armed intervention.

> At the outbreak of the insurrection all that I did was to give every possible support to the Palma government, the regularly constituted authorities, even going to the length of facilitating their getting cartridges from this country—for I felt that a successful insurrection, or indeed a long and dragging civil war in Cuba would be a serious calamity for Cuba and a real evil to the United States; but the Palma government proved helplessly unable to protect itself. It seems to have almost no support among the Cubans; it had taken no steps in advance which would enable it to put down the crisis with nerve and vigor.[62]

Taft and Bacon agreed. The Rural Guards, they concluded, "were distributed in small detachments in the various towns of the island and were thus unable to cope with the insurrection where they were organized in any numbers at all. This weakness of the Government left it naked to its enemies and critics." The government "was utterly unprepared to meet this attack."[63] Provisional Governor Charles E. Magoon reached similar conclusions. The "Cuban Government," he wrote to Roosevelt, "was unstable because it lacked even the ordinary means and agencies by which stability is secured."[64]

The absence of an adequate military force had rendered the Cuban government vulnerable to armed protest and incapable of discharging its obligations under the Permanent Treaty. The condition of Cuban armed forces received early attention, partly because there existed an obvious remedy. Under the Root interpretation of the Platt Amendment, Cuba had no need for an army because U.S. forces were committed to its defense. The inefficacy of the Root interpretation meant that Cuban authorities would have to assume a larger share of military responsibility for the defense of constituted government. The creation of a formal military establishment, capable of suppressing internal disorders, efficiently and effectively, without U.S. intervention, offered an appealing guarantee of stability in Cuba.

The provisional government immediately turned its attention to reorganizing the Rural Guard. The worst features of the outpost system were eliminated. Training missions and military schools were established in all provincial capitals. New arms were distributed. Enlistment requirements were revised and new appropriations were allocated to expand the guard.[65] "If it is necessary to make an additional appropriation," Taft counseled, "I would make it because the truth is that Palma had not a large enough force, and the appropriation was not sufficient."[66] In early 1907, Taft outlined plans to organize an armed force capable of defending the Cuban government. "What we want you to do," Taft instructed the provisional governor, "is to go ahead and recruit the Rural Guard up to 10,000, no matter what objection is made to it, so that when we leave the government there we shall leave it something with which to preserve itself."[67]

But it soon became apparent that a Rural Guard, however much reformed and reorganized, remained substantially a constabulary force. After 1906, political considerations required the establishment of a regular military force. Magoon explained to Roosevelt, "A military force pure and simple is a reasonable and necessary agency for the stability of the Government. The necessity of such a force was demonstrated by the insurrection of 1906."[68] "Upon the outbreak of the insurrection of 1906," Magoon stated in his official report, "it was necessary for the President of the Republic to guard Havana and the larger towns of the island and also to have a force sufficient to send against the insurgent forces. To do this he was obliged to concentrate the Rural Guard, leaving the country without patrol and the small towns without protection. This would not have been the case if a small military force had been available in each of the provincial capitals."[69]

In April 1908 the provisional government promulgated the decrees reorganizing the armed forces. The Rural Guard remained intact, expanded to 5,000 officers and men distributed in 380 detachments. A new permanent army consisted of one infantry brigade, to be subsequently expanded by a gradual transfer of men from the Rural Guard.

In 1908, too, elections established Liberal ascendancy over the island. The Liberal party won the presidency, obtained control of both houses of congress, and prevailed in provincial and municipal positions across the island. In January 1909 the new congress assembled and certified the election of José Miguel Gómez as president and Alfredo Zayas as vice-president.

5.

The Republic
Restored

I

The restoration of the republic in 1909 did not signify the recovery of sovereignty any more than the creation of the republic in 1902 signaled independence. Conditions in the intervening years had changed, and these changes bode ill for the exercise of Cuban sovereignty.

U.S. hegemony shifted to a new set of approaches, based on different assumptions. Many of the new assumptions, to be sure, were nothing more than reformulations of old attitudes. But in 1909 they acquired a renewed vigor in the pursuit of new objectives. William Howard Taft had arrived at some rather pointed conclusions during his mediation efforts in Cuba in 1906. "The whole thing demonstrates the utter unfitness of these people for self-government."[1] "The absence of patriotism and the exaltation of selfish pride and love of place and power and greed are the most discouraging traits we have seen here."[2]

These sentiments, in part culturally determined, in part ideologically derived, characterized official thinking in the United States about Cuba for the better part of the decade. They served, too, as the central assumptions of policy, the justification for a growing U.S. presence and the rationale for an expanding hegemony. But even as Cuba prepared to reclaim national sovereignty in 1909, premises of another sort were shaping the policy approaches to the Caribbean and the political purpose of the Platt Amendment in Cuba.

Conditions had changed between January 1899 when Spain relinquished Cuba to U.S. rule and January 1909 when the United States restored the island to Cuban rule. In the course of that decade the United States enjoyed uninterrupted success in establishing mastery over the circum-Caribbean region. It had been a comparatively easy task; the United States had not encountered serious obstruction from either the remaining colonial powers of Europe or the emergent new states in the Caribbean. The defeat of Spain had expelled an unstable colonial power and ended a troublesome source of recurring political disorder. In the Treaty of Paris of 1899, the United States gained sovereignty over Puerto Rico. In the Permanent Treaty of 1903 it acquired sway over Cuba. Together the two islands established a U.S. naval presence along the four principal sea approaches to the Isthmus of Panama. The Hay–Bunau Varilla Treaty in 1903 settled the central strategic issue of the region by guaranteeing to the United States undisputed control over the Panama Canal. The proclamation of the Roosevelt Corollary in 1904, moreover, gave policy form to the U.S. claim of paramount interest in the region.[3] "Brutal wrong doing," Roosevelt wrote to Elihu Root, "or an impotence which results in a general loosening of the ties of civilized society, may finally require intervention by some civilized nation, and in the Western Hemisphere the United States cannot ignore this duty."[4] Six months later, Roosevelt outlined in full the policy implications of these musings. The "insurrectionary habit" of those "wretched republics," the president proclaimed in his annual message to Congress in 1904, had created conditions potentially hazardous to U.S. interests in the region:

> Chronic wrongdoing . . . may in America, as elsewhere, ultimately require intervention by some civilized nation, and in the Western Hemisphere the adherence of the United States to the Monroe Doctrine may force the United States, however reluctantly in flagrant cases of such wrong doing or impotence, to the exercise of an international police power.[5]

Control over Cuba announced hegemony over the region. The injunction that placed the region off limits to Europe also created, certainly in the minds of policy officials, Caribbean accountability to the United States. This was the purport of the Roosevelt Corollary. In early years of the new century, the quest for conditions of sovereignty over the Caribbean drew the United States deeper into the vortex of local national systems. Security over the whole required surveillance of the parts. Sporadic involvement in the internal affairs of the Caribbean republics became sustained and permanent. What was earlier the defense of the region as a means of hegemony became hegemony as a means of defending the region.

Annexationism had outlived its time. It had been a nineteenth-century policy formulation, one that rested on an expanding but yet undefined policy for the whole region and on the proposition that U.S. interests would be served best by formal absorption of Cuba. But much had changed since the United States evacuated Cuba in 1902. The United States had formally proclaimed the Caribbean as a sphere of influence, if not with Europe's approval, then with its acquiescence. Acquisition of Cuba through annexation was no longer an urgent issue; U.S. interests in the Caribbean had been defined in broader geopolitical terms.

II

This newfound supremacy was the cause and effect of needs of a different sort. Interests proclaimed paramount for security were now affirmed essential for prosperity. Rapid economic development and surplus production in the United States required new markets, and the Caribbean region became a necessary extension of the North American economic system. "No picture of our future," Assistant Secretary of State Francis B. Loomis asserted in 1905, "is complete which does not contemplate and comprehend the United States as the dominant power in the Caribbean Sea."

> In considering the position of the United States on the American continent you will ultimately have to reckon . . . [that] the vastly augmented power of production on the part of the American people has rendered insufficient the home market. We are being driven, by necessity, to find new markets, and these economic problems must be given due, if not commanding place, in considering in a rounded, broad and comprehensive way the relations of the United States to the rest of this hemisphere and to the rest of the world.[6]

The economic necessity to expand into the Caribbean created its own set of policy imperatives. The United States demanded open economies with free access to resources, favorable market conditions, a docile working class, a compliant political elite, and a friendly climate of investment that included minimum competition, maximum protection, and political stability.

The export of surplus production as a means of promoting political stability abroad and peace at home early captured the imagination of the Taft administration. On this issue political considerations converged with foreign policy. U.S. politico-military control in the Caribbean coincided with mounting economic difficulties in the United States. Production was overtaking consumption, and lagging consumption threatened to impede continued economic expansion. The panic of 1907 underscored the need for both new investment opportunities and new markets. Economic expansion at home demanded political expansion abroad.

President Taft and Secretary of State Philander C. Knox early recognized that economic prosperity and social order in the United States required mastery over Latin America. To this purpose the State Department devoted its mission in Latin America. This was the stuff, too, of dollar diplomacy. In 1909, Knox established the Bureau of Trade Relations. In the same year, the State Department created a Latin American Bureau, to sercure for the United States "its share in the almost boundless possibilities of Latin American trade to which it is entitled." Knox proclaimed: "[The] Bureau of Latin-American Affairs . . . is expected to be a most effective way of stimulating commercial relations with the countries in question. . . . With the creation of the Latin-American Bureau the producers of the United States will have at their command facilities which will enable them to understand just the sort of market offered to them and what is to be done in order to secure customers in that quarter."[7]

The expansion of trade and the export of capital were also seen as the way to reduce European influence in the Caribbean, which would, in turn, eliminate economic competitors and political rivals.[8] Taft proclaimed of the Caribbean in 1912:

> It is, therefore, essential that the countries within that sphere shall be removed from the jeopardy involved by heavy foreign debt and chaotic national finances from the ever-present danger of international complications due to disorder at home. Hence the United States has been glad to encourage and support American bankers who were willing to lend a helping hand to the financial rehabilitation of such countries, because this financial rehabilitation and the protection of their customhouses from being the prey of would be dictators would remove at one stroke the menace of foreign creditors and the menace of revolutionary disorder.[9]

A similar note was struck by Knox in 1910: "True stability is best established not by military, but by economic and social forces. . . . The problem of good government is inextricably interwoven with that of economic
prosperity and sound finance; financial stability contributes perhaps
more than any other factor to political stability."[10] "The logic of political
geography and of strategy, and now our tremendous national interest created by the Panama Canal," Knox reiterated two years later, "make the
safety, the peace, and the prosperity of Central American and the zone of
the Caribbean of paramount interest to the Government of the United
States. Thus the malady of revolutions and financial collapse is most
acute precisely in the region where it is most dangerous to us. It is here
that we seek to apply a remedy."[11]

But stability remained always a means, for its object was to create an
environment in which trade and investment would flourish. And it was
this goal to which the State Department committed itself in the Caribbean. Dollar diplomacy, Assistant Secretary of State F. M. Huntington
Wilson explained in 1911, "means use of the capital of the country in the
foreign field in a manner calculated to enhance fixed national interests. It
means the substitution of dollars for bullets. It means the creation of a
prosperity which will be preferred to predatory strife. It means availing of
capital's self interest in peace. It means taking advantage of the interest
in peace of those who benefit by the investment of capital. It recognizes
that financial soundness is a potent factor in political stability; that prosperity means contentment and contentment repose."[12] Peace in the Caribbean also promised profits in the United States. Taft predicted:

> The . . . advantage to the United States is one affecting all the southern
> and Gulf ports and the business and industry of the South. The Re-
> publics of Central America and the Caribbean possess great natural
> wealth. They need only a measure of stability and the means of financial
> regeneration to enter upon an era of peace and prosperity, bringing
> profit and happiness to themselves and at the same time creating condi-
> tions sure to lead to a flourishing interchange of trade with this country.[13]

The relationship between economic prosperity and national security in
the United States, on one hand, and economic expansion and stability
in the Caribbean, on the other, was indissolubly linked in the policy approaches to the region. "The theory that the field of diplomacy does not
include in any degree commerce and the increase of trade relations," Taft
asserted in 1910,

is one to which Mr. Knox and this administration do not subscribe. We believe . . . that [our foreign policy] . . . may well be made to include active intervention to secure for our merchandise and our capitalists opportunities for profitable investment which shall inure to the benefit of both countries involved. . . . If the protection which the United States shall assure to her citizens in the assertion of just rights under investment made in foreign countries shall promote the amount of such investments and stimulate and enlarge the business relations, it is a result to be commended.[14]

It was also the purpose to which Taft committed the foreign policy of the United States: "Our trade has grown quite beyond the limits of this country. With an annual foreign trade exceeding $2 billion, our State Department could not vindicate its existence or justify a policy in which in any way withheld a fostering, protecting, and stimulating hand in the development and extension of that trade."[15] "The homemarket," warned L. W. Strayer, a close associate of Knox, "has long ceased to be able to consume the home production and the production is growing out of all proportions for the population. . . . If there are not enough buyers at home we must find them abroad."[16] Assistant Secretary of State Huntington Wilson also pledged official support to investments in Latin America that "promote vital political interests." Wilson identified three principal characteristics: first, activities that "establish permanent and valuable markets for trade while at the same time subserving political strength where the policy of the country demands that it be strong if we are to have security and tranquility"; second, investments that "serve in giving us a commercial standing in some valuable market where development may be preempted by others if a foot be not early obtained," and, lastly, activities that "bring profit and employment to the American people in general." Investors that "lend themselves as instrumentalities of foreign policy," Wilson promised, would receive "rights of protection of especial dignity."[17]

These were, to be sure, always important considerations in the formulation of U.S. policy in the Caribbean. But during the Taft years, and continuing thereafter, these became central. "The investment of our surplus capital," Knox predicted, "and the exploitation of our products not absorbed by the home market, . . . which increase with the slackening of the domestic demand for their activities, should vitalize our commerce with the other American republics."[18] Knox was especially mindful of the relationship between foreign policy and domestic prosperity. "For the prosperity of those who labor and those who sell, we must have uninter-

mittent production and to avoid the perils of over-production and congestion we must find foreign markets for our surplus products." He added:

> The time is coming when the foreign market will be more important to
> our prosperity than at present, and as that time approaches the foreign
> market will be less open to us because there will be keener competition.
> Nothing equals our home market but we need foreign markets as a bal-
> ance wheel. . . . Latin America is one of the regions of greatest poten-
> tiality as a field for foreign commerce and investment in the near future
> and it is a field conspicuously adapted to American enterprise. . . . The
> present magnitude of Latin America is probably seldom appreciated,
> while its potentiality in the not distant future is almost beyond esti-
> mate. . . . If efforts be not now made there is a very real danger that op-
> portunities will be pre-empted and that American commerce will fall so
> far behind as to make it well-nigh impossible for us to overtake our
> rivals. . . . There is no impropriety in the advancement of American
> trade by the effective cooperation of the Government in finding openings
> abroad, in insisting that our money have an equal chance with all other
> money. . . . Now, as always, in order to secure investments abroad and to
> build up a trade with foreign countries, the protection of Government is
> required.[19]

Dollar diplomacy rested on several key assumptions. The flow of U.S.
capital to the Caribbean, in the form of loans and/or direct investments,
was intended to promote financial stability that, in turn, would eliminate
European capital and end political instability. This condition, further,
would enhance U.S. influence by promoting indebtedness to and dependency on North American capital. The displacement of European capital
and the reduction of political instability, moreover, promised to decrease
international tensions in the region. Capital would promote financial stability and open economies, which would encourage political stability,
international tranquility, and receptivity to U.S. exports. The connection
between investment and trade was sharply drawn in the United States'
policy approach to the region. Knox proclaimed:

> If we want foreign trade, a share in foreign investments, a chance to ex-
> ploit the riches of other lands, our share in the wealth of other nations,
> we must buy their bonds, help float their loans, build their railroads, es-
> tablish banks in their chief cities. In South America the giving of good
> advice and the Monroe Doctrine should be made to yield a financial har-
> vest by the establishment of banks in population centers. When their
> people want money they should come here for it. As a consequence,

> when railroads are to be built, our mills will furnish the equipment;
> when mines are to be opened, bridges to be constructed, great enter-
> prises started, the finished materials and machines will come from our
> plants.[20]

Dollar diplomacy was also intended to eliminate the conditions requiring U.S. armed intervention. The proposition that financial stability produced political stability was an article of faith central to policy calculations. So too was the belief that capital would eliminate the cause of
disorder. "Whether this Government likes it or not," Knox insisted, "by
the common consent of the Republics of Central America and the Caribbean and according to the fixed idea of the world at large, this Government is regarded as responsible under the Monroe Doctrine as a matter of
course and as the inevitable result of its position in the Caribbean, for the
conditions existing in those republics. The obligation cannot be escaped.
Is it better to meet it with dollars or with guns? . . . The moral effect of
the right to act coupled with the material benefits realized from financial
regeneration diminishes more than anything else could the occasions
when it is necessary actually to act."[21]

U.S. capital in the Caribbean, for its part, needed the promise of assistance and assurance of protection. Other foreign fields offered capitalists
comparable returns with incomparably fewer risks. Policymakers sought
not only to induce capital to invest with the prospect of profit, but also to
enlist investors with the promise of protection. Public men summoned
private men to participate in a collaborative enterprise in which the needs
of state and the interests of capital fused indistinguishably in the pursuit
of policy. The lines between public and private were often vague, and at
any given time it was impossible to determine if policy conformed to the
requirements of capital or if capital complied with the needs of policy. Nor
was this distinction important. In fact, it was both, and this ambiguity
underscored the degree to which assumptions were shared in common
and objectives pursued in concert.

Enlisting capital to promote political control required, in turn, an increase of political control to protect capital. The use of capital to reduce
the necessity of armed intervention increased the need for political intervention. "Both the sanction and the ultimate justification for the interference of the United States close to its doors," Knox stressed, "has
invariably been the perpetuation of conditions of disorder and lawlessness. . . . That the continuance of such a condition at our doors could not
fail to concern us became speedily apparent. The first justification of in-

terest always rests on material grounds, and herein, the presence of numerous Americans and the employment of American capital to very considerable extent, has made it desirable in behalf of the legitimate rights of our citizens to ensure the preservation of law and order wherever this was disturbed."[22]

No potential source of political disorder, no possible cause of fiscal instability could be overlooked. This inevitably expanded the scope of U.S. intervention in the internal affairs of Caribbean states. The guarantee of financial stability required supervision over fiscal administration, including collection of revenues, budget preparation, and credit transactions. Foreign capital needed guarantees against prejudicial legislation and militant labor, against threats to life and property, against political instability—against anything and everything likely to interrupt profits and endanger property.

III

The restoration of Cuban sovereignty in 1909 coincided with the formulation of new U.S. policy approaches to the Caribbean. Certainly the central assumptions of dollar diplomacy had direct relevance to Cuba. But Cuba was different in several important respects. Nowhere else in the Caribbean did industrial capital represent such a large portion of the total share of North American investment. U.S. capital in Central America consisted principally in the form of direct loans and credits to governments. In Cuba, U.S. investments took the form of industrial capital, most of which was distributed among sugar and tobacco property, railroads, public utilities, mines, and a variety of industrial and manufacturing enterprises.

The precise form of the U.S. capital stake in Cuba had direct policy implications. Industrial capital was especially susceptible to the destruction attending political instability and armed strife. Sugar mills, cane fields, railroad facilities, mines, and public utilities were exposed and vulnerable to attack, and inevitably were among the earliest casualties of insurrection. Moreover, armed intervention was not as much the consequence of property losses as it was the cause. Foreign property was vulnerable to destruction precisely because the United States was committed to its defense by terms of the Platt Amendment.

The United States' intervention in Cuba in defense of its property, sanctioned by precedent and prescribed by treaty, offered under the best of circumstances only belated protection and passing security. And when conditions required armed intervention, they were never the best of circumstances. The best of circumstances were those in which political stability endured and order prevailed, when access to local economies remained unobstructed, and authority over the national political system passed unopposed. The best of circumstances, Washington understood, were those in which the conditions of hegemony assumed totally the appearance of normality.

This was the purpose to which U.S. policy in Cuba was given. This served as the inspiration for the creation of the permanent army: the establishment of a Cuban military force to assume responsibility for order and replace the U.S. military. Policy emphasis shifted away from armed intervention to restore political order to political intervention to prevent armed disorder. The shift announced, too, a change both in the interpretation of intervention and the function of the Platt Amendment. The search for stability propelled the United States to seek an end to the causes of instability.

To prevent the rise of conditions necessitating armed intervention, the United States sought wider authority over local administration. Assistant Secretary of State Huntington Wilson stressed, "The Government of the United States, as an act of friendship, has pointed out to the Government of Cuba where dangerous pitfalls be and has thus adopted what has been well called a 'preventive policy,' that is a policy of doing everything in its power to induce Cuba to prevent any reason for possible intervention at any time."[23] The pursuit of stability in Cuba required the creation of an infrastructure of hegemony in which the United States appropriated authority over the national system. At the same time, these structures created new sources of political conflict, social unrest, and economic dislocation. Ironically, the exercise of hegemony in the pursuit of stability became itself the principal source of instability.

IV

The preventive policy announced fundamentally a new function of intervention, and in turn signaled a new form. The very meaning of intervention changed to accommodate changing U.S. needs in Cuba. Inevitably, this necessitated a new interpretation of the Platt Amendment. Any condition capable of creating the circumstances requiring military intervention passed under the purview of Article 3. No longer would the

United States wait for instability to reach the point of a "state of anarchy," as Root had pledged in 1901. Attention now centered on remedying the causes of instability before the disorders appeared. The terms of intervention originally defined by Root offered capital too little too late. If the Platt Amendment was to have any value, it was precisely in the prevention of conditions that Root had earlier used to justify intervention.[24]

The effects of the new approach to Cuba were immediate. Most important, it provided policy sanction to promote U.S. capital penetration as a function of political requirements. If, indeed, as Washington believed, political stability derived from financial stability, private capital became a necessary complement of public policy. "The problem of good government," Knox insisted, "is inextricably interwoven with that of economic prosperity and sound finance; financial stability contributes perhaps more than any other one factor to political stability."[25] Moreover, the policy of preventive intervention assured capital maximum returns with minimum risks.

Intervention thus shifted from the specific to the general, from the prescriptive to the normative. The Platt Amendment, in turn, underwent fundamental redefinition as the central clauses were adjusted to fit the needs of capital and adapted to meet policy objectives. This necessarily required new structures for influence over and new points of entree into Cuban internal affairs. U.S. policy turned on the need to scrutinize public administration, supervise public officials, and stabilize public order.

The United States claimed a vastly augmented authority over the Cuban national system, using new definitions of intervention to justify new modes of intervention—all in the name of preventing the rise of conditions requiring intervention. The original interpretation of Article 3 was no longer adequate to policy needs. The United States sought a broader sanction for a wider scope of intervention under the Platt Amendment. The State Department Solicitor asked rhetorically in 1912, "The question arises whether 'intervention' in this article [3] means only actual occupation of Cuban territory by American forces or whether it has also the broader meaning . . . which comprehends the giving advice or the making of demands or requests by diplomatic representation." The State Department conceded that Congress in 1901 originally "had in mind actual occupation of Cuban territory." But neither was there any specific injunction against other interpretations, and the solicitor concluded portentously: "These statements concerning the interpretation of Article III are so general in their nature as to furnish little certain warrant for a precise definition of 'intervention' at the present time. It may be said, however, that negatively at least, there are no obstacles to adopting the broader meaning of 'intervention' now under discussion."[26]

The "broader meaning" was applied to reinterpret entirely the definition of intervention, its purpose, and the conditions demanding it. The Permanent Treaty, the State Department proclaimed, did not confine U.S. intervention to the limits stipulated in Article 3:

> The treaty provision is not a *grant* of a right but a consent to the *exercise* of a right. In other words, the treaty distinctly recognizes the right of the United States to intervene irrespective of the terms of the treaty itself, the treaty stipulation being nothing more than an anticipatory consent of the Cuban Government to the exercise of that right. The treaty, therefore, need not be primarily invoked to establish the right of intervention but only to meet any objection which the Government of Cuba might at any time be disposed to raise, in the absence of such a treaty stipulation, to the exercise of such admitted right.[27]

The United States possessed interests yet unrevealed: "It may well be, and such is probably the fact, that neither the Platt Amendment, the constitution, nor the treaty is to be regarded as containing a schedule of all the conditions and circumstances under which this Government has the *right* to intervene, and that it may well be that conditions will arise where it will be necessary for this Government to intervene in the affairs of Cuba under conditions not specified in any of the documents named."[28]

The State Department also expanded the meaning of intervention to include considerably more than the deployment of armed forces. The essential linkages were thus artfully constructed:

> The term "intervention" includes not merely the use of armed forces or the military occupation of a country, but that it comprises also such pacific measures as may in any case be taken by a government in its interference with the internal domestic affairs of another government. It therefore follows naturally that this Government may *intervene* in Cuba in other ways than by landing forces and undertaking a military occupation, and that by its constitution and the Treaty, the Government of Cuba has given an anticipatory consent to such intervention.[29]

Under the terms of binding treaty relations, Washington insisted, Cuba had sanctioned U.S. intervention to preserve Cuban independence, to protect life, property, and individual liberty, and to discharge obligations with respect to Cuba imposed on the United States by the Treaty of Paris.

This construction conformed generally to the intent of the Platt Amendment as outlined in the discussions of 1901 and Root's assurance to the Cuban constituent convention that same year. But the State Department continued:

> No argument is necessary to establish that the intervention here contemplated, whether it be pacific or armed, is to be exercised for the purpose of *preserving* Cuban independence and not for the purpose of restoring it. This being true, it is the right of the Government of the United States, to the exercise of which right Cuba has consented, to intervene in Cuban affairs by either warlike or pacific measures, whenever it considers that conditions arise threatening the independence of Cuba, in order that such independence may be preserved. It need not wait until the independence is lost before acting. That is to say, to make use of a homely illustration, the barn door is to be locked *before* and not *after* the horse is stolen.[30]

The new interpretations of Article 3 provided subtle and implicit sanction for a new definition of the requirements necessary to maintain a stable government. Indeed, the new interpretation served as the basis of U.S. policy:

> This stipulation . . . contemplates preventive measures and not measures of restoration,—that is to say, the treaty recognizes the right of this Government to intervene to maintain a government adequate for the purposes named, and not merely to intervene to re-establish a government of required effectiveness. In other words, Cuba has consented that this Government shall intervene not to re-establish an efficient government, but to preserve and maintain an efficient government. So that whenever, in the estimation of this Government, the maintenance of a government adequate for the protection of life, property, and liberty in Cuba is threatened, the Government of Cuba has consented that the Government of the United States shall intervene for the purpose of maintaining such a government and, from the discussion already had, it must be admitted that such intervention may be either pacific or by force of arms.[31]

The relationship between financial and political stability, further, was a central factor in the reinterpretation of the Platt Amendment. If the fiscal policies of the Cuban government imperiled the island's independence or threatened life, property, and personal freedom, the United States reserved the authority, "by reason of its recognized right to intervene," to "make declarations in order to make certain the preservation of such a government, and that such declaration being made is the duty of Cuba to follow the same."[32] And in the absence of Cuban acquiescence to these recommendations, the State Department concluded, "then this Government has the right to intervene in such form as it sees fit."[33] Indeed, the United States assumed authority "to advise the Government of Cuba in all matters" affecting the island's independence and orderly government, a claim from which no sphere of public administration was exempted:

> This right extends over and includes the right to give to Cuba, as occasion may in the opinion of this Government require, counsel and advice regarding the fiscal administration of that Republic; that such advice being given it is the duty of the Government of Cuba to observe and follow such advice, just as it is the duty of the Government of Cuba to observe and follow counsel and advice on any other matter touching and affecting Cuban stability, integrity, or sovereignty, in which this Government has, by reason of treaty stipulations and otherwise, a vital concern and interest; that Cuba, failing to heed and following such advice, it is the right of the United States, as recognized by the Treaty of 1903 (to which exercise of which right Cuba has in the treaty consented) to take such measures, peaceful or otherwise, as may be necessary to see that the untoward internal conditions contemplated in the treaty do not arise in Cuba.[34]

The final change was not long in coming. The degree to which Cuba complied with treaty obligations, and hence relieved the United States of the necessity of armed intervention, was measured by the well-being of foreign property in Cuba. The Platt Amendment acquired a new purpose, and in the course of repeated renderings emerged as the instrument through which to promote and protect U.S. capital. Stability was a necessary condition for the security of foreign capital. Soon a corollary prevailed: security for foreign capital served as the measure of stability. A challenge to continued U.S. economic expansion in Cuba by whatever means, the disruption of economic growth from whatever source, offered sufficient grounds for U.S. intervention under the terms of the Platt Amendment.

The relevance of fiscal stability and Article 3 to U.S. economic interests and intervention stood in sharp relief. This was both the sense and essence of Knox's interpretation of U.S. treaty obligations:

> The United States has a direct and vital interest in the preservation of Cuban independence and the maintenance of a government adequate for the protection of life, property and individual liberty, and for the dis-

charge of the obligations with respect to Cuba imposed upon the United States by the Treaty of Paris. This interest of the United States, however, arises out of and is dependent upon its economic and commercial relationship to Cuba, and upon the imperative necessities attendant on and growing from the geographical propinquity of Cuba and the considerations inseparably inherent to the general problem of national defense. The Government of the United States recognizes that whatever benefits and makes for the growth and prosperity and stability to Cuba and its people is likewise beneficial to the United States. So also, on the other hand, it is clearly understood by this Government that conditions threatening the permanency of Cuban independence or the establishment and promotion of domestic tranquility, security and the general welfare of the Cuban people, involve in a greater or less degree the welfare and interests of the United States.[35]

V

The expanded scope of the Platt Amendment met specifically the needs of dollar diplomacy and preventive intervention. The widened sanction to intervene offered the United States direct access to the levers of policy formulation in Cuba. The principal purpose of intervention was to exact Cuban conformity with the terms of treaty obligations, implement directives from home, and report infractions from abroad. The normal conduct of diplomacy became the nominal exercise of sovereignty. Through the U.S. minister Washington prescribed and proscribed behavior, proposed laws and pressured lawmakers, advised the president and admonished public officials. The minister supervised fiscal transactions, oversaw legislative proceedings, and presided over executive policy. He met with legislators and openly discussed bills pending in congress, pressed for passage of some and demanded defeat of others.

Such extensive supervision was necessary, presumably, because the mismanagement of any aspect of public administration seemed capable of producing unstable conditions. This was the purport of Knox's brief but pointed instructions to the U.S. minister in Havana in May 1911:

> You are informed that because of its special treaty relations with Cuba, and of its interest in the welfare of the Cuban Republic, the Department considers that besides the direct protection of American interests you are to endeavor, by friendly representations and advice, to deter the Cuban Government from enacting legislation which appears to you of an undesirable or improvident character, even though it seems improvi-

dent or ill-advised purely from the Cuban standpoint, especially if it is likely in any degree to jeopardize the future welfare of revenue of Cuba.[36]

VI

The expansion of U.S. authority over the Cuban national system occurred simultaneously with the ascendancy of new political forces. The election of José Miguel Gómez in 1908 signaled more than vindication of the Liberal party—it announced nothing less than the triumph of the armed wing of the old separatist coalition. These were the populists, the men who appropriated the political symbols of *patria* and seized control of government as a means for collective economic security and individual mobility. On two previous occasions, in 1898 and 1906, the United States had prevented them from seizing power. In more than symbolic terms, the United States represented their principal political rival for control of the state, and twice before the United States had not hesitated to use superior political and military resources to prevent their rise to power.

The victory of José Miguel Gómez and the Liberal party brought to power the veterans and their allies, men of modest social origins who had earlier attained senior grades in the Liberation Army. These were, too, precisely the Cubans for whom control of the state promised economic security and social mobility. In 1909 Liberals seized political power and secured the means with which to confer institutional form and occupational function to the party rank and file. The Liberal constituency demanded the expansion of public services and an increase in the public payroll. These were the necessary emoluments to accommodate the countless thousands, mainly veterans and other dependents, who had served the cause of Cuba Libre and who had not fared well in the subsequent distribution of resources.

The new Liberal administration rapidly expanded public programs and state-sponsored development projects, established new government agencies, increased public services, and added public positions. Between 1909 and 1913, more than twenty-five new municipalities were created.[37] Public school facilities were expanded and new teachers were appointed. A wide range of public works programs were inaugurated, including rail expansion, road construction, and port improvements. New post offices and government telegraph stations were established across the island.[38] Within a year of the inauguration of the Gómez administration, the U.S. minister commented: "There is a marked tendency to increase the number of public functionaries—by the creation of new offices and the re-establishment of municipalities which had been dissolved in 1902. It is said that fully two-thirds of the revenues of the Republic go toward paying the salaries of its personnel."[39]

Liberals launched several major developmental programs, variously involving government subsidies and public revenues. In 1911, the Cuban congress authorized vast public works programs for dredging the major harbors of the island. Cuban ports, and especially Havana, were in desperate need of improvement. An estimated three hundred abandoned wrecks, the accumulated debris of several centuries of maritime traffic, littered Cuban harbors and created hazardous shipping conditions. The completion of the Panama Canal promised new possibilities of increased trade and commerce, and Cubans moved with dispatch. A government charter established the Cuban Ports Company, a private company operating under a thirty-year public license charged with dredging and maintaining service in the principal harbors. Payment would be in the form of increased port dues of one dollar per ton on general merchandise and twenty-five cents per ton of coal.

In a related bill, the House of Representatives introduced a measure authorizing the president to create a monopoly concession for salvage operations and emergency relief service to vessels in distress along the Cuban coast. Two salvage stations were to be established, in Havana and Baracoa. The bill further stipulated that the proposed salvage concession would be awarded to Cuban citizens.

An irrigation bill in April 1911 proposed mandatory irrigation systems throughout the island. Under the terms of the bill, the president was empowered to commission a private company to undertake the project at a cost of $25 million. To encourage investment in agriculture in newly irrigated lands, further, the state guaranteed an annual interest rate of 5 percent on capital invested, a percentage to decrease by the amount received from taxes until 2.5 percent.

In 1912 another bill authorized government subvention for the construction of a new railway system linking Nuevitas with Caibarién. A project deemed essential to the development of rich agricultural lands of northern Las Villas and Camagüey, the proposed railway was to receive a public subsidy of some $5,000 per kilometer.

Still another project later in 1912 authorized a government concession for the reclamation of the Zapata swamp, some 1,000 square miles on the south coast of Matanzas province. By terms of the eight-year grant, a locally organized firm, the Compañía Agricultura de Zapata, was to reclaim swamp lands and develop natural resources, in return for which the company was given license for forest privilege and public lands.

VII

These programs represented some of the more important legislation during the Liberal administration. They shared several features. First, they marked the active state participation in national development programs. They also promoted Cuban interests over U.S. interests and tended to favor British over North American capital. Lastly, they were opposed by the United States. The Cuban programs created direct obstacles to U.S. capital at the precise moment that dollar diplomacy demanded the expansion of North American investment in the region. The proposed bills threatened existing U.S. interests in Cuba and prejudiced future ones. The Ports Company bill planned to raise revenue by increasing duties on imports, much of which originated in the United States. This levy was passed on to the consumer in the form of higher prices, thereby offsetting the advantages acquired in the reciprocity treaty. The proposed salvage monopoly concession discriminated against U.S. interests. Charles C. Burlingham, an attorney representing U.S. shipowners and underwriters, protested the proposed bill. "I appreciate that it is a delicate matter to question the right of Cuba to exclude foreigners when we do it ourselves," Burlingham explained to the State Department, "but it is worth looking into. Possibly there are existing treaties which would limit the right of Cuba to exclude the United States and its citizens, but I have not looked into this."[40] The compulsory irrigation bill required landowners to undertake improvements according to specifications devised by Cuban authorities. Undeveloped property owned by land speculators and absentee landowners, property held by real estate companies, and land owned by U.S. sugar companies would be required, by the terms of the bill, to undertake extensive, and expensive, land improvement measures. The U.S. minister warned, "Its operation might be extended in such a manner as to amount to practical confiscation and to a pretense of irrigation of private lands where no irrigation is called for or where a system already exists or may in the future be put into effect."[41]

The United States' attempts, further, to displace European capital faced a serious setback as the Cuban projects created new opportunities for British investors. The Ports Company, for example, proposed to finance the operations by selling $6 million worth of bonds in England. State participation in the proposed projects, moreover, through either financial exemptions and public concessions or direct subsidies and outright grants raised the spectre of misuse of public resources and misappropriation of public funds, all of which, Washington contended, threatened the fiscal integrity of the republic and, ultimately, public order and political stability.

The United States' worst fears came together in the Caibarién-Nuevitas railroad project. The proposed construction called for direct government subvention of $5,000 per kilometer as an incentive to promote railroad development of the region. The government favored the North Coast Railroad Company, directed by José M. Tarafa, a close associate of President Gómez who was identified as part of the "palace clique." The North Coast Railroad was also believed to have heavy British backing. Belief was general, too, that the new lands to be opened for development by the railroad project were owned by ranking Liberal leaders.

Few denied the need or doubted the benefits of establishing railway service between Nuevitas and Caibarién, and ultimately through all the eastern provinces. The future of the Cuban economy, many believed, depended on the development of the eastern third of the island. The issue raised by the Caibarién-Nuevitas project was not the desirability of railway expansion, but the origins of the capital. Virtually all of Cuba's public railroads, as U.S. Consul General James L. Rodgers warned Washington in June 1911, were controlled by British capital. To permit the Cuban government to construct the Caibarién-Nuevitas railway threatened to give British capital an incomparable advantage in developing the rich sugar regions of Camagüey and Oriente. Rodgers elaborated:

> It can be seen from this that English and foreign capital is exploiting Cuban railroads now, and that means controlling to a great extent the sugar business of Cuba—the great hope of the future. . . . The great development of the future . . . must take place in the section through northern Camaguey and northern and eastern Oriente provinces. The value of such a line can hardly be overestimated. . . . There are enormous areas of highly fertile and virgin land, there are vast deposits of iron ore, and there are almost untouched forests, waiting for transportation. . . . Eastern Cuba needs all these things and they will be given by capital other than American in the near future if no effort is made by our own people to secure that to which it would seem we have a better right than any others. . . . I am willing to admit that I am influenced in this

matter to some extent by the desire to see American capital own and operate and make a success of an American railroad in Cuba, and assist thereby in a great development which is sure to come. As it is now, such opportunity is being seized by English capital and in a short time there will be an end to such good things. But five days ago Jose M. Tarafa announced that he had succeeded in England in securing the sum of $18 million, for railroad and sugar mill exploitation in Cuba provided proper subsidies are given. We know that England has nearly all the existing lines and if the statement of Tarafa is true, such an addition would about clinch control. I want to see Amerian capital in Cuba in such matters—not English, or French, or Spanish—and so if the proposition under discussion is a legitimate thing—as I believe it to be—I want to see it accomplished if it can be done with entire justice to Cuban and American interests.[42]

Two weeks later, as the Cuban congress debated the railroad bill, Rodgers was explicit: "If these concessions should be granted it can be depended upon that only English capital will be used and that the opportunity for American exploitation of extensive new railroad territory in Cuba will be ended."[43] Similar sentiments were expressed by Minister John B. Jackson: "The principal question seems to be, are we to permit the extension of British control to the whole railway system of Cuba, or should advantage be taken of what is apparently an opportunity to interest American capital in railway construction in this island."[44]

The proposed railway project not only bode ill for future U.S. capital expansion in Cuba, but also challenged U.S. interests in Las Villas province. The North American Sugar Company (Central Narcisa), controlled the sugar lands north of the Sierra de Bamburanao, a total of some sixty kilometers of rich sugar properties between Caibarién on the west and the Jatibonico River to the east. North American Sugar also owned and operated a network of several narrow-gauge railroads in the region, designed originally for private commercial use. In 1911, it was preparing to consolidate and convert its system into a public service railroad, a project that involved a complete conversion to standard gauge and the organization of a common carrier linking Caibarién with Morón. North American Sugar protested the proposed Caibarién-Nuevitas link.[45] The new U.S. minister, Arthur M. Beaupré, drew the obvious moral to the attention of the State Department in 1912: "We have, on one hand, a public railroad, largely—if not entirely—*owned by American interests*, built without State aid which must under the terms of its charter as a common carrier, be practically rebuilt (for conversion of gauge) without State aid; and, on the other hand, a bill in congress contemplating the construction of a *subsidized* railroad from Caibarién to Nuevitas which would, through about one-fourth its length, parallel the former." The proposed rail project, Beaupré concluded, "would seriously harm its interests, if indeed the competition of a subsidized road running parallel to its existing lines through a very narrow valley would not render the latter wholly useless as a common carrier."[46]

There were rumors, too, of large-scale corruption. The total proposed subvention amounted to some $500,000 a year, a subsidy that many charged would find its way back to government officials.[47] Then, too, as Beaupré reported, "indefinite and vague" rumors alleged that President Gómez and "members of the Palace clique" stood to gain directly from the proposed rail line. Persisting charges alluded to vast land transactions in which ranking members of the Gómez government had acquired public lands and private mills in the districts to be traversed by the projected route of the railroad.[48] By late 1912, the State Department had concluded that the "so-called 'Palace Clique' is deeply interested in the whole proposition by reason of unworthy motives."[49] This view was corroborated by the U.S. minister in Havana: "I have not and do not now doubt that some of the Palace Clique are more or less interested in this matter, and that their motives are unworthy and despicable because founded upon the hope of or realizaion of graft."[50]

VIII

In raising objections to Cuban development projects, the State Department gave new scope to the United States' claim over Cuban internal affairs as a function of the Platt Amendment. Washington found the amendment a useful instrument through which to promote continued U.S. economic expansion and to protect existing investments.

The United States' assertion that the Cuban projects violated treaty requirements provided an unlimited sanction for intervention. The compulsory irrigation bill, Secretary of State Philander C. Knox protested in April 1911, appeared "to be an ill-advised and improvident measure and perhaps in conflict with the Platt Amendment." Knox instructed Minister Jackson to "discreetly discourage its passage" pending further study in Washington.[51] A week later the State Department was categorical. Assistant Secretary Huntington Wilson instructed the legation, "You will immediately inform President Gómez that the Government of the United States . . . considers proposed compulsory irrigation bill ill-advised and improvident, and its passage, as drawn, undesirable." To "avoid any possible future complications," Wilson warned, "the passage of the measure should be postponed until such time as this Government shall have had full opportunity to give the bill careful consideration."[52] In Cuba, Jackson explained the meaning of "future complications": "I explained to [President Gómez] . . . that because of our general interest in the welfare of Cuba, we felt obliged to give advice which might prevent future complications. In reply . . . as to what I meant by future complications, I added 'complications' such as might arise from the creation of feelings of unrest among the Cubans themselves and of uncertainty among foreign landowners."[53]

The belief that fiscal irresponsibility would produce political instability was also invoked to justify the United States' proscription of Cuban legislation. The single largest threat to fiscal integrity, Washington charged, was the administration of government as a spoils system by incumbent Liberals. The link between fiscal responsibility and political stability required regulation of Cuban public policy as a corollary mandate of the preventive policy. "The real danger to the stability of the country," Beaupré warned, "lies in the great mass of irresponsible and vicious laws, contracts and concessions, by means of which the executive and legislative branches of the Government are mortgaging the future of the country." Beaupré urged the "assumption by the United States Government over public contracts, concessions, and other legislation," a policy that promised to "stop . . . the steady increase of the public burdens of Cuba and would greatly lessen our difficulties in regard to this country."[54]

The Zapata swamp concession raised many of these issues. The southern marshlands, Beaupré reported, contained vast quantities of valuable timber and mangrove and was Cuba's principal source of charcoal: "The project of reclamation is merely a specious pretext for giving away incalculable millions in timber and charcoal woods." And, from this conclusion, Beaupré urged action: "Therefore, the only apparent way to stop this gigantic and barefaced steal—for as such it must be regarded viewed from any light—is for us to enter without delay an emphatic protest that will leave no doubt as to our disauthorization of the measure."[55]

"Disauthorization" was immediately forthcoming. "Address note to Government of Cuba," Knox cabled the legation, "saying that upon such examination as the Department has been able to make, the project seems so clearly ill-advised and improvident and such a reckless wasting of revenue and of natural resources which Cuba can ill afford to lose that this Government is impelled to express to the Cuban Government its strong disapproval of the scheme."[56]

The Zapata swamp concession provided the occasion to establish the widest sanction yet for the management of Cuban internal affairs under the auspices of the Platt Amendment. At a cabinet meeting in July 1912, the Taft administration adopted a comprehensive policy approach to relations with Cuba in which elements of the preventive intervention policy were subsumed into treaty relations with Cuba. The United States, the State Department indicated, conscious of its rights and obligations, sought to influence the Cuban government informally by communicating its disapproval of "various ill-advised, ill-considered and dangerous fiscal measures." The State Department continued:

> These feelings of apprehension and disapproval have come from fears of the United States that these various projects, if perfected and put into operation, were calculated, owing to their improvidence, to plunge the Cuban nation, contrary to the desires of its people, into a state of hopeless bankruptcy, from which it could not of its own power extricate itself and which would, by reason of the practical anarchy almost necessarily following such a condition, compel the United States, contrary to its real wishes and disposition, again to occupy Cuba, at an enormous expense, for the re-establishment of peace, law, and order, and a government adequate from the protection of life, liberty, and property.[57]

This approach was entirely consistent with preventive intervention. In the context of the Platt Amendment, however, it was a formulation of another type. It employed quite unabashedly the threat of force—armed intervention and military occupation—to manage Cuban administration. Conformity to State Department demands was exacted by threatening Cuba with the suspension of sovereignty and the ouster of the government from power. In short, if the existing government was unwilling or unable to meet State Department demands, the United States would intervene militarily to install a government that would. After 1898, and especially after 1906, Cuban political authorities could not dismiss the spectre of U.S. armed intervention. In failing to acquiesce to U.S. demands, Cuban officeholders, were charged with defaulting on treaty obligations, thus jeopardizing the sovereignty of the republic. To avoid "another active intervention," the State Department warned, it was necessary for the United States to make "timely and friendly suggestions."

> The United States has . . . called to the attention of the Cuban Government the improvidence and unwisdom of the proposals, because it was convinced that if this course of diverting national revenue and wasting natural resources was persisted in, the time would soon come when the Cuban national income from the portions of the Cuban revenue remaining free and unencumbered, would be wholly insufficient to meet the current needs of the government, which would thus be reduced to a condition of absolute bankruptcy; and because the history of popular republican government in the Americas absolutely demonstrates that a bankrupt government . . . leads either to such despotism or to such a state of anarchy as, in either event, is equally incapable of maintaining a government able to secure to the people . . . those blessings of life, liberty and property which are contemplated by the Treaty of Relations of 1903.[58]

To avoid conditions requiring U.S. military intervention, therefore, and in pursuit of treaty rights and international obligations, Washington claimed authority "to give to Cuba . . . counsel and advice regarding the fiscal administration of that republic," and, once given, that advice had to be followed. Otherwise:

> Cuba failing to heed and follow such advice, it is the right of the United States, as recognized by the Treaty of 1903 . . . to take such measures, peaceful or otherwise, as may be necessary to see that the untoward, internal conditions contemplated in the treaty do not arise in Cuba; and that, necessity arising by reason of Cuba continuing the dangerous fiscal policy now followed, such measure must, pursuant to its duties and obligations, be immediately taken by the United States; however much of its natural inclination might be otherwise.[59]

Cuba's refusal to heed the United States' counsel thus became a sufficient cause for intervention—"peaceful or otherwise." "Apart from any question as to legality or illegality of the concessions and fiscal measures adopted or projected by the Cuban Government and objected to by this Government," Secretary of State Knox warned Cuba, "it must be evident to the Cuban Government that if the apprehension of this Government as to the effect of these concessions and measures is well-founded, then it is inevitable that ultimately a situation will result requiring intervention by the United States." Knox continued:

> In any event this Government believes that the Cuban Government is pursuing a fiscal policy which will ultimately lead to a situation requiring intervention, and therefore, inasmuch as from the standpoint of both

> Governments intervention is not desired, it must be evident to the Cuban government that the United States is not only justified but is acting in accordance with its rights and obligations in warning the Cuban Government against the course it is pursuing. . . . [The] right of intervention, which was accepted and recognized by the Cuban people . . . entitles this Government to caution the Cuban Government against adopting an improvident or otherwise objectionable fiscal policy on the ground that such policy might ultimately either by itself or in connection with general conditions in Cuba, produce a situation there requiring the United States to intervene.[60]

The State Department protested the Ports Company concession for the same reasons. The "contract is on its face so manifestly improvident and one-sided," the State Department contended, "that it so lacks in equity and reasonableness, that imposes such burdensome and excessive taxes on the ordinary revenues of Cuba which were already scarcely adequate to defray the expenses of the Government, as to raise grave doubts regarding its ultimate validity and legality."[61]

The Caibarién-Nuevitas railroad project raised similar objections. Indeed, in responding to the proposal, the United States pressed its authority to supervise Cuban internal affairs on still another rendering of the Platt Amendment. Washington linked the issue of fiscal solvency addressed in Article 2 directly to the intervention clause of Article 3. "Under any or all of these proposed forms of government assistance to private enterprise," State Department Solicitor J. Reuben Clark contended, "Cuba might easily bring about the situation which presumably the treaty article was intended in some measure to prevent, i.e., a state of national bankruptcy caused by improvident pledging of the national credit, or even the situation which was specifically intended to be met by the article, namely, the creation of a foreign owned debt against the Government which upon default might induce the governments of foreign creditors to demand participation in the administration of island's revenues for the purpose of discharging its obligations." Clark concluded that Article 2 provided sufficient grounds to protest the proposed railroad project, and added: "Ground for such protest may also be found in Article III of the Treaty. . . . That is, it may well be argued . . . that a bankrupt government is not a government 'adequate for the protection of life, property, and individual liberty,' and that accordingly Article III of the Treaty becomes operative in the face of any measure which imminently threatens to bring about such a condition."[62] But, Clark hastened to acknowledge in an internal memorandum, this was a matter of interpretation. In construing the language of Article 2 strictly and literally, Clark conceded, "there would appear to be considerable strength in the position that none of various [Cuban] projects are within its operation." Article 2 sought specifically to prohibit only a bonded debt involving the payment of interest and sinking charges incurred by the government. "An agreement to pay interest on the debt of a private corporation or to grant a stipulated annual subsidy to the corporation," Clark suggested, "would not seem to be literally the creation or the assumption of a public debt by Cuba. . . . It would seem impossible to lay down a hard and fast rule, the application of which will automatically establish that Cuba is or is not incurring a public debt when it agrees to act as guarantor or surety of a private corporation."[63]

Assistant Solicitor E. H. Harrison adopted a similar position. "The questions, now raised in this matter would seem to be, in the main, ones of policy rather than law." Harrison conceded that certainly the argument could be made that a promise of subvention equalled the assumption of a debt. The more judicial view, however, would depend on the determination of Cuban ability to make the disbursement required. This, of course, "would seem to be largely a matter of conjecture."[64]

Harrison was correct on both counts. It was a matter of conjecture, and a question of policy. It was not so much the United States' concern that the proposed subvention would create a public debt as much as its opposition to indebtedness in favor of British capital. The United States desired a postponement of the proposed bill, "particularly in view of the added burden it contemplates imposing on the Cuban treasury in favor of capital which is neither Cuban nor American."[65]

The linking of Article 2 with Article 3 provided a convenient construction of the Platt Amendment to bolster the United States' contention that fiscal responsibility was essential to political stability. "The Government of the United States," Knox informed Cuban authorities, "is unalterably of the opinion that a bankrupt Government would not be a Government adequate to the protection of life, property and individual liberty, within the meaning of the treaty, and that extravagant and improvident action by the Executive and Legislature of Cuba, or an inclination to deal wastefully with the natural resources, to grant ill-advised and extravagant concessions, and to encourage the undertaking of unnecessary and expensive projects, could as well bring the Cuban Government into a position where it would be no longer capable of discharging its international obligations as any domestic or foreign complications could possibly do." Knox drew some portentous conclusions:

> In adopting a policy of friendly counsel and warning, a policy preventive of those things which would inevitably change the status of Cuba, the Government of the United States has wished to refrain from any undue assertion of rights. Now, however, . . . the Government of the United States must declare that it deems its high duty and indubitable right that such friendly counsel should be given and should be received in a manner to protect that economical and financial stability which in, modern times, are the cornerstone of national responsibility. The Government of the United States cannot assume the heavy obligations which it bears towards Cuba and at the same time, be denied the means of discharging duties in a situation in which it must be remembered there is mutuality in the rights, duties and obligations involved in the relations between the two countries.[66]

Similarly, in its opposition to the Ports Company concession, the State Department artfully linked Articles 2 and 3 to threaten the Cuban government with armed intervention. An insolvent government, Knox insisted, lacked the means to discharge its minimal treaty obligations, thereby creating the conditions ultimately requiring the United States to intervene militarily. He protested that the ports project created a "tax burdensome to Cuban commerce" and alienated revenues vital to the national treasury. Knox also objected to and passed judgment on Cuban legislative procedures. The project, "involving matters of the gravest national import," had been before the Cuban congress and executive for "the brief period of 21 days," and within six days of enactment collection of taxes commenced. "That a law of such far reaching possibilities should be enacted not only without mature study and deliberation," Knox protested, "but with such inconsiderate haste, and that such a valuable franchise should have been granted a private corporation without resort to open competition would in themselves seem sufficient to cause those striving for the welfare of Cuba the gravest concern."[67]

A similar linkage was made in the Zapata swamp concession. This was simply one in a series of projects, Knox charged, "calculated to plunge the Cuban nation into a state of hopeless bankruptcy not only jeopardizing the maintenance of any government in Cuba, but also in so far as the interests of foreign governments are affected." The end result was obvious—"tending to threaten the independence of Cuba,"—and the necessary remedy was clear: the exercise of "the right of intervention."[68]

Washington also used the argument to oppose the salvage monopoly concession. In an intra-agency memorandum, the Department of Commerce responded directly to the substantive issue raised by the proposed Cuban legislation: "In the opinion of this Department, in view of our proximity to Cuba, our construction of the Canal, and our political relations to the Republic, Americans should have the privilege of salvaging their own vessels in Cuban waters."[69] The State Department responded, too, but couched its objections within the context of treaty relations: "The project from the fiscal aspect is open to the criticism which has applied to so many of the projects which have of late been the subject of consideration and action by the Cuban congress, namely that it provides for an improvident pledging of the national resources to a private concessionaire. In this connection this Government of the United States is compelled to state that it finds it difficult to perceive the reasons which apparently have induced a policy of repeated hypothecation of the Cuban revenues and Treasury receipts on a manner which would seem scarcely justifiable upon any criteria of fiscal administration."[70] Several months later, Secretary Knox instructed the Legation to inform the Cuban government:

> It is not the United States Government's intention nor its desire to hamper the Cuban authorities in the administration of the domestic affairs of the Republic. In view, however, of the provisions of the Treaty of May 22, 1903, between the United States and Cuba whereby there have been granted to and imposed upon the Government of the United States certain unmistakable rights and obligations, that Government believes that it would be indeed remiss in its duty did it not formally and energetically bring to the attention of the Government of Cuba a state of affairs which, if permitted to continue, it is believed, will ultimately bring on in Cuba a state of national bankruptcy. The Government of the United States is unalterably of the opinion that a bankrupt government is not a government adequate to the protection of life, property, and individual liberty within the meaning of Article III of the Treaty, and that extravagant and improvident action by the Executive and Legislature of Cuba can as well bring the Cuban Government into a position where it will be no longer capable of discharging its international obligations as any domestic or foreign complications can possibly do.[71]

IX

The State Department protested virtually every bill involving the disbursement of public funds and the creation of public contracts that favored local interests over U.S. enterprise. The Platt Amendment served as the policy instrument to maintain an open economy and a subservient political elite. U.S. investors viewed the Permanent Treaty as a guarantee of privilege and immunity, and the State Department did not discourage this view. In 1910, a U.S. contracting company that was threatened with the loss of a lucrative sewerage concession to a Cuban firm believed it entirely proper to appeal to Washington for assistance. The company's attorney was confident that the State Department would make "every endeavor to guard and protect the interests of contracting company in this great enterprise and that it will enforce the rights of the United States as set out in the Platt Amendment and the Treaty between the United States and Cuba."[72] In mid-1910, the Cuban congress contemplated raising the minimum wage to $1.25 for all workers employed by national, provincial, and municipal governments, as well as laborers employed by private contractors paid with public funds. A U.S. contractor protested the proposed pay increase, charging that the measure would cause interminable delays in the work, if not its ultimate cancellation. "It is needless to say," the company insisted, "the completion of this contract is of great concern and importance to the people of the United States, and that the duty of the Government, under its treaty with Cuba, is to vigorously object to collateral attacks being made upon the contract which will impair the terms and conditions thereof."[73]

The State Department agreed, and protested the proposed bill. The United States, Huntington Wilson wrote, was "directly and keenly interested" in the completion of the construction work in Havana without interruption: "The right of this Government to have such interest is derived from the fact that the proximity of Cuba to the United States makes the healthfulness of Cuban ports a matter of vital, practical concern to this Government and people, and also from the fact that the provisions of the Treaty of 1904 [sic] give to this Government the legal right to have and exercise such an interest."[74]

In 1911, the contract between the Cuban government and the American Bank Note Company of New York for the printing of internal revenue stamps expired. A newly organized Cuban company, headed by a known associate of President Gómez, secured the government option to a new five-year contract to produce the stamps at a lower price. American Bank Note protested that the new contract awarded had been as the "result of irregular transaction with certain high officials." Warren L. Green, president of the American Bank Note, charged that a bribe of some $80,000 had been paid to Cuban authorities, thereby resulting in his company's loss of the contract.[75] When urged by the U.S. minister in Havana to formulate the charges in writing, American Bank Note declined. In part, the refusal to press forward with a formal complaint against the Cuban government was due to a postage stamp contract still held by American Bank Note. More important, American Bank Note had itself engaged in some questionable financial transactions to obtain the postage stamp contract, and feared the adverse consequences attending public disclosure.[76] The State Department nevertheless lodged an official complaint. In May 1911 Knox protested the irregularities and complained of the "absurdity of giving work the quality of which is so vitally important to the fiscal safety of Cuba to a firm possessing no adequate apparatus or experience and offering an absolutely negligible difference in price." Washington instructed the Legation to use "every effort consistent with the general interests of this Government to gain for American bidders the honest opportunity to which they are entitled."[77] This point was reiterated several months later by Assistant Secretary Huntington Wilson: "The Cuban Government must . . . realize the importance of giving to American concerns the honest opportunity to which they are entitled."[78]

In 1912, the Cuban government contemplated a measure to restrict the award of public contracts, including national, provincial and municipal grants, exclusively to Cuban citizens. Immediately the United States protested, couching its objections in Article 5 of the Platt Amendment, the provision concerning sanitation. "You will discreetly discourage the legislation contemplated," the State Department instructed the legation, "pointing out, as among its objectionable features, the unfriendly character of the bill in its tone and in its proposal to bar American enterprises from government work in Cuba and the serious embarrassment and obstacles it might create with respect particularly to the carrying out of works of sanitation, in which matter the Government of the United States has a vital interest and concerns as recognized by the Treaty of Relations of 1903."[79]

A proposed bill in 1912 that favored a Cuban company over Lykes Brothers also raised U.S. objections. This was palpable "abuse of power," the U.S. minister protested, "a clear attempt to force an American concern out of business for the benefit of a rival Cuban firm composed of corrupt personal friends of the President." Beaupré explained to the State Department:

> "Discreet oral representations" and efforts to "discourage" legislation are only relatively effective in carrying out what I conceive to be the wishes of the Department—to protect the fiscal stability of Cuba and the rights of Americans here. . . . So far as I am able to see, there is now no way to ensure a proper deference to the expressed wishes to the American Government will demand from him in the future a regard for at least the decencies of administration, an observance of truthfulness in dealings with the American Government, and due consideration for such representations as the American Government may see fit to make from time to time.[80]

The Platt Amendment had been transformed into an instrument to facilitate U.S. capital penetration and the appropriation of local resources. The Cubans responded accordingly.

6.

The Pursuit of
Politics

I

The attempt by the United States to increase control over public administration in Cuba as a means of economic mastery occurred simultaneously with the rise of new political forces determined to expand control over public office as a means of economic mobility. Not that these goals were necessarily mutually exclusive. Both U.S. and Cuban officials sought to control the state apparatus as a means through which to expand competing claims over local resources. These were also years during which some of the more prominent features of skewed class development in Cuba assumed political form. The generation of Cubans that had participated in the patriotic gesture of '95 sought political office as a function of its social character and economic cohesion. This was the origin of a state bourgeoisie organized around the control of the state and public administration as the principal source of wealth and security. Herein was one of the more anomalous features of the early republic. Economic power did not produce political power; rather, political power created riches and an economically powerful class. The state thus served at once as a source and instrument of economic power. For the political class, the state assumed the functions of the "means of production."

This central reality gave Cuban political culture its distinctive character. Public office symbolized opportunity in an economy where opportunity was limited to outsiders with capital or insiders with power. The overwhelming presence of foreign capital all but totally excluded Cuban participation in production and control over property. Thus the group holding political power became a class unto itself, in which control of the state was principally, and vitally, an economic pursuit.[1] Government was the only enterprise wholly Cuban. "Foreigners (resident or absentee) own," Irene Wright wrote from Cuba in 1910, "I am convinced, at least 75 percent of Cuba,—fully three-fourths of the very soil of the island. I have heard their real estate holdings estimated, by an office whose official business it is to know conditions here, at 90 or 95 percent of the whole. Foreigners (Americans and Europeans of many nationalities) are the owners of the far-reaching sugar fields, of the tobacco *vegas* of account, of the bristling ruby pineapple fields, of the scattered green citrus fruit orchards." Wright continued:

> We have, then, in Cuba, a country owned by foreigners, the government of which is supported by foreigners, but administered by Cubans. . . . As at present constituted this is the most expensive government on earth, and those who operate it (the Cuban office-holding class) have every reason to labor to make it even more so, since its extravagancies run to salaries, which they received, and to even more outrageous contracts and concessions, on which they get liberal "rake-offs."[2]

Writing several decades later, Ruby Hart Phillips struck a similar theme:

> Cubans really have little they can call their own in the island, with the exception of the government. Wall Street owns all the sugar mills or controls them through having loaned far too much money on them; English and American capital own the railways; the Electric Bond and Share have a practical monopoly of electric power in the island; the International Telephone and Telegraph have a telephone monopoly; the bulk of city property and much farm land is owned by Spaniards; all commercial firms are owned by Spaniards or Jews. The servant class, clerks, waiters, etc., are foreigners.[3]

The war for independence signaled the political ascendancy of a mixed social amalgam. It destroyed the creole bourgeoisie, but did not replace it. The U.S. military intervention prevented the consummation of the social revolution, and promoted the continuation of colonial property relations. Foreigners prevailed over production and property, and Cubans controlled the state, from which a new class would form.[4] Miguel de Carrión wrote in 1921:

> The Cuban political class sprang to life among us because we had to construct artificially a democracy with our native elements, and democ-

racies need a middle class in order to subsist. In fact, we possessed a group of professionals and landowners, almost all ruined; but it was too weak to be the sustenance of the regime that had been adopted. The State was in need of many functionaries, and many leaders for the political parties, and it was necessary to recruit them from among our population. . . . The true middle class, the possessor of money and the resources of the Republic was not Cuban, and was not and will never be nationalist. Thus, we had to pursue an abnormal course in the building of our country: instead of bringing to public power a proportional representation of wealth, we brought wealth to the hands of representatives of public power. . . . We made politics our only industry and administrative fraud the only course open to wealth for our compatriots. . . . This political industry . . . is stronger than the sugar industry, which is no longer ours; more lucrative than the railroads, which are managed by foreigners; safer than the banks, than maritime transportation and commercial trade, which also do not belong to us. It frees many Cubans from poverty, carrying them to the edge of a future middle class, which is still in an embryonic period, but that will necessarily form.[5]

Political sinecures and patronage had their own internal logic, not without historically determined and functionally defined roles. Some antecedents reached deep into the colonial experience. Under Spain, public office symbolized the joining of position, prestige, and power. But in the main, developments in Cuba conformed to the social reality of the republic. Patronage served as the principal method of consolidating the old separatist constituency into a cohesive political force. It served, too, as a means of discipline and direction. The hope of public office and the expectation of personal rewards derived from political power served to consolidate the political class.[6] "Cuban politics and politicians," the U.S. Consul James L. Rodgers reported in 1911, "are concerned only with efforts to secure possession of the powers of the government, national, provincial and municipal, with a view to private profit from the control of the public funds and, to a greater degree, for the opportunities for corrupt gain which the possession of public office affords." Rodgers continued:

It would be difficult to enumerate all of the so-called political parties. . . . Without exception such parties have been mere factions composed of the personal followers of a leader or group of leaders and held together only by the hope of sharing in the spoils of the public purse and in the opportunity to prey on private property by illegal and corrupt exercise of the power of public office. So long as any such faction has been able to secure and retain possession of some share of power, it has been able to maintain its organization at a strength proportional to the amount of plunder, public and private, which has been at its disposal. When its ability to acquire and distribute spoils is lost, the "party" disintegrates. The leaders of such "parties" disappear from public life immediately on losing their hold on public office and their followers seek refuge in other factions in the hope of sharing again in the harvest under new leadership. . . . The sole visible purpose of government in Cuba is the personal advantage of the individuals in possession, for the time being, of the powers of government. . . . [The president's] sole concern is to keep his followers satisfied with such share of the public plunder as he concedes to them and to keep them within the limits of oppression beyond which the exasperation of the people might result in violent outbreaks.[7]

These were matters of economic and social urgency. Political demand on public administration was the price of chronic unemployment and underemployment, of a political economy unable to accommodate national needs. The necessity to distribute political sinecures and public revenues to create public jobs was like a state subsidy of social welfare programs. The swelling civil service rolls were the most visible social cost of imperialism, serving directly to relieve potential political discontent. It disguised unemployment, for it created jobs for the otherwise unemployed and unemployable, and in the process provided social equilibrium to an otherwise unbalanced political economy by muting conflict. From contractors to cabinet ministers, from piece workers to the president, tens of thousands of Cubans together with hundreds of thousands of dependents relied on the state for their livelihood and well-being.[8] Public positions multiplied and government spending increased, and any interference with this process threatened the republic with social calamity. Writing in 1921 of a new public works program under the Zayas administration, the U.S. minister noted: "Dr. Zayas is inspired to undertake this work in order to safeguard his administration against possible unrest due to the large percentage of unemployment which is likely to exist in the near future."[9] This system was nothing less than improvisation institutionalized—not particularly stable, not especially rational, but eminently functional. If it offended the sensibilities of those outside of government, it was universally recognized that the system worked. "The Cuban government is badly managed," Manuel Rionda commented in 1911, "many political jobs and graft, but the country is peaceful."[10] The system had to work. The alternatives were so palpably few and so limited as to make distributive politics the principal source of stability in the republic and a deterrent to political disorders.

II

Thus the Liberals assumed power in 1909 determined to expand their control over the state just as the United States increased its political intervention as a means of renewed economic expansion. In principle, the United States did not initially protest the distributive imperative of Cuban politics. The conflict was fundamentally between two rivals competing for the benefits, legal and illicit, of political power. And inevitably—the corollary of distributive politics in a socially truncated and economically skewed system—corruption followed. The drive for wealth was reinforced by a sense of impermanence, particularly at the upper reaches of government, where four years was the ordinary time clock against which incumbents raced.

Political corruption functioned as an allocative mechanism—an often inefficient but nevertheless effective method of capital accumulation. Certainly not all capital found constructive application in the local economy. Much of the wealth obtained through corruption was expended on consumption and investments abroad, but much was not, and was applied to local enterprises. In an economic environment in which Cuban access to capital was limited, political corruption was a method of funneling capital from established property holders to a new entrepreneurial class either with political antecedents or political connections. One source of bribes originated with foreigners anxious to obtain local franchises, concessions, licenses, and titles. An immediate effect of this collaboration, to be sure, was to facilitate the penetration of foreign capital into Cuba. But corruption also permitted Cubans to accumulate capital through which to challenge foreign control over property and production.

Cubans who used public office to pursue private property did so directly as competitors to foreign capital. Indeed, through government posts, officeholders found a strategic noneconomic route to possession of property and participation in production, despite the foreign domination of economic opportunity. Political positions provided an entree into commerce, industry, and manufacturing, and enabled officeholders to buy real property, including sugar estates, tobacco farms, ranches, and mines. José Miguel Gómez used his years in power to considerable personal advantage, acquiring sugar property, railroad stock, and industrial interests.

The president subscribed to the stock of the Compañía de Minas de Petróleo at 80 percent of par. From Compañía Carbonera de Cuba he obtained shares at 25 percent of par.[11] Orestes Ferrara, president of the House of Representatives, acquired possession of several sugar estates, including "Ciego de Avila," "Algodones," "María Luisa," and "Carmita."[12] Charles Hernández, the director general of post and telegraphs under Mario G. Menocal, acquired title to 175,000 acres of henequen land in Pinar del Río.[13] During these years, Manuel de la Cruz, Carlos Miguel de Céspedes, and José Manuel Cortina organized the development firm of Compañía Urbanizador "Playa de Marianao," and secured all the coastal property between Miramar and La Concha.[14]

Government contracts and state concessions created vast opportunity for new wealth. A new group of wealthy Cubans came into existence during the Gómez administration, enriched from the control of the perquisites derived from public office.[15] The expansion of government development programs and extensive public works projects, moreover, and the distribution of franchises, licenses, and concessions stimulated Cuban enterprise. The state possessed vast purchasing power through taxation, customs, and borrowing, and used this power to employ private firms to implement policy. It used taxes, subsidies, penalties, and loans to divert resources and promote development. Much of the capital used to stimulate local entrepreneurial activity came from government sources. Indeed, many Cuban enterprises initiated in the early decades of the republic were essentially concessionary in character and depended upon public revenues.[16]

Political position was translated into economic power by a variety of means. Officeholders could enter business directly or through friends and family, either during or after government service. They organized the public monopolies, awarded state subsidies, established legal quotas, distributed government contracts, and they endeavored mightily to be the principal beneficiaries of these policies. This was state intervention of massive proportions, providing employment, creating jobs, providing most of all direct subsidy and sustaining support to national enterprise. This pattern was reproduced on a lesser scale at the provincial and municipal levels. A new entrepreneurial sector, largely Cuban, took form around government contracts—printers, clothing manufacturers, builders, and shoe manufacturers, among the most prominent. Officials benefited from their privileged positions. Public administration created lucrative possibilities for formalized bribery and informal appropriations of state funds in the management of public revenues. The sale of public concessions, public works contracts, specifically the construction of new roads, new bridges, new government buildings (which during the Gómez years included the lavish presidential palace and two stately Italian renaissance ministry buildings for Gobernación and Justice), provided lucrative profits for officeholders. An estimated 25 percent of customs revenue, approximately $8 million, was lost annually through corruption.[17]

This, in turn, subsidized patronage and the expansion of the public rolls. In sum, an extensive network linked tens of thousands of state employees in a common endeavor. Patronage was practiced on a vast scale. It was the exercise of political power, the means by which the president governed the nation, presided over the legislative process, preserved control over the government party, and procured a working majority in congress. Any diminution of the power of patronage in a political system that was predominantly distributive in function and primarily executive in form would weaken enormously the power of the president. Gómez complained more than once that U.S. demands threatened to weaken his authority and make his political position untenable.

Still another form of aggrandizement was the exploitation of existing wealth, from both foreign and local capitalists. The positions that allowed public officials to confer privileges on themselves also allowed them to sell favors to others. Thus, additional remuneration was garnered in the form of bribes and kickbacks for government contracts, concessionary grants, and economic policies of all kinds favoring special interests.

Officeholders exploited not only capitalists, but also peasants and small farmers. Blocked on one side by foreign capital from expanding control over natural resources and land, the political class used the state to expropriate the lands of Cuban farmers. Through state policies, they organized local sugar enterprises, railroad companies, and other agricultural and ranching concerns from land wrested from small landowners. By controlling political power, they presided over the maintenance of the legal system and directed the activities of a repressive apparatus.

III

Throughout the early decades of the republic, the United States sought to expand control over the course and content of state policy in Cuba to guarantee an open economy, reduce competition, and preserve a cheap and plentiful supply of labor in a peaceful, orderly, and prosperous environment. To some extent the United States succeeded. But this success served also to create new conflicts and exacerbate old contradictions, and these tensions accumulated.

Just as the United States represented the principal political rival to the state bourgeoisie, the political class offered potentially a significant economic challenge to the United States in Cuba. The United States' insistence upon public honesty may have been in part morally inspired, but it also had an economic imperative. Indeed, "honesty" and "integrity" would have obliged officeholders to serve with disinterest the needs of the hegemonial class—in this instance, foreign capitalists. The Cuban political class possessed interests of its own, however, and it pursued them aggressively, often in direct conflict with U.S. capital. Attempts by the United States to restrict the authority of Cuban public officials, and especially to regulate their control over public administration, had fateful consequences. A government under unremitting pressure to defend foreign interests could not adequately respond to national ones.

In defending its collective needs by supporting its members through sinecures, patronage, and payroll jobs, the political class clashed headlong with the objectives of U.S. policy. Political instability may have indeed been related to fiscal responsibility, but not quite in the fashion Washington believed. U.S. efforts to manage Cuban administration, specifically to obstruct legislation that was unabashedly political in inspiration and self-aggrandizing in intent, promised to limit the beneficiaries of state policies to those of the United States' choosing. Washington's threat of armed intervention threatened the political class with removal. The moral was unambiguous: if Cuban officeholders were unwilling or politically unable to accommodate foreign needs, the United States would install others who would.

IV

Not all members of the old separatist polity shared equally in the distribution of public positions and state sinecures. The army veterans in particular never wavered in their claim over public office. Much of this was a demand for preferential employment for those who had served the cause of Cuba Libre in arms. It also had symbolic national value, an insistence that positions in the republic should be reserved exclusively for those who had sacrificed in behalf of its realization. In 1911, the Cuban Council of Veterans, representing the former officers and soldiers of the

Liberation Army, petitioned the Gómez government for a more equitable distribution of public office at all levels of national, provincial, and local administration. Veterans initially asked for the dismissal from office of all Cubans who had served in the Spanish armed forces. These were largely appointments made earlier, during the course of the two previous U.S. occupations and subsequently ratified by civil service regulations. The veterans' protest quickly generalized into a popular call for the removal of all officeholders, Cuban and Spanish, who had opposed independence and a demand that they be replaced with veterans.[18] "We only ask," the veterans insisted, "that Cubans who loved Cuba and who did not dishonor its existence replace the disloyal . . . who fought against Cuba."[19]

The veterans' protest in 1911 was not only about preferential appointment and public office, although these certainly were the immediate issues. In a larger sense, the sources of Cuban dissatisfaction in the early twentieth century were not dissimilar to those of the late nineteenth century. Too many Spaniards and too many Cubans who had opposed independence remained in office. Much remained unchanged in the administration of the island since the colonial regime. "Our fundamental purpose," General Emilio Núñez, president of the Veterans' Council, insisted, "is singularly to Cubanize public administration. . . . Without the predominant influence of virtuous Cubans in public affairs . . . nationality is a myth, for the Republic lacks the security to oppose all future eventualities."[20] The veterans' demands went beyond the Cubanization of public administration. As the veterans themselves suggested, Cuban control of government was a necessary first step toward establishing the primacy of Cuban interests in the republic. Veterans complained of the growing foreign presence in Cuba, and demanded the Cubanization of public office, property ownership, the economy, and culture.

This was a movement of enormous popular appeal, and difficult to resist. The government did not even try. In December 1911 the Cuban congress voted to suspend the relevant sections of the civil service law to permit the discharge of all public employees who had supported Spain during the war.

The action prompted an immediate protest from the United States. The State Department again invoked the threat of armed intervention, this time taking the unusual step of publishing the note simultaneously with its delivery to the Cuban foreign office:

> The situation in Cuba as now reported causes grave concern to the Government of the United States. That the laws intended to safeguard free

republican government shall be enforced and not defied is obviously essential to the maintenance of the law, order, and stability indispensable to the continued well being of which the United States has always evinced and cannot escape a vital interest. The President of the United States therefore looks to the President and Government of Cuba to prevent a threatened situation which would compel the Government of the United States much against its desires to consider what measures it must take in pursuance of the obligations of its relations with Cuba.[21]

The Gómez administration yielded to U.S. pressure, and withdrew support for the proposed civil service reorganization. The publication of the State Department note in Cuba caused widespread protest. Emilio Núñez denounced the threat of intervention to obstruct Cubanization. Carlos Velez, also of the council of Veterans, asked why if the U.S. patriots had expelled Tories after 1776, Cubans could not expel loyalists in 1912.[22]

V

The veterans' protest was eclipsed by a new crisis later in 1912, one of similar origins. No single group suffered as much from the inequitable distribution of political office in the early republic as Afro-Cubans. The separatist summons to black Cubans to serve the cause of Cuba Libre had raised the promise of social justice, political freedom, and racial equality.[23] Afro-Cubans had responded as much to the promise of a new society as to the prospects of a new country. "No one will be excluded from public positions for reason of color," one PRC official had vowed in 1896.[24]

The war itself gave black Cubans an opportunity for rapid advancement and mobility. Afro-Cubans registered notable gains within the separatist polity during these years. On the island and abroad, in the army, in the party, in the government, Cubans of color occupied positions of prominence, prestige, and power.

The U.S. intervention in 1898 dealt a rude blow to the hope of social justice. The dissolution of the PRC, the disbandment of the provisional government, and the demobilization of the army during the military occupation effectively suppressed the institutional structures in which the triumph of the revolution, the intervention nullified the gains registered by vast numbers of the poor and propertyless, many of whom were Cubans of color. Like white veterans, black soldiers also suffered destitution and displacement after the war.

But Afro-Cubans also confronted racism. And very early in the occupation, this difference had telling consequences. Black veterans were victims of discriminatory hiring practices and finished second best in the distribution of public office. Blacks were routinely excluded from the police and the Rural Guard. Where it was not a practice, it was policy. When establishing the Artillery Corps in early 1902, U.S. military advisors stipulated, "All officers will be white."[25]

Conditions for Afro-Cubans did not materially improve with the establishment of the republic. For Cubans of color the need for positions in public administration was especially urgent, for in the competition for jobs in the republican economy, blacks continued to suffer from discrimination. "After the war ended," ex-slave Esteban Montejo later recalled, "the arguments began about whether the Negroes had fought or not. I know that ninety-five per cent of the blacks fought in the war, but they started saying it was only seventy-five per cent. Well, no one got up and told them they were lying, and the result was the Negroes found themselves out in the streets—men brave as lions, out in the streets. It was unjust, but that's what happened."[26] State assistance was vital; unable to find adequate work in the republican economy, Afro-Cubans understood their only recourse to be government service.[27]

Very early blacks demanded a fair share of public positions. In June 1902, within a month of the inauguration of the new administration, representatives of several Afro-Cuban organizations met with Estrada Palma to protest their shabby treatment by the government. The absence of blacks from the police and the Rural Guard, Generoso Campos Marquetti complained, and their exclusion from the civil departments of government, underscored the neglect "towards a race that had valiantly spilled its blood in defense of the Cuban cause. . . . The truth is, Mr. President, this is not what we expected from the Revolution and things can not continue like this."[28]

But they did. Of a population of some two million people, Cubans of color represented 30 percent, approximately 610,000. In the two categories of occupations listed in the 1907 census identified wholly as public service workers, teachers, and members of the armed forces, blacks were underrepresented:[29]

	Teachers	Soldiers and Policemen
Whites (Cuban and foreigners)	5,524	6,520
Cubans of color	440	1,718

In both categories, foreign whites (828 teachers and 1,135 soldiers and policemen) numbered almost as many as Afro-Cubans.

Blacks were also displaced from the private workplace. In fact, the material conditions of Afro-Cubans seems to have actually deteriorated with independence. Traveling to Cuba in 1905, Arthur Schomburg remarked:

> During the colonial days of Spain the Negroes were better treated, enjoyed a measure of freedom and happiness than they do to-day. Many Cuban Negroes curse the dawn of the Republic. Negroes were welcomed in the time of oppression, in the time of hardship, during the days of the revolution, but in the days of peace . . . they are deprived of positions, ostracized and made political outcasts. The Negro has done much for Cuba. Cuba has done nothing for the Negro.[30]

The Estrada Palma administration not only failed to ameliorate conditions for Afro-Cubans, it exacerbated them. As the government purged the civil service ranks to make room for Moderates on the eve of reelection, countless hundreds of blacks found themselves dismissed. One of the central issues of the 1906 rebellion involved the question of race, and the failure of the republic to accommodate the needs of Afro-Cubans. That the insurgent Liberal army was overwhelmingly Afro-Cuban underscored some of the more urgent socioeconomic aspects of the August revolution.[31]

But rebellion in 1906, like the revolution a decade earlier, did not improve conditions for blacks. During the U.S. military occupation of 1906–1909, Afro-Cubans continued to suffer from discrimination and racism. Across the island, black veterans of the wars of 1895 and 1906 demanded positions commensurate to their contribution to the successful efforts. In Pinar del Río, a nonpartisan committee of Afro-Cubans demanded one-third of all public offices. In the city of Trinidad, blacks protested the lack of recognition in the distribution of municipal positions. In Havana, black members of the Liberal party demonstrated against under-representation in public office with the cry, "We will have the jobs or we will make this another Santo Domingo."[32]

It was during the second intervention that Afro-Cubans organized politically, outside the established party system, first in the Agrupación Independiente de Color in 1907, and later into a full-fledged political party, the Partido Independiente de Color, offering a full slate of candidates for national, provincial, and municipal office. In its first effort at electoral politics in the 1908 elections, the Agrupación fared poorly. But it persisted, and expanded the size of its organization and scope of its activities. The party advocated generally better government, improved working conditions, and free university education. But its principal concerns centered on combating racial discrimination, and specifically demands for increased representation of Afro-Cubans in public office and appointive positions, including the armed forces, the diplomatic corps, the judiciary, and all civil departments of government.[33]

The Partido Independiente de Color posed an immediate threat to the Liberal party, for it challenged the Liberals' traditional hold over the Afro-Cuban electorate. Indeed, the challenge was sufficiently formidable to prompt the Liberal administration to move against the new party. In 1910, the government enacted the Morúa Law, prohibiting the organization of political parties along racial lines.

The Morúa Law was the first in a series of measures designed to force the Partido Independiente de Color to dissolve. Party leaders were harassed and arrested. Party newspapers were banned. In early 1912, the party leadership appealed to the United States for assistance by invoking Article 3 of the Platt Amendment. "Pray tell President Taft," the petition enjoined the U.S. minister, "to accept our most solemn protest in the name of the 'Independent Party of Color' against outrages against our persons and our rights by armed forces of the Cuban Government. We protest to civilization, and ask for guarantees of our lives, families, interests, rights and liberties. Weary of injustice and abuses, we look to the protection of your Government under article three of the Platt Amendment."[34]

In May 1912, the Partido Independiente de Color despaired of a political settlement and resorted to armed protest. The government responded swiftly and ruthlessly. Fighting lasted several months, mostly in Oriente, and when it was all over some 3,000 Afro-Cubans had been slain in the field.[35]

The short-lived race war revealed the depth and breadth of social tensions in the early republic. It represented manifestly a political failure to accommodate an important segment of the population in the republic. The failure of the state to function adequately in its distributive capacity set the socioeconomic deficiencies of the republic in sharp relief. Rebellion was the inevitable recourse of a population unable to find sufficient opportunity as field hands, factory workers, farmers, or functionaries in public administration. In every sense, the republic betrayed the hopes of Afro-Cubans. The rebellion served, too, as a portent of what could and would happen when, set against foreign control over property and production, the state lost the capacity to accommodate the needs of a large number of Cuban citizens.

VI

The Platt Amendment offered the United States virtually un-limited sanction for the supervision of Cuban public administration. But the threat to U.S. interests was not confined to the policies of office-holders or their politics. The challenge to foreign capital originated of-ten as much from below and outside government as it did from within government.

Cuba early attracted foreign capital for the promise of its resources, and Cuban workers were expected to serve this promise. From the estab-lishment of the republic, the Cuban labor market displayed several notable features very much in demand by foreign capital. Immigration policies provided an abundant supply of cheap labor. Depressed wages and weak labor organizations, persisting legacies of the colonial system, offered ad-ditional inducements. These were not merely preferred conditions for for-eign capital, they were essential, and formed part of an economic en-vironment the United States was committed to maintaining. It was not sufficient to have preferential access to local markets and resources. It was also necessary to depress wages, discourage strikes, and deter union-ization. And because North American capital so greatly dominated pro-duction and so largely controlled property, any attempt by labor to im-prove its condition involved a confrontation with the United States.

VII

Labor gains came hard to Cuban workers, but gains came. Each advance strengthened the resolve of labor to advance, and capital to re-sist. The republic was hardly six months old when a strike by cigar work-ers brought production at the United States–owned Havana Commercial Company to a halt. Cuban cigar workers demanded an end to preferential employment of Spanish immigrants as apprentices, a practice that all but guaranteed Spaniards privileged positions in the factories. Cigar workers who had supported the cause of Cuba Libre in the cigar factories of Key West, Tampa, Ocala, and Jacksonville returned to Cuba after the war and found that Spaniards remained a strong presence in the factories. The "apprentice strike," as it became known, enjoyed popular support, and

quickly assumed general proportions. The strike expanded to Guanabacoa, Marianao, Santiago de las Vegas, Bejucal, and San Antonio de los
Baños, and involved coachmen, printers, bakers, and icemen, ending
only after armed clashes between workers and the police resulted in the
death of 6 workers, injury to another 114, and the arrest of 80 others.[36] In
another strike in 1907, cigar workers, construction workers, and stevedores protested against the system whereby wages were paid in Spanish
bills while consumer goods were sold in U.S. currency.[37]

Early labor organizing in the republic proceeded haltingly, mainly in
larger cities, and principally in Havana. During the early decades of the
republic, workers in most crafts and trades organized into local unions,
including cigar workers, typesetters, laborers in building trades, bakers,
stevedores, and railroad employees. During these years, too, labor moved
toward the establishment of regional and national federation of local
unions. In Havana, some thirty unions representing the principal crafts
and trades formed a local syndicate. Most of the twenty unions in Cienfuegos and the ten unions in Matanzas established local federations. So,
too, did the unions of Santiago and those of Cárdenas.[38] In 1914, the first
National Workers' Congress met in Havana. An estimated 1,700 delegates approved a variety of resolutions calling for a nationalization of labor bill, an eight-hour work day, a reduction of the cost of living, and the
establishment of a government ministry to support labor demands. More
important, however, the occasion encouraged the organization of new
craft unions and the establishment of a national federation.[39]

The expansion of unionization was both cause and effect of growing
labor militancy. Strikes, work stoppages, and boycotts announced the
growing power of Cuban trade unionism. By the late 1910s, strikes rever-
berated across the island. During January and February 1919 there was
always a strike somewhere in Cuba: stevedores in Cárdenas, ceramic
workers in Rancho Boyeros, construction workers in Havana, cigar workers in Matanzas, United Railway workers in Santa Clara, carpenters in
Havana, miners in Oriente, typographers in Havana, bakers in Cienfuegos, stevedores in Matanzas, textile workers in Havana.[40]

VIII

U.S. capital interests perceived the labor developments in Cuba
with foreboding. The most conspicuous labor advances of the decade
were registered precisely in those sectors most heavily capitalized by for-

eign investment. Strikes against shipping and wharf facilities halted trade, interrupted sugar exports, and suspended delivery of vital machinery, equipment, and spare parts. Rail stoppages paralyzed the internal movement of supplies and crops. Strikes against sugar mills threatened the *zafra*. In fact, U.S. capital had so thoroughly penetrated the national economy that it was not likely that a strike in any sector of agriculture, commerce, manufacturing, communication, transportation, mining, and utilities would not somewhere, somehow, adversely affect U.S. interests. In a very real sense, the growing strength of labor threatened foreign interests as directly or with as much loss as political disorders. Strikes suspended normal business activity and, whether they were wholly peaceful or accompanied by local or national violence, they interrupted production and endangered property. A strike among stevedores in Havana in May 1912 led to sympathy strikes in Santiago de Cuba, Guantánamo, Manzanillo, and Cienfuegos, and ultimately to the suspension of all shipping along the Cuban south coast. U.S. interests were among the principal casualties. "Present strike," Minister Arthur M. Beaupré cabled the State Department, "seriously damages horticultural interests, which are almost entirely American, and important American shipping interests."[41] A strike among sugar workers in early 1919, at the height of the harvest, interrupted the zafra and resulted in the loss of millions of dollars.[42] Another strike along the Havana waterfront in 1920 paralyzed all maritime traffic, causing damages to North American interests estimated conservatively at $300,000 a day.[43] In 1922, the Department of Labor estimated that strikes and work stoppages in Cuba resulted in a loss of some $200 million to U.S. investors.[44]

The growing strength of labor and increasing success of unions were not, thus, matters of trivial importance to U.S. capital. At issue were the very assumptions upon which foreign capital operated in Cuba. Labor demands for power over the workplace, demands for increased wages and improved work conditions, and demands for the right to organize found expression in strikes, boycotts, and, increasingly, violence and sabotage. U.S. businesses looked immediately to local authorities to protect property against labor demands. Ultimately, however, investors relied on Washington to hold the Cuban government to the task of defending U.S. interests. And, inevitably, the inability of Cuban authorities to provide assistance deemed adequate for the protection of foreign property created conditions that justified the invocation of the Platt Amendment and ultimately sanctioned the resort to armed intervention. Recalling the 1902 general strike, Orestes Ferrara later wrote that many believed that "its prolongation directly threatened nationhood and the Republic." But for the government to have made concessions "would have proved its weakness, and incapacity . . . thereby provoking and thus justifying the intervention specified in the deleterious Platt Amendment."[45]

Increasingly, workers' advances set the stage for a confrontation between labor and capital—more specifically, a clash between Cuban workers and U.S. capitalists. In this conflict, the defense of foreign property served as a measure of the republic's capacity to discharge its treaty obligations, and thereby guarantee national independence. By directly challenging foreign capital, labor indirectly challenged Cuban sovereignty. If indeed the final measure of political stability turned on security to property, per the requirement of Article 3, labor strikes no less than political disorders threatened sovereignty with extinction. When action by labor resulted in loss to property, these distinctions were further blurred. Hence, labor threatened more than the assumptions under which foreign capital operated in Cuba; it threatened also the premises upon which the political class ruled. By challenging foreign capital, labor could create the conditions inviting armed intervention and the displacement of incumbent officeholders.

IX

The Platt Amendment therefore stood for more than a guarantee of political stability. It also represented a commitment to the defense of foreign capital. Inevitably, labor-capital relations had direct implications for United States–Cuban relations. "The political problem Spain failed to solve in Cuba," Special Representative Enoch H. Crowder asserted in 1922, "was intimately connected with an economic problem, and this in turn depended upon social and industrial conditions closely connected with the labor question." Crowder drew an obvious moral:

> If the above is true, then we can assume that the maintenance of the Government and the protection of property in the country is, to a certain degree, in the hands of the labor elements. For this reason, beside the economic one, our Government has a direct interest in labor conditions because of article Three of the Platt Amendment.[46]

From the first organized strike in the republic, the United States displayed little reluctance to threaten the Cuban government if it failed to end labor disturbances. Cuban authorities were held directly responsible for the actions of workers, and if the government proved unable or unwilling to end the threat to property, U.S. military intervention to restore order to the workplace would be necessary. During the apprentice strike of 1902, the United States congratulated the Estrada Palma government for its "vigorous action" in ending the dispute and preventing the general strike from expanding into the sugar districts. "A strike in the cane fields," Minister Herbert G. Squiers warned, with a thinly disguised allusion to Article 3, "would mean the greatest possible danger to life and property in this island, a danger with which this Government could not cope with its available forces." The vigor with which the Estrada Palma government proceeded to crush the strike, Squiers reported, was in no small way owing to Cuban fear of U.S. armed intervention:

> This Government by its prompt action discouraged a great strike, one which if allowed to reach a certain point would have spread over the island and might have terminated in such a state of disorder as to bring the United States face to face again with the question of intervention. . . . Probably this fear induced the Cuban Government to act more promptly and vigorously than it would otherwise have done. The same action may always be counted upon under similar circumstances for the reason that the intervention of the United States is more feared by the Government than a crisis more serious than the one which has ended so fortunately.[47]

During the stevedores' strike in 1912, the State Department demanded Cuban authorization to permit local shippers to recruit strikebreakers to unload cargoes. "The necessity of adequately protecting life and property in this situation," Assistant Secretary of State F. M. Huntington Wilson warned in a paraphrase of Article 3, "will doubtless be self-evident to the Cuban Government which should perceive the wisdom of strong decided action to avoid untoward eventualities."[48]

Almost from the inauguration of the republic, foreign capital soon came to perceive organized labor as the single largest threat to the security of property. One traveler to Cuba reported as early as 1902, "The unions have been aggressively opposed principally by American and English managers and capitalists."[49] Either labor organizations were suppressed, the United Railways manager warned after a general strike in 1918, or "foreign interests will be compelled to withdraw from Cuba. We are therefore confronted by a situation which I consider very serious. It means that the entire laboring element is prepared to assist the demands, just or otherwise, of any unit or units of their organization. . . . Such conditions afford no guarantee whatever to foreign capital and are intolerable."[50] Nor did it much matter that strikes were often wholly peaceful, orderly, and within the law. Indeed, peaceful strikes were particularly odious, often forcing management to precipitate violence as a means of securing government intervention against strikers. "The fact that these strikes are carried peacefully," the United Railways manager complained to the home office, "only makes them more dangerous because it is difficult for the Government to find grounds on which to employ the public forces."[51] This was also the lament of U.S. Minister William E. Gonzales, who during a railroad strike in March 1919 complained that the "condition so far maintained of peaceful nonaction on the part of workmen is difficult to react with force."[52]

Nor was foreign capital unmindful of the implications of labor success. Between 1917 and 1919, workers along the waterfronts, on the railways, in the cane fields, and in the building trades registered important gains: wages increased, benefits improved, unions won recognition.[53] The success of one union served as incentive for others. Labor organizing expanded and union membership increased. So did strikes. In late 1918 U.S. intelligence sources warned the State Department of the implications of labor successes:

> The government is not able to take a stand against labor. Every victory obtained by labor adds more recruits to its ranks. There are about 50% of laborers who do not belong to the laborers' union, but . . . every victory adds to the list of the union. It is estimated that within the last four weeks the union membership has increased 25%.[54]

U.S. armed intervention responded typically to conditions of disorders, specifically, conditions beyond the control of local authorities that posed imminent danger to property, including political violence, armed uprisings, and military rebellions. The Platt Amendment allowed the United States to include labor activity in a similar category, and thereby to justify the threat of armed intervention. For purposes of policy, the distinction between politicians organizing an uprising and the proletariat organizing a union, on one hand, and sedition and strike, on the other, was a moot point, a subtlety too fine to distract policy officials from the larger task of protecting foreign capital. In both cases the effects were similar: profits declined, production diminished, and property values decreased. Indeed, the link between political disorder and labor unrest was itself a policy construct that enlarged the sanction for intervention, all properly within the purview of the Platt Amendment.

The analogy between strikes and rebellion, particularly as they both adversely affected property, thereby coming properly under the purview of treaty obligations, soon became a fixed feature in the application of the Platt Amendment. In 1917 a strike of mill mechanics in Cienfuegos interrupted local sugar production. Because it came only months after political disorders in February 1917, U.S. Consul Charles S. Winans drew the obvious conclusion. "This strike is believed to be quite as serious, or even more so, than the recent revolution, since the work in the sugar mills cannot proceed without the mechanics; they state openly they do not wish to work, hence the Government has no claim upon them, as in the case of rebellion."[55] A railroad strike in early 1919, Minister Gonzales informed Washington, "by paralyzing railroads is curtailing sugar production and causing tremendous losses to American interests." This "menace to property interests . . . is as great as would be active revolution." Gonzales urged the State Department to issue a public manifesto directly to the Cuban people:

> Apart from treaty obligations of the United States to maintain and uphold in Cuba a Government adequate for the protection [of] life and property, it has a most direct and compelling interest in the orderly harvesting and shipment of the present sugar crop, it views with grave concern and displeasure the unpatriotic and base motives of those who, whether for anarchical or political ends or both, have inveighed the workers in essential industries to paralyze the productive life of the country on the empty pretext of abetting the demands of workers in nonessential industries. The Government of the United States has therefore determined in exercise of its treaty rights to suggest to the Government of Cuba, if work on the railroads, in the harbors and in other essential industries is not resumed within twenty-four hours, the adoption of certain drastic and thorough-going measures to enforce such resumption, and to lend the Government of Cuba the necessary moral and material aid and support to carry out these measures.[56]

Labor activity was characterized in terms calculated to elicit opposition and evoke apprehension, but most of all to establish grounds for armed intervention. Unions were characterized as forces of sedition, strikes as sieges, and labor leaders subversives—forces with which there could be neither compromise nor conciliation. The 1912 stevedores' strike, the U.S. minister reported, was the work of the "agitation of foreign anarchists and socialists."[57] A strike in Santiago in 1918 was portrayed as a political movement designed to overthrow the government.[58] Consul General Henry H. Morgan agreed, insisting that strikes "have been in much greater part political agitations than purely movements by labor to improve its condition or benefit itself."[59] Strikes were the work of a "certain class of politicians," the military attaché reported, "who control the ignorant people."[60] After the Russian revolution, Cuban workers were perceived under the influence of "Bolshevist propagandists."[61]

These policy constructs placed labor activities beyond the pale of legality. Labor threatened foreign property, and the United States expected local authorities to protect property from all sources of danger, and labor was no exception. The Cuban government was enjoined to oppose labor militancy with as much vigor and force as it would employ to combat armed rebellion. The relationship was manifest. Consul Morgan warned Washington in 1918: "Conditions in Cuba regarding the strike situation is giving me considerable anxiety and a feeling of unrest in this country. The vacillating policy pursued by the government here in treating with this subject leads only to revolution and destruction of property, which is the form a revolution generally takes in this volcanic island."[62] During World War I, Washington proclaimed Cuban sugar a strategic commodity, a decision that all but proclaimed a moratorium on strikes on the island. "Cuba is at the present time the main source of the world's supply," the U.S. Food Administration declared in late 1917, "and any labor trouble or revolutionary disturbances in that island during the coming crop will have a far reaching and disastrous effect on the welfare of the nations at war with Germany."[63] Cuban authorities responded, and outlawed all strikes, pledging to invoke martial law to combat labor demonstrations.[64]

Washington freely invoked the Platt Amendment to bestir Cuban authorities to repress strikes and resist unions. Cuban unwillingness to use strike breakers during the stevedores' strike of May 1912 drew a sharp reprimand from Washington, and the obligatory allusion to armed intervention.[65] In 1920, on the occasion of another waterfront strike, the U.S. legation convened a meeting of U.S. shipping interests to prepare a list of demands for the Cuban government. "The intimate relations, commercial and otherwise," Chargé d'Affaires Harold L. Williamson reminded the Cuban government, existing between Cuba and the United States is "sufficient reason if none other obtain for a keen interest on the part of my Government in the harbor difficulties of Habana." The United States demanded quick action. "The labor trouble in the bay," Williamson warned, "is in danger of becoming a disease which it is thought should be stamped out now before the difficulty becomes malignant." The U.S. legation demanded immediate deportation of foreign labor leaders and prompt arrest, trial, and conviction of Cuban leaders, with the imposition of maximum prison sentences and without the possibility of early parole. To facilitate the proposed purge of the union leadership, the legation provided Cuban authorities with a list of all the strike organizers compiled by the shipping companies. The United States demanded, lastly, "as many soldiers as possible for work at the harbor front, the soldiers to be paid by the employers at the same rate as usually accorded the regular workmen. Prisoners . . . might be used for unloading coal and doing other work of a dirty nature."[66]

Government repression of labor increased during the late 1910s. Strikes often became occasions for bloody confrontations. Violence against labor was freely threatened, and threats frequently fulfilled. Periodic suspension of constitutional guarantees and rule by martial law facilitated wholesale arrest and detention of Cuban labor organizers and strike leaders. Soldiers often replaced workers in stricken services. Foreign strikers were deported. Union offices and labor halls were sacked and gutted.

U.S. participation in antilabor activities also increased. Intelligence was shared with Cuban authorities, and military personnel assigned to the legation collaborated with Cuban army officers in the development of government antilabor measures.[67] Leaders of striking mill mechanics in 1917 learned from President Mario G. Menocal that the "Government of the United States does not want strikes of any kind," and that he had received encouragement from Washington "to prosecute any laborers who promote any movement of this sort." Workers were threatened with violence, a threat for which, striker organizers reported, Menocal claimed to have U.S. support.[68]

But the United States could not always rely upon Cuban authorities to deal expeditiously with labor militancy or strikes. When local armed forces revealed themselves incapable of controlling labor demonstrations, the United States stepped into the breach. A general strike in 1919 prompted the mobilization of some 6,000 marines in Philadelphia and Quantico for possible deployment in Cuba.[69] An additional 1,000 marines arrived in

Cuba to reinforce the garrison at the Guantánamo naval station. Warships made "friendly visits" to port cities affected by strikes in the hope, the secretary of the navy wrote, that they "might have a good effect in easing the condition brought about by a number of strikes now going on."[70] Naval vessels visited the stricken cities of Havana, Cienfuegos, and Gibara, and their presence served to intimidate workers and to force them to return to work.[71]

Marine units stationed in eastern Cuba during World War I participated actively in combating labor activity in Oriente province. The marine comand organized "practice marches" and reconnaissance patrols to provide a U.S. military presence in districts affected by strikes. The movement of marines from Santiago de Cuba to Camagüey in one "practice march" was organized in such a manner as to give the deliberate impression that U.S. armed forces had arrived to crush a local strike.[72] A strike in Manzanillo in December 1917 led to the establishment of a permanent marine camp near centers of labor activity in western Oriente.[73] Colonel M. J. Shaw, the local marine commander wrote: "It appears to me that it is desirable that the presence of our troops on Cuban territory be known to the fullest extent with a view to exercising a deterrent effect upon those who would foment strikes or disorders."[74] In January 1919 U.S. military authorities recommended the transfer of marines from eastern Cuba to Santa Clara, the center of Cuban sugar districts commanding the important railroad junctions linking the western provinces with the east. "Evidence of a thorough [labor] organization," the military attache warned, "capable of quick united action as demonstrated during the recent general strike in Cuba, rendered the question of our being prepared for another such strike and being in a position to protect lives and property should the occasion arise one which warrants the moving of the regiment of Marines now stationed at Guantánamo Naval Station into Cuban territory and placing them at Santa Clara."[75]

X

The stirrings of Cuban workers in the early twentieth century were new manifestations of old discontents, grievances with antecedents in the late nineteenth century. Indeed, the issues that drove Cuban labor to the picket lines in the republic were not dissimilar to the ones that had propelled workers to the battle lines in the colony. Workers had sacrificed

selflessly and unstintingly in behalf of Cuba Libre, only to find the republic little more than a new political carapace of the old colonial system.

Labor had shared the fate of the separatist coalition in which it played
such a decisive part. The circumstances that perpetuated colonial property relations also preserved colonial class relationships. Workers were divided by nationality and culture; wages were depressed by immigration.
Workers in Cuba remained weak as a class and Cubans were weak within
that class. These were different facets of the same phenomenon, namely
the incomplete conquest of nationhood. Everywhere Cubans had encountered obstacles to their integration into the republic they had sacrificed to create. Workers were no different. The exclusion of Cuban workers signified nothing less than the loss of livelihood.

Central to labor strategy, and upon which so much else depended, was
the completion of the process of decolonization and the establishment of
control over the workplace. This was possible only through the restriction
of immigration generally and the nationalization of labor specifically—
that is, the establishment of a mandated Cuban preponderance in the
factories and fields. This was the central objective of the apprentice
strike in 1902, an effort by Cubans to appropriate for themselves all jobs
in the cigar industry.[76]

During the early decades of the republic, the nationalization of labor
became an increasingly significant issue. Nothing had higher priority on
the national agenda of organized labor than the restriction of foreigners
in the workplace, an idea that periodically surfaced as national legislative
proposals, and obtained support in congress. On several occasions, congress sought to nationalize labor through legislation. These efforts sought
to prescribe a legal formula mandating the employment of a Cuban
majority in industry, commerce, and agriculture. But the presence of foreign workers served the needs of foreign capital. Foreign employees depressed wages and divided workers, precisely the conditions that had
contributed to making Cuba so attractive to foreign capital. Investors
were determined to preserve them.

The first nationalization of labor bill was introduced in congress in
1910. It specified a formula whereby 75 percent of all apprenticeship
positions would be reserved for Cuban workers. This proposal possessed
the virtue of providing for Cuban control of crafts and trades on a gradual
basis, without threatening foreign workers with immediate displacement.
Foreign investors immediately opposed the bill. In response to protests
from foreign property owners, including British and German investors,

the State Department enjoined Cuban authorities to defer passage of the proposed bill. Minister John B. Jackson met directly with the president of the House of Representatives to discourage the lower house from enacting the bill into law.[77] In Washington, Secretary of State Philander C. Knox challenged the constitutionality of the proposed legislation, insisting that it violated Article 10, "which seems to place foreigners residing in Cuba on the same footing as Cubans." It was "not improbable," Knox added, that the bill "will be found seriously to interfere with the development of the great natural resources and wealth of the Island."[78]

The nationalization of labor bill languished in committee for another year, rewritten with restrictions, revisions and exemptions. In the end, the bill died in committee. Several subsequent attempts to nationalize labor met a similar fate. Through the late 1910s and early 1920s, however, as the power of labor increased, as newly drawn class lines delineated the growing complexity of national politics, congress made new attempts to legislate a nationalization law. Introduced in 1925, and now known as the Lombard bill, the measure provided for the employment of a 75 percent Cuban work force with 75 percent of salaries, wages, and fees paid to Cuban nationals.

The Lombard bill, like its predecessors, encountered U.S. opposition. The Chamber of Commerce in Havana denounced the bill as "generally detrimental to American business interests and in some respects confiscatory."[79] U.S. firms appealed directly to the State Department to block passage of the measure, insisting that the bill would "gravely prejudice" foreign interests in Cuba.[80]

In Cuba, the U.S. embassy organized a campaign to weaken the provisions of the bill. Members of the Chamber of Commerce lobbied ranking legislators. Ambassador Enoch H. Crowder carried the State Department protest directly to President Gerardo Machado, urging the president to use his influence to secure senate postponement of the bill.[81] Secretary of State Frank Kellogg informed Cuban authorities that the United States was "vitally interested" in the proposed legislation and hoped that no further steps would be taken "towards its enactment until this Government has had an opportunity to study the text of the law and make its views known to the Government of Cuba."[82]

Like previous attempts, the Lombard Law failed. Machado reassured the State Department that the bill, if passed, would be so framed as to offer U.S. interests in Cuba full guarantees.[83] The issue would not come up again until 1933.

XI

The fate of legislation to nationalize labor was neither unique nor isolated. In fact, virtually all legislative efforts to revise old labor laws, many going back to colonial times, as well as efforts to formulate new ones in behalf of workers' interests, met sustained opposition from foreign capital. The Platt Amendment served foreign capital well, for under its provisions the United States could properly denounce concessions to labor as inimical to the interests of property, and therefore a violation of Cuban treaty obligations. Foreign capital greeted most labor legislation with hostility, for in one form or another these efforts threatened to restrict foreign property and regulate foreign investments. Legislation in 1910 proposed raising the national minimum wage to $1.25 a day for public employees at national, provincial, and municipal levels. The bill also included workers employed under contract in projects involving public funds. U.S. contracting companies immediately denounced the proposed guidelines.[84] Alluding to the Platt Amendment, the State Department lodged a formal protest with the Cuban government. "If the bill becomes law," Assistant Secretary of State F. M. Huntington Wilson warned, "various complications will arise between the Government and those who have made contracts based upon the conditions of the labor market heretofore existing." Washington instructed the legation "to present this matter informally, but correctly, to the attention of the Cuban Government, and to indicate clearly to that Government that the enactment of such legislation is all but certain to bring both Governments difficulties and entanglements of a serious character."[85] The bill was defeated. In 1927 another bill mandating recognition of trade unions and establishing compulsory arbitration also met opposition from foreign capital. John H. Edwards, representing the Consolidated Railroads of Cuba, protested personally to the State Department, characterizing the measure as the result of "Red activities." Edwards insisted, using a familiar analogy, "Legislation of this character . . . would be a matter of vital concern and of great harm to the American investments of over a billion dollars in Cuba. It might well lead to disputes between capital and labor of such a character as to result in disturbances, perhaps even revolution."[86] This bill, too, failed to pass.

The growing power of labor led directly to increased pressure to control labor. The more militant the workers, the more insistent foreign capital was for government repression. Thus it was under Machado that the rising power of labor intersected with the expanding prominence of foreign capital. And it was to Machado that investors looked to contain labor. Within days of Machado's inauguration in 1925, several ranking representatives of foreign sugar interests met with the new president to convey, in the words of one participant, concern for the "labor problem which is most difficult and important." Wrote Antonio G. Mendoza of Czarnikow-Rionda: "General Machado approved all our points and he reminded us that he was right back of us . . . and would continue to help us."[87] Indeed, Machado understood well what foreign capital expected of his administration. At a luncheon reception organized by the National City Bank of New York in 1925, Machado pledged bluntly: "My administration will offer guarantees to all business and enterprises which are worthy of the protection of the Government, and there is no reason to fear that any disorder will occur, because I have sufficient material force to stamp it out."[88]

The exercise of hegemony, even as the power of labor increased, contributed to a national environment surcharged with tension. Hegemonial pressure from the top allowed Cuban officeholders little margin either to mediate mounting social unrest or manage new political forces. Nor could the traditional political parties of the early republic or the new middle-class groupings later in the 1920s consummate strategic electoral alliances or social democratic pacts with a working-class movement that was growing daily more formidable. The phenomenon that characterized much of Latin American politics during the early 1920s did not take hold in Cuba. Because Cuban control of government was not unrivaled, officeholders and office seekers were not in position either to promise or to deliver reforms and relief to Cuban workers. Unable to bargain an accommodation with the new social forces of the republic, labor was effectively denied a role as a political pressure group. The Plattist system sanctioned few alternatives. Strikes were repressed and unions attacked. Confrontations increased. By the 1920s, the contradictions of the Plattist system were deepening, and everywhere in evidence. The political class found itself situated between conflicting forces—from above and without and from below and within. Authorities could neither sanction strikes nor support concessions without risk of provoking the United States' ire and, they feared, armed intervention and political displacement. The violent repression of a railroad strike in 1927, Machado insisted, was necessary because "foreign firms had appealed to the government of Washington and of other nations soliciting protection, which signified the threat of a new intervention."[89]

At the same time, labor was emerging increasingly as a formidable national force. It was a source of pressure to which the political class could not long remain indifferent or unresponsive. Continued resistance to resolving fundamental social problems, many with roots in the nineteenth century, contributed to increasing labor strength and deepening class conflict. More important, labor was emerging as a power contender in the republic.

7.

Free and Honest
Elections

I

Politics in the republic continued to arouse controversy through the 1910s, and nothing more than the issue of reelection. In 1912, José Miguel Gómez and the Liberals relinquished power to Mario G. Menocal and the Conservatives, a wholly proper compliance with the protocol of the political exchange.

Four years later, however, Conservatives opted for reelection, and again Cuba plunged into civil war. Through a combination of fraud, coercion, and violence, Menocal obtained a second term of office. Counting on popular support and the endorsement of a large sector of the army command, Gómez and the Liberals once more took to the field of armed protest. The "February Revolution," as the 1917 uprising became known, erupted on the eve of the United States' entry into World War I, at the height of the sugar harvest, and persisted through the spring. An estimated $200 million was registered in property damages.

However, the incumbent government did not collapse as it had in 1906. But neither did it prevail swiftly and totally over the insurgent armies. In fact, during the early days of the February uprising, the Menocal government was in serious difficulty. Liberals had established complete mastery over Oriente and Camagüey and partial control over Las Villas. Insurgent bands operated everywhere across the island. A quarter of the army had deserted to the Liberal cause, and no one in the government was certain of the loyalty of units that had not defected. Scores of Liberal legislators, provincial officials, and municipal authorities abandoned elected office to take up military positions. In all, some 30,000 men had taken up arms to support the Liberal protest.[1]

The Conservative government survived, but just barely. And immediately it was evident in Washington that the survival of the Menocal administration was the minimum requirement for avoiding armed intervention. The possibility of the government falling, either through defections from within or defeat from without, threatened to create conditions for intervention.

The object of U.S. policy, hence, was twofold: first, to raise the morale of government forces and arrest the erosion of administration support; and second, to assure insurgent Liberals that the United States would not intervene, as it had done in 1906, to preside over their return to power.

The first goal affected two distinct groups: the Liberal party and the armed forces. Although many members of the Liberal congressional delegation had joined the party leadership in the field, many more had delayed a final commitment to arms pending an outcome of early fighting. The course of early events was crucial, for the success of Liberals in arms would encourage Liberals in congress to defect, thereby depriving both houses a quorum and crippling national legislative process.

The same considerations applied to the armed forces. The scope of the first defections from the army jolted government leaders, and not a few in the administration feared that the initial desertions foreshadowed larger ones. Liberal sympathizers remained in the armed forces, awaiting the outcome of early developments before committing themselves to the insurgent cause. Few observers believed Menocal capable of retaining the loyalty of the armed forces for long, and certainly not at all if the administration fared poorly in early field operations. Minister William E. Gonzales cabled Washington, "General and widespread doubt exists of army's loyalty. . . . The president's nearest friends, even some cabinet members, are not confident and I know many of them would be glad of almost any compromise. All of them doubt the army and are apprehensive of result of uprising here."[2]

Very early the State Department resorted to public diplomacy, releasing official policy communiques directly to the Cuban press. In a series of diplomatic notes, the United States conducted a propaganda campaign in behalf of the beleaguered Conservatives. Directed principally at Liberals in rebellion and contemplating rebellion, as well as army officers considering defection, the U.S. notes were categorical. On February 13, Secretary of State Robert Lansing expressed "the greatest apprehension" over events in Cuba. "Reports such as these of insurrection against consti-tuted Government," Lansing warned, "cannot be considered except as of the most serious nature since the Government of the United States has given its confidence and support only to Governments established through legal and constitutional methods."[3] In a second note five days later, the State Department reiterated its support of constituted govern-ment, this time in greater detail:

1. The Government of the United States supports and sustains the con-stitutional Government of the Republic of Cuba.
2. The armed revolt against the Constitutional Government of Cuba is considered by the Government of the United States as a lawless and unconstitutional act and will not be countenanced.
3. The leaders of the revolt will be held responsible for injury to foreign nationals and for destruction of foreign property.
4. The Government of the United States will give careful consideration to future attitude towards those persons connected with and con-cerned in the present disturbance of peace in the Republic of Cuba.[4]

To give maximum publicity to the condemnation of the revolt, the State Department authorized the distribution of thousands of copies of the message throughout the island.[5]

The State Department notes had immediate effects. Many Liberals who had earlier delayed their decision to join the insurrection now aban-doned plans to take to the field. In addition, a number of ranking insur-gent chieftains in arms, without hope of favorable U.S. intercession, mindful too of the implications of the fourth clause of the February 18 note, surrendered to government authorities.[6] The notes also served to stabilize the government internally. The publication of the February 13 note, Gonzales cabled two days later, had a "beneficial effect in abating ardor of revolutionary party."[7] Both notes contributed to halting further defections in the armed forces.[8] "Publication of statement giving position of the United States regarding revolutions," Gonzales wrote Washington, "has had more clarifying effect upon public mind and the Government officials are deeply grateful."[9] With the publication of the second note on February 18, the U.S. legation expressed confidence that the Menocal government could completely dominate the political situation in a matter of weeks.[10]

Concurrent with diplomatic support, Washington also rushed mili-tary equipment to Cuba. Within days of the rebellion, the United States shipped some 10,000 rifles and 2 million cartridges. Several weeks later, Cuba purchased an additional 28 machine guns and 10 million rounds of ammunition.[11] Military assistance provided an additional moral boost to the armed forces, providing in still another fashion an expression of U.S. support.

Fighting continued in desultory fashion through the early spring, leading ultimately to a series of U.S. military interventions designed to assist Cuban field operations. Aware that Menocal lacked the means at once to defend foreign property and prosecute the war, Washington assumed responsibility for the protection to foreign holdings in Camagüey and Oriente, thereby permitting the government to devote its military resources to the pursuit of insurgent bands. Throughout the early spring, U.S. forces assumed garrison duty on the sugar plantations, at the mines, and along the principal rail lines.

These were limited armed interventions designed to prevent the necessity of a larger armed intervention, and inevitably military occupation. By lending selective military assistance to Cuban authorities, the United States released Cuban troops for field duty against the insurgent Liberals and thereby assisted in suppressing the insurrection. On a limited basis, the United States had again assumed responsibility under the Platt Amendment for the well-being of foreign property. Army Chief of Staff General Hugh L. Scott wrote in March, "There seems to be no prospect of our going into Cuba at the present time."[12]

II

The February Revolution underscored the persisting volatility of Cuban politics, and specifically electoral politics involving presidential contests. Within two years of the 1917 uprising, these were again hotly debated issues as Cuba prepared for presidential elections in 1920. U.S. officials followed electoral developments in Cuba with growing uneasiness. No one in the State Department needed reminding that on two previous occasions disputed elections had resulted in armed uprisings. Confronting the prospect of another electoral crisis in 1920, and hence the possibility of another armed protest, Washington prepared to increase supervision of Cuban internal affairs, specifically to regulate the conduct of elections. State Department policy calculations were based on the belief that supervision of the electoral process would encourage honest elections, thereby encouraging participants to abide by the results and forego the resort to arms that attended fraudulent elections in the past. As early as January 1919 the State Department outlined to President Menocal the minimum requirements for orderly elections. Undersecretary Frank L. Polk enjoined Menocal to organize and preside over elections capable of inspiring national confidence. This involved, first, public assurances from the president pledging his administration to fair elections, without which, Polk stressed, revolution "was almost certain."[13]

But more than public assurances, Washington demanded a far-reaching overhaul of the electoral system. Indeed, the State Department's hope for peaceful presidential elections depended largely on a proposed reorganization of election procedures. These were minimum measures deemed essential for the credibility of Conservative commitments to honest elections. The inability of regulatory agencies to investigate Liberal charges of fraud in 1916 had encouraged abuse of the electoral code. Recurring allegations of irregularities in voter lists, moreover, including counts in several *municipios* where returns exceeded the number of registered voters, underscored the need to review the voter registration lists around which the 1920 elections would be organized. Lastly, the State Department sought an invitation from the Menocal government for a U.S. commission to supervise the proposed reform of the electoral system and to assist Cubans in conducting the elections. All these measures, Polk emphasized, were "absolutely necessary to secure peace in Cuba."[14]

These proposals were received with a mixture of apprehension and aversion in Havana. On the question of election reform, the government was amenable. Within a week, Menocal pledged electoral reforms and invited General Enoch H. Crowder, the U.S. legal adviser during the 1906–1909 occupation, to visit Cuba to revise the electoral code.[15] On February 12, 1919, Menocal dutifully requested U.S. assistance to reorganize Cuban electoral laws in order "to remove the constant source of irritation, criticism, and mortification" attending past elections.[16]

On the question of supervised elections, however, Menocal balked. The presence of U.S. officials monitoring the administration's conduct of elections, Secretary of State Pablo Desvernine protested, would itself promote political unrest and compromise national sovereignty, for which Conservatives would be held accountable by the electorate.[17] The Menocal position was supported by Minister Gonzales. "Where would he or his party stand before these people," Gonzales asked rhetorically, "if he invited intervention in his own administration and himself openly impugned the sovereignty of the state!"[18] Gonzales urged a compromise in the form of the "solicitation of friends having vital concern in the peace and welfare of Cuba and as necessary for our personal confidence."[19] Under the proposed arrangement, the legation would secure from Menocal an informal pledge to conduct honest national elections.

Cuban objections notwithstanding, the State Department hoped that the Crowder mission in 1919 would set in place the procedure and personnel to supervise the elections the following year. Polk's oral instructions to Crowder stressed the importance of a new electoral code to avoid a repetition of previous political difficulties.[20] The State Department was also eager for Crowder to remain in Cuba through the 1920 election to supervise the enforcement of the new code. Polk privately discouraged Crowder from making any public statement proposing supervision of elections for fear that premature disclosure would antagonize Menocal. "[I] told him," Polk entered in his diary, "it would be better to recommend certain reforms publicly and make private recommendations to the President of Cuba that it would be useless unless this Government controlled elections."[21]

General Crowder arrived in Cuba in March 1919. For the better part of six months, he studied the political context of the electoral code through consultation with the president, cabinet ministers, political leaders of both parties, and Cuban jurists. By August 1919, after an exhaustive study of all elections since 1908, in which virtually every known fraud was catalogued, Crowder had completed his work.[22] The new law placed greater responsibility on judicial agencies to resolve electoral disputes. The reorganized electoral board drew representatives from all parties equally. The code strengthened the authority of the local appellate system over election quarrels. Presidential candidates could not seek office on more than one party ticket. Additional reforms included new voter registration cards, improved communications to relay outlying returns to Havana immediately, and safeguards against the padding of voter registration lists.[23] Crowder also recommended a new census preliminary to the reorganization of voter registration lists. In July 1919, the Cuban government established a census bureau under the supervision of the United States. With the completion of the census in early fall, the government allotted several months for party registrations and the distribution of new voter identification cards.[24] In early 1920, revised voter registration lists based on the new census figures were completed.[25]

III

Liberals received the reorganization of the electoral system with reservations. They hailed the electoral reforms as vindication of their charges in 1916.[26] But even the elimination of some of the most obvious defects of the electoral code inspired little more than guarded optimism for honest elections in 1920. In the end, Liberals argued, Conservatives still retained full custody over the electoral administration, however much reformed and reorganized. Liberals carried their argument one step further: responsibility for honest elections in 1920 rested with authorities in Washington.[27] Having neutralized the deterrent value of the threat of arms to protest electoral fraud, having eliminated rebellion as both a restraint of government excesses before the elections and as a means of redress for government abuses after the elections, Liberals insisted, the United States was now required to guarantee the integrity of elections. As early as December 1918, José Miguel Gómez outlined in tentative form the party position:

> If we must tolerate in Cuba intervention in everything, whether in the sanitary department or in the treasury, or in the supply department; if the American army occupies the country, if Minister Gonzales addresses manifestos and dictates to the Cuban people, if the Executive himself has to tolerate intervention by Desvernine and others, and if all this with the consent of the present government; if they rob us of the result of the elections, if they dictate restrictions on the free exercise of electoral rights, if they do not permit us to resort to revolution in order to carry out sane reforms; then in this lamentable case, let us hope they intervene in the only thing in which they have never intervened before and that is real elections which form the only method to save the country. Elections directed by the present government would not make it worthwhile for me to accept a nomination as there would be no justice exercised.[28]

Several months later, the Liberal National Assembly authorized the party leadership to seek U.S. assistance if prospects for honest election deteriorated.[29]

Pressure mounted within the Liberal party to secure U.S. supervision of the election.[30] In October 1919, the executive committee dispatched Fernando Ortiz to Washington to present the Liberal case directly to the State Department. The Liberal party, Ortiz stressed, had little expectation for honest elections. Under these circumstances Liberals were prepared to request U.S. supervision, without which, he predicted, Cuba would experience new political disorders.[31]

The State Department was sufficiently moved by Liberal arguments to revive the issue of U.S. supervision. Assistant Secretary of State William Phillips feared "the alternative of facing serious political disturbances or a condition equally serious." Doubting Menocal's ability if not perhaps his willingness to guarantee honest elections, the State Department pressed again for an official invitation for Crowder to supervise the conduct of the campaign. "What would be more natural," Phillips asked rhetorically, "than for Cuba to invite General Crowder (who is now thought to enjoy, as he long has done, the confidence of the majority of Cubans), to interpret and apply the new law."[32]

Renewed U.S. efforts to supervise the election met continued opposition in Havana. Gonzales reported that Menocal appeared "astonished" at the United States' proposal. The appointment of Crowder as election supervisor would be interpreted in Cuba as a defeat of his policies, Menocal held, perhaps impairing his ability to govern for the balance of his term. Indeed, Menocal threatened to resign before submitting to the humiliation of U.S. supervision.[33] Secretary of State Desvernine protested the proposed supervision as a Liberal plot to discredit the Conservative government. Writing directly to Crowder, Desvernine pleaded Havana's case privately, warning that imposed supervision would inevitably result in Menocal's resignation. Only the *miguelista* faction of the Liberal party, Desvernine insisted, stood to benefit from the chaos certain to result from the collapse of the Conservative government.[34]

The issue of supervision divided U.S. policy officials. Crowder himself expressed reservations about imposing supervision on recalcitrant Cuban authorities. Without the cooperation and participation of all political parties, he warned, supervision was "unthinkable" and doomed to failure.[35] The Conservatives' position was also endorsed by the U.S. minister in Havana. The issue of supervision, Gonzales wrote, represented nothing more than a clever Liberal political maneuver. To acquiesce to Liberal demands for supervision was effectively to generate "a boom for the presidential aspirations of José Miguel Gómez."[36] This new pressure for supervision relaxed in November 1919 when Gonzales obtained a personal pledge from Menocal guaranteeing the integrity of national elections.[37]

IV

Election-year politics moved at an accelerating pace. A power struggle between the rival candidates for the Liberal party nomination, José Miguel Gómez and Alfredo Zayas, ended when Gómez prevailed and thereupon expelled Zayas from the party. Zayas immediately organized a new party, the Partido Popular Cubano (PPC), obtained the PPC presidential nomination, and cast about for allies. In one of the more improbable developments, Menocal seized the opportunity to thwart Gómez's presidential hopes by endorsing the PPC candidate and delivering the support of the Conservative party to Zayas. The PPC and the Conservative party joined together to form the Liga Nacional. In return, Zayas pledged to help Menocal return to the presidential palace in the 1924 national elections.[38]

Only the newly enacted electoral code, specifically the clause prohibiting a candidate from seeking office on two tickets, stood between Zayas and the Conservative party nomination. In early March 1920, the Conservative-controlled congress introduced legislation designed to amend the code to permit dual party nominations. The proposed change evoked immediate opposition in Washington. Menocal's partisan assault, Secretary of State Bainbridge Colby protested, threatened to undermine national confidence in the electoral system so laboriously prepared by General Crowder. Colby denounced the contemplated revision of the law as "unwise and unnecessary to the conduct of fair and honest elections in Cuba, giving rise to misunderstanding and capable of jeopardizing the national elections later in the year."[39]

Over Washington's objections, however, the Conservatives secured rapid congressional passage of the administration's revision of the electoral code. On March 27, Menocal signed the amendment into law. In Havana, a new U.S. minister, Boaz W. Long, disappointed and very much vexed over the swift course of events, expressed to Menocal his personal regrets that the president had chosen to disregard Washington's counsel. Menocal's "very precipitous" act, Long feared, was an ominous augury early in the election year.[40] "I am terribly disappointed at Menocal's action," he admitted. "Apparently the man has played the game very fairly with us for seven years, but in this case, the first I recall of its kind, our word has been disregarded."[41] The State Department protested Menocal's action and cautioned against any "further tinkering" with the electoral code.[42]

Washington's second warning, however, fared no better than the first. Between March and April 1920, Conservatives laid siege to the electoral code. New amendments and additional changes were rushed to the floor of congress, all designed to rewrite the code to the advantage of the government ticket. One amendment authorized the administration to hire temporary employees for the duration of the election campaign—a practice outlawed in the Crowder code for having previously led to the recruitment of political thugs to harass the opposition. Another amendment suspended the prohibition against absentee registration, a move designed specifically to facilitate enrollment in the new PPC. By late April, a very much disheartened Crowder concluded that all the "evils of 1916 are, in all probability, to be practiced in 1920 upon a scale undreamed of in Cuban politics."[43]

The rush by administration supporters to revise the electoral code immediately revived Liberal demands for U.S. supervision. Their worst fears had been confirmed: the government had no intention of organizing honest elections. In March 1920, Liberal party president Faustino Guerra asked for an appointment to meet informally with Secretary of State Colby in Washington. Without minimal assurances from the State Department, principally a commitment to supervise the balloting, Guerra explained, the Liberal party would not participate in the elections.[44] Colby rejected the Liberal request, insisting that any effort to "transfer the forum of political activity from the Island of Cuba to Washington is harmful to the best interests of Cuba and is fruitful of endless misunderstandings."[45]

The purport of Guerra's communication did not go unnoticed, however. For the first time, a prominent Liberal had given clear if only private expression to a tactic rumored to be under active consideration in the inner councils of the Liberal party—a boycott of elections. "Such a withdrawal," Minister Long warned the State Department, "might be a prelude to civil war."[46] Colby was sufficiently concerned about a boycott to address himself directly to the Liberal threat:

> The withdrawal of any political party from participation in an election . . . is regarded by this Government not only an undemocratic, but as tending to undermine the foundations of popular government. Such withdrawal would in the view of this Government, mean that the leaders of the party thus counseling their followers to abstain from exercising the political duties of citizenship have in reality urged them to withdraw from the political life of the country. Such a proceeding would be regarded in the United States as a grave injustice to the Cuban people, and

would place any party adopting such a policy not only beyond the place of the political life of the country, but as indicative of their incapacity to participate in a fruitful and constructive way in the development of democratic institutions. The withdrawal of any element from the national elections will in no way influence the policy of the United States to regard the result of a fair election as expressive of the national will.[47]

When informed of the State Department's refusal to meet with Liberal representatives, Guerra responded tersely: "If there is no supervision, we cannot go to the polls."[48]

V

In mid-1920 the implications of Menocal's determination to frustrate a Liberal victory aroused considerable concern in Washington. By April 1920, with ballotting little more than six months away, there seemed little prospect of averting civil war. What alarmed the State Department most was not so much the enmity among the power contenders, but the realization that Menocal was prepared, if necessary, to provoke political disorders to block a Liberal triumph. More and more reports reached Washington that the Conservatives would not under any circumstances relinquish power to the Liberals, whatever the outcome of the elections. Indeed, the government was reported predisposed to provoke U.S. intervention rather than yield power to the opposition.[49] In Washington, Colby reported learning that Menocal was prepared to "be the first man in Cuba to revolt" if Gómez won the election.[50]

Nor were Liberals, for their part, reconciled to defeat through fraud. Many advocated a more aggressive policy against conservatives and alluded freely to armed protest. In Santa Clara and Camagüey, Liberals threatened to destroy every cane field and sugar mill in the eastern third of the island.[51] The U.S. consul in Antilla reported learning that in the event of wide-scale electoral fraud, the Liberals plotted the destruction of foreign property and attacks on U.S. citizens.[52]

Tensions mounted as the campaign moved into the summer months. Government misconduct escalated. *Botelleros* in the form of armed civilian henchmen protected by the army and police intimidated Liberal voters and illegally seized voter registration cards. *Municipios* where registered Liberals outnumbered the combined strength of the PPC and Conservative coalition were placed under the control of progovernment military supervisors.[53] In many districts the registered voters far outnumbered the count of the recently completed population census, raising doubts among Liberals about the accuracy of the new census enterprise. In July, a Liberal judge serving on the electoral board was murdered under mysterious circumstances. Government abuse, Liberals warned, had created an intolerable situation, one certain to erupt into civil war unless remedied immediately by the United States.[54]

The State Department watched events in Cuba with an unaccustomed helplessness. The prospects for postelection violence increased, and Washington seemed powerless to stem the tide of events. "Since coming here," Minister Long reported as early as March 1920, "I [have] learned of past happenings which indicate that many Cubans feared, in approaching elections, a repetition of the 1916 experience."[55] From Washington, an impatient Secretary of State Colby reminded Menocal of his "solemn assurance" of the previous November to guarantee honest elections. Colby protested the apparent lack of official concern over the death of the Liberal judge, asserting that the administration's indifference to the case had created an "unfavorable impression" in Washington. He warned that "nothing short of the most diligent activity on the part of all the Government authorities in Cuba . . . will remove this impression."[56] By mid-1920, moreover, the State Department had concluded that the government candidate lacked the support to win the election legally. Assistant Secretary of State Sumner Welles decided that developments in Cuba justified Liberal fears of fraud and violence in the absence of supervision. "A revolt by the Liberal Party is a contingency that may be expected if Zayas should appear to be elected." Only "radical measures," Welles concluded, could save the rapidly deteriorating political situation in Cuba.[57] In late summer, a satisfactory settlement of growing political crisis reached a new urgency as the Cuban postwar economy collapsed. Mass unemployment, street demonstrations, and rising prices added economic stress to political tensions. Labor militancy heightened concern in the United States that economic grievances would ignite political disorders. Undersecretary of State Norman H. Davis wrote the White House, "We are advised that widespread alarm exists lest the attempt be made by party leaders to use the dissatisfaction of this element in order to promote serious disturbances in connection with political meetings which are not being held."[58] Suddenly, in August, the Liberal party announced its decision to withdraw from the campaign and boycott the election. This resolution, Guerra warned the United States, inevitably meant revolution.[59]

The first serious election crisis had erupted, and the State Department responded immediately. Alluding to the Platt Amendment, Secretary of State Colby warned Liberals that responsibility for maintaining a government adequate for the protection of life, property, and individual liberty precluded U.S. sympathy for "any attempt to substitute violence and revolution for the process of government." At the same time, the State Department rebuked the Menocal administration, declaring that Washington was "no less opposed to intimidation and fraud in the conduct of elections as such a procedure might be effective in depriving the people of Cuba of their right to choose their own government." Once again the issue of supervision was revived, and this time the State Department was unequivocal. Treaty obligations, Colby argued, made it "incumbent on the Government of the United States to use all available means to observe the conduct of the electoral procedure in Cuba, as well as the spirit in which the electoral law is being enforced."[60] Under the proposed plan, the United States would appoint agents to observe election proceedings in all six provinces and report their findings directly to the legation.

The State Department response ended the crisis. On the strength of the U.S. pledge to observe the elections and the State Department's denunciation of fraud and intimidation, the Liberals agreed to remain in the campaign and go to the polls.[61]

Throughout the fall, the legation forwarded to Washington periodic summaries of electoral abuses reported from the field. Relying on the information received from Havana, the State Department in turn lodged diplomatic protests with Cuban authorities, demanding immediate investigation and correction of specific abuses.[62] In this manner, the State Department took an increasingly active role in the elections. On October 20, recalling the events of 1916, Davis emphasized to Menocal the "highest importance" of publicly releasing election returns as quickly as possible.[63] Two days later, the State Department protested the theft of vote registration cards and the appointment of military supervisors. Menocal was urged to order military personnel to observe the strictest neutrality. "It is feared," Colby warned, "that these occurrences, which appear to be well substantiated will give rise to general popular discontent with the manner in which the elections are being conducted."[64] On October 25, Davis again urged Menocal to order the army to abstain from political activity.[65] Three days later, Colby vigorously protested an illegal appointment of a Conservative as mayor of Havana in defiance of a decision by the electoral board and the Supreme Court.[66] Several days before the election,

Davis protested the administration's plan to employ military personnel to observe the ballotting, a direct violation of the Crowder code.[67]

The State Department's attempt to orchestrate honest elections through normal diplomatic channels had no effect in Cuba. The presence of U.S. observers did little to restrain Conservative excesses. The Ministry of Gobernación, the politicized nerve center of the government, issued an inordinate number of permits for firearms to government partisans.[68] Menocal continued to disobey the electoral laws and disregard the constitutional rights of the opposition. Liberal officeholders, including judges, mayors, and governors, were summarily removed from elected office. Army units harassed Liberal voters in remote districts. Murders of Liberals increased.

VI

Ballotting ended on November 1 with neither party winning a clear mandate. Both candidates claimed victory. Communication difficulties and procedural tangles delayed announcement of election results for almost two weeks. The preliminary results released in mid-November indicated a Conservative-PPC sweep in five provinces, with only Havana in the Liberal column—results challenged immediately by the Liberal party. In the midst of charges and countercharges of fraud and corruption, the authenticity of municipal returns, including those from several key districts, was in dispute. Allegations by Liberals of government fraud, with supporting documentation, poured into the U.S. legation. Ten days after the inconclusive ballotting, Liberals appealed to Washington to mediate the election dispute.

By late 1920, the State Department no longer believed Cubans capable of resolving the election dispute without a resort to arms. Disillusioned by the inability to direct the course of events from afar by diplomatic means, the United States dropped all further solicitude toward Cuban sovereignty and bluntly invoked the Platt Amendment. Cuban indifference to U.S. counsel, the State Department held, had created conditions threatening life, property, and individual liberty, and therefore justified a suspension of sovereignty. In late December, the State Department appointed General Crowder as President Wilson's "special representative" to Cuba.[69]

These were policy variations of the theme of preventive intervention, only in 1920 they had failed to prevent the conditions creating the need for military intervention. In 1920, Undersecretary Davis artfully paraphrased the Root interpretation of the Platt Amendment to insist that U.S. treaty obligations included responsibility to "prevent action on the part of Cuban authorities which if permitted or continued would jeopardize the independence of Cuba, or the maintenance of a government adequate for the protection of life, property, and individual liberty."[70] Since disputed national elections had on two previous occasions resulted in armed protest, Washington moved quickly in 1920 to assert control over the resolution of the crisis. "Experience in the past has shown very plainly," Secretary of State Colby concluded, "that free and honest elections are essential 'to the maintenance of a government adequate for the protection of life, property, and individual liberty'"—another interpretative twist to Article 3.[71] Cuba was politically "on the rocks," Long later wrote, and only Crowder's arrival "in the nick of time . . . [saved] Cuba from intervention."[72]

8.

Reason to Rule

I

The 1920 political crisis unfolded just as U.S. capitalism was undergoing a transformation that would, in turn, alter the form of U.S. capital in Cuba and modify again the function of intervention. The United States emerged from World War I with a vastly expanded industrial capacity. But the end of the war also brought recession, and with it new pressures to expand production as essential to sustain prosperity. Several corollary concerns served immediately to frame policy formulation, central to which was the conviction that foreign trade was indispensable to continued economic development. Control of foreign markets promised to underwrite production, relieve overproduction, maintain full employment, and sustain economic growth. "For the first time in our history as a nation," the National Bank of Commerce proclaimed in 1919, "the assurance of our continued prosperity rests with the future of our foreign trade. The period of our industrial isolation is as completely behind us as is the period of our political isolation. Our industries were expanded and speeded up during four years of war in order to supply not only our own markets but also to meet a share of the world's demand. . . . We have surplus to sell."[1] A special committee of the National Foreign Trade Council arrived at substantially similar conclusions:

> Foreign trade is an absolute necessity if the development of American life is to continue along the lines of which it has proceeded ever since the first white man landed on these shores. The alternative is so unthinkable that its mere statement is all that is needed to expose convincingly

its ridiculous impossibility. . . . There would be enforced upon us an inconceivable reorganization of our manner of existence. On the day when that was done we should revert to a life of savagery and nothing more.[2]

After the war, the United States was transformed from a debtor nation into a creditor, with surplus capital in search of investment opportunities abroad. This development shaped a second corollary to foreign policy, namely that finance capital, in the form of credit, foreign loans, and investments abroad, occupied a strategic place in promoting foreign trade and facilitating U.S. economic expansion abroad. This was also an issue to which the National Foreign Trade Council gave its attention:

> Finance performs two great services in the maintenance and promotion of foreign trade. It facilitates purchases and sales, and it paves the way for new transactions. . . . It is the field of investment in foreign countries that American finance has its largest opportunities for the promotion of American foreign trade. This is the second of the two great services. . . . One effect of the flotation of foreign loans in this country seems fairly well developed. . . . Their proceeds go abroad sooner or later in the form of exports of American products.[3]

The National Bank of Commerce announced: "We have surpluses to sell . . . and a way must be found to finance those purchases on credit. Such credit, whatever the financial machinery set in motion, must eventually be based on the savings of the American people."[4] One banker stated, "The key to foreign trade expansion is the foreign loan. We have the means to obtain that key if we only will. So far we have neglected a priceless opportunity."[5]

The proposition that finance capital would create opportunities for trade and commerce and that both would provide preferential access to markets and appropriation of resources influenced the shape of postwar policy calculations. Overseas economic expansion was directed principally at establishing control over vital primary materials necessary for U.S. industry and manufacturing and markets for surplus production, whether in the form of capital or goods themselves. One executive officer of Fenner and Beane underscored this relationship:

> We no longer borrow foreign money. We now have surplus billions to lend and to invest abroad. That gives us the status of world banker. Our mills are now capable of producing an enormous surplus of finished articles of commerce required by the remainder of the world. More and more we will need the raw materials of other countries. More and more

we will need favorable markets in foreign countries for our manufacturers. . . . Our mills must produce a surplus of the finished articles of
commerce if we would keep our labor and our capital employed. They
cannot do this unless there is an ample overseas outlet.[6]

One other consideration was important, namely, that the markets most
available, the investment opportunities most attainable, and resources
most desirable were those of Latin America. European preeminence in
Latin America collapsed after World War I, thereby creating new opportunities for U.S. commerce and capital. "The major manufacturing and
exporting nations of Europe still are comparatively prostrate and beset by
the ills of war," wrote banker E. Pennington soon after the war. "It is the
golden hour for the United States. The opportunity is ours for the taking."[7]
Latin America seemed to offer unlimited prospects for the exploitation of
raw materials and new markets.

Foreign policy became an extension of capital needs, and capital offered
the instrument through which to expand U.S. hegemony. A convergence
of interests and an integration of policy joined manufacturers, merchants,
industrialists, bankers, and the State Department. The expansion of economic interests abroad bcame an element essential to the growth of the
economy at home. Secretary of State Charles Evans Hughes assured the
National Chamber of Commerce in 1922, "It is my most earnest desire
that all practicable measures shall be taken to promote American commerce and disseminate through all appropriate channels the essential information which the American merchant needs." Hughes affirmed categorically: "The Department of State is carrying the flag of the twentieth
century. It aims to be responsive in its own essential sphere to what it
recognizes as the imperative demands of American business. It aims at
the coordination of the work of all departments bearing upon the same
great object of American prosperity."[8] Career diplomat Joseph C. Grew
stressed the importance of informing the public what "diplomatic service
stands for and what it can, if properly supported, accomplish," namely, "to
ensure business, better business, bigger business."[9] Assistant Secretary
of State J. Butler Wright agreed: "The interest of the Government of the
United States [is] . . . the promotion and support of legitimate American enterprise in foreign countries . . . to protect and support reputable
American enterprises abroad."[10] Assistant Secretary of State W. R. Castle,
Jr., elaborated further in a speech before the National Foreign Trade
Council:

> The Department of State [is] primarily, for you, an attorney, an advocate abroad of your interests. Whenever a legitimate American business enterprise in any foreign country gets into difficulties which cannot be settled by ordinary processes of law we are ready to take up the cudgels for it. The Department of State has always stood for the open door. . . . But all your Government can do is to open the door and hold it open. We cannot pass through the door and do business for you.[11]

These were elements, to be sure, not dissimilar to past policy. The difference after World War I, however, was the degree to which policymakers and capitalists collaborated. Different, too, was the growing interest by the State Department in exporting finance capital in the form of loans and credits to Latin America. Washington sought to take immediate advantage of the collapse of the region's traditional European creditors by urging U.S. banking interests to furnish capital to the region. This was the purport of Sumner Welles's counsel in early 1922:

> Conditions in all [Latin America] are such that their Governments must in the near future sell government bonds to obtain money for funding accumulations of budgetary deficits, and the other current debts, paying maturing obligations, and for financing the construction of railways, port works, sanitary systems, etc. The United States appears to be the only market for their securities. . . . The United States Government, on behalf of its nationals, seeks in these South American countries reasonable opportunities and protection in commercial intercourse, in obtaining concessions, in profitable investment, and in all undertakings that will be mutually beneficial to American citizens and to the citizens of the South American countries concerned.[12]

The Division of Latin American Affairs explained that the United States was crucially interested in the rapid developments in Central and South American countries since the war:

> Our political relations with those countries in certain respects are quite distinct from our relations with other countries of the world. The economic development of Latin-American countries presents problems in the Old World. It is quite reasonable that the Government should have a distinct policy with reference to economic relations with Latin American countries. . . . Every dollar invested to promote the development of Latin-American countries, whether it be for materials made in the United States, or for public works, or improvements in lands or industries in Latin-America will mean an additional bond of material and mutual interest between North and South America. This would not be true neces-

sarily of dollars invested in European countries, for there they might be used to rehabilitate enterprises that enter into direct competition with North American interests.[13]

By late 1921, the State Department prepared to coordinate policy with banking interests so that, according to the Office of the Foreign Trade Adviser, "both the government and business can obtain mutual advantages from being mutually informed regarding their respective operations and policies."[14] Sumner Welles elaborated:

> I have for some time been anxious that this Department adopt a definite policy with respect to the financing by American banking interests of Latin American governments, states, provinces and municipalities. It is of particular and immediate importance at this time that some policy be determined upon which will enable this Department, as well as the Treasury and Commerce Departments, to be fully advised of all negotiations conducted by American banks in Latin America for the flotation of such loans, both in order to render assistance in such cases to the banking interests involved and likewise to exert as much influence as may be possible and proper over the manner in which the proceeds of such loans are expended and to prevent, so far as may be possible, American bankers taking up propositions which this Government believes to be unsound or undesirable, and likewise, to restrict such financing in Latin-America to American banking interests in which financial stability and integrity the Department has confidence.[15]

In an attempt to promote cooperation between banking interests and the State Department, policy officials pledged assistance and complete confidentiality of all transactions.[16] In 1921, the State Department requested banks to provide information concerning contemplated foreign loans, stressing that the "Department will not be able intelligently to assist American enterprise unless it is so informed, and that it may be embarrassed in some of its general policies and in caring for the interests of the United States unless it is so informed."[17]

II

These were developments with far-reaching implications in Cuba. The island had enjoyed extraordinary prosperity during the war and the immediate postwar period. The value of the sugar crop in 1920, at the peak of the boom, was more than double that of the previous year, from

$455 million in 1919 to $1 billion. This sudden increase in the value of sugar required a larger volume of financing. Sugar producers and speculators accounted for much of this credit. But during the "dance of the millions" all values had become inflated and property changed ownership in rapid succession. Speculation was rampant. New enterprises were launched, construction projects expanded, and banks extended operations and opened new branches across the island.[18] The Banco Nacional managed 130 branches and in 1920 claimed total deposits approaching $200 million. The Banco Español controlled 55 branches and represented some $112 million in deposits. The Banco Internacional operated 104 branches accounting for $30 million. As the Cuban economy expanded between 1915 and 1920, the number of older North American banks increased, while the operations of new ones enlarged. The Canadian Bank of Commerce opened an office in Havana.[19] The National City Bank also opened an office in Havana in 1915 and quickly established branches elsewhere on the island. National City was followed by the Mercantile Bank of the Americas and the American Foreign Banking Corporation, a Chase subsidiary. As sugar production increased and prices soared, competition among lenders grew particularly fierce. Credit to mill owners and farmers was cheap, and virtually unlimited. Some 50 mills, more than a quarter of the 198 *centrales* in operation, were acquired by new owners between 1919 and 1920.[20] Every banking house owned portfolios thick with notes of mortgaged sugar property, notes on standing and future crops, and liens on the bagged sugar that already in 1919 began to accumulate ominously in Cuban warehouses. By late summer of 1920, there was some $80 million in loans upon sugar made at a valuation of twenty cents a pound.[21] Years later, the former U.S. consul in Havana recalled the period:

> Everybody in Cuba had money. . . . New machinery was ordered, banks loaned money on sugar taken at the prevailing market price, lending up to half the amount, and gold flowed in every direction. A Cuban family that I knew went abroad at the time for a part of the summer taking a letter of credit for forty thousand dollars, and telegraphed back for twenty thousand more. People started to erect sumptuous villas in Country Club Park, Almenares and elsewhere, magnificent automobiles were imported from the north, house rents increased enormously, six to eight hundred being regarded as practically giving the premises for nothing and prices of everything were on the same scale, even a room with bath at the hotels costing twenty dollars a day.[22]

The end was not long in coming. Sugar that sold for twenty-two cents a pound in the spring of 1920 fell to four cents in the autumn. Commodity imports ordered during the peak of the sugar boom arrived to Havana as prices collapsed, and were left unclaimed at the Havana shipyards. The docks became congested and trade and commerce came to a halt. Sugar surpluses increased as prices decreased, and planters and mill owners found themselves with sugar that could not be sold and debts that could not be serviced. Banks that had advanced loans to planters with abandon during the sugar boom were left overextended and undercapitalized. In early October 1920, a run on the principal banks, including the Banco Nacional, the Banco Español, and the Banco Internacional, threatened Cuba's principal lending institutions with collapse. The very solvency of the republic appeared at stake as the government fiscal agent, the Banco Nacional, struggled to stave off bankruptcy. On October 11, the government proclaimed a moratorium through December, later renewed through February 1921.

The collapse of sugar prices in 1920 signaled a new expansion of U.S. control over Cuban sugar. Investments increased 536 percent between 1913 and 1928, from $220 million to $1.5 billion. The portion of the total sugar crop produced by U.S.-owned mills increased from 15 percent in 1906 to 48 percent in 1920 and 75 percent in 1928.[23] But the difference was not only the expanding scope of U.S. capital but also its changing source. Sugar production expanded during and immediately after the war as a result of credits and loans provided by U.S. banks. The principal casualties of the sugar debacle were independent local producers, and in time smaller U.S. mills failed and were absorbed by larger properties. Even the powerful Cuba Cane Corporation passed under the control of an executive committee of bankers. By 1925, some thirty-three *centrales* that had participated in the 1920–1921 crop had ceased operations. Many others survived only at the expense of ownership. The National City Bank and Chase National foreclosed on scores of mills to settle debts. In 1920–1921, National City alone had some $35 million in loans that could not be paid. By 1922, it had assumed ownership of some sixty sugar mills, and soon thereafter established the General Sugar Company. In the following decade, National City floated some fifteen bond issues for U.S. companies in Cuba, including sugar, railroads, and utilities.[24]

Other banks also acquired title to insolvent sugar properties. New bank-controlled corporations assumed control over the consolidation of old sugar mills. Between 1921 and 1922, $67 million in bonds were marketed for Cuban sugar companies in New York.[25]

These developments foretold of other far-reaching changes overtaking sugar production. Newly organized sugar syndicates responded to declining prices by improved efficiency and increased production, both of which depended upon expansion, consolidation, reorganization, and modernization. As debt-ridden estates and mills surrendered ownership to banks, a new push toward concentration of property placed sugar production in fewer hands.

But this change was not limited to the sugar industry. By the spring of 1921, calamity struck the banking system, and with devastating consequences for Spanish and Cuban banks. Eight banks with a total of 123 branches failed in May. Three others closed in June. In all, some eighteen banks totaling some $130 million failed, including the Banco Internacional, the Banco Español, and the Banco Nacional. And almost immediately, the National City Bank became the leading bank in Cuba.[26]

U.S. investments of other types followed. The Electric Bond and Share Company acquired branches and property across the island. The Cuban Telephone Company, a subsidiary of ITT, established control over communications. Under the auspices of the National City Bank, a railway merger brought the principal railroads into the Consolidated Railroads of Cuba. U.S. banks also floated securities for the Cuban government. J. P. Morgan, the Chase National Bank, and Continental Bank and Trust Company handled loans and public works. The United States' control of mines, tobacco, and ranches increased. Trade expanded, reaching a high in 1920 when 73 percent of all imports came from the United States.[27]

III

When presidential elections ended inconclusively on November 1, 1920, the stage was set for a new civil war. For weeks, tensions mounted. Both parties proclaimed victory. The candidates exchanged invectives and traded threats. The electoral dispute threatened political upheaval, and social discontent deepened. Unemployment, food shortages, and rising prices left no one unaffected. Strikes increased and public demonstrations became commonplace. And the longer the delay in processing the votes, the greater the possibility of fraud, and the larger the prospects of civil strife.

U.S. authorities watched the deepening crisis in Cuba with a mixture of disbelief and despair. Minister Boaz W. Long issued an urgent appeal for instructions, admitting, "I find myself at somewhat a loss to know what to do."[28] Somehow—and no one was quite certain how—Cuban politicians had outmaneuvered the State Department and eluded the constraints so effectively applied in the past. These maneuvers had precipitated precisely the conditions so long dreaded by U.S. policymakers. The electoral system had failed and the economy had faltered.

The State Department responded quickly. In conditions reminiscent of the crisis of 1906, Washington appointed General Enoch H. Crowder "special representative of the president" in Cuba. Invested with the full sanction of the Platt Amendment, Crowder received sweeping authority over the Cuban administration, including supervision over the pending partial elections, reorganization of national, provincial, and municipal governments, and revival of the Cuban economy. On December 31, the State Department instructed the legation to inform President Menocal—"without comment"—of Crowder's arrival and to make all necessary preparations for the special representative to meet with ranking Cuban leaders.[29] When Menocal protested the United States' disregard for the customary diplomatic courtesies prior to Crowder's arrival, Undersecretary Norman H. Davis responded tersely: "On account of the special relations existing in Cuba and the United States it has not been customary, or is it considered necessary, for the President of the United States to obtain prior consent of the President of Cuba to send a special representative to confer with him regarding conditions seriously affecting the interests of both Cuba and the United States."[30]

Crowder arrived to Havana on January 6, 1921, aboard the battleship *Minnesota,* properly ostentatious, purposefully ominous. The official reception was cool but correct, for Cuban authorities were much too sensible to allow a protocol peccadillo to add to their political problems with the United States. But gone was the customary graciousness with which Cubans characteristically greeted U.S. envoys. Gone, too, was the desire to cooperate with the North Americans. Stated simply, Enoch Crowder was not welcome in Havana. This was intervention, again; some would say armed intervention, albeit in slightly modified form—one battleship, not a navy, one major general, not an army—but it was a warship and not a passenger vessel, and the special representative was a soldier, not a diplomat, and the implications of these details were not lost on the Cubans. A proconsul had arrived, with full authority, everyone knew, superseding that of the U.S. minister to Cuba. There was speculation, too, that this authority exceeded even that of the president of the republic. For the better part of that year, Crowder conducted official business aboard the *Minnesota*, receiving delegations and issuing decrees from a stateroom somewhere deep within the battleship. It was an ominous presence, this single warship anchored in Havana harbor. Certainly not an unfamiliar sight in the brief history of the republic, but still unsettling, for the Special Representative imperiously conducted affairs of state—affairs of the Cuban state—with the *Minnesota*'s guns trained (coincidentally, the North Americans said, symbolically, the Cubans charged) on the presidential palace.

Unresolved elections brought the government to a standstill, at the brink of political collapse presiding over an economy that had already collapsed. Minister Long attributed the deepening crisis to short-sighted government authorities who were "either unwilling or unable to prevent catastrophes," the "reckless buying of Cuban merchants, the Bolsheviki tendency of Havana harbor workers (the Government being unable to handle them) and the corruption among Government officials." Long concluded: "Such are the elements which combine to defeat the purposes of those who are properly inspired. Added to these conditions were the inefficiency and obstinacy of certain Cuban officials who will not or cannot realize that it is appropriate to maintain cordial relations with the United States."[31] Secretary of Commerce Herbert Hoover also spoke of the necessity to relieve the apprehension attending imminent "Cuban government bankruptcy and social chaos."[32] What made the prospect of paralysis in Cuban administration so alarming was the urgent necessity of decisive state intervention to resolve the expanding economic crisis. These conditions also threatened U.S. capital interests. "It is thought to be particularly desirable," the State Department instructed Crowder before his departure, "that emphasis be laid upon the fact that the present situation in Cuba is proving harmful to commercial intercourse between the United States and Cuba . . . and that the resultant detriment to the prosperity of Cuba cannot but be a matter of close concern to the United States."[33] In late 1920, Washington concluded that Cuban authorities could not be depended upon to resolve the deepening crisis in a manner satisfactory to the United States. On the contrary, Cubans themselves were perceived to be a source of the problem.

Crowder's arrival in early 1920 as special representative also reflected the changing nature of U.S. capital in Cuba. He was charged with adjusting state policy to the changing requirements of foreign capital in Cuba. Only through direct appropriation of the policy apparatus of state could the State Department hope to create the necessary conditions for the security of U.S. economic interests. As early as December 1920, Minister Long complained of Cuban "inexperience in dealing with large Governmental problems." Under the Platt Amendment, he insisted, the responsibility for rescuing the floundering republic fell to the United States:

> The future of Cuba is fraught with many perils. The greatest of these, at the moment, is the economic peril. Our Government, therefore, as sponsor for the well-being and independence of this nation, which has been created as a result of our genuine belief that Cubans were able to govern themselves, is doomed to sad disappointment, unless the Cubans are big enough to accept and follow the advice of a nation which created her.[34]

Long would return to this theme some weeks later, this time in private correspondence with considerably less tact:

> Conflicting interests, political and economic, threatened the life of the nation, but few of the Cubans seemed to realize it. The "Liga" party was absorbed in sustaining the election returns; the Liberal party was struggling to prove irregularities; both were so engrossed in serving their ends that they appeared to have forgotten the fate of the nation. Politically Cuba was "on the rocks." Petty officials were reaching for their last sure moments to graft in every department of the Government. The banking interests, each struggling for its own selfish advantage, even though some were in the throes of death, continued to fight for points of advantage while economic ruin threatened the only great industry of the country.

Presupposing a satisfactory settlement of the electoral crisis, Long concluded: "We must recognize that the new incumbent will be no better than his predecessors, unless we show him the way."[35]

The authority conferred on Crowder had been exercised previously only by Wood and Magoon, and both of them had ruled during military occupations without the slightest pretense of maintaining the fiction of Cuban sovereignty. Full-scale armed intervention had delivered to the United States total and unencumbered control of the state through which to pursue the institutional development of hegemony. Each suspension of sovereignty announced a new interpretation of both the scope and function of intervention and signaled a shift of U.S. interests in Cuba.

In 1920, however, armed intervention and military occupation were no longer necessary to obtain Cuban acquiescence to U.S. demands. The unresolved election in 1920 created unsettled political conditions. Both parties appealed to Washington for assistance, thereby facilitating the United States' entree. This was a government paralyzed and susceptible to the imposition of political authority from abroad and an economy prostrate and vulnerable to increased foreign capital penetration. But, more important, by 1920 U.S. participation in local policy formulation had acquired institutional vigor, and increasingly it was impossible to determine where Cuban initiative ended and North American influence began.

The Crowder appointment represented the most sweeping sanction for the appropriation of Cuban administration ever read into the Platt Amendment. It was not necessary—or desirable—to suppress Cuban sovereignty as long as the exercise of that sovereignty did not obstruct U.S. hegemony. "A continuation of the present situation," Undersecretary Davis proclaimed, "would prove most detrimental to the prosperity of Cuba and harmful to the relations between the United States and Cuba. As this cannot but be a matter of the closest concern to this Government because of the special relations existing between the two countries, the President has instructed General Crowder to confer with President Menocal as to the best means of remedying the situation."[36] The invocation of treaty rights did not require the displacement of Cuban government, only Cuban acquiescence, and as long as the Cuban government heeded the advice of the Special Representative there would be no "intervention." "You may state to President Menocal," the State Department instructed the Legation in Havana, "that it is the earnest desire of this Government to avoid the necessity of taking any measures which could be construed as intervention in Cuba or as supervision of the domestic affairs of that Republic, which we still feel confident can be avoided, provided President Menocal assumes a receptive attitude in respect to the advice and just recommendations which the President has instructed General Crowder to convey to him."[37]

IV

In many important respects, the Crowder mission employed the methods developed earlier as preventive measures. The threat of armed intervention, with its attending implications to Cuban sovereignty, was used freely against local officeholders. But the larger purpose, Washington insisted, remained to end conditions capable of requiring armed intervention.[38]

What was different in 1921, and what distinguished the Crowder mission from earlier intervention, was that while the United States intruded into Cuban internal affairs more often and for more reasons than before, the circumstances under which Washington contemplated armed intervention had greatly decreased. In short, Washington was increasingly loath to exercise the military option in Cuba. Reluctance to exercise the specific treaty right of armed intervention, in turn, increased the need to exercise wider control over a greater scope of Cuban internal affairs, more directly, more efficiently, and more completely—to avoid the necessity of armed intervention.

Nor was this difference only one of degree; the very mode of intervention was transformed. Supervision of Cuban authorities was no longer exercised by the legation implementing directives from Washington. Cuban authorities had already demonstrated a readiness to dismiss and disregard diplomatic counsel. Crowder arrived in Cuba with objectives no less sweeping than those of the military interventions of 1898 and 1906—the total reorganization of Cuban administration. And for this, the United States required the election of a president who, in the words of Sumner Welles, was thoroughly acquainted "with the desires of this government" and was amenable "to suggestions or advice which might be made to him by the American Legation."[39]

Different, too, was the nature of U.S. capital stake on the island. The early 1920s witnessed the growing concentration and centralization of industrial capital, the tendential elimination of free competition through monopolies and trusts, and the increasing power of banks and finance capital. U.S. capital had not only enlarged its economic control over the island, but also that control took new forms. Banks had displaced individual and corporate investors in Cuba and quickly prevailed as the principal mode of U.S. investment in Cuba. By 1920–1921, over $100 million had been invested in Cuban sugar alone by New York banks, including $10 million from National City, $8 million from the American Foreign Banking Corporation, and $15 million from the Royal Bank of Canada. The balance was distributed among Park National, Chase National, Irving National, the Equitable Trust Company, and the First National Bank of Boston.[40] In all, some 400 banks in the United States had funds invested in Cuban sugar, mostly through the New York banks. The crisis in the Cuban economy, specifically the decline of sugar prices, Secretary of Commerce Herbert Hoover concluded, was due to "a great lack of confidence in the stability of the Cuban government."[41]

And it was to this task that the Crowder mission was given: to promote political stability by establishing a regimen of administrative integrity and fiscal responsibility. This would become known as the "moralization program," an attempt to create the proper environment to promote Cuban prosperity and protect U.S. property.

Once more, the United States found in the Platt Amendment adequate sanction for the new moralization program. Secretary of State Charles Evans Hughes insisted:

> This Government's position with regard to Cuba is that of a special friend and adviser by reason of our relation to the establishment of the Republic and of the Platt Amendment. Counsel has been given to the President of Cuba with a view to assisting his administration to become more effective and economical, and to end corruption and graft. The hope has been cherished that Cuba would accept the disinterested advice tendered by the United States in an endeavor to create a habit of sound government among the Cuban people.[42]

Crowder was appointed as adviser to provide counsel generally, but, more important, to preside over political stability and economic solvency. His immediate objective was to resolve the electoral dispute and preside over a smooth transition of power. By early January, delays in tabulating election returns had resulted in ad interim governments in many municipalities and created the possibility that provincial administration and, ultimately, national government itself would be de facto and without constitutional sanction—conditions many feared would require armed intervention.[43]

Through January and February, the Electoral Board and the Cuban courts disposed of most of the cases involving fraud, a total of 250 districts representing some 20 percent of the total. On March 15, new partial elections in the disputed *municipios* gave Alfredo Zayas the popular majority.

But it was the stability of the republic, specifically the state of fiscal administration and the solvency of the national treasury, that quickly preoccupied Crowder. "It is only through the enactment of such a program of drastic economy and honest administration," Secretary of State Hughes instructed him, "that the Government of Cuba can be placed on a sound basis with the restoration of its former prosperity." Hughes outlined Crowder's responsibility within the context of United States treaty obligations:

It is the intention of this Government that you advise the Cuban Government in particular as to solutions which may be found for the present disturbing financial conditions which obtain in the Republic and report to this Government upon the phase of the financial crisis. Since the financial rehabilitation of Cuba . . . affects very directly the stability of the Government of Cuba which it is the obligation of the United States under the Treaty of 1904 [sic] to maintain, President Zayas will doubtless appreciate the reasons for the special interest this phase of the situation in Cuba causes this Government.[44]

The settlement of the electoral dispute allowed Crowder to turn his attention to matters of fiscal policy and public administration. Indeed, Crowder set the tone of his mission by asserting that national and local treasuries throughout the island were insolvent and that "drastic reforms, beyond the power of any Cuban administration to establish, are necessary to the continuance of self-government in Cuba." The rationale of intervention had thus been formulated. If, indeed, it was beyond the capacity of the Cuban government to institute the reforms necessary for continued independence, it was the responsibility of the United States, committed by treaty to guarantee Cuban independence, to rescue the beleaguered island from the recklessness of Cubans themselves. Crowder wrote the State Department, doubtless speaking of his mission, "We need here the very type of man whose very presence would announce to the Cuban people the new conception our Government has come to entertain of the duty it owes Cuba; and that hereafter the authority of the Platt Amendment is to be used to *maintain* and not simply *restore* stable government."[45]

V

If authority to manage Cuban internal affairs found sanction in Article 3 of the Platt Amendment, the means to exact Cuban compliance to United State counsel rested on Article 2. National finances had reached desperate conditions. The collapse of sugar prices and the ensuing economic dislocation combined to diminish drastically government revenues. While the crisis may have accelerated new consolidation of existing property, there was actually little new investment. Government receipts for fiscal year 1920–1921 amounted to $108 million and expenditures surpassed $182 million. In 1921, Cuba defaulted on its bonded debt for the first time.[46]

Almost immediately upon his arrival, Crowder assumed direction over preparation of the government budget. Crowder opposed the government proposal of $136 million for fiscal year 1921–1922. Convinced that the proposed budget would only exacerbate financial conditions, Crowder recommended the adoption of whatever "steps as may be necessary to prevent [Cuban] Congress from enacting this extraordinary budget."[47] Washington warned the Cuban government of the "very grave anxiety" with which the United States viewed the new budget proposal.[48]

The defeat of the new budget settled one issue, but created a new one. The failure to pass a new appropriations bill for 1921–1922 meant that the Cuban government would continue operating under the constraints of the previously enacted budget, in this case, the revenue bill of 1918–1919, some $64 million. Effectively, the United States had cut the proposed budget allocation by more than half, a sum Crowder believed "amply sufficient" to meet government expenses, if revenues were "economically disbursed."[49]

Related to new budgetary restrictions were mounting deficits, estimated by Crowder at $46 million, and almost certain to increase in the upcoming fiscal year.[50] Zayas assumed control of a government with an empty treasury. Claims of several hundred public works contracts remained outstanding. Government funds estimated conservatively at $12 million—and perhaps even as much as $24 million—were hopelessly tied up in the insolvent Banco Nacional. Salaries and other ordinary government expenditures added further pressures. Then, too, there was the necessity of meeting interest and amortization payments. This alone amounted to $2 million in the first two months of the Zayas government. In addition, the new administration was obliged to remit $200,000 a month to New York bankers in accord with a previous external loan agreement. The government did not default; rather it issued treasury checks, and continued to fall hopelessly in arrears: some $2 million by June 1921 on the internal debt, and $4.5 million by June 1922.[51]

By mid-1921, the Cuban government was in urgent need of a new loan. Indeed, as early as November 1920, the Menocal administration had applied to J. P. Morgan and Company for a $50 million loan. But Cubans were not alone in their desire for a loan. U.S. commercial interests also urged the Department of State to facilitate a new loan as a means of reviving the economy and improving the Cuban market for American exports. Secretary of Commerce Herbert Hoover urged President Harding to endorse a loan as a means of restoring business confidence in the Cuban government and reviving economic prosperity. According to Hoover, this issue was "so important that we would be well justified in at once instructing General Crowder to be more liberal in the requirements (no doubt very properly set up) as a condition of American government approval for this loan."[52]

Neither Crowder nor the State Department disputed the efficacy of a new loan. The Zayas government did indeed face serious financial problems, and a loan offered some prospects of immediate relief. Certainly new revenue promised to contribute to recovery of the economy, restore political stability, and revive trade and investment. But a new loan, the State Department feared, the immediate benefits notwithstanding, would only ease Cuba through difficult times without addressing the causes of the problem. Certainly one source of economic distress originated with worldwide conditions over which Cuba had little control. But many of Cuba's problems, Washington insisted, were wholly of local origins, the results of two decades of maladministration and misgovernment.

The occasion was auspicious, hence, to exact from Cuban authorities widescale concessions for reform and reorganization. By invoking Article 2 of the Platt Amendment, whereby Cuban indebtedness was linked to the ordinary revenues of the island, the State Department held the Cuban government to the brink of impending insolvency in exchange for reform. The magnitude of government deficits all but totally precluded Cuban eligibility for a new loan without U.S. approval. In this period of growing bank and State Department cooperation, banks would not make a loan without prior U.S. sanction. State Department insistence upon reform became a condition of the loan negotiations, and both propelled the United States deeper into the internal affairs of the republic.

A thorough study of the Cuban budget in mid-1921 disclosed a total deficit of $46 million, and the need of a foreign loan of approximately $65 million: $25 million to rescue the sugar crop and the balance to supplement the ordinary revenues in meeting normal obligations and extinguishing the deficit.[53] But U.S. approval of the loan was not unconditional. Secretary of State Hughes insisted on a further reduction of the 1918–1919 budget and an increase of national revenues to assure

> that the ordinary revenues of the Republic would be adequate to provide for the current expenses of the total public debt, including any new loan which may be desired. The Department of State would necessarily, in view of Article II of the Platt Amendment, be unable to approve any

> increase in the public debt until such assurances were forthcoming. Nevertheless, the Department regards the Cuban financial situation . . . as being so grave that it believes all possible expedition should be used in providing remedies. It now appears that the flotation of a government loan will be a necessary portion of such remedies.[54]

The invocation of Article 2, and specifically the allusion to the need of approving an increase in the public debt, meant deeper U.S. involvement in Cuban affairs. "I cannot imagine," Crowder mused, "the Department sanctioning loans approximating this amount except upon the condition precedent that Cuba accepts some form of American supervision over Cuban revenues." Crowder conceded that an attempt to establish a customs receivership similar to one the United States imposed earlier on the Dominican Republic would meet with "very strong opposition" in Cuba, and "if imposed would result in a political crisis and a probable yielding up of the Government to an American intervention."[55] But some form of supervision of public revenues was necessary and, as Crowder certainly must have recognized, supervision over revenues was effectively supervision over virtually every aspect of Cuban administration.

The United States' interpretation of Article 2 maintained fundamentally that it was the responsibility of the United States "to safeguard the solvency of Cuba."[56] The Cuban government was not to contract any public debt, foreign or interior, until sanctioned by the United States. Only if Cuba's revenues were deemed sufficient would sanction be granted. In Crowder's words:

> That today the ordinary revenues are notoriously insufficient for these purposes is made abundantly clear. . . . The loan proposition which I have recommended will, if accepted, result in more than doubling the present national debt. We are warned by past failures of the revenues that we may no longer accept, in support of an application for authority to negotiate additional indebtedness, piecemeal revision of the revenues such as has been proffered in connection with past applications of this character.[57]

Crowder insisted upon a reduction of government expenditures with an increase in revenues. But this was only part of the problem. Just as important, Washington charged, was the graft and corruption that prevailed in every aspect of public administration. Corruption drained government revenues and depleted public morale as effectively as wasteful spending,

Crowder insisted, and posed as great a threat to the republic as insurrection, annually diverting millions to the maintenance of "corrupting sinecures." [58] He found his sanction in a new reading of the Platt Amendment:

> The stable government which we are obligated to maintain in Cuba under article three of the Platt Amendment is as much imperilled by insolvency as by armed revolution. . . . Our policy of non-interference has permitted extravagance and corruption to expand to the point of constituting a danger for the existence of the Republic. . . . The situation of Cuba is approaching insolvency and can be remedied only by the most rigid economy and the ruthless elimination of extravagance. Failure to adopt such a source will tend to aggravate or at least prolong the existing crisis. [59]

But the attempt to reform Cuban administration was not unopposed in Havana. Pressure to reduce the 1918–1919 budget to $55 million met immediate obstacles from both the Cuban congress and the Zayas administration. The attack on the political patronage system, in the name of combating corruption, encountered particular resistance. Crowder singled out the *botellas*—sinecures and political appointments—and the *colecturías* of the national lottery as the two principal threats to the solvency of the national treasury. The collectorship served as the outlet for lottery tickets to vendors. In the early 1920s, some 2,000 *colecturías* accounted for some $10 million, most of which never returned to the treasury. [60] Any plan contemplating fiscal reorganization, Crowder insisted, could not leave the issue of *botellas* and *colecturías* unattended. He thought both should be abolished, "saving only such as are in the nature of pensions and stand in the name of persons who have a claim as pensioners upon the public treasury." [61] Two months later, Crowder prepared a list of recommended reforms, including a reduction in congressional expense accounts, a cut in congressional employees, a 25 percent reduction of civil servants, reorganization of the judicial system to eliminate municipal judges, a 25 percent cut in the appropriation for materials, and a reorganization of the pension rolls. "By putting into effect the economies listed above and others which a closer investigation of the Government's departments would certainly suggest," Crowder predicted confidently, "the budgetary expenses would easily reduce to between 45 and 59 millions, with an ample provision for an efficient administration." [62]

Crowder's advice, however, remained largely unacted upon. "Almost daily I am called upon to intervene with Congress and the President to prevent action prejudicial to the public credit," Crowder complained in June 1921.[63] By August, he elaborated:

> It was clearly the hope and the expectation of the Department that the more essential reforms in the Government here could be accomplished through the Cuban agencies by advice firmly and insistently given. I have endeavored in good faith to carry out this policy which in the three month period that has elapsed since Zayas was inaugurated has, I think, been given a fair trial. The results are disappointing to me and can hardly be satisfactory to the Department.[64]

The time had arrived "to speak to the Zayas administration upon important matters more or less in terms of an ultimatum." Zayas could not be counted upon to conform to U.S. counsel voluntarily. "I am convinced," Crowder wrote, "that Zayas is first a politician and second a patriot; that he will always subordinate, even in this great crisis, essential reforms to party expediency; that he will never on his own initiative be aggressive in suppressing the graft and corruption which is sapping the foundations of government here and threatening the perpetuity of the Republic; that, unless unrestrained by our Government, he will always yield in these more essential matters to the urgings of political groups allied with him and that we must speak to him and more in terms of an ultimatum in all important matters."[65]

In early fall Crowder appealed for the adoption of a "firmer attitude" in U.S. dealings with Cuban authorities: "My effort thus far has been to accord the fullest and fairest opportunity to the Cuban Government to bring about these reforms and to make its failure to do so, under all the circumstances, a *demonstration* of either incapacity or unwillingness and a logical basis and justification for the firmer and more insistent attitude on our part." Crowder again evoked the spectre of intervention, now as a means to elicit concurrence in Washington and exact conformity in Havana, for in fact neither government could entertain the prospect of a military occupation with equanimity. Crowder asserted:

> In his present mood (created for him largely by a hungry political following) it is certain that [Zayas] will continue to obstruct many of the reforms . . . unless coerced into a more compliant attitude by pressure from Washington. Eventually Zayas must be told in unmistakable terms that his policy of a $65 million budget, with a continuation of governmental extravagance and fraud, with insufficient resources for present and possible future needs, and with liquidation of the floating and con-

> tractual indebtedness protracted over a long period of years . . . imperil
> the kind of stable government which we are pledged by treaty stipula-
> tion to maintain in Cuba and must yield to a policy of definite and spe-
> cific reforms which, of course, will be outlined by the Department only
> after the gravest deliberation and which ought, I think, under the policy
> of utilizing Cuban agencies to embody the minimum of essential re-
> forms compatible with maintaining a solvent Government here.[66]

The opportunity to "coerce" Cuban authorities into "a more compliant attitude" presented itself shortly. In late September, the Zayas govern-ment applied to J. P. Morgan and Company for a short-term loan of $5 million. Early in June, the State Department had invoked Article 2, warning Cuban authorities that approval for new loans would not be forthcoming until Cuba raised additional revenue to meet the added indebtedness.[67] Hughes sent a similar communication to Morgan and Company:

> In view of the obligations of this Government under the Platt Amend-
> ment . . . the Department will feel itself obliged, before authorizing any
> increase in the public debt of the Republic of Cuba, to assure itself that
> the ordinary revenues of the Republic are sufficient to meet the service
> of such debt. The Department of State is advised that measures are now
> contemplated by the Cuban Government for the reduction of the na-
> tional expenses and the increase of the national revenues to such an ex-
> tent as to make possible the service of the proposed Cuban loan from
> ordinary revenues of the Republic. When the Department is advised that
> such measures have become effective, it will consider further, in the
> light of its obligations above referred to, any proposals which you may
> desire to bring to the attention of the Cuban Government in connection
> with the flotation by you of the desired Cuban loan.[68]

Bankers endorsed State Department insistence on fiscal reform as a nec-essary means to guarantee the proposed loans. Some form of control over national finances was necessary before favorable action on the Cuban ap-plication was possible. "Without this safeguard," Morgan and Company asserted, "it has seemed to us, as well as to the bankers whom we have consulted, impossible to consider an issue of a Cuban Government loan to the American public."[69]

A convergence of interests joined the State Department and J. P. Morgan behind demands for reforms in Cuba. In September, Morgan rep-resentatives Dwight W. Morrow and former Undersecretary Norman H. Davis informed the State Department that the bank was prepared to consider the loan as part of a "preliminary step in constructive reform in the administration of Cuba's finances." Morgan and Company expressed a willingness to cooperate with Washington in promoting good government in Cuba and, to that end, offered to place the $5 million loan at the service of the State Department. The loan offered a means through which to exact Cuba's compliance with reform proposals. Morrow and Davis wrote to Secretary Hughes:

> [J. P. Morgan and Company] felt it possible that this application for a loan from Cuba might afford them the opportunity of cooperating with you in impressing upon the Cuban Government, if the foreign credit of the Government is to be maintained, the necessity of prompt and substantial improvement in the Cuban budget. They add that if you think it advisable for Cuba to have this temporary assistance in order to maintain credit, pending the adoption of the constructive measures necessary to put Cuba on a stable basis, J. P. Morgan and Company express their willingness to assist, provided they are assured that Cuba will adopt such a measure.[70]

Morgan and Company in future negotiations would encourage the Cuban government "to take such constructive measures as will insure fiscal stability of Cuba."[71] The $5 million loan, lastly, was also a way of securing reforms as preliminary to continued negotiations for a larger bond issue.

Hughes gave cautious endorsement of the proposed loan and the use to which it could be put. "The negotiations of the bankers," he suggested to Crowder in late September, "might well be of assistance to you."[72] Within a week, the State Department outlined the minimum requirements necessary to approve the loan: a budget not to exceed $59 million with an additional appropriation of $6 million for unforeseen expenditures and the creation of additional sources of revenues through a "comprehensive revision" of internal revenue legislation. Otherwise, Washington warned Zayas, the United States would oppose the proposed loan.[73]

By mid-October the negotiations in Havana involving representatives of the State Department, J. P. Morgan, and the Cuban government arrived at a tentative agreement. Speaking for Morgan, Morrow informed Zayas that the $5 million loan was to be considered as "a step towards and a part of more comprehensive constructive measures which are to be taken." The measures included:

> (a) A budget for the fiscal year of $59 million with the provision that an additional amount not to exceed $6 million may be included for unforeseen expenditures. . . .

(b) Legislation for such changes in the existing customs and internal revenue laws, and for such additional taxes as may be agreed upon.

(c) A loan not to exceed $50 million for the purpose of liquidating the floating debt of the Government, including repayment of the $5 million loan and of carrying out with the balance such public works or other constructive measures as may be agreed upon.[74]

On October 16, Zayas acceded to U.S. demands.[75] "His commitments," Crowder exulted, "which he understands are conditions precedent to securing the Department's sanction of the projected loan, carry him further than I anticipated he would go."[76] Several days later, Hughes informed J. P. Morgan and Company:

> I take pleasure in advising you that this Government has received from the President of Cuba certain assurances which satisfy the Department of State that the President of Cuba is committed to the constructive financial program recommended by this Government. The assurances received from President Zayas contemplate budgetary reduction and an increase of the ordinary revenues of the Republic, and entail the obligation on the part of the Executive to maintain a safe margin of receipts over expenditures. In the opinion of the Department of State these pledges of the President provide a sufficient guarantee that the ordinary revenues of the Republic will be ample to meet the service of the proposed addition to the public debt of the Republic, as contemplated in Article II of the Platt Amendment, and upon this understanding, when the proposed contract has been approved by the Cuban Congress, this Government will advise the Government of Cuba that it sanctions the temporary advance of $5 million offered by your company to the Cuban Government and will interpose no objection to the Cuban Government proceedings with the negotiations with your company for the permanent loan of $50 million.[77]

But celebration proved premature. Within a month, the State Department concluded that only "more sweeping and drastic economies than originally contemplated" would avert "a greatly increased deficit." Cuban reluctance to make further reductions in public spending, Washington warned, would force the State Department to withdraw its sanction to the proposed $5 million loan.[78] The dispute continued for another month. In mid-December, Dana G. Munro, chief of the Latin American Division, warned that continued delay in negotiating the temporary loan threatened Cuba with imminent insolvency, could mean the failure of the State Department's constructive efforts, "and might lead to a financial and possibly a political intervention."[79]

Hughes responded by recalling Crowder to Washington for a conference on the mounting crisis in Cuba. Crowder was instructed to communicate to Zayas the "utmost concern" with which Washington viewed the president's failure to make deeper cuts.[80] Crisis was again averted when negotiations secured for a second time Cuban acquiescence to new budget reductions and creation of new sources of revenue.[81]

VI

The difficulties attending the settlement of the $5 million loan had a sobering effect in Washington and augured ill for the pending negotiation for the $50 million loan. The moment was propitious, therefore, to review the developments of the previous year and define the policy context of relations with Cuba. Immediately Washington served notice on Cuban authorities that sanction of the temporary loan did not necessarily entail approval of the permanent foreign loan:

> Any decision as to the advisability of the flotation of this larger loan by the Cuban Government must necessarily be postponed by the government of the United States, in view of its obligations under Article II of the Treaty of May 22, 1903, until such time as this Government is advised by the Government of Cuba that the revision of its internal revenue and tariff schedules, now being undertaken, has been completed and that the total revenue of the Republic obtained as the result of such revision will be adequate to meet the service of this proposed addition to the public debt of the Republic of Cuba.[82]

Reviewed at length, too, was the treaty context of U.S. policy. Cuban actions, Hughes chided the Zayas government, had edged the republic to the brink of insolvency. To prevent this from recurring, and because of the "peculiarly close and special relationship to the Cuban Government," Hughes urged Cubans to be mindful of and responsive to the counsel offered by the special representative. Crowder's mission in Havana was to supervise the finances of the republic, consistently with the terms of the Platt Amendment. "It has seemed at times," the Secretary indicated bluntly, "during the past few months, as if the Cuban Government could have more effectively availed itself of such assistance had that Government clearly comprehended that such aid and counsel was offered not only through friendly interest but also by virtue of rights vested in this Government by Article II of the Permanent Treaty of 1903," which "are no less imperative than those imposed by Article III."[83]

Having sanctioned the Crowder mission as an extension of Article 3, the State Department proceeded to expand the scope of Article 2. "Since 'any public debt' might call for interest and sinking fund for which the 'ordinary revenues' would be 'inadequate,'" Hughes paraphrased the second clause, "it is clearly necessary that the United States should inform itself in advance of the contraction of any public debt whether the conditions required both by the aforesaid permanent treaty and the Constitution of Cuba are complied with." The United States, therefore, was entitled to know prior to any new Cuban indebtedness, "what the 'ordinary revenues' are, from what sources they are derived, and what said sources have produced and may be expected to produce." This proposition led Hughes to a new meaning of the Platt Amendment:

> It is in the light of the clear provisions of the Treaty and the duties it imposes that the Government of the United States is maintaining the Special Mission near the Cuban Government, and it feels it desirable upon this occasion to emphasize in this manner its belief that in order that the said Mission may be enabled to act effectively in its effort to render profitable aid to the Cuban Government, it should have free and full access to any and all sources of information which it may require, before the Government of the United States can either take intelligent action regarding whatever loan may be proposed, or determine what measures may be necessary for the appropriate protection of those who have extended credit to the Government of Cuba. To this end, it is essential that said Mission should at times offer suggestions and recommendations regarding needed fiscal measures and appropriate legislation and make such inspection of actual government operations as may in its judgment be required.[84]

This pronouncement as the condition preliminary to a new and much-needed loan effectively if not formally conferred parallel executive authority on Crowder. In a special memorandum to Zayas entitled the "Proper Construction of Article II of the Permanent Treaty," Crowder affirmed the special authority conceded to him by virtue of the second clause.[85] But Crowder's claim went beyond the second clause and, indeed, together with his interpretation of Article 3, provided the basis for the most sweeping authority ever advanced by the United States over Cuban internal affairs. "The interest of my Government in the framing of the Constitution of Cuba," Crowder explained to Zayas, "was not confined to those parts of it which fix Cuba's relationship to the United States, but extended to each and every provision whose authority could be invoked in the maintenance of a Government adequate for the protection of life, property, and individual liberty, and for the discharge of the obligations developing upon the United States under the Treaty of Paris."[86]

VII

Crowder lost no time exercising his new power. Armed with sweeping authority over Cuba based on a new interpretation of Article 3, aided too by the Cuban urgent need for a loan, authorization for which the United States claimed by virtue of a new interpretation of Article 2, Washington pursued the most far-reaching reorganization of Cuban government since the military occupation of 1899–1902: an attempt to eliminate what the State Department perceived as the deficiencies accruing in the two decades of self-government. The time was right, Crowder counseled Secretary Hughes, to proceed "with the necessary justification to employ the ultimatum in demanding of the Zayas Administration the accomplishment of certain essential reforms."[87]

But, in fact, it was to be more than the adoption of "certain essential reforms." Crowder aspired to nothing less, in his words, than an "era of moral readjustment in the National Administrative life of the Cuban Government," to be accomplished by "coercive influence" and "insistent advice, recommendations, and finally the virtual demands of the United States through my Special Mission."[88] In March 1922, Crowder dictated the first of fifteen memoranda—ultimatums directed to the Cuban government demanding reforms and reorganization of virtually every key aspect of national, provincial, and municipal administration. Several memoranda called for the collection of trade and commerce data pursuant to changes in the commercial relations, the reorganization of municipal government, and reform of the electoral board. Others insisted upon constitutional amendments reforming administrative procedures. Two memoranda demanded sweeping reorganization of the lottery system to eliminate graft and corruption associated with the *colecturías*.

Several memoranda were advisory and exhortative; some were prescriptive and threatening. All were pronounced with the expectation of Cuban compliance. Memorandum 7, entitled "The Executive and the Budget for 1922–1923," insisted upon a $55 million ceiling on the national budget. Reductions were to be attained through lowering fixed expenditures, reorganizing the diplomatic service and the armed forces, suspending civil service law to permit dismissal of unnecessary government employees, and ending all political sinecures and appointments. The Cuban crisis, Crowder warned Zayas, "failed to produce that demonstration of capacity for progressive self-government so sorely needed after the glaring errors of past administrations." Failure to adopt the budget restrictions "would be fatal to the possibility of averting imminent financial disaster to Cuban Treasury and could not but be regarded by my Government with the gravest concern." A failure to act would "bring responsibility upon both the Congress and [Zayas] for financial disaster to the Treasury and for the consequences following a further demonstration of the incapacity of the independent republican government to meet the national crisis."[89]

In memorandum 8, "Graft, Corruption and Immorality in the Public Administration," Crowder attacked the system of *botellas* and sinecures, "so general and so scandalous as to undermine the credit of Cuba and to constitute a stain on the honor of the Republic." Zayas was enjoined to use the power of the executive to remove from office all unworthy employees. "Public office," Crowder admonished the president, "is a public trust and incumbents thereof have the duty and obligation to so administer their respective offices as to disarm all except captious and irresponsible criticism." The United States was "constrained to insist" upon the adoption of measures that would eliminate public malfeasance, including:

1. The immediate removal from office of every official who
   (a) is found living at an expense exceeding any known income which he may have;
   (b) purchases property of considerable value and beyond his known capacity to pay;
   (c) is found to have permitted sinecures or corrupt influences to continue in his Department or Bureau;
   (d) ignores long continued accusations against his personal and official honesty in the administration of his office;
   (e) has demonstrated his inability to protect his Department or Bureau against charges of graft, corruption and immorality which have persisted for a considerable period and tend to bring his office into disrepute;
   (f) has not been aggressive in maintaining the reputation of his Department for efficiency and honesty.
2. An active, thorough, impartial investigation of the activities of the various Departments and Bureaus of the Government, and especially a searching inquiry into charges of corruption to generally made. . . .

3. The relentless dismissal from office and criminal prosecution of all persons found implicated in the corruption practices which may be discovered.

4. The institution of effective methods to eliminate fraud in the collection of revenues and assure an honest disbursement of public funds.[90]

Crowder called for more than the dismissal of dishonest public servants. He demanded the appointment of honest ones, and claimed authority to appoint them. In June 1922, Crowder concluded that members of the Zayas cabinet could neither inspire confidence in or induce compliance with the moralization program. He insisted upon a cabinet reorganization and the selection of new ministers, especially for the departments of treasury, public works, and *gobernación*. The new secretaries were to be selected for "the purpose of waging a relentless war on the graft, corruption and immorality especially prevailing in these three departments." The appointments, Crowder further stipulated, would be made "only after conference with me as to their availability to carry out these important reforms."[91] Zayas dutifully reorganized his cabinet, as requested, but failed to submit his nominees first to Crowder's approval. Crowder promptly rejected the new cabinet.[92] Duly chastened, Zayas prepared a second list of candidates, and again Crowder demurred. "I was not impressed by his list," he cabled the State Department. Crowder responded with a list of his own, nominees he believed to be "appropriate to include in the discussion of eligibles for appointments to Cabinet positions."[93]

These were men known personally to Crowder. He had met with all of them and they had all committed themselves in advance to hold the Cuban government to the moralization program. Crowder's method of selection was suggested by his choice of Ricardo Lancis for the portfolio of Gobernación. "I was less confident of him than any other member of the new cabinet," he explained to the State Department. "I did not consent to his appointment until I had had a prolonged interview with him and until I had cross examined him upon his policy. . . . His answers were satisfactory in every respect and I withdrew my objection."[94]

So it was, too, with the other members of the cabinet. Secretary of State Carlos Manuel de Céspedes was born in the United States and had served as Cuban minister in Washington late in the Menocal administration. Secretary of Public Works Demetrio Castillo was educated in the United States and a graduate of West Point. A naturalized U.S. citizen and married to a North American, Castillo operated a school of commerce in New

York and owned interests in the Juraguá iron mines. Manuel Despaigne, secretary of the treasury, had served the military occupation government as assistant secretary of state and government. During World War I he headed the Cuban economic mission in Washington. Arístides Agramonte, a physician, was educated in the United States and served in the U.S. army during the war with Spain.

Thus the "honest cabinet," as it became known, was summoned into existence. And immediately it created an anomalous situation. These were ministers not of Zayas's choosing committed to programs not of Zayas's making. The new cabinet members assumed control over the besieged but still bloated bureaucracies of the executive department, determined to discharge employees and decrease expenditures. But their appointments also threatened traditional power of presidential patronage. And immediately the new ministers encountered opposition from above and below.

The results were predictable. Government became a war of positions. Cabinet ministers refused to countersign presidential appointments. Public officials appointed earlier in the Zayas administration were dismissed summarily. Many of those discharged were friends and relatives of influential legislators and party leaders, thereby weakening the ability of the administration to govern. Public works programs were revoked and contracts rescinded. The cabinet purposefully obstructed presidential programs.

Crowder's intervention in local administration increased, if only to support the policies of his cabinet appointees. In early 1923, the secretary of the treasury complained that the administration of the newly organized Sales Tax Bureau of the Treasury Department continued subject to pernicious presidential interference. Crowder immediately denounced Zayas for the political meddling and technical inefficiency. In a comprehensive study noteworthy for its detail, Crowder documented scores of infractions and violations of the law. Only nine of the forty-three appointed inspectors possessed adequate qualifications, Crowder complained. Ten had failed their examination, twelve were never examined, two were too young, one was too old, eight were on payroll but had never reported to work. Crowder demanded scores of dismissals, starting with the bureau chief, and full reorganization of the division under the direct supervision of the treasury secretary.[95]

The Zayas administration became quickly the means through which the United States governed the island. Crowder presided over the executive and prevailed over the legislature. He met regularly with congressional leaders, lobbying legislators in behalf of reform measures. Just as often, he protested bills incompatible with the moralization program. When the Cuban congress balked at reform legislation, the State Department publicly criticized the "obstructionist action" of the Cuban congress. Alluding purposefully to Cuban need for a new loan, Washington insisted that the reforms were "vitally necessary for stamping out corruption" and that "no progress can be made towards the financial rehabilitation of the Island until this program is carried out."[96]

This was more than preventive intervention. It was preemptive, with sanction in the Platt Amendment as a means necessary to avoid military intervention. "We have always to consider the eternal vigil," Crowder exhorted, "and that must be exercised by America's representative in Cuba to prevent conditions which menace the kind of stable Government we are pledged by Treaty to maintain."[97] "The object of my efforts here," Crowder wrote in early 1923, "is to save the United States from a costly military intervention and the loss of prestige incident to failure of the experiment of Republican government in Cuba, which by Treaty stipulation is placed under the guardianship and protection of the United States."[98] The banks concurred in this view. "The primary thing to accomplish," Morrow wrote Crowder in mid-1922, "is to avoid intervention."[99]

VIII

It was the Platt Amendment that sanctioned U.S. intervention; it was financial distress that exacted Cuban acquiescence. By mid-1922, the Zayas government had conformed to most of the United States' demands. The Cuban congress had adopted a new $55 million budget for 1922–1923. New legislation created additional sources of revenue. The new cabinet held executive departments to the tight leash of moralization. Not all the reforms, to be sure, had been adopted, but certainly sufficient conditions had been met to justify U.S. faith in Cuban intentions. At least this was Zayas's argument. So was not the moment propitious to commence negotiations for the $50 million loan?

The U.S. response came in the form of memorandum 13, entitled "Conditions Precedent to Approval of a Loan." The United States demanded assurances that the Cuban government would provide guarantees for prompt payment of interest and sinking fund charges, including the passage of new laws providing for the loan, assigning permanent revenues to service it, and a continuation of the reform program.[100]

The Zayas government complied with the terms of the memorandum and negotiations commenced. By early autumn the State Department had reviewed Cuban accomplishments and approved the loan.[101] But now it was the turn of the banks to raise conditions. Both Speyer Brothers and J. P. Morgan, the banks bidding on the Cuban loan, insisted that the proposed loan prospectus contain a statement asserting: "Pursuant to the Permanent Treaty between the United States and the Republic of Cuba, the Department of State has been advised of the negotiation of this loan and has given its consent thereto."[102] The use of this phrase, the banks argued, would permit a better rate and inspire confidence among lenders. When J. P. Morgan finally received the loan, Dwight Morrow secured State Department authorization to include in the *New York Times* announcement of the sale of coupon bonds the assurances: "Issued with the acquiescence of the United States Government under the Provisions of the Treaty dated May 22, 1903." At another point, the advertisement read: "Under these provisions, commonly referred to as the 'Platt Amendment,' the Republic of Cuba agrees not to contract any public debt the service of which, including reasonable sinking fund provision, cannot be provided by the ordinary revenues."[103] The Platt Amendment had come to represent the public guarantee of U.S. investment in Cuba.

J. P. Morgan had one more request. "The bankers with whom I have talked," Morrow informed the State Department, "are satisfied that Cuba is fundamentally sound, but that her immediate problems are most intricate." To his point:

> They believe that the service of the loan and the general conduct of Cuban finances depend to a large extent upon the ability of the American representative, backed by the Department of State, to guide the Cuban administration to satisfactory performance. They are satisfied that General Crowder is capable of doing this, but the approach of his retirement from the United States Army creates some doubt in their minds as to the ability of our Government to retain him in Havana. These circumstances, coupled with the report that he is to be succeeded by a minister, esteemed to possess less experience than he, tend to lessen their confidence. These misgivings reflect themselves clearly in their present attitude toward the proposed loan. If some assurance could

be given that General Crowder will be retained in Cuba it would materially improve the position and prospect of the proposed issue.[104]

In January 1923 the loan negotiations between Cuba and J. P. Morgan were completed. A month later, by a special act of Congress, Enoch Crowder was appointed to fill the newly created ambassadorship to Cuba.

9.

For High Reasons
of State

I

Nineteen twenty-three was a good year in Cuba. The Zayas government received the coveted $50 million loan. It was also a good harvest year, and a good sugar harvest in a year of good sugar prices. Government receipts increased, unmistakable evidence of economic recovery and prosperity restored. In fiscal year 1922–1923, $73 million dollars were collected. And conditions improved further the following year, when the government collected an additional $90 million in new revenues. In one year the surplus in the national treasury increased from $3 million to $34 million.[1]

Gone were the chronic deficits of the early 1920s and the spectre of uncertainty under which the Cuban economy had languished. But gone, most of all, was the need for Alfredo Zayas to continue to acquiesce to policy directives from the United States. He seized the opportunity. Within weeks of the completed loan transaction, he reorganized his cabinet and dismissed Agramonte, Castillo, Despaigne, and Lancis, the four ministers most closely associated with the moralization program. Members of the Zayas family—no fewer than fourteen relatives—returned to government payrolls.[2] A flurry of legislative resolutions announced the resumption of government spending, including new public works programs, supplemental budget allocations, the award of new franchises, and a series of salary increments. A new lottery law was enacted, and the president's son was appointed director general of the lottery. In 1923, the president's wife won the second prize of $200,000 in the Christmas lottery. *Colecturías* returned to legislators, cabinet members, and political leaders of all parties. *Botellas* were distributed anew, and apace. The growth industry of government revived, a certain sign of economic recovery. It was necessary, Zayas explained, to reassert control over his government for "high reasons of state."[3]

But more than economic recovery was occurring in Cuba. Under way, too, was a political revival, for in a very real sense Zayas moved to reassert his power and to reclaim possession of the government. For two years the president had endured restricted executive authority with reduced expenditure allocation—a fateful combination that brought government to a standstill, and almost to its downfall. The magnitude of the usurpation of authority by the United States served to deepen the contradictions in a skewed institutional order.

Patronage was more than the perquisite of power—it was the prerequisite of politics. *Botellas* served as the medium of the political exchange, and interrupting of the transaction threatened government with insolvency. *Botellas* were routinely distributed to political supporters, party members, and just about anyone else who had contributed to the president's past success or whose support was necessary for future success. Patronage also offered an important means of consolidating political alliances between the executive and ranking legislators. Congressional allies, in turn, used access to presidential levers of resource allocation to consolidate local alliances. This was true, too, of government contracts, public works programs, and revenue-sharing projects. Programs to benefit local constituencies and aid congressional districts were used—or withheld—to induce congressional conformity to executive policies.

Authority over the distribution of public office and the disbursement of public funds, more perhaps than any other executive prerogative, was central to the credibility of presidential authority. The system fostered political consensus, facilitated the passage of administration programs, and forged political alliances.

By the early 1920s, the world created by the political class had its own intrinsic purpose and internal procedure. State position no longer represented a hedge between employment and indigence, although certainly for the lower echelon of the political class this always remained a source of powerful social control. More important, public office created opportunity for amassing wealth through the manipulation of state resources and public revenues. Graft, bribery, and embezzlement combined to serve as the medium of political exchange.

All public agencies involved in the collection and management of revenues were special objects of political interest, and none more than the Bureau of the National Lottery. Established in the republic in 1909, the lottery was transformed immediately into a source of political pressure and personal enrichment. The lottery was organized into some 2,000 *colecturías*, collectorships that conferred on each owner the privilege of selling sixteen tickets for each of the three monthly drawings. Each ticket was purchased at discounted costs from the lottery administration, and resold to the public at inflated prices.

Of the approximate total of 2,000 *colecturías*, some 800 were reserved by the director general of the lottery, acting in behalf of the president, for direct sale. Through this means, an incumbent administration generated some $250,000 monthly for personal and political use. Another 500 *colecturías* were distributed among senators and representatives. While the number assigned to any one legislator varied, the average allocation was ten *colecturías* to each senator and five to each representative. Thus a senator holding ten collectorships stood to supplement his salary by some $54,000 during good economic times. The balance of the *colecturías* was distributed by the administration as favors and recompense. Recipients included family and friends of the president, cabinet members, ranking officials of government, army and police officers, members of the judiciary, and newspaper editors.[4] Estimates concerning the total sums of revenue raised by the lottery varied, but all agreed the total was staggering. The sum of $11 million was the figure most commonly cited, although it was also among the more conservative estimates.[5]

Control of an agency capable of generating such vast sums of money placed a powerful political weapon in the hands of the president. Certainly, the lottery was not without a useful social purpose, particularly in a distributive political system. The lottery employed thousands of Cubans as vendors. Vendorships were usually reserved for the aged and infirm as well as for retired civil servants and pensioners. But the opportunities for wealth were at the top, and the president used the funds purposefully. Opposition to administration legislation resulted typically in the withdrawal of *colecturías* from uncooperative legislators. So, too, with judicial officials who rendered unpopular decisions. Newspaper editors holding *colecturías* treaded lightly on their editorial pages, lest they risk the suppression of their collectorships.

These were also years of spectacular revelations of graft and corruption in all branches of public administration. A reading of the Havana press during the early 1920s provides compelling evidence that corruption ran deep and wide. Smuggling was rampant in custom houses and among the port police. Allegations of corruption in the post office were routine. The Treasury Department was rocked by several scandals at once, including the disappearance of retirement pensions, misappropriation of tax revenues, and padded payrolls. One incident of misappropriation of funds almost forced a suspension of services by the Department of Communications. Corruption was especially rampant in the Department of Public Works, in which kickbacks and rakeoffs were normal aspects of awarding government contracts. So were bidding irregularities, misappropriation of funds, and cost overruns. Vast expanses of state lands were illegally transferred from the public patrimony to private possession. The vast employment opportunities provided by public works offered virtually unlimited political benefits. In 1924, the Department of Public Works granted Celso Cuéllar, Zayas's son-in-law, 2,000 appointments at $50 a month to distribute in behalf of his senatorial campaign in Matanzas province. Senator Juan Gualberto Gómez from Oriente also received employment positions to distribute in his campaign for reelection.[6]

Periodically, public officials were prosecuted for misconduct and malfeasance. Indictments were often partisan affairs, especially during a turnover of administrations, for criminal prosecution was one method of forcing out of office incumbents otherwise protected by civil service regulations, and thereby creating new employment opportunities for the incoming government. During the administrations of José Miguel Gómez and Mario G. Menocal, a total of some 372 indictments were brought against public officials, dealing with a wide range of offenses, including embezzlement, fraud, homocide, infraction of postal regulations, violations of lottery law, misappropriation of funds, and violation of electoral laws. By 1923, the number of indictments had increased to 483.[7]

But indictments were typically empty gestures, and even when convictions were obtained, sentences were rarely served. Most legislators enjoyed constitutional immunity from criminal prosecution. When congressional immunity failed, there were ample alternative devices through which to elude prosecution and escape punishment. No type of bill was more popular with Cuban officeholders than congressional amnesty measures, for this was a class mindful of the need to defend itself and its interests. Amnesty bills set aside convictions for past criminal wrongdoing and, second, absolved officials of crimes committed while in office, thereby foreclosing future prosecution. Six amnesty bills were passed during the administration of Estrada Palma. The Gómez government enacted twenty-nine measures, while another thirty were passed under Menocal. The Zayas administration passed a total of thirty-three. One of the last amnesty laws enacted under Zayas awarded immunity from prosecution to the former mayor of Havana and the city council for corruption, to the former governors of Matanzas and Oriente for graft, and to Alfredo Zayas, Jr., the son of the president, for fraud while he served as director of the lottery.[8]

Presidential pardons served the same purpose as amnesty bills, and through the first four presidential administrations of the republic, successful prosecution of misconduct by public officials was increasingly rare. Estrada Palma issued a total of some 324 pardons covering a variety of political offenses. Gómez proclaimed 1,500 pardons while Menocal issued 2,900. In the first two years of the Zayas administration, before the harness of moralization was set in place, the president issued a total of 825 pardons.[9]

Thus it was not uncommon for Cuban officeholders to have been, at one time or another, under criminal investigation and indictment. Indeed, fully one-fifth of all candidates for political office in the 1922 elections had criminal antecedents.[10]

These were, moreover, years during which the political class expanded and consolidated its hold over public revenues. Lawmakers devoted an increasing part of their activities to legislation designed to guarantee themselves and their dependents continued state support. These were largely personal bills dealing with special appropriations, retirement laws, and pension provisions. Duing the eight years of the Menocal administration, over 400 donation and pension laws were enacted.[11] In the first half of 1923 alone, the Cuban congress enacted a total of 349 special pension acts, involving a total disbursement of $357,000.[12] In the preceding decade, an elaborate set of pensions bills passed into law, providing for the retirement of public officials and all inheritable by the spouse, children, and parents of the pensioner. Among the most important retirement bills passed included the following: the Retirement Law of the Land and Sea Forces (June 1913), the Retirement Law of Officials and Auxiliaries of the Judiciary (May 1917), the Retirement Law of Employees and Officials of Postal and Telegraphic Departments (March 1918), the Veterans Pension Law (April 1918), the Civil Employees' Retirement Law (June 1919), the Teachers' Retirement Law (August 1919), the Retirement

Law of Havana Police (February 1920), and the Retirement Law of Diplomats and Consuls (July 1921).

The legislative proceedings of one work day, December 16, 1925, in the House of Representatives, set in relief one of the principal activities of Cuban lawmakers: [13]

> *Bills passed by the House formerly passed by the Senate or reported by Mixed Committees and forwarded to the Executive for signature:*
>
> Granting a pension of $2,400 per annum to Mrs. Adolfina Veulens, widow of Senator Carnot, and of the same amount to Argelia Batista, widow of ex-Senator Guillén.
>
> Authorizing payment of the funeral of General Alberto Nodarse and transferring his pension to his widow.
>
> Granting a pension of $6,000 to General Lope Recio Loynaz.
>
> Creating a Municipal Court of the 4th Class at Santa Lucía, Sancti Spíritus.
>
> Granting a pension of $6,000 per annum to the widow of the ex-Chief Justice of the Supreme Court Angel Betancourt.
>
> Granting a pension of $600 per annum to the son of Captain Miguel Campanioni.
>
> Creating the post of a Second Class Inspector for the Normal Schools.
>
> Reorganizing the personnel of the Botanical Gardens of the University.
>
> Amending Article 273 of the Organic Law of the Judiciary and creating additional District Attorneys.
>
> Granting a pension of $600 per annum to Angelina González.
>
> Authorizing the inclusion in the ternaries proposed by the Supreme Court for Clerks of Audiencias and of Courts of First Instance.
>
> Amending Article 1 of the law of April 8, 1919, which granted a pension to Rafael José Maceo.
>
> Granting a pension of $2,400 per annum to Amelia Martí, sister of José Martí.
>
> Granting a pension of $6,000 per annum to ex-Senator Figueroa.
>
> Turning over to the Tourist Commission 30% of the proceeds of the lottery drawing of May 19, 1926.
>
> Granting a pension of $3,600 per annum to Leonor García Velez daughter of General Calixto García.
>
> Appropriation of $2,500 to be given to Domitila García in order that she may terminate publication of a book on Cuban Women Writers and Artists.

Postponing collection of 2% real estate tax until the coming fiscal year.

Adding a paragraph to Article 63 of the Judicial Law providing that time of services of attorneys in Department of Justice shall be considered as time of practice of the law.

Granting pensions of $6,000 per annum to the widows of Generals Rafael Manduley and Castillo Duany.

Setting aside surplus pensions funds on hand in the Treasury for payment of pensions now granted.

Bills passed and sent to the Senate:

Providing that Secretaries of Electoral Boards shall be appointed for an unlimited time and fixing salaries therefore.

Appropriation of $300,000 for payment of pensions due members of the judiciary.

Modifying the consular tariffs and increasing the salaries of officials and members of the diplomatic and consular corps and of the State Department.

Appropriation of $13,200 for fulfillment of the law which created the posts of Delegate and Sub Delegate of Immigration in Europe and establishing a head tax of $2.00 for every person going abroad.

Donation of a parcel of land to the Veterans Council.

Amending Article 148 of the Organic Law of the Judiciary to increase rank of subordinate employees of the Courts.

Amending Article 8 of the Workmens Compensation Act and providing that laborers will be entitled to indemnity from the day in which they are disabled.

Authorizing the payment of the funerals of Colonels Dupotey, Gómez Rubio and Arango.

Reestablishing the Municipal District of Catalina de Güines.

Placing all persons passing the examinations for Registrars of Property on the ranking of said service.

Providing that the Secretary of War may revise, upon petition of parties interested, all trials under the military jurisdiction.

Making a donation of $12,000 and a pension of $250 per month for Colonel Emilio Giró.

Granting a pension of $6,000 to Miguel Coyula.

Creating a Court of First Instance for Jatibonico.

Granting a pension of $100 per month to Enrique Gravier.

Increasing the salaries of the members of the Police Corps of the House of Representatives.

Creating a Municipal Court at Meneses, Yaguajay.

Increasing the assignment for expenses of Municipal Courts of the fourth class.

Providing that public service companies which demand deposits from subscribers pay six per cent interest thereon.

Raising the rank of the Court of First Instance and of Instruction, and of the Registry of Property of Palma Soriano.

Creating a Municipal Court of the 4th Class at Dos Caminos del Cobre (Oriente).

Granting an appropriation of $25,000.00 for the construction of a public slaughter house at Bayamo.

Amending Article 47 of the Provincial Organic Law, and fixing the re-muneration which provincial counsellors may receive.

Granting an appropriation of $3,310.00 for the payment of the obligation contained in the Message No. XVIII of May 16, 1925. (Payment of sala-ries due Mr. Pérez, employee replaced in office by the Civil Service Commission.)

Providing that entry and search referred to in article 550 of the Law of Criminal Procedure be made by the Judge himself.

Transferring to the widow of Dr. Juan Guiteras the pension paid to him.

Granting a subsidy of $30,000.00 for four years to the provincial councils of Pinar del Río, Matanzas and Camagüey.

Transferring to the widow of Manuel Sanguily the pension paid to him. (Returned to the Senate with amendments).

Increasing the category of the Judicial District of Sancti Spíritus.

Granting exemption from customs duties for machinery for *La Prensa* and *Heraldo de Cuba*.

Granting a pension of $100.00 per month to Mrs. Juana Báel Viuda de del Río and $50.00 to each one of her three children.

Granting a donation of $10,000.00 to Dominga Maceo, sister of General Maceo.

Authorizing the purchase of the Moncada Mansion in Santiago de Cuba.

Granting a pension of $3,600.00 per annum to the widow of General Pedro Díaz, and $600.00 per year to each one of the legitimate and natu-ral children of the General.

Authorizing a credit of $100,000.00 for the construction of public school buildings in Cienfuegos.

Creating the Municipal Districts of Chambas and Punto Alegro in Camagüey.

Equalizing the rank of secretaries of Courts of First Instance who are lawyers with more than ten years practice with the Judges thereof.

Creating a Municipal Court of the 4th class at Baguanos (Oriente).

Establishing a single half-day session at the government offices from April to October of each year.

Raising the rank of the Court of First Instance of Jaruco.

Modifying several articles of the Organic Law of the Executive Power relative to the organization of the Auditor General's office.

Creating new fiscal districts.

Providing that owners of city property pay 6% interest to lessees on sums required as security.

Creating the Municipal Courts of the 4th class at San Germán, San Ariba, and Omaja.

Providing for the assimilation of technical posts discharged by civil employees in the Army and Navy.

Exemptions of Customs duties on lighting fixtures for Caibarién.

Granting a parcel of land to the Veterans' Council at Holguin.

Providing that aspirants for entry in the Judiciary shall include all persons passing examination with more than 50 points credited them.

Fixing at $6,000.00 the bond to be furnished by Notaries Public in the Judicial District of Havana.

Providing that surplus funds for personnel in the Department of Communications be placed in the Retirement Fund thereof.

Raising the rank of the Courts of First Instance and Municipal Courts of San Cristobal.

Assigning certain properties belonging to the government in Manzanillo under life estates.

Creating the Municipal District of Jose Miguel Gomez in Camagüey.

Amending paragraph 14 of Article I of the Law which reorganized the Medical School.

Creating Municipal Courts at Cueto, Caimanera, and Felicidad (Oriente).

Authorizing the payment of funeral expenses of the following veterans: Major General Agustín Cebreco, Colonel Rafael Manduley, Colonel

Braulio Peia, Colonel Salvador Díaz, Colonel Fernando Certino, Colonel Rafael Benítez, Colonel Alcibiades de la Peia, and ex-Congressman Francisco Menchero.

Creating a Court of First Instance of the Third Class at Florida (Camagüey).

Granting a life pension of $3,600.00 per annum to the widow of General Aguirre.

Granting a credit of $27,400.00 for the Institute of Horticulture at Oriente.

Granting a pension of $18,000.00 per annum to the daughter of Victoriano Betancourt.

Creating the Municipal District of Majagua.

Authorizing the inclusion of Secretaries of the First Class who are lawyers in the ternaries for the 8th and 9th grades of the judicial scale.

Dividing the Court of First Instance of Sagua la Grande into two sections.

Dividing the Court of Instruction of Bayamo into two sections.

Creating several posts in the House of Representatives.

Increasing the pay of certain posts in the House of Representatives.

Creating posts of Justices and auxiliaries for the Audiencias of Havana and Camagüey.

A pension of $600.00 per annum to Mrs. Ursula Sola.

II

Moralization dealt a body blow to government in Cuba, and all but paralyzed the Zayas administration. The suppression of sinecures was tantamount to a divestiture of executive authority. In depriving Zayas of the power of patronage, the United States undermined his power to govern.

But more than the Zayas administration suffered. All of government faced crisis and the political class confronted calamity. In using the Platt Amendment to combat what it perceived to be misgovernment, the United States threatened to undermine all government in Cuba. "There is no more serious menace to the maintenance of stable government in Cuba," Crowder warned, "'adequate for the protection of life, property, and individual liberty,' in the sense that phrase is used in Article 3 of the Permanent Treaty, nor to the maintenance of a solvent Republic, able to discharge its obligations under Article 2 of that Treaty, than is to be found in the inefficiency and corruption of the legislative branch."[14] The Platt Amendment was also summoned as the basis through which to attack the lottery system:

> Protection of life, property and individual liberty is dependent upon the compliance with their public duty of the officials of all of the three branches of the Government. When considerable portions of the six million dollar fund derived from the illegal *colecturía* system now in force are distributed, not only among members of the Executive and Legislative branches, also among numerous members of the judiciary, . . . the adequate protection of life, property and individual liberty which the United States Government is pledged to maintain cannot be said to exist. . . . When, as at present, the President of Cuba is in absolute control of the distribution through the *colecturía* system of more than six million dollars annually . . . and when this enormous total of more than $7,000.00 per annum can be utilized in its major portion if the President so desires for the control of political parties and political electoral campaigns, the result of general elections in Cuba cannot ever be said to represent the expression of popular will.[15]

The suppression of *botellas* was only one aspect of moralization. The other, the reduction of the budget through cuts in expenditures, also had far-reaching effects. The required reorganization of government departments resulted in reduction of budget allocations and, inevitably, large-scale personnel layoffs. Thousands of public employees were dismissed. Others retained their jobs but at reduced salaries, while the salaries of many others fell hopelessly in arrears. Especially hard hit were the diplomatic corps, postal workers, teachers, and day laborers. But, in fact, all public employees were affected. Retired civil servants and the thousands of army veterans on pensions suffered. And all suffered commensurately fewer opportunities for personal enrichment from public funds. The reorganization of the lottery system, particularly the suppression of the *colecturías,* a time-honored source of supplemental income, weakened all levels of government. The suppression of *botellas,* the reduction of the *colecturías,* and cuts in government expenditures occurred, moreover, at a time of deepening economic dislocation. Sugar prices collapsed, production contracted, unemployment increased. Many banks closed permanently, and the savings of thousands of depositors were hopelessly tied up in liquidation proceedings. Old taxes increased, new ones were instituted. Imported consumer goods and foodstuffs decreased and the price for imports still available increased. And everywhere the cost of living was on the rise.

This was the bleak economic landscape against which the moralization program unfolded. State maintenance of the polity, the traditional and increasingly institutionalized means of containing social conflict and controlling political dissent, was no longer capable of subsidizing the republican consensus.

Most immediately, the president lost control of the government. The imposition of the "honest cabinet," a body designed to function as the instrument of U.S. political control, in more than symbolic terms announced that the president was no longer in charge. Indeed, it effectively denied Zayas control over the executive branches of his administration. The suppression of *botellas* and the vastly curtailed powers of patronage, together with a reduced budget, also meant that Zayas lost influence over the congress, the judiciary, the armed forces, and the press. The combined effects were telling. Zayas lost control of his administration and the administration lost control of government.

By appropriating control over the state apparatus and asserting authority over the principal levers of resource allocation, the State Department exacted Cuban acquiescence to the reorganization of national administration in conformity with U.S. needs. No need of armed intervention in 1920, although certainly it was a spectre summoned often to induce Cuban compliance. The collapse of sugar prices, and the ensuing economic crisis, and the Cuban need for a loan within the context of the Platt Amendment, made the Zayas government enormously vulnerable to pressure from the United States.

III

In the course of two decades, the political class had acquired definitive form around the pursuit of and possession over political office. It continued to expand as both a cause and effect of the expansion of state services and revenues. In 1911, more than 31,000 Cubans were on the payroll of the national government. The distribution included: [16]

Legislature	340
Judiciary	1,432
Office of the Presidency	53

Department of State	205
Tax Bureau	231
Department of Government	12,685
Treasury	2,179
Public Instruction	8,319
Public Works	508
Sanitation	4,383
Agriculture, Commerce, and Industry	324

This total did not include an estimated 4,200 municipal employees across the island. Nor did the figures include the employees of provincial government, day laborers employed in the departments of public work and sanitation, or workers hired by private contractors engaged in government work, for which no reliable statistics exist.[17] As much as two-thirds of total national expenditures in 1910 went for personnel salaries.[18] Another set of figures for fiscal 1914–1915 are equally telling. Of a total population of 931,000 Cubans between the age of 18 and 64, some 31,700 were employees of the state. An additional 7,000 day laborers, 1,000 lottery employees, and 5,000 temporary workers brought the total to almost 45,000 Cubans—more than 20 percent of the working population, without including provincial and municipal employees and public contract workers. Out of a total national budget of $38 million, $21 million went toward the payment of salaries and wages.[19] By 1924, the size of the national government payroll increased to 42,000 employees, including 2,000 in the judiciary, and another 1,000 in the legislature. The executive branch accounted for the vast part of public positions and personnel payrolls—a total of some 39,000 functionaries, from cabinet officers to clerks distributed among ten government ministries and departments.[20] Two years later, the size of the public payroll had increased again, reaching 48,000: 2,000 in the judiciary, 1,200 in the legislature and 45,000 in the executive branch, accounting for a total of some $38.5 million in salaries.[21] The data for the 1920s did not include provincial and municipal government employees, day laborers, private contract workers, and pensioners.

Political power in Cuba provided more than control over patronage and authority over the development of public policy. It offered, in fact, the institutional structures around which the political class acquired its definitive characteristics. And across the island this was reproduced from provincial governors to municipal mayors to *ayuntamiento* presidents. The state served as the source of high salaries, status, privilege and power. Tens of thousands of functionaries served in government departments, as well as on boards, commissions, delegations, and councils. Their principal concern was with the preservation of positions.

The existing class structure of the early republic meant that for two decades, the political class enjoyed virtual monopolization of power, facing neither social challenge from below nor political competition from without. An economically dominant national class did not exist at the time of the establishment of the republic. Thus the state came to represent the interest of two distinct and not necessarily compatible groups: the newly emergent political class and foreign capitalists. Other competitors had all but ceased to exist. The planter class had nearly disappeared by the end of the nineteenth century. What remained of it was absorbed into or eclipsed by a nonresident foreign dominant class, and its interests had become intimately identified with U.S. interests; it was incapable of articulating and defending its needs. The old colonial commercial and industrial bourgeoisie that survived, made up principally of Spaniards, did not develop into a rival political force. They neither organized separate parties nor sponsored candidates within existing parties. From the moment of their redemption in 1898, Spanish property owners functioned under the guarantees provided by U.S. hegemony. At the same time, the working class remained weak and divided. Labor activity during the early years of the republic was confined largely to trade union issues—organizing workers of a single trade, often at the same work site, against local management with specific grievances. In the early republic, attempts by labor to organize politically produced parties with few members and of short duration.[22]

Within the interstices of the skewed social structure, the Cuban political classes exercised considerable freedom of action. Nothing underscored the scope of state autonomy more than the lack of institutional constraints on executive authority. Through the exercise of its power and vast resources, the executive easily prevailed over other elements in the state system, without pressure either to share power internally or accommodate state policy to the needs of other national groups. Its members were not typically recruited from the dominant landed, industrial, and commercial classes, and the separation of officeholders from the propertied classes of the republic and their dependence on the state promoted the development of a relatively autonomous state bureaucracy. Only on the occasion of the organization of the Partido Independiente de Color and the Afro-Cuban rebellion of 1912 was this hegemony challenged, and the thoroughness with which the PIC was dissolved and the uprising suppressed ended the threat to the political class.

But the Plattist state did not enjoy complete autonomy, nor was the political class entirely free from pressure and challenge. It faced a formidable competitor in the United States. The dominant class in Cuba was a sector of the North American bourgeoisie that did not exercise hegemony directly from within and through the Cuban state apparatus, but indirectly through the political structures of the United States. Foreign capitalists established control over strategic sectors of the national economy and asserted their dominant position over public policy in Cuba through the vast power of the U.S. government. In 1898–1902 and in 1906–1909, the United States had forcibly displaced Cubans from control over the state. These antecedents made the threat of U.S. military intervention an effective instrument of hegemony. Manuel Rionda wrote shortly after the evacuation of the United States in 1909, "The last American intervention was not much to the Cuban liking, and they will look twice before they will risk a third intervention."[23] The prospects of displacement threatened the political class with calamity. "The spectre of intervention was of such potence," former President Gerardo Machado later wrote of these years, "that no one ever dared to oppose it. It was believed . . . that the act of rejecting an unjustifiable [United States] supervision could bring to Havana harbor warships and marines from the United States."[24]

The Platt Amendment functioned as the vital fulcrum of the hegemonial system, the final measure by which the United States judged the performance of the political class in the defense of foreign property—a judgment, too, that determined the solvency of sovereignty. But officeholders not only favored foreign capital as a function of political hegemony, but also had parlayed political power into economic privilege. Many were integrated directly into the structures of U.S. capitalism.

The quest for and expansion over public office distinguished the form of the political class. These pursuits also defined the function of politics in Cuba. Political power promised the means through which to acquire property and attain wealth by controlling the enactment and enforcement powers of government. In this sense the political class possessed the means of its own transfiguration and the potential to expand control over property and production.

It was this potential of the political class to constitute itself into a rival bourgeoisie that posed the greatest source of competition to foreign capital. Foreigners, too, coveted the concessions, franchises, licenses, and contracts. In this second sense, the services of officeholders were obtained through collaboration with foreign capital. One form was through direct payoff, principally in the form of bribery and graft. Another was to allow political leaders to serve as officers, directors, and administrators of foreign corporations. Power brokers joined with money makers in strategic alliances. President José Miguel Gómez sat on the board of directors of the Cuba Cane Sugar Corporation. The Liberal party's vice-presidential nominee in 1920, Miguel Arango, managed Cuba Cane properties. Arango served also as president of the Violet Sugar Company. Speaker of the House of Representatives Orestes Ferrara was secretary of the Violet Sugar Company and sat on the boards of Cuba Cane and DeGeorgio Fruit Company.[25] President Mario G. Menocal was a director of the Cuban-American Sugar Company. Representatives Carlos I. Párraga and Pelayo García sat on the Board of Cuban Telephone Company. Representative Antonio San Miguel served as director on the Havana Electric Railway, Light and Power Company. Senator Domingo Méndez Capote was a director of Central Sugar Corporation and legal counsel for Cuban Portland Cement Company. Senator Antonio Sánchez de Bustamante served as director of the Ferrocarriles Unidos de La Habana and Cuba Cane. Antonio Berenguer served as Cuban Counsel to the Cuban Railroad Company. Gerardo Machado was vice-president of the Cuban Electric Company.

These circumstances contributed to the ambivalence of the political class. On one hand, it aspired to the monopolization of public office as a means of self-aggrandizement and expand its control over resources. On the other, it was perforce obliged to share the prerogatives of public administration and policy formulation with foreign capital as a condition of its local hegemony.

These relationships were not without tension. The source of virtually every diplomatic dispute in the early republic turned on conflict over the function of the state: the political class seeking to use it as a means of capital accumulation and the foreign bourgeoisie, through the U.S. government, seeking to employ it as a means of capital penetration. On occasion, the objectives were complementary. But just as often, they were contradictory. It was during these instances that the Platt Amendment, with its expanding sanction for intervention based on the threat to suspend sovereignty and displace power holders, served its most vital role.

IV

By the 1920s, contradictions of this anomaly were rapidly over-taking the Plattist state. As the scope of U.S. intervention widened, as its authority penetrated deeper into Cuban internal affairs, the very exercise of hegemony contributed to the conditions weakening the internal position of the political class. The United States could not preempt Cuban political leadership on the scale it had between 1921 and 1923—that is, proceed to shut down the very sources of capital accumulation indispens-able to the political class—without inflicting irreparable harm to the in-ternal hegemony of the officeholders. What was not perhaps entirely evi-dent in the United States during the early 1920s was that this was the class upon which the well-being of foreign capital rested, and in weaken-ing the ability of the political class to exercise local hegemony, the United States also weakened its capacity to defend foreign property. Any chal-lenge to the rule of the political class represented no less a challenge to the dominant class, in this case North American capitalists.

These were years, too, of renewed economic growth and expansion in Cuba—though uneven, to be sure. The prosperity of the war years and recovery after the war stimulated new economic development and re-leased new social forces out of which emerged a more complicated social order.[26] A new Cuban entrepreneurial bourgeoisie took form during these years. The precipitous decline of trade with Europe during the war cre-ated conditions favorable to the rapid development of an import substitu-tion industry for consumer goods. Local manufacture and light industry expanded during the war years, providing new opportunities for local capital. Imports from the United States dropped from $404 million in 1920 to $120 million two years later.[27] By the mid-1920s, Cuban capital dominated some 1,000 factories and businesses across the island. Na-tional ownership prevailed in such enterprises as confectionery shops, ice plants, shoe manufacturing, soap, furniture construction, paper, per-fume, match factories, beer breweries, glass and bottling plants, distill-eries, simple pharmaceuticals and drugs, cigarette factories, tanneries, bottled soda and water and a variety of food processing plants. Land speculation and a building boom in Havana, moreover, provided a boost to Cuban construction-related enterprise. Local capital expanded into the building-material plants, including cement, tiles, brick, metal works, rig-gings, and limestone blocks.[28]

By the time of the 1919 census, Cuban males over the age of fifteen had registered important gains in the economy, overtaking foreigners in all major occupational categories: [29]

Male Workers	Agriculture Mining and Fishing	Commerce and Transportation	Industry and Manufacturing	Professional Services	Personal Services
White Cubans	239,215	53,840	63,425	18,175	31,559
Cubans of color	126,804	18,648	58,752	2,549	21,681
White foreigners	67,178	59,058	35,694	3,818	18,304

For the first time, Cubans surpassed foreigners in industry and manufacture, while enhancing considerably their majority in commerce and professional services.[30]

The new entrepreneurial class enjoyed diverse origins. In part it drew membership from the continued decomposition of the old planter class, a process accelerated by World War I.[31] Many small investors had obtained short-term credits, funds that proved vital to the organization of new commercial and industrial enterprises. Capital was readily available during the boom years, and together with the opportunities of local market conditions provided powerful incentive for the expansion of Cuban industry and manufacturing. Representatives of the political class, both in and out of office, also came to constitute another sector of this entrepreneurial bourgeoisie, using public power to acquire private wealth in a variety of economic ventures: sugar, mining interests, urban real estate, manufacturing, industry, and commerce. These developments produced a genuine local bourgeoisie with strong ties to the state. These men prospered from controls, revenue policies, public credit facilities, and government franchises and grants.[32] One last development that added to the apparent expansion of national growth over property and production, but difficult to assess, was the rise of Cuban ownership through second-generation immigrants. These were the children of foreigners, moving into family businesses, who had reached maturity in the republic and identified themselves as wholly Cuban.

Admittedly tentative, the emergence of this Cuban entrepreneurial bourgeoisie gave shape to a new political constituency, representing capital largely local, advocating goals entirely national, but most of all demanding state support of interests wholly Cuban. These were private men with an agenda for the public men. No longer did pressure on officeholders come only from above and without. It now came from below and within, mounting impatience with government inattention and official indifference to national economic interests. This was also a class increasingly susceptible to the appeal of economic nationalism and for which U.S. intervention on behalf of foreign capital was becoming increasingly noxious.

The 1920–1921 crisis served to galvanize the nascent entrepreneurial bourgeoisie into political action. Cuban property owners became alive to the necessity for greater involvement in public affairs in defense of local economic interests. This new advocacy reflected growing concern with uncertainty and a desire to extend control over local resources and national markets. The postwar crisis also exposed the magnitude of state autonomy, for, in fact, there existed neither institutional forms nor political forums through which the new entrepreneurs could adequately influence the course of government policies. Throughout the crisis, that is, during the years of Crowder's sway, officeholders remained primarily responsive to foreign interests as the means of defending incumbency.

VI

By the early 1920s, Cuban property owners, growing in strength, found themselves reduced to onlookers of political events over which they had little control. Increasingly frustrated, they lacked the political means with which to obtain consistent and favorable state policy. Certainly bribery and corruption offered one obvious possibility of influence, but even through graft local entrepreneurs could not hope to compete successfully with foreign capital. Nor could Cuban local property interests expect to secure favor through campaign donations. This was irrelevant in Cuban politics. Widescale corruption and coercion against the electorate, a growing trend of political violence and assassination, and wholesale electoral fraud underscored the degree to which the political class acted independently to perpetuate itself and depended on the manipulation of state agencies rather than the subsidy of local property interests.[33] In 1922 three successful mayoral candidates, Antonio Garriga of Sagua de Tánamo, Manuel Sala of Guantánamo, and Asencio Villalón of Santiago, were murdered. The routine rigging of elections meant, too, that even the value of the ballot was in question, and certainly of limited utility as a means of orderly political change. The deepening involvement of the United States in Cuban internal affairs, moreover, in large part a response to charges of political misconduct, meant also that state policy would perforce continue to favor foreign capital interests. Only government indifference to the defense of national economic interests irked the entrepreneurial bourgeoisie more than U.S. intervention, and the relationship between the two was manifest.

The spectacle of republican politics was played before an incredulous national audience. These were years of political excesses, revelations of spectacular graft, and seemingly endless accounts of official corruption. The political mischief of the officeholders plunged the island into revolution in 1917 and threatened another one in 1920. By the early 1920s, the new entrepreneurial bourgeoisie had reached the limit of its patience. They demanded a greater voice in public affairs, and prepared to increase their participation in the political process. They were stronger numerically and economically, and they intended to use their newfound strength to defend their interests.

VII

The Crowder mission had come to symbolize effectively the suspension of sovereignty. The political class had lost control of government at the precise moment that demand for state policy in behalf of national economic interests was greatest. In the early 1920s, key sectors of the local bourgeoisie took the first step to challenge the political class for control of the state. The emergence of associational interest groups created new pressure for policies in behalf of national needs, including state intervention in the defense of local enterprises, currency stability, fiscal reform, administrative integrity, and political order. In January 1920, Havana merchants organized into the Asociación de Comerciantes de La Habana to press for improved trade conditions. Their principal concerns involved the paralyzing port congestion and negotiating a more favorable trade relationship with the United States. In 1922, a prestigious Committee of One Hundred was established. Made up of young businessmen led by Porfirio Franca, the committee demanded an end to political misconduct and the adoption of a merit system in government. In late 1922, industrialists organized the Asociación Nacional de Industriales de Cuba, joining all national industry in one organization. Under the direction of Ramón F. Crusellas, a leading soap manufacturer, the Asociación Nacional de Industriales urged the adoption of strong protectionist policies to defend national industry. At about the same time, merchants across the island organized into Federación Nacional de Detallistas and added their voice to the growing clamor for favorable government policies, including the establishment of a merchants' bank and the abolition of the monopoly enjoyed by company stores on the large sugar estates. In 1923, Cuban producers and property owners established the Federación Nacional de Corporaciones Económicas de Cuba. Representatives from the new associations, moreover, together with members of older organizations, including the Sociedad Económica de Amigos del País and Cámara de Comercio, Industria y Navegación de la Isla de Cuba, joined to promote cooperation among agricultural, commercial, and industrial sectors of the island. These developments were occurring also at the provincial and municipal level. Perhaps the most important was the organization in September 1923 of the Federación Provincial de Entidades Económicas de Oriente, bringing together in one organization local chambers of commerce, planters, merchants, and industrialists to defend Oriente's economic interests.

The new associations were primarily pressure groups committed to the defense of local economic interests. More than this, however, they provided the basis of a national constituency for a new movement that challenged the power of the political class. The first tentative steps toward organization occurred in January 1922 with the establishment of the Asociación de Buen Gobierno in Havana. Made up of young professionals and businessmen, the organization launched a campaign against corruption and graft in public office.[34] Later that year, the association made its debut in electoral politics, joining with a dissident faction of the Conservative party to sponsor a candidate for Havana's 1922 mayoral election. The new Republican party candidate, José Eliseo Cartaya, a founder of the Asociación Nacional de Industriales de Cuba, finished inauspiciously a distant third in a field of five.[35]

Defeated but undaunted, reformist elements continued to pursue political change through alternative channels. Within a year, the reformist urge surfaced again in the newly organized Junta Cubana de Renovación Nacional. Under the direction of University of Havana professor Fernando Ortiz, the Junta issued a lengthy manifesto denouncing the accumulated ills of two decades of republican misgovernment. In economic matters the Junta called for protection of Cuban industry, commerce, and agriculture, and the renegotiation of reciprocal trade relations with the United States as a means to promote balanced national economic development. It drew up a social agenda that demanded reform in industry, agriculture, education, and the penal system, advocated the expansion of health services, and defended women's rights. On political matters the Junta called for an end to graft and corruption, judicial reorganization, and electoral reform. The Junta also gave expression to early nationalist stirrings by protesting "with alarm" the growing domination of Cuba by the United States, a direct allusion to the Crowder mission: "The Cuban people want to be free as much from the foreigners who abuse the flag as from the citizens who violate it and will end up burying it."[36]

The summons to national renovation united representatives from virtually all sectors of commerce, industry, finance, and professions: in commerce the Asociación de Comerciantes, the Cámara de Comercio, Industria y Navegación, the Federación Nacional de Corporaciones Económicas de Cuba, the Asociación de Viajantes del Comercio, the Sociedad Económica de Amigos del País, the Asociación Nacional de Detallistas, and the Asociación de Importadores; in industry the Asociación Nacional de Industriales de Cuba, and the Unión de Fabricantes de Tabacos y Cigarros; in finance the Clearing House of Havana and the Bolsa Privada de La Habana. Among professional associations represented were physicians, pharmacists, architects, lawyers, notaries, primary and normal school teachers, university professors, journalists, historians, editors, and painters. Represented also were feminist organizations, Afro-Cuban associations, and Catholic groups. Among the individual signatories who endorsed the manifesto were Ramón Grau San Martín, Raúl de Cárdenas, and Jorge Mañach.

VIII

The promise of reform swept over and seized hold of the republic. Reform was in the air, offering the hope of a total regeneration of the republic. Its appeal was irresistible, and the possibilities were unlimited. It soon reached the university campus. In January 1923 students at the University of Havana seized control of several buildings and demanded university reforms, including the dismissal of incompetent faculty, free higher education, and autonomy for the university. The newly organized Federación de Estudiantes de la Universidad de La Habana (FEU) convoked the first National Student Congress, bringing to Havana some 138 delegates representing forty-nine educational institutions across the island. Among the resolutions passed were demands for student participation in school governance, establishment of high professional standards for faculty, and increased government support of education. But not all resolutions were confined to matters of education. The FEU also demanded the abrogation of the Platt Amendment, decried U.S. intervention in Cuban internal affairs, and denounced corruption in government.[37]

The dissent on the university campus shared common antecedents with disquiet in intellectual circles. During the early 1920s, and initially at the margins of the national debate, intellectuals explored the possibilities of revival in national literature and art. At the Café Martí near Central Park in Havana, writers, poets, and artists under the leadership of Rubén Martínez Villena engaged in passionate discussions on the essential form and function of national literature. The debate on form would persist unresolved for another decade. But on the matter of function, the consensus was striking, and immediate. More than advocates of cultural revival, writers assumed for themselves the role of agents of national rejuvenation. In extolling things Cuban, they added content to the emerging nationalist revival; by denouncing corruption in Cuba, they added conscience to national reform.

By 1923 intellectuals had joined the reform swell. In March, a score of writers led by Martínez Villena walked out of a literary function to protest the participation of a Zayas cabinet minister. The "Protest of the Thirteen," as the incident became known, soon generalized to a blanket indictment against the government. In a subsequent manifesto, the writers denounced corruption in the Zayas administration and solicited the support of all Cubans who "feel indignant against those who mistreat the Republic . . . and who believe that the time has arrived to react vigorously and punish in some manner the delinquent rulers."[38] A month later, Martínez Villena organized the Falange de Acción Cubana, a political action group intended to organize opposition to the government.[39]

Later in 1923 the Grupo Minorista united the republican generation of intellectuals around the goal of cultural rejuvenation and national redemption. Calling for a reexamination of national values, the Grupo Minorista identified itself with educational reform and university autonomy. Minorismo also denounced U.S. imperialism, called for labor and agrarian reform, and demanded an end to political corruption and electoral fraud.[40]

IX

These were the powerful currents swirling about the republic in the early 1920s, and when flowing in the same direction they formed a tide that was irresistible. The organization of the new entrepreneurial bourgeoisie into economic interest groups and the articulation of intellectual dissent, together with their mobilization for political action, announced the emergence of new forces in the republic. This was an ill-conceived coalition, to be sure—more an expression of the mood of the moment than a meeting of the minds. For the time being, however, it provided a constituency for reform dedicated to the defense of national interests and the redemption of national ideals. As it gathered momentum, power holders faced mounting internal pressure to share political power and accommodate policy to the needs of a new constituency.

During the early 1920s, the working class also organized and expanded, gained strength, and emerged as another formidable force for change. Led by cigar workers, stevedores, carpenters, drivers, mechanics, and railroad workers, the ranks of organized labor increased in membership and militancy.

Economic conditions in Cuba after World War I had contributed much to the rising militancy among Cuban workers. For many workers, the crisis was well advanced at the time of postwar depression. The European war had caused cancellation of Cuban tobacco products, resulting immediately in the closing of cigar factories and unemployment for the thousands of workers engaged in the planting and harvesting of tobacco and the manufacture of cigars. But even for workers who enjoyed continued employment through the war years, the economic boom was not an unmixed blessing. The cost of living increased. The price of basic commodities soared, and workers' wages failed to keep pace with the increases. One observer commented in 1919:

> A visitor to Cuba is immediately impressed with the high cost of living which in Havana exceeds even that prevailing in the city of New York, and investigation readily reveals that this increase is not only confined to the luxuries of the rich but affects also the necessities of the poor. Staples of food of the laboring classes, such as beans, rice, cod-fish, etc., and that of most necessary articles of clothing, such as shoes and cotton goods, have all risen in price from 200 to 400 percent since the outbreak of the world war. . . . The increase in the cost of necessities is greater than the increase in the wages of the laboring classes, so that it is very difficult for the poor to balance the weekly budget. The result is discontent, economic unrest, and a productive ground for the seeds of political agitation.[41]

The postwar depression made a difficult situation impossible. Unemployment struck suddenly and spread swiftly. Shops closed, factories ceased production, and construction stopped. The bank moratorium meant that employers could not draw on more than 10 percent of cash reserves, a sum wholly inadequate for many to meet standing payroll requirements. The result was mass layoffs. In the building trades alone, some 5,000 workers were immediately without jobs. By mid-October 1920, some 10,000 workers were without employment, and observers predicted the number would increase to 50,000.[42] Many businesses remained open only by reducing personnel and lowering salaries and wages. "The easy-going mode of living at many of these workers," the U.S. minister reported in 1920, "finds them without money; the stores will not give them credit; the result is that they will be hungry, and hunger respects no law or government."[43]

But even as changing conditions outside the working class accelerated workers' militancy, changes inside the proletariat facilitated labor organizing. Over the preceding two decades, the size of the working class increased in all strategic sectors of the economy. More important, the 1919 census suggests considerable advances registered by Cuban workers over foreigners. The 1919 census revealed that for the first time Cubans represented a majority among railroad workers and maritime employees. The total number of mechanics, machinists, bricklayers, masons, and printers almost doubled, and in this expansion Cubans expanded their numbers significantly.[44] The net effect was increased stability for workers, continuity at the workplace, and homogeneity in the composition of the working class. By the early 1920s, the effects of these developments were beginning to tell.

Not unlike bourgeois interest groups, workers organized initially in the pursuit of improved working conditions and living standards. The principal demands called for an eight-hour day, wage increases, better working conditions, and miscellaneous social benefits. The economic crisis of 1920–1921 served to accelerate labor organizing. Caught between increasing unemployment and rising living costs, workers responded with renewed militancy. A strike in 1920 in Havana harbor paralyzed maritime traffic. A typographers' strike the same year brought Havana presses to a halt. Strikes in sugar *centrales* closed mills in Las Villas, Camagüey, and Oriente. A railroad stoppage in August 1920 interrupted rail transportation across the island. Resistance to labor demands, and repression of labor demonstrations, added to workers' grievances as they called for the right to organize and strike, freedom for imprisoned workers, and an end to deportation of foreign labor leaders. Increasingly strikes, boycotts, and, most of all, the general strike were transforming labor into a formidable political force.[45]

Against this backdrop, the second National Labor Congress convened in Havana in 1920. Representing an estimated 90,000 workers in 102 unions, labor leaders passed a variety of resolutions calling for government assistance programs, public housing, an eight-hour work day, price controls on basic commodity staples, equal pay for men and women, the abolition of piecework, and denunciation of U.S. imperialism.[46]

Through the early 1920s workers continued to organize and unions increased in size and strength. In late 1920, some eighteen unions in Havana consolidated into the anarchosyndicalist Federación Obrera de La Habana (FOH). As the strike movement gathered momentum, workers in similar trades and industries across the island began to organize in national unions. In February 1924, railroad workers organized into the Hermandad Ferroviaria de Cuba, the first organization to bring together in one national union all workers of a single industry. A year later, port workers followed its lead and organized nationally into the Federación Nacional Marítima de los Puertos de Cuba.

At the third National Labor Congress in 1925, resolutions called for the nationalization of labor, affirmed the right to strike and use of boycott and sabotage in defense of workers' interests, and adopted an anti-imperialist plank. By far the most important accomplishment of the third congress, however, was the consolidation of Cuban trade unions into a single national organization. Delegations from eighty-two trade unions attending the congress, with the endorsement of another forty-six others not present, representing an estimated 200,000 workers, consolidated into one national labor federation, the Confederación Nacional Obrera de Cuba (CNOC).[47]

Labor also organized politically. As early as 1920, the newly formed Partido Socialista Radical (PSR) called for the socialization of property, equality for women, the construction of public housing, improvement of work conditions for women and children, amnesty for workers arrested in strike activity, and government regulation of strategic national industries, including sugar, mining, railroads, and shipping.[48] In March 1923, José Peña Vilabod, founder and secretary general of the FOH, and Alejandro Barreiro, treasurer of the FOH, joined with Carlos Baliño and Julio Antonio Mella to establish the Agrupación Comunista de La Habana. In the following two years, new communist *agrupaciones* were established in San Antonio de los Baños, Guanabacoa, Manzanillo, and Media Luna. In August 1925, within weeks of the founding of CNOC, the *agrupaciones* met in Havana and consolidated into the Partido Comunista de Cuba (PCC). The founding delegates included Pena Vilabod and Alejandro

Barreiro of the FOH, Venancio Rodríguez and Alfredo López of the cigar workers' union, Emilio Rodríguez, a delegate of the third workers' congress, Baliño, and Mella. That same year, the PCC formally applied for membership in the Comintern.[49] The PCC developed strategies of organizing political support among unions, rejected electoral politics, established educational programs for workers, and organized a youth movement. During the late 1920s, the PCC expanded its influence into the CNOC and established leadership over many constituent unions.[50]

X

Simultaneously, the political class confronted a threat from a newly organized bourgeoisie and a newly mobilized proletariat. Suddenly the premises upon which the officeholders had traditionally presided over the polity fell into desuetude. Their power and position were no longer unassailable. New social groups aspired to hegemony, and they could not be ignored. The immediate effect of these developments was to situate the political class between outside restraints imposed by the United States and internal pressures from the bourgeoisie and the working class. These forces were themselves at odds. The new power contenders challenged as much the hegemony of the United States as the continued rule of the Cuban political class. They threatened the authority of the class through which the United States had exercised power and upon which it depended for the defense of foreign interests.

But the challenge to the political class was within itself at cross-purposes. The contradictions were insuperable, for the bourgeoisie was as much concerned about the expanding power of the working class as it was committed to reducing the power of the political class. Bourgeois reformists could not view the rising power and expanding militancy of labor with equanimity. Even as it pressed for reform and denounced U.S. intervention, the new entrepreneurial bourgeoisie was mindful that to a lesser or greater extent, certainly in the short run, it depended upon the officeholders, and behind them, the United States, to contain the growing power of the mobilized working class. Certainly bourgeois reformers advocated labor reforms, but as a strategic means to mobilize the urban working class into a political constituency for reform politics. As the opportunity for leadership over the working class passed from the advocates of reform to the agents of revolution, labor was transformed from a potential ally into a probable adversary. And in a very short time, bourgeois reformers found themselves isolated and vulnerable, and with a decision to make.

XI

The national mood was in flux in the early 1920s—uncertain and unsettled. The murmurs of discontent were everywhere audible, the auguries of change were everywhere visible. Zayas could not have chosen a more inauspicious moment to reorganize his cabinet. The unabashed purposefulness with which the president and his family amassed personal fortunes from public funds, the manifest cynicism with which legislators passed special-interest bills, and the magnitude of corruption that returned to government generally, offended the sensibilities of even those long inured to such excesses. Zayas gave corruption a bad name. This was too much, too fast, too public—all palpable evidence that the political class remained incorrigibly corrupt.

The tenor of the times was different in 1923, and no longer was public incredulity an adequate response to the excesses of power holders. This most recent display of official misconduct consolidated the advocates of national renovation into a coherent constituency and summoned proponents of reforms to participate in politics. Reform had become a political issue, but it was not at all certain that traditional politics could accommodate reform. Reformist groups could not rely on the traditional political parties and electoral mechanisms to remove incumbents from power. Presidential elections scheduled for 1924 offered no prospect of reform, for Zayas had already expressed interest in a second term. Reformists needed an alternative political vehicle. The opportunity soon presented itself.

In August 1923, the prestigious and powerful Veterans' Association met in Havana to protest rumored pension cuts. The protest expanded and quickly became a general indictment of all aspects of public life. The veterans called for the regeneration of Cuba and adopted a twelve-point resolution. The most important items included the repeal of the lottery law, honest collection of taxes, the abolition of *botellas,* honest elections, competitive public bidding for government contracts, an independent judiciary, legal accountability in the disbursement of public funds, limitations on congressional immunity from criminal prosecution, laws favoring Cuban workers over foreign labor, abolition of presidential reelection, political rights for women, and the defense of national industry and commerce. The veterans established the National Association of Veterans and Patriots to coordinate political action and press for the enactment of their demands.[51]

The Veterans and Patriots movement gave immediate political expression to national stirrings of reform. It received the endorsement of scores of organizations, including the Federación Nacional de Corporaciones Económicas, the Asociación de Industriales, the Asociación de Buen Gobierno, the FEU, the Falange de Acción Cubana, the Federación de Asociaciones Femeninas, as well as local veterans' groups, professional organizations, and a variety of civic clubs. General Carlos García Velez, a ranking veteran leader, assumed the presidency. The six active vice-presidents included Alejo Carreño, president of the Asociación de Hacendados y Colonos, Carlos Alzugaray, head of the Asociación de Comerciantes de La Habana, Lorenzo Nieto, historian Manual Sanguily, and philosopher Enrique José Varona. The majority of the forty honorary presidents consisted of former officers of the Liberation Army. Also included among the honorary presidents were Enrique Hernández Cartaya, a member of the "honest cabinet," Porfirio Franca, Julio Antonio Mella, Antonio G. Mendoza, Vicente Soler, Fernando González, Manuel Enrique, and Carlos Zaldo. Manuel Despaigne, the secretary of the treasury in the "honest cabinet," assumed the treasury position. Oscar Soto and Gustavo Gutiérrez of the Asociación de Buen Gobierno served as secretaries and Ruben Martínez Villena directed propaganda. Signatories to subsequent pronouncements in 1923 included representation from the full spectrum of the reform stirrings of the early 1920s: Manuel Despaigne, Hortensia Lamar, Federico Laredo Bru, Alejo Carreño, Carlos Alzugaray, Aníbal Escalante, Rubén Martínez Villena, and Juan Marinello.[52]

The establishment of a formal organization with duly elected officers and a publicly ratified program underscored the central feature of the Veterans and Patriots Association. It was more than a passing protest. This was a political movement in the makng, one that immediately captured the popular imagination. By September there was growing sentiment to transform the Veterans and Patriots Association formally into a political party.[53] Behind its official slogan—"For the Regeneration of Cuba"—the Veterans and Patriots movement gained momentum and gathered supporters. Provincial delegations were organized, municipal committees established, and neighborhood councils created. Public endorsements and financial donations came from across the island.

By early autumn the Zayas government had arrived at some understanding of the threat posed by the Veterans and Patriots movement. The president did not hesitate. Leaders were harassed and meetings were disrupted. Printing shops publishing propaganda for the association were closed. In October 1923, Zayas issued a presidential order prohibiting the Veterans and Patriots Association from holding public meetings. When the association defied the executive decree, government authorities moved quickly to arrest the leadership. Some twenty officials were immediately imprisoned and others fled into hiding. In late autumn, at one of the last public meetings, the Veterans and Patriots Association's governing council proclaimed itself frankly revolutionary and vowed to take whatever steps necessary for the regeneration of Cuba.

The Veterans and Patriots movement now plotted the overthrow of the Zayas government, and the prospects were good. As early as 1922, the U.S. legation in Havana warned the State Department that reformist forces "carry sufficient weight with the people to endanger the existence of the present Government, in the event that they should take radical steps to accomplish the elimination of corruption."[54] Disaffection ran deep, too, within the government. Two years of budget restrictions, expenditure reductions, and personnel retirements had taken their toll on the morale of public employees and not a few were receptive to political change. Wrote the second secretary of the U.S. legation:

> There are in Cuba large numbers of Government employees dissatisfied with the Government, among such being members of the Army, Police, Postal Service, etc. The principal reason for their dissatisfaction is the failure of the Government to pay their salaries. Similarly affected are the numbers of private citizens who have been creditors of the Government for a number of months. Because of this condition, there is an excellent field in which to start an organized action against the Government.[55]

Discontent deepened after Zayas reorganized the "honest cabinet." While much of government continued under a regimen of austerity, the executive unabashedly pursued stunning schemes of graft and corruption.

Nowhere was this discontent as deep or dissent as ominous as in the armed forces. In July 1923, U.S. Military Attache Major W. H. Shutan reported conversations wth senior Cuban officers in which they expressed "dissatisfaction with the policies of the Chief Executive and disgust over the official acts of both houses of the Cuban Congress."[56] A reduction of government expenditures affected the military directly. The officers' retirement pension was reduced by two-thirds. Salaries had fallen into several months' arrears. Rumors abounded of impending pay cuts and imminent troop reductons. "In the event that the present opposition movement should result in open rebellion against the Zayas Government," U.S. military intelligence concluded two months later, "there is every assurance that the Cuban Army would either lend its active support to the opposition or else remain neutral."[57] In late October, Shutan reported learning that key officers of regimental commands in Oriente, Camagüey, and Matanzas had committed themselves to lead their garrisons against the government. Plans were in progress to recruit commanders of Camp Columbia in Havana, and if successful all but guaranteed the overthrow of the government.[58]

Congressional leaders also moved quickly to distance themselves from the beleaguered president. In good part, this was a reaction against two years of unpopular austerity measures. But legislators also feared the success of the Veterans and Patriots movement. Concern increased further, that the protest would provoke U.S. military intervention. In early September, Ramón Zaydín, the majority leader of the House of Representatives, met with U.S. diplomatic officials in Havana to volunteer congressional action against the president. As many as seventy-four members of both houses of congress, Zaydín disclosed, had met secretly and agreed that "if the president were an obstacle to retaining friendly relations with the United States, they would endeavor to find grounds to impeach him."[59]

XII

The United States reacted to events in 1923 with ambivalence. Reports early in the year that Zayas contemplated the dismissal of the "honest cabinet" had been received in Washington with disbelief and discouragement. Undersecretary of State William Phillips summoned the Cuban chargé in Washington on the eve of the rumored cabinet reorganization to protest "a step which was contrary to the solemn assurances" given by Zayas. Phillips wrote: "I said that I could hardly believe that the President of Cuba would go back on his understanding with this Government, and with the bankers, and that if he did do, it will be a very serious and indeed an alarming situation."[60] Secretary of State Charles Evans Hughes warned Zayas directly: "This Government would reserve complete liberty to take such further steps as might be necessary should it learn that a change in cabinet was definitely determined upon."[61] In

Havana, Crowder warned Zayas of the relationship of the United States to Cuba—"that of a special friend and adviser by reason of its relations to the establishment of the Cuban Republic, and further by reason of the Permanent Treaty between the two countries, likewise a part of the Cuban Constitution, and usually designated as the Platt Amendment." Crowder stressed the importance of the "honest cabinet" to the implementation of the moralization program—a program, he reminded Zayas, to which the president had committed himself. With that commitment in mind, Crowder suggested disingenuously to Zayas in early April, "I must assume . . . that such [cabinet] changes as you now have in mind are individual changes for the better enforcement of the moralization program."[62]

But Zayas was undeterred. Appealing to the necessity of defending national sovereignty and redeeming national honor, the president proceeded to purge his cabinet.[63] The Cuban foreign ministry responded tersely, almost indifferently: "The President of the Republic could not conceive how the possible exercise of his constitutional powers in regard to any of his own Secretaries could cause unpleasantness and alarm to the Government of the United States."[64] To Crowder, Zayas explained simply that his previous commitment did not obligate him "to discuss in advance the fitness of proposed new cabinet members, but only to explain away, after their appointment, any doubts [the United States] Government might have."[65] The dismissal of the "honest cabinet" delivered the final blow to U.S. efforts. With this, moralization came to an end, and Zayas recovered control over government.

But it was not to be an uncontested control. The process of reasserting Cuban authority over national administration, accompanied as it was in 1923 by the revival in unrestrained form of *colecturías, botellas,* and corruption, set in motion the forces that threatened the survival of the Zayas administration. Zayas freed his government from foreign influence only to face a mounting internal challenge gaining popularity through the Veterans and Patriots movement. Reform was now an issue that would not go away. And nothing represented more the object of reformist abhorrence than the Zayas regime in 1923. The position of the government became immediately tenuous. Powerful national economic interests had arrayed against the president, the army moved closer to mutiny, congress contemplated impeachment. Zayas found himself isolated, his support shrinking, and his backers defecting.

Any likelihood that Zayas would survive the crisis now depended on an expression of support from the United States. As early as August 1923 Celso Cuéllar, Zayas's son-in-law, visited Washington to urge the State Department to condemn the Veterans and Patriots movement and express public support for constituted government in Cuba.[66] In Havana, Gerardo Machado urged the U.S. government to intercede in behalf of the beleaguered administration. "Unless the United States Government immediately disavows the veterans movement," Machado warned, "an early revolution is inevitable."[67]

In the Cuban context, U.S. support had its own logic, and expression of this support was essential if only to prevent the Zayas government from collapsing from within. Legislators and army officers would be less inclined to defect if it were publicly known that the constituted authorities retained U.S. backing. But Washington remained silent purposefully. And official silences possessed as much meaning as public utterances. As early as September 1923, Manuel Despaigne visited the embassy to urge the United States to do nothing to prejudice the Veterans and Patriots movement.[68] And silence implied consent. As long as Washington remained uninvolved, the conspiracy would gain momentum—the circle of conspiracy widened and the base of government support narrowed.[69]

Policymakers viewed political developments in 1923 with some ambivalence. Certainly Zayas had fallen into disfavor in Washington. No one expected moralizaion to revive under his government. "It is evident," Assistant Secretary of State Francis White lamented in July 1923, "that the moralization program which progressed splendidly from June 1922 to February 1923 has, since April of this year, gradually been put aside, and that the work accomplished is little by little being undone."[70] Crowder in Havana agreed: "No one here believes that the Moralization Program will be carred out by President Zayas."[71]

In fact, however, the banner of moralization had been raised anew—but it had been appropriated by a reformist, nationalist, and anti-imperialist constituency. Crowder understood this. "Attention might well be invited," he suggested to Secretary of State Hughes, "to [the Veterans and Patriots] twelve point program and to the fact that they are advocating many of the reforms that have been suggested by the United States in the diplomatic correspondence of the past two years."[72] But it was not at all certain that the United States desired moralization under these circumstances. The choice before the United States was clear: either a weak and corrupt government committed to the defense of foreign interests or the promise of a strong government committed to the defense of national interests and predisposed to honesty. In a very real sense, the Veterans and Patriots protest threatened more than the authority of the Zayas government. At stake were the premises and practices of hegemony, for the political class represented the front-line defense of vital U.S. interests. This was a nationalist movement, a bid to promote reform through a program of regeneration by advocating the primacy of national interests. Forced to choose between a lax corrupt government defending U.S. interests or an efficient honest one challenging those interests, Washington did not hesitate. In October 1923, Assistant Secretary White warned against creating a situation which "would make this Government appear to support the Veterans against constituted authorities of Cuba."[73] Several months later Crowder urged Washington to invoke the Platt Amendment in defense of the Zayas government:

> Further development of the revolutionary movement can be prevented by a timely statement by the Department . . . that the efforts of the Government of the United States near the Cuban Government have heretofore been primarily directed toward the reestablishment and maintenance of a solvent government, as provided in Article II of the Permanent Treaty between the two countries; to the maintenance of a stable government, adequate for the protection of life, property, and individual liberty, as provided for in Article III of said Treaty; and to the reestablishment and maintenance of the adequate system of sanitation implanted by the First Intervention, as provided for in Article V of said Treaty; and to the adoption and enforcement of the Moralization Program vitally necessary to the accomplishment of these three primary purposes; that it has sought at all times to obtain these ends through the Cuban authorities, and would view with disapproval any effort among the Cuban people to accomplish the same purpose by acts of violence.[74]

In April 1924, the leadership of the Veterans and Patriots movement made good on its threat to rebel. The long-awaited summons to rebellion was issued in the form of a *pronunciamiento* in Las Villas province. By then, however, the effects of the U.S. condemnation of rumored rebellion had had its impact within the government. The army remained loyal; congress proclaimed its support of the president. With key reformist leaders in prison or exile, without hope of securing army backing, the Veterans and Patriots movement collapsed within days, and with it collapsed reform.[75]

It was almost a stillborn effort—but not quite. The reform surge had been contained, at least for the time being. Over the next decade, the headwaters of political change would flow into different currents, and Cuba would never be the same. The political class had survived a serious challenge, the first threat to originate outside its ranks since the short-lived uprising by the Partido Independiente de Color. Both threats had considerable political appeal, and were both outlawed and ultimately crushed by force.

XIII

Nineteen twenty-four was a presidential election year in Cuba. Political conditions may have obliged the United States to support Zayas, but only to the end of his term. U.S. policymakers agreed: "His reelection is undoubtedly undesirable," the U.S. chargé in Havana warned, "principally because, first, the two revolutions [1906 and 1917] were due to reelections and that of Zayas would be reasonably certain to cause a third one. Second, Zayas will misuse and is misusing his present position with all its facilities, including the lottery and all available funds, to bring about his reelection. Third, his first administration shows that a second one would not be for the peace or good of Cuba."[76] Crowder struck a similar note: "Everyone here believes that through the secret administration of the National Lottery by himself and his son, he will be able to divert all the corruption funds necessary to control nominations in his favor, and his own election. It is reasonably certain that if Zayas brings about his own nomination by these methods, the opposition party . . . will have very substantial support from the people, financial and otherwise, in establishing a condition of civil war in the Island."[77]

And so Washington let it be known, discreetly and unofficially, that it would not welcome a second term for Zayas. The president complied. And this was apparently the quid pro quo: Washington would see Zayas through the end of his term on the condition that he would not seek another one. The Conservative party nominated Mario G. Menocal and the Liberals chose Gerardo Machado. No one doubted that the Liberals would win. No one was disappointed.

XIV

The early 1920s were watershed years. Interpretation of the Platt Amendment had undergone its final transfiguration. Never before had intervention been so broadly interpreted or so widely exercised. More intervention seemed to beget more intervention, without limits. But the utility of the Platt Amendment as an instrument of hegemony gradually weakened from overuse, and because the object of intervention soon included everything, the means of intervention excluded nothing. It was also true, however, that intervention on this scale was creating profound contradictions in the hegemonial system conditions capable of neutralizing U.S. authority. These years demonstrated that hegemony could be neither fully exercised nor wholly sustained through intervention. Certainly this was the lesson of 1906, and resulted in the application of the policy of "preventive intervention." But this, too, was soon found wanting, and necessitated increasingly direct supervision over and appropriation of state policy. Far from producing stability, however, the exercise of hegemony contributed to instability. The United States was making the position of local powerholders increasingly tenuous and the task of government increasingly unmanageable. But more than this, it was jeopardizing the very solvency of the class upon whose continued political success foreign interests depended. Pressure from outside was undermining the power of the political class. To have insisted upon probity in administration, an end to political corruption, and the integrity of electoral process meant nothing less than the abolition of the bases around which the state bourgeoisie had organized, dismantling the very structures that sustained its solvency as a ruling class. The Veterans and Patriots movement set the alternatives in stark relief: corrupt political leadership defending U.S. interests or honest political leadership defending Cuban interests.

In fact, by the mid-1920s the Platt Amendment had become an uncertain means through which to pursue shifting policy objectives. If the system of hegemony was to survive, the practice of intervention had to change. Defense of U.S. interests required the support—not subversion—of local power holders.

This view slowly acquired adherents in Washington. The policy pendulum now returned to nonintervention, and specifically the revival of the original Root interpretation of the Platt Amendment. Even as Zayas purged the "honest cabinet" and suspended the moralization program, Washington responded cautiously, and under new constraints. Secretary of State Hughes refused Crowder authorization to issue a new ultimatum to Zayas, adding:

> While the Department desires you to make strong representations for the loyal carrying out of the moralization program, it does not desire that

you should deliver an ultimatum or intimate intervention. The Department does not wish to be placed in a position where it has to make good a threat. Intervention could come only as the result of a complete breakdown of the Cuban Government which would clearly leave no other alternative.[78]

This was in essence a restatement of the Root interpretation. Hughes concluded with one last telling thought: "This Government could not contemplate intervention for merely the purpose of eliminating graft and corruption from the Cuban Government much as it desires and will earnestly urge the complete carrying out of the moralization program."[79] Corruption was no longer as much a source of concern as stability. Washington also rejected Crowder's recommendation that the State Department appoint a supervisor to the Cuban Central Electoral Board to monitor the tabulation of ballots in the 1924 elections.[80] "In the absence of any request from the Cuban Government or an intimation from them that a suggestion to that effect would be welcomed," Hughes explained in an unusual display of solicitude to Cuban sensibilities, "the Department is unable to take any action on [your] suggestion . . . that this Government be represented upon the Cuban Central Electoral Board by an unofficial member, and advisor thereof." Hughes concluded: "You will understand that this Government does not desire to intervene in the internal affairs of Cuba but is ready to exert its proper influence on behalf of peace, order and constitutional government."[81]

Treaty-sanctioned intervention had outlived its usefulness. More than this, the practice of intervention had become incompatible with the preservation of hegemony. The constraints that the United States had imposed on Zayas weakened presidential authority in a system preeminently executive and predominantly prescriptive. The suppression of the system of traditional benefit allocation undermined both Zayas's ability to preside over the apparatus of government and the government's capacity to prevail over the polity.

The consequences of intervention were immediately apparent. If the political class was deprived of autonomy, government would be denied control over the polity. For almost two decades, the United States had intervened in all aspects of public administration, demanding political reforms and fiscal honesty as a means through which to promote local stability and protect foreign interests. By the 1920s, however, the usurpation of political authority from above in the name of reform almost resulted in the overthrow of constituted government from below, also in the name of reform. The fear that administrative corruption would cause resentment and that political fraud would give rise to frustration and popular discontent gave way to the view that honesty in government would cause disintegration at the top. The Zayas government may have been guilty of reprehensible behavior, but nobody in Washington doubted Zayas's commitment to the defense of U.S. interests. The only issue in question was his ability to do so, and this, Washington realized, was itself the result of U.S. policy.

Accordingly, pressure for reform ended and the United States made tacit peace with its local political allies, and called it nonintervention. In effect, the political class had to enjoy nominal autonomy from U.S. control if it was to succeed in the defense of U.S. interests. The policy of nonintervention, and specifically the revival of the Root interpretation of the Platt Amendment, responded to developments in and out of Cuba. Most immediately, its formulation came at a time when the political class was under internal pressure. It was inexpedient to create additional strain on the besieged officeholders. Intervention in the early decades of the republic had encountered few political obstacles; indeed, the only opposition came from the political class itself. Evolving through various forms, intervention gave the United States authority over state policies as a means of accommodating foreign interests. In the end, hegemony worked well principally because the United States freely threatened military intervention to displace the political class from power. The principal challenge to the power of the officeholders originated with the United States, and it was to Washington that political elites perforce responded.

However, by the mid-1920s the United States was no longer the only power contender with demands on the state bourgeoisie. New social forces had appeared in Cuba, equally able to displace the political class from power. The United States also acquired new rivals, competitors advancing demands antithetical to foreign interests. Washington was obliged to retreat from intervention in local affairs, lest continued intermeddling weakened the internal position of its local political elites.

Intervention created other conditions that served to weaken hegemony. Such overdrawn interpretations of the intervention clause that had come to characterize Washington's construction of the Platt Amendment could not help but set in sharp relief the feebleness with which the political class defended national sovereignty. So much of the surge of Cuban nationalism during the 1920s derived directly from an abiding abhorrence of the Platt Amendment—a sentiment that translated quickly into revilement of the political class and its U.S. backers. For the first time since the debates at the Constituent Assembly of 1901, the Platt Amendment had become the object of national discontent and the subject of political debate. A vast corpus of literature—some of it polemical, much of it scholarly—detailed the Cuban case against the Platt Amendment. All Cubans of all political persuasions agreed on one central proposition: the necessity to abrogate the Platt Amendment. A source of enduring injury to Cuban national sensibilities, it quickly became the focal point of growing nationalist sentiment.[82]

Through the 1920s, attacks against the Platt Amendment increased in virulence and frequency. Crowder reported as early as 1922, "There can be no question but that discussion of American relations as established by the Platt Amendment is becoming quite acute."[83] On few other issues had Cuban public opinion arrived at such unanimity of purpose. Machado stood for office in 1924 on a Liberal party platform committed to a "revision of the Permanent Treaty, eliminating the appendix to the Constitution, and winning Cuba an independent place in the world."[84] In 1926, the League Against the Platt Amendment was organized in Havana to mobilize public opinion.

Cubans carried their protests beyond the national arena. Opponents of the amendment appealed for international support. In 1922, University of Havana law professor Luis Machado urged Cuba to submit its case against the Platt Amendment to an arbitration commission of the League of Nations.[85] In that same year, the amendment was the subject at the annual meeting of the Association of International Law of Cuba. Pressure also mounted for placing the Platt Amendment on the agenda of the Sixth Pan American conference, scheduled to convene in 1928 in Havana.[86]

These national stirrings readily received hemispheric sympathy, for they were the stirrings, too, of the continent. Cuba's was only one of many Latin American voices in a rising chorus condemning U.S. intervention throughout the hemisphere. Pan American conferences during the 1920s were given to Latin American attempts to establish binding legal means through which to limit U.S. interventionism. At the Fifth Pan American conference in Santiago, Chile, in 1923, Uruguay proposed multilateral enforcement of the Monroe Doctrine. Costa Rica advocated the establishment of a Pan American court of justice to arbitrate all Western Hemisphere disputes. The 1927 meeting of the Inter-American Committee of Jurists in Rio de Janeiro passed unanimously a resolution condemning intervention and affirming the inviolability of national sovereignty.

These were developments impossible for the United States to ignore. In Cuba, the Platt Amendment had become a source of passionate debate. Political elites could neither dismiss rising nationalist sentiment nor remain neutral in the national debate. Nor could they acquiesce to continued U.S. intervention without impairing their ability to govern. This also imposed, as a corollary imperative, new restraints on U.S. power. Intervention in Cuba could not be exercised without causing further embarrassment to the political class, and perhaps, ultimately, undermining its very authority to rule. This meant, further, that if the Plattist system was to survive, power holders would require greater local autonomy. This was a necessary concession to rising Cuban nationalism and the growing demand for reform. This was also the meaning of U.S. acquiescence to the end of moralization.

Intervention anywhere in Latin America became the subject of debate everywhere in the hemisphere. And everywhere anti-American sentiment was on the upswing. Increasingly, too, U.S. policy was becoming a live political issue. The United States could not remain indifferent to the repercussions of its Cuba policy in Latin America. Restraints on intervention in Cuba, as indeed elsewhere in Central America and the Caribbean, responded in part to larger political considerations in Latin America. U.S. policy in Cuba was now assessed against its larger implications. As early as 1921, Crowder recognized the importance of reconciling policy needs in Cuba with political requirements in the hemisphere. "I realize that the policy to be pursued here," Crowder wrote from Havana, "will be profoundly influenced by our own general Latin American policy and that the Department, out of deference to that policy, may find it necessary to modify the more important recommendations that I have . . . made or which I may make in the future." [87]

Through the 1920s, nonintervention served to protect U.S. interests both in Cuba and in Latin America. Three decades of intervention had provided neither political stability nor economic security. On the contrary, intervention had created widespread hostility in Latin America. "Time and again," former Undersecretary of State Norman Davis lamented, "the nations of Latin America have been aroused by our methods, and have even upon occasion formally protested against our disregard for the sovereignty of one of their number." The Nicaraguan intervention of the 1920s, Davis noted, had raised Latin American animosity "to a fever pitch due to a belief that the action taken by the United States was dictated solely by its ambitions for commercial expansion and economic domination." It was necessary to put to rest the notion that the United States entertained imperialist pretensions in the hemisphere: "If one . . . recognizes further that the general sentiment of Latin America towards the United States is one of suspicion, fear, and latent hostility, the logical query must be: 'how can they be corrected.'" Davis responded: nonintervention.[88] A similar note was struck by Sumner Welles: "Can it be a cause for wonder or astonishment on our part that the belief that the United States would continue to disregard the most inalienable rights of sovereign peoples in the American continents was widespread, caused bitter and lasting resentment, not only on the part of the other republics of this hemisphere, and created an attitude of hostility toward the United States which it will take some time to overcome?"[89] By 1926, Assistant Secretary of State Francis White could derive some satisfaction over shifts in U.S. policy: "I think that in the last five years we have really accomplished a great deal, especially in making evident that we have no imperialistic designs. . . . The more we can do to be most circumspect in our relations and avoid any impression of imperialism will I think help tremendously."[90]

Nor was this new solicitude to Latin American sensibilities without economic sources. By the end of the 1920s, U.S. investments in Latin America had reached $5.3 billion, two-thirds of which were in the form of direct investment in properties and the balance in securities. By the 1920s, the U.S. capital stake in Latin America had surpassed investments in Europe.[91] "No foreign trade region holds out greater promise for the business of the United States as Latin-America," exulted Lawrence A. Downs, president of the Illinois Central Systems. "Latin-America is coming with every passing year to play a larger part in the economic life of the United States."[92]

Intervention in the Caribbean was no longer a regional affair. It now had hemispheric repercussions. And as the U.S. trade and investments increased in Latin America, those implications assumed a new urgency. Nonintervention found champions from the most improbable sources— U.S. capitalists. Palmer E. Pierce of Standard Oil of New Jersey warned: "The fear in imperialism of economic exploitation, of political domination to the prejudice of the Southern neighbor must be dissipated. . . . We should endeavor to convince Latin-America of our good intentions."[93] "Now as to this fear of imperialism" Francis R. Hart of the United Fruit

Company exhorted, "there should be no such fear, and we must so act that the fact that we have no desire for, or faith in, such a policy will be self-evident. Our faith must be expressed in behavior, not in words."[94] In 1927, during the Nicaraguan intervention, the *New York Times* urged a change of policy for fear that intervention "might easily tip the balance in favor of European exporters."[95] Dana G. Munro of the Latin American Division of the State Department wrote in 1918:

> Our Caribbean policy had also aroused much unfriendly feeling toward the United States in other parts of the Continent. The people of the more stable Latin American countries naturally felt a strong interest in the fate of the small tropical republics. . . . Moreover, they bitterly resented what they described as our pretension to the hegemony of the Western Hemisphere. . . . Throughout the Latin republics, therefore, there was a widespread, and perhaps an increasing, dislike of the United States.[96]

A similar tone was struck by Secretary of State Henry L. Stimson. Repeated intervention, he lamented, particularly during these years of rising nationalism and growing anti-Americanism, threatened to undermine the position of the United States in Latin America: "Each [intervention] has been used by the enemies and critics of the United States as proof positive that we are an imperialistic people prone to use our power in subverting the independence of our neighbors. And these accusations, however unjustified, have damaged our good name, our credits, and our trade far beyond the apprehension of our own people."[97]

XV

Nonintervention in Cuba did not announce an abandonment of U.S. policy objectives. On the contrary, it signified only a new approach to hegemonial relations. Power holders certainly acquired greater autonomy, but assumed in the exchange greater responsibility for the well-being of U.S. interests. This was possible, too, at a historical juncture in Cuba, in the presidential election year 1924. Assistant Secretary of State White discussed what he admittedly recognized as "a somewhat cynical view" to have the United States "back any strong man who comes in on the theory that a dictator will preserve peace and order as Diaz did in Mexico for so many years and as Gomez is now doing in Venezuela and so long as they respect American rights and interests give them our unqualified backing." White found this approach to possess obvious virtues, if only for the larger countries. "If a strong man is in office," White suggested on November 7, 1924, "I think we should by all means be friendly to him and if he continues in office more than the constitutional period . . . I feel that we should by all means be on friendly terms with him so long as he protects our interests."[98] These policy propositions were dated one week after the election of Gerardo Machado.

10.

Promise Without Proof

The election of Gerardo Machado was a favorable augury for the policy of nonintervention. Nonintervention boded well, too, for Machado. Each required the other to succeed—or succeed for as long as both did.

Machado represented the climax of an age. His claims to prescience made him something of a clairvoyant who foresaw a national future under the pall of disorder and dissolution. His presentiment was not without an intimation of ambition, for it served to exalt his indispensability to social peace. But it also conformed to a Manichean view of the world in which Machado aspired to lead the forces of good over the followers of evil. Machado was also one of the last representatives of the officeholding class shaped by the nineteenth-century wars for independence. His political antecedents did not differ markedly from those of his contemporaries. He held the rank of brigadier general at the conclusion of the war and was active in Liberal politics in Las Villas province. Machado previously occupied a number of positions in the early republic, including mayor of Santa Clara, inspector general of the army, and secretary of *Gobernación,* the latter two posts in the government of José Miguel Gómez. He passed his years out of politics in successful collaboration with a variety of U.S. enterprises, most notably the Electric Bond and Share Company.

Machado stood at the threshold of the presidency in 1924 as the climax to an undistinguished career in politics. But Machado was different—if only because the times were different. Reform was in the air, an ethereal presence to be sure, formless and leaderless. Machado the candidate intuitively adopted the rhetoric of reform and the role of redeemer. Reformism entered mainstream politics via the program of the Liberal party and the platform of the Liberal candidate.

Machado called it the "Platform of Regeneration" and summoned all Cubans to participate in what he proclaimed a crusade for national revival. He pledged an end to political corruption, repudiated reelection, and committed himself to new schools, new roads, new social services. The army was to be professionalized and the civil service modernized. The candidate favored the development of new local industry, the protection of existing industry, and the diversification of the economy. Throughout the campaign Machado invoked nationalism, defended the integrity of the republic, and—again and again—called for a revision of treaty relations and the abrogation of the Platt Amendment.[1]

These themes struck a responsive chord in 1924. Many who only twelve months earlier had seen no prospect for reform except through revolt returned enthusiastically to electoral politics and endorsed the Liberal candidate. Machado won endorsements from Fernando Ortiz, organizer of the Junta Cubana de Renovación Nacional, Ramiro Guerra, the Federación Nacional de Corporaciones Económicas, and the Federación de Estudiantes de la Universidad. Several members of the Supreme National Council of the Veterans and Patriots Movement joined the new Machado government, including Rogelio Zayas Bazán, as secretary of the Gobernación, and Enrique Hernández Cartaya, as secretary of the treasury.

But Machado was too clever to allow advocacy of political reform and defense of national interests jeopardize relations with the United States. North American capital interests in Cuba had swollen to sums estimated in 1925 as ranging between $1.1 billion to $2 billion, distributed through every key sector of the Cuban economy. Two-thirds of the 1926 sugar crop was produced by U.S. mills. U.S. interests owned 22 percent of all Cuban land and supplied 90 percent of electrical power. Eight banks— five North American and three British—controlled 75 percent of the banking interests. By 1927, U.S. capital was distributed as follows: investments in the sugar industry amounted to $600 million; in railroads, $120 million; in public utilities, $150 million; in real estate, $65 million; in tobacco, $20 million; in commerce, $30 million; in mines, $50 million;

in agriculture, $25 million; in industry, $15 million; and of the government debt, its share was $100 million.[2]

Candidate Machado was careful to temper public addresses to Cubans with private reassurances to North Americans. Crowder wrote of a conversation with Machado before the election, "He gave me further assurance that he would, if elected, choose a Cabinet of the most responsible men in Cuba, and would give to each of his Secretaries sixty days in which to 'clean house.'" "He proposed to utilize my services and advice upon all questions which arise within the sphere of relations between the two countries, or had any bearing thereon."[3] Soon after the election Crowder wrote: "In many if not all of the conferences I have had with the President-elect of Cuba, he has emphasized his desire that I should disregard all limitations upon me as Ambassador and feel entirely free to advise him as to any matter affecting the relations of our respective countries and, as well, as to matters which pertain to the internal affairs of Cuba."[4] Two months later Crowder described Machado as a man "who has been outspoken as to the reforms he will initiate and most outspoken as to the friendly attitude of cooperation which he proposed to maintain with the Embassy and the Government of the United States."[5]

But most of all, Machado reassured U.S. capital. He was fundamentally a businessman, Machado was fond of reminding his audiences, committed to creating an environment in which all economic interests, foreign and Cuban, would flourish. In April 1925, prior to his inauguration, Machado visited the United States to present his credentials personally to the State Department and ranking representatives of U.S. capital in Cuba. To the State Department Machado committed his administration to the improvement of commercial relations between both countries.[6] During a reception by the Bankers' Club of New York, Machado pledged:

> I wish to assure the businessmen present here . . . that they will have absolute guarantees for their interests under the administration of Cuba. Among the problems to which I wish to refer is the question of strikes. I intend, as soon as I take office, to send a message to Congress recommending that a law be passed providing for the settlement by means of arbitrators, of all difficulties which may arise between capital and labor, so that neither the interests of capital nor those of the laboring classes may be injured by prolonged strikes, and so that the tranquility of the Government and the peace of the country may not be disturbed by agitations which interrupt the harmony under which industrial activities

should be carried. . . . The public forces . . . will lend to capital and the laborers every assistance to which they are entitled.[7]

At a luncheon reception organized by the National City Bank, Machado was blunt: "My administraton will offer full guarantees to all business and enterprises which are worthy of the protection of the Government, and there is no reason to fear that any disorder will occur, because I have sufficient material force to stamp it out."[8] "Like the majority of you," Machado assured the Merchants Association of New York, "I have been a businessman, and have been all my life. . . . And so, one of your class, a merchant like yourselves, will shortly occupy the presidency of your sister republic." To North American sugar interests, Machado exhorted: "I wish sugar mill owners to study their problems, I am also, on a small scale, a sugar manufacturer; so that by finding the right solutions we may be able to defend our sugar interests."[9]

II

Not a few rushed to proclaim the victory of Machado as vindication of reform—a perception not entirely without merit. Many persuaded themselves, at least during the early years of the new administration, that in Machado they had found the redemption of reformism.[10] Certainly Machado played the part deftly. He recognized the symptoms of national discontent, and by adopting the role of proponent of reform and protector of national sovereignty, Machado successfully brought a measure of political legitimacy to the goals of a movement outlawed only months earlier. For its part the political class needed a stable political environment to guarantee its continued hegemony. By necessity Machado gradually appropriated the symbols and substance of reform. But it was also necessary to reassure foreign capital that the old rules remained substantially intact, albeit in slightly modified form. Machado's repeated public call for revision of treaty relations together with recurring private reassurances to U.S. capitalists served to mobilize North American economic interests behind Machado's form of nationalism as the greatest guarantee of foreign investments. In 1925, no one less than Dwight W. Morrow of J. P. Morgan and Company called for a return to the Root Interpretation of the Platt Amendment: "It is of the utmost importance that American businessmen who have property interests in Cuba should assist our government in every way to keep its pledge to the Cuban people. . . . They should remember that Secretary Root, whom no single person had more to do with the passing of the Platt Amendment, assured the Cuban people while their constitutent convention was in session that it was not the purpose of that amendment to lead to intermeddling or interference with the affairs of the Cuban Government." [11]

But Machado's advocacy of national interests was neither wholly specious nor entirely cynical. Machado differed from his predecessors in still one other respect. In three decades of politics, he had amassed a considerable personal fortune. Machado represented a success story, a member of the political class who had profitably used the opportunities of public office. In this sense, he represented something of a transition, a member of the state bourgeoisie passing into the ranks of the new entrepreneurial bourgeoisie. Machado owned the "Santa Marta" sugar *central,* a construction company, a paint factory, newspapers (*El País* and *Excelsior*), a bank (Banco del Comercio), a shoe company, a contracting business (Mestre y Machado), a market (Mercado Union), and held investments in several other local enterprises, including a soap factory and a beer brewery. [12]

Machado's portrayal of himself as a businessman was not entirely without substance. Nor was his defense of national economic interests. Those sectors of the bourgeoisie that had only twenty-four months earlier organized to demand state support for national interests now looked to the Machado government to implement these goals. And they were not disappointed. During the first two years of his administration, Machado continued to extol the virtues of national industrial development and the need for economic diversification. "Cuba needs to diversify production to live well and without the periodic anxieties of sugar crises that endanger its economic stability," Machado proclaimed in 1926. He encouraged the development of new industry and diversification of agriculture because "without economic independence there is no true political independence." He committed the government to the support of economic growth in the form of developing communication and transportation facilities, most notably the Central Highway, providing agricultural credit, and, most important, tariff support. [13] In 1927, the government enacted the Customs-Tariff Law, easily one of the most important pieces of economic legislation of the early republic. For the better part of a decade, Cuban industrialists had clamored for protectionist measures. Machado delivered. The Customs-Tariff Law provided state support and government subsidy for the expansion of national industry and agriculture. Duties on raw materials decreased as a means to promote local manufacturing. The tariff on crude oil was reduced to encourage the expansion of refining facilities. Sisal was exempted from duties to promote the local rope and cordage manufacturing. Duty on cotton was lowered to encourage textiles. Lower duties on the import of machinery and heavy equipment stimulated the expansion of industrial facilities. Tariff imposts on manufactured goods increased, producing generally a salutary effect on local production. A variety of new manufacturing enterprises developed behind the tariff shield, including the production of cheese, condensed milk, butter, shoes, starch, paint, paper, clothing, knitting fabrics and hosieries, and glass containers. Among the existing industries that expanded were soap, beer, lubricants, furniture, and cement. By 1929, permits for fifty new industries had been issued by the government.[14]

Livestock and agricultural production diversified and expanded. Production of meat and milk increased. Under tariff protection, tannery facilities expanded operations. The production of salted meat (*tasajo*) increased and reduced foreign meat imports. Imports of fowl and eggs declined. Duties on cacao and coffee remained set at high levels to protect and promote national producers. A new tariff rate on rice provided a direct stimulus to rice production in Havana and Matanzas provinces. The production of textile fibers increased. The use of rice flour and yucca flour increased over more expensive wheat flour imports. Fruit and vegetable production expanded. A year later, the government created a national commission for the protection and promotion of tobacco. The construction of the Central Highway provided an alternative to the railroad system, and facilitated the distribution of locally produced fruits and vegetables.[15]

III

Not all the proponents of change found redemption in the Liberal party, however. In fact, the ill-starred Veterans and Patriots Movement split into two political tendencies. One group returned to electoral politics and found in the Machado government adequate fulfillment of earlier reform aspirations. The second tendency evolved into revolutionary politics. For many participants of the Veterans and Patriots Movement, the failure of reform in 1923–1924 underscored the futility of seeking political change in collaboration with discontented sectors of the new bourgeoisie and disgruntled members of the old political class. Julio Antonio Mella, member of the Supreme National Council of the Veterans and Patriots movement, participated in the organization of the Communist party a year after the collapse of the reform movement. Ruben Martínez Villena and Juan Marinello, likewise members of the Supreme National Council, also joined the PCC. All three played important roles in the founding and development of CNOC.[16]

For the first time since the last quarter of the nineteenth century, politics in Cuba gave expression to deepening social tensions. Social lines were sharply etched across the political terrain. Certainly the emergence of new pressure groups in the form of bourgeois and labor organizations challenged the hegemony of the traditional officeholding class. But labor also threatened the bourgeoisie. And without the political means to defend its interests, the bourgeoisie was compelled to return to the old politics as the best defense against revolution. Machado made it easy. He offered reconciliation, even redemption, the best defense of economic interests and guarantee of social order. Representatives of the bourgeoisie wanted political reform and economic development, but they wanted social stability more. In Machado they believed they were securing all three.

IV

The coincidence was compelling. In 1925, all within months of each other, Machado was inaugurated, the Communist party was founded, and CNOC was organized. And the coincidence was not lost on Machado. A convergence of interests joined the political class, the local bourgeoisie, and foreign capital in a common undertaking. The means was the Machado government and the end was to contain a newly mobilized and increasingly militant working class.

Machado did not hesitate. Immediately upon his inauguration he turned on the Communist party, arresting PCC organizers and deporting foreign party members. In August 1925, PCC secretary José Miguel Pérez was imprisoned and deported to Spain. A month later, some forty members of the Communist party were arrested on charges of conspiracy. From the time of its founding, and through the *machadato*, the PCC was a proscribed party, its activities outlawed, and its members persecuted.

But it was labor, just as he had promised, that Machado pursued most relentlessly. A wave of strikes greeted the new Machado government. Sugar workers in Camagüey mills struck for recognition of local syndicates. Railroad workers in Guantánamo paralyzed provincial transportation. Bakers in Santiago and trolleymen in Camagüey proclaimed strikes. In Havana, the Federación Obrera de La Habana (FOH) supported the Sindicato de la Industria Fábrica (SIF) in a strike against textile producers.

The government reacted immediately. In September Machado dissolved the SIF, arrested FOH members, and outlawed FOH publications. Efforts were made to dissolve the CNOC. In an attempt to combat the growing militancy of Cuban labor, Machado worked with the State Department and the American Federation of Labor to organize a progovernment union, the Federación Cubana del Trabajo (FCT).

But in the end, the government principally relied on force and violence. Foreign leaders were deported. By 1926, a presidential decree authorized the use of the armed forces against strikers. Military supervisors assumed control of municipalities in which strikes occured. The imposition of martial law subjected strikers to military arrests and trial. A railroad strike in Morón was broken by military force. And increasingly, terror against labor leaders: Enrique Varona, head of Sociedad de Empleados del Ferrocarril del Norte, was assassinated. In March 1926, some forty sugar workers were killed in Ciego de Avila. Several months later, also in Ciego de Avila, Tomás Grant, a railroad worker organizer, was assassinated. In Cienfuegos, Baldomero Dumenigo, treasurer of the Hermandad Ferroviaria, met a similar fate. In July 1926, Alfredo López, the secretary general of CNOC, was abducted on a Havana street, tortured at the Atarés military prison, and subsequently killed. By early 1927, some 150 labor leaders and workers had been killed. William Green, president of the Pan American Federation of Labor, denounced the Machado government, insisting that "a condition of virtual terrorism existed."[17]

This strategy won approval and assistance from the United States. Early in the Machado administration, the State Department devised a plan to report the activities of anti-Machado groups operating in the United States to Cuban authorities. This surveillance, an internal department memorandum suggested, would monitor the activities of "revolutionists who tend to destroy American capital." It concluded: "The United States is interested in maintaining a stable government in Cuba . . . in order that American investments . . . may not be lost or destroyed through revolutionary activities."[18]

V

The alliance was sound in its design and, at moments, even compelling in its function. But the structure was faulty, largely because the premises were flawed. Machado's attempt to govern at the behest of the local bourgeoisie while acting in behalf of the foreign bourgeoisie, and, at the same time, seeking to maximize the autonomy of the political class, represented a ingenious effort to resolve the outstanding contradictions of the Cuban political economy. Labor's challenge to this scheme was self-evident, and in large part explains the ruthlessness with which Machado crushed strikes and repressed unions—an indication that open class warfare had broken out in Cuba. But in a larger sense, it was also an experiment conceived at a time of prosperity, one that required continued economic growth of sufficient vigor to permit both foreign and national capital to expand. Cuban capital expanded tentatively, always under the spectre of dominant foreign interests and dependent on favorable state policies. As long as the economy continued to grow, foreign investors and local interests could coexist. The political class could serve both without apparent contradiction, and still maintain its dominant internal position. It was a short-lived experiment, however. Machado could crush labor but he could not control the world price of sugar.

The depression came early to Cuba. Starting in the mid-1920s, the price of sugar began to drop, a decline that would not end until the following decade. The government responded to the brewing crisis with the Verdeja Act, an effort to halt declining world prices by decreasing Cuban supplies. Machado secured authority to establish a quota system for production in each province and mill based on estimated acreage. The length of the harvest season was shortened from 136 days to 87 days. The 1926 crop was fixed at 4.5 million tons, a 10 percent reduction from the 1925 harvest. Subsequent decrees imposed a moratorium on new planting and fixed the start of the harvest for January 1927, a month later than usual.[19]

Cuban efforts proved futile. Instead of stabilizing world prices on reduced supplies, the curtailment of Cuban production stimulated increased sugar exports elsewhere, and prices continued to drop. The 1924 price of 4.19 cents a pound fell to 2.57 cents in 1926 and 2.46 cents in 1928.[20]

Machado found himself in a dilemma. Cuba was producing bumper crops, a growing portion of which could not be absorbed by the U.S. market. Increasingly, Cuban producers found themselves with surplus sugar, in search of new markets, at a time of declining prices. Machado wrote as early as December 1925:

> The sugar problem is the most important problem I have been called upon to decide and I deem it unquestionably necessary to seek new markets, at least for the portion the United States cannot consume. This portion can in time be a large one since lands are available for a very large production. This year the drought caused considerable damage, thus reducing our harvest. However, had the weather been favorable the sugar problem would have assumed larger proportions. I noticed that when a bumper harvest seemed imminent the price of sugar dropped to one cent per pound below the cost of production.[21]

Cuban efforts to conform to international production strategies as a means to combat declining world prices, however, exacerbated internal contradictons. Social tensions increased. The economy slumped and stopped expanding. Hardest hit were sugar workers. The shortened *zafra* meant effectively less work for tens of thousands of Cubans already suffering from underemployment. This meant, too, that the quota system would leave *colonos* with greater quantities of unsold sugar cane. It also marked the beginning of the end of the collaboration between the old political class and the new entrepreneurial bourgeoisie. As the crisis deepened, local capital turned to state agencies for relief only to find the government authorities preoccupied with the defense of foreign interests.

A chilling consensus emerged. Cuba appeared moving ineluctably toward a catastrophic economic crisis. Across the island, U.S. consular agents reported mounting distress and growing dissatisfaction. Francis R. Stewart wrote from Santiago de Cuba in mid-1927:

> Importers find themselves suddenly overstocked and the market going down. Restriction of the sugar crop . . . has failed to alleviate conditions in this territory. Field hands upon whom merchants depend for a large portion of their trade have received the lowest wages in many years, in many cases barely sufficient to support their families, and as a majority of the mills of this district have already ceased operations, the men thrown out of work are facing eight months of idleness.[22]

In Guantánamo, Stewart reported, the "poorer classes already are subsisting on sugar cane and boniatos, and the diet must continue until the next crop." Poverty was "apparent everywhere" and business was stagnant with "many firms being particularly bad off."[23] A similar condition prevailed in Antilla. "Due to the presidential decree limiting the current sugar crop by several months," Consul Horace J. Dickenson reported, "unemployment and destitution is everywhere in the province." The closing of the sugar mills and increasing unemployment affected everyone in Antilla. "One of the oldest and soundest firms at Antilla," Dickenson wrote, "recently closed its doors owing to inactivity in trade, and it is thought that this will be the first of a series of such failures. . . . Merchants generally . . . are extremely pessimistic over the outlook during the remainder of the year. The local bank reports that trade seems paralyzed, and local steamship companies report practically no movement is to be noted in imports." Dickenson continued:

> To date centrals Marcaen, Alto Cedro, Cupey, Miranda, Maceo and Preston have terminated their crops, so that a large number of unemployed men have been left in those localities to face a period of enforced idleness. . . . Conditions will become worse during the coming months when the savings of the workingmen accumulated during the brief period of the past crop have been exhausted. It is anticipated then that there will be a large influx of labor into the port towns and other centers offering hope of employment in other agricultural lines. Such a tendency has already been noted in Antilla, where vagrancy and mendicancy are more marked than at any previous period of the town's history.[24]

In Nuevitas, the twenty local *centrales* suspended operations months earlier than usual, producing large-scale unemployment. Local joblessness led to a decline in import and retail trade, which in turn resulted in the discharge of countless numbers of employees in those sectors.[25] The U.S. consul in Matanzas reported local business conditions as "dull," with merchants in all lines complaining of poor sales at a time when receipts were typically high. "There has been very little movement of sugar so far this year from the Ports in this district," the consul reported. "The slow movement of sugar . . . tends to increase the unemployment as the stevedores and sugar warehouse workers are forced into idleness awaiting the shipping period. There is considerable unemployment in this district and it has been stated that the poor and laboring classes are finding difficulty in providing a livelihood."[26] William B. Murray, the vice-consul in Havana province, predicted that "the coming months of 1927 . . . will be a very trying period both for the businessmen and working men of this consular district. . . . There has been a period of economic depression throughout Cuba."[27] This view was corroborated several months later by C. B. Curtis, the U.S. chargé d'affaires: "For the last year or two world production of sugar has exceeded demand, so that the price for Cuba's principal commodity has not been satisfactory. The result has been extreme economic depression throughout the Republic."[28]

These were portents that Crowder could not dismiss. Repeatedly through 1927, he wrote of the "bad economic situation prevailing in this Republic, a state of affairs which cannot be ignored and which, if it is to become aggravated, is capable of producing grave consequences." And elsewhere: "I am of the opinion that the contemporaneous situation is one which may well give cause for anxiety."[29] Crowder was mindful, too, of the social and political implications of these developments:

> What has been gained by some individual mills through crop restriction and the consequent slight augmentation of the sugar prices has been lost to this country as a whole as a result of the curtailment of the length of the grinding season. Not only has the colono been forced to leave much of his cane standing in the fields but the laborers who usually work in the fields or mills from December well into the summer were this year not employed until January and are as a whole already thrown out of work or will be this month because of the mills having reached their quota. Many of the field hands are said to have given their services for little more than payment in food. What will become of them and their families during an eight or nine month dead season when no savings have been accumulated is not pleasant to contemplate.[30]

Nor were the effects of the slumping economy confined to the working class or provincial burghers. All suffered from the decline of sugar production and curtailment of the flow of currency. Imports and internal consumption dropped. Professionals lost clients, merchants lost customers, and white-collar employees lost jobs. Living standards that had increased steadily since 1923 suddenly faltered and gradually declined. Government employees faced growing prospects of salary cuts and, increasingly, discharge—an ominous portent, for the expansion of the state bureaucracy had traditionally absorbed the expanding ranks of new professionals. This signified the loss of the means by which the political class had traditionally recruited allies and renewed itself in power. By the late 1920s, public employment declined as government revenues decreased. And as a certain sign of distress, in 1927 many of the wealthier families were forced to forego their annual summer vacations in Europe and the United States.[31]

The auguries of calamity were everywhere. Crowder warned the State Department in May 1927: "It seems wise to report upon the economic conditions since an aggravation of the crisis might well find its counter-part in disturbance of the political situation. Indeed, the Administration's problem is no longer one solely of policies but it partakes more and more of an economic nature. If discontent from unemployment and depressed business conditions greatly increases the people are likely to place blame upon the shoulder of the Government. . . . As is well known the popula-tion looks too much to governmental agencies for economic miracles."[32]

VI

Crowder was correct. As the economy continued to contract, many of the entrepreneurs previously allied with Machado grew increas-ingly restless. Impatience with government policies mounted, and strikes spread. Political opposition increased. In 1927, former Liberal Carlos Mendieta organized a new political party, La Asociación Unión Naciona-lista, to oppose the government. This was a significant development, for Mendieta had been one of the central figures of the Veterans and Patriots Movement. The organization of the Unión Nacionalista was in many ways the recrudescence of earlier reformist stirrings. Significant, too, was the organization in 1927 of the Directorio Estudiantil Universitario (DEU), a new student organization opposed to the Machado government.

But even as political opposition to the government increased, plans were under way to extend Machado's term of office. In April 1927 the Cuban congress approved a series of constitutional amendments that in-cluded augmenting the term of office of senators from eight years to twelve and representatives from four years to eight. Terms of provincial and municipal elective officials were similarly extended from two to four years. Presidential reelection was abolished and replaced with a single six-year term. The most controversial features of the proposed amend-ments involved the prorogation of incumbent terms of office: four years for the president, four to six years for senators and representatives, and two years for provincial and municipal officials. All elected officials in Cuba, their staffs, their appointees, and their dependents stood to gain from the amendments: an unexpected boon for the political class across the island. New general elections were rescheduled for November 1, 1932. A constituent assembly, lastly, was summoned to convene in April 1928 to consider ratification of the proposed amendments.[33]

U.S. policy officials reacted to the proposed amendments with a mix-ture of favor and foreboding. In Cuba, Crowder reported periodically of growing discontent, a mood that suddenly acquired the proportions of a movement with congressional passage of the constitutional amendments.[34] The issue at hand was reelection, for that was the net effect of the prorogation of the presidential term: four additional years in office. Reelection had been always a hazardous enterprise, U.S. officials understood, leading twice before to revolution and armed intervention. But Machado enjoyed considerable popularity in the United States, and the potential gains attending a second term more than offset the risks of reelection. As early as February 1927, Machado met unofficially with Crowder to discuss his plans for a second term. He reaffirmed his opposition to reelection in principle, but hastened to add that extraordinary circumstances required him to rise above conviction. The republic was approaching crisis, Machado asserted, and it required his presence. Pressure for a new term came from Cubans of all political persuasions, he added, a summons that conscience could not permit him to decline.[35]

Crowder reacted sympathetically to Machado's case. He encouraged Machado to discuss the matter with President Calvin Coolidge and Secretary of State Frank B. Kellogg during a visit to Washington planned later that spring. Crowder wrote to the State Department: "I do not feel that he is seeking the aid or endorsement of our Government of his reelection but rather wished to receive informal assurance that the Department would not be hostile to his reelection and I suggest that such informed assurance might be appropriately given him on the occasion of his visit to Washington." Crowder reminded Washington that Machado "desires the closest possible cooperative relation with the United States." Machado would not escape accusations of misuse of executive power, Crowder acknowledged, especially if Mendieta—whom Crowder characterized as "a noted anti-Americanist"—were to be a candidate. And in face of contrary historical precedents, Crowder proclaimed: "Personally I am convinced that the whole power of his office will be exerted to promote honest elections in 1928."[36]

But that was in February, and in the intervening months political discontent seemed to cast a pall over Machado's reelection prospects. It was to these conditions that the prorogation provisions responded— another four-year term without the necessity of submitting to an electoral mandate.

U.S. policymakers were not oblivious to the intent of the constitutional amendments. Indeed, at one point Crowder stated bluntly that the provisions "relating to the prorogue of contemporaneous terms of office . . .

vitally strike at the stability of Government and in their unfortunate precedent at the principle of Republican Government which the United States is pledged to uphold."[37] For the most part, however, these concerns did not seem to arouse undue concern in Washington. On the contrary, policymakers, and Crowder among them, directed their attention more to the political consequences of the amendments rather than their content. Crowder's objections rested on the "danger to the stability of the government through the creation of popular resentment and consequent disorder than in the body of the amendments themselves."[38] This opinion also prevailed in the State Department. R. Morgan of the Latin American Division wrote:

> While speaking more or less academically, we look with disfavor upon any amendments which would appear to impair the representative form of Government in Cuba, it is well to bear in mind that with a large illiterate electorate a truly representative Government in the literal meaning of the term will probably be impossible for many years and from a practical point of view, therefore our chief interest consists in the maintenance of an honest Government and the avoidance of disorder. While the amendments if put through in their present form would appear to be somewhat objectionable on account of maintaining the present regime in power for a period considerably longer than that for which it was elected, nevertheless, by prohibiting the reelection of a President, they contain a safeguard against the establishment of a dictatorial regime; and therefore if it proves that the amendments can be passed by a Constituent Assembly without creating disorder and revolution I consider it undesirable for us to object to the passage of these measures.[39]

These were the central topics of conversation during Machado's visit to the United States in April 1927. In discussions with Latin American Division Chief Morgan, Machado reiterated his personal preference to retire from office, but added that it would be impossible to complete the important work of his administration by the expiration of his term in mid-1929. The prorogation provision allowed him to complete the task of his government, but not violate the antireelectionist principle. When urged to seek another term through election rather than an extension of his term, Machado proclaimed himself "unalterably opposed in principle to reelection" and desired to see that principle written into the constitution. He raised one other objection to new elections. In view of the generally unsettled conditions in Cuba, Machado insisted, "another election in the near future would be a bad thing for Cuba." Elections "always led to disturbances, dislocation of business, and a great expenditure of money which Cuba could not afford."[40]

Machado expressed these views again during his meeting with Coolidge. Repeating his opposition to the principle of reelection as much for himself as for others, Machado asked only for the opportunity "to complete the reform work" inaugurated by his administration. Coolidge reassured Machado that the United States had no intention of interfering in Cuban internal affairs. The matter of the proposed amendments was "a question for the Cuban people and their government to decide; that the United States only desired that the people of Cuba should have whatever Government and Constitution they themselves generally wanted."[41]

VII

Machado could not have interpreted his visit to Washington as anything less than a success. Not an indication of reproach, not even an intimation of restraint—only an injunction to prevent disorders; the United States was preeminently concerned with stability. "The only interest of the Department," Latin American Division Chief Morgan informed Machado, "was in feeling assured that nothing would occur in Cuba which might prejudice peace and order."[42] Only weeks after Machado's departure from Washington, Secretary of State Kellogg cabled the purport of U.S. policy to Crowder: "As regards the attitude of the Department towards the proposed constitutional amendments, you are informed that for reasons of policy the Department does not consider that in the circumstances it would be justified in raising any objections."[43]

The trip to Washington apparently also encouraged Machado to modify his plans. Instead of pursuing an extension of his term through the proposed prorogation amendments, he decided to seek a new term through reelection. He had, after all, been counseled in Washington to submit himself to the will of the electorate.

But reelection was admittedly a hazardous enterprise, one not to be undertaken without prudent planning. Through the remainder of 1927, Machado resorted to a combination of intimidation, coercion, and bribery to secure from the traditional parties the joint nomination of his bid for a second term. *Cooperativismo*, as the arrangement became known, joined the Liberal, Conservative, and Popular parties behind Machado's candidacy for reelection. All political factions were thus promised in some form guaranteed access to sinecures of state, party affiliation notwithstanding.[44] But most important, it ended all semblance of party independence and political competition, the traditional sources of anti-reelectionist violence.

Against this background the Constituent Assembly convened in April 1928 to consider the proposed amendments. Instead of enacting the specific congressional resolutions, however, the assembly adopted a new amendment and declared on its own authority that the reelection prohibition could not be applied retroactively. Machado could seek reelection for a new six-year term in 1928, to expire in May 1935, at which time the prohibition would take force. The assembly concluded its deliberation with a tribute to Machado, passing a resolution urging him to seek another term in accordance with the newly amended constitution. It was a summons Machado could not reject.

In fact, however, the constituent assembly had exceeded its authority. Article 115 of the 1901 constitution specified that the function of a constituent assembly was limited to the adoption or rejection of congressional amendments, not the introduction of new revisions or formulation of additional modifications. The 1928 amendment, critics charged, was unconstitutional and, by extension, the term of any executive serving under its provisions was illegal.

The State Department also subscribed to this view, but only privately. "The Constitution clearly contemplates no power in the Convention to modify an amendment and approved it as modified," the State Department solicitor concluded. "It must either approve or reject. Otherwise it will usurp the functions of the Congress and violate the previous provisions of Article 115."[45] From Havana, the United States chargé d'affaires wrote: "With reference to the Department's inquiry whether the procedure accorded strictly with the provision of Article 115 of the Constitution, it appears to me that its procedure violated that part of the article which states that the duties of the Constitutional Convention shall be limited to either approving or rejecting the amendments voted by the co-legislative body."[46] The new U.S. ambassador in Havana, Noble Brandon Judah, concurred: "Article 115 specifically limits the powers of the Convention to approving or rejecting the amendments proposed by Congress." Judah continued:

> It certainly does not authorize the Convention itself to propose amendments or to reach the same end by substantially modifying those referred to it. It is equally certain that the amendments as finally adopted by the Convention have been modified. . . . In inserting such new matter,

the Convention, in my opinion, clearly exceeded its authority and such new matter in my opinion, is, therefore, unconstitutional.[47]

Judah added, too, that there was little likelihood that anyone in Cuba would challenge either the constitutionality of the amendments or the candidacy of the incumbent. Nor would the Cuban supreme court rule against the president. "There is at this time," Judah wrote privately to Francis White in the State Department, "no outstanding individual candidate for the Presidency against Machado, nor is there any individual or organization which would have the courage to raise the question in the Courts. . . . Probably the only way the constitutionality of the re-election could be brought up in (otherwise than by us) would be by revolution before or after the election."[48] Having reduced the alternatives to objections from the United States or revolution, Judah nevertheless counseled the State Department:

> The United States ought not, at this time, to take the responsibility of maintaining that it, and not the Supreme Court of Cuba, is the proper interpreter of the constitutionality of the acts of the Cuban Congress, or of the Cuban Constitutional Convention, or of the candidacy by authority of the exact wording of the amendment Constitution of any presidential candidate. Any action by us, based on our own interpretation of the point, would certainly be considered by all classes of Cubans and by the people of other Latin American countries as well, as an unwarranted interference on our part in the internal affairs of Cuba. They would consider it, moreover, as an interference based solely on our own decision of a close technical question as to which there might well be two answers and as to which we had no authority to make the decision.[49]

Judah described the political situation privately to Francis White in slightly different terms:

> Unless the United States were ready to take a firm position as to Cuban affairs it would seem an unwise policy to claim the authority to interpret the Cuban Constitution. Our interference would be resented by practically all classes of Cubans. From the point of view of our own interests, admitting for argument's sake, that the Machado administration is open to criticism, nevertheless, from all I am able to learn, it is by far the best administration that Cuba has ever had. Also, if Machado, because of our interpretation of the constitution, should be eliminated by us as a candidate to succeed himself, I do not see at this time any Presidential possibilities strong enough to have a chance of being elected, who are as able as Machado, or who are not already subject to more criticism in the per-

formance of their public duties than he has been. The elimination of Machado at this time would mean, in my judgment, either the election of one of these possibilities, which would be bad both for Cuba and for the United States, or else the bringing about of such chaotic conditions that some form of government intervention by the United States would then be necessary.[50]

The position was an anomalous one—this was intervention by nonintervention. For decades the United States had freely and frequently rendered judgments on the constitutionality of Cuban statutes, offered unsolicited opinions on the legality of legislation, and passed on the propriety of administration all under the provisions of various clauses and a variety of interpretations of the Platt Amendment. It was not so much that the United States declined to invoke treaty rights in pursuit of nonintervention, but rather that Washington chose nonintervention as the means through which to attain policy objectives. But there was another aspect to nonintervention. For decades the United States had exercised its treaty rights as a method of regulating the powerholders. The political class had accommodated itself to the institutional presence of the United States as something of a power contender. So deeply had three decades of intervention penetrated the national system that a change in this policy had far-reaching political significance. And in this sense, Cubans understood clearly the meaning of nonintervention policy. There could be no interpretation of non-intervention other than approval and endorsement.

The State Department's response to the passage of the amendments was official silence. Privately, Washington seemed prepared to endorse Machado as long as he controlled the situation. "Should a difficult political situation result down there from such action as Machado may take," White privately suggested to Judah in June 1928, "so that there might be a likelihood of disturbance of public order and appeals to the United States, then we might have to look into it somewhat differently, but until that situation arises I think we can well keep hands off."[51]

Nor did Machado misconstrue nonintervention. He could not have interpreted the silence as anything other than a signal of approval. In 1928, Machado carried his reelection drive a bit deeper into the realm of dissimulation and subterfuge. In July, congress enacted the Emergency Law, prohibiting presidential nominations by parties other than the Liberal, Conservative, and Popular—a law designed to prevent Carlos Mendieta and the Unión Nacionalista from lawfully opposing Machado in the general elections.

On November 1, 1928, as the *candidato único*, Machado secured uncontested reelection to a new six-year term. To the already dubious proposition of pursuing a second term and the palpably coercive methods employed in that enterprise was added a questionable constitutional procedure for presidential succession. Machado began his second term under the pall of unconstitutionality. The reelectionist proposition that was in principle politically ill-conceived was now in fact constitutionally illegitimate.

VIII

In many ways, the reelection of Machado represented a collective response by the political class to the profound changes overtaking Cuban society. *Cooperativismo* was itself a necessary coalition among the embattled traditional parties designed to overcome the mounting challenge to their continued internal hegemony. It was also sanctioned by the United States, which came increasingly to recognize the necessity of underwriting the political solvency of its local allies. For thirty years, the veterans of the wars for independence had dominated the island's politics, bargaining among themselves political accommodations to ensure their continued dominance. In 1928 this community of interests found its logical conclusion in the *cooperativista* consensus. Their ranks were thinning, and it was now possible for the state to accommodate all of them. Indeed, *cooperativismo* promised to stabilize intraelite politics at a time when the old political class was itself under siege and facing the most serious challenge to its thirty-year rule of the republic.

Reelection was not without opposition. Some of it originated with members of the old-line parties, for whom Machado had violated a canon central to the standing political protocol of the republic. Old-line party leaders, including disaffected Liberals Federico Laredo Bru and Roberto Méndez Peñate and former Conservative president Mario G. Menocal, denounced reelectionism and fled into exile to organize opposition to Machado. But it was to Carlos Mendieta and the Unión Nacionalista that the disaffected turned first. A former member of the Supreme National Council of the Veterans and Patriots Movement, a large landowner, Mendieta appealed to the old reformist constituency. The Unión Nacionalista advocated time-honored principles of reformist politics: honesty, political democracy, integrity of elections, and a return to the original 1901 constitution. Mendieta denounced the government for failing to provide adequate "guarantees to property rights," and called for the restoration of civil rights.[52]

Reelection delivered, too, one more blow to the short-lived collaboration between old political class and the new entrepreneurial bourgeoisie. At the time of Machado's second inauguration in May 1929, disaffection was widespread. Reelection had always precipitated crisis, and the addition now of the spectre of political disturbances to the growing economic dislocation and deepening social tensions cast a pall over the republic. *Cooperativismo* underscored the self-serving tendency of the political class to act for itself, without regard to the consequences of those actions, even if in so doing it knowingly created the conditions of crisis.

The old political class closed ranks and reasserted the traditional exclusivism over the state. There were two results. First, the Machado government aligned itself closer to the United States, committing itself first and foremost to the defense of foreign interest, but not abandoning entirely its nationalist stance. Indeed, continued pressure against the Platt Amendment served Machado well, for it counteracted any attempts by the United States to intervene in Cuban internal affairs. Nonintervention had significant propaganda value, for it was freely used by Machado as evidence of U.S. support. This was enormously useful to deter defection within the regime and discourage opposition within the political class.

Events in Cuba produced a second development. Even as the stance of nonintervention assumed definitive policy form, increasingly the beleaguered bourgeoisie looked to Washington for relief and redemption. Intervention was now called for against the Machado government. As political oppression increased, as social tensions deepened, as the island moved ineluctably closer to revolution, the call for intervention grew more insistent. Only intervention, many believed, could save Cuba from the threat posed by a mounting revolutionary situation. At the same time, U.S. capital insisted upon a policy of nonintervention, and continued support of the Machado government.

IX

Between the time of Machado's reelection and his inauguration, Washington had come to recognize the nature of the growing dilemma in Cuba. It was manifestly self-evident to many that Machado had crossed over into the nether world of vague illegality, a passage enormously facilitated by U.S. policy. The constitutional amendments were illegal, the political opposition was outlawed, and the presidential election was fraudulent. "Further information received by the Embassy," the U.S. chargé d'affaires C. B. Curtis reported tersely on the eve of the election, "indicates more and more that President Machado has developed into a Latin-American dictator of a type not far removed from the worst." Curtis proceeded to detail accounts of government terror, assassination, and press censorship, and added: "President Machado appears to be endeavoring to convey in every way possible the impression that he is the choice of the United States to succeed himself in the coming elections and that he is receiving our firm support."[53] And from Nuevitas a day after the election, the local U.S. consul reported: "The elections held yesterday for President of Cuba were fraudulent in that the returns were prepared without regard to any votes cast and that nobody, or practically nobody, voted at the polls."[54] The consul in Santiago estimated that less than one-fourth of the voters in the district cast ballots.[55]

The reports were not conclusive, but they were compelling. A sense of foreboding and frustration was overtaking Washington. In a detailed policy review, Undersecretary J. Reuben Clark detailed the central issues before the State Department. "A really serious condition exists in Cuba," Clark acknowledged, "and a revolution may break prior to Machado's inauguration." Clark reviewed the "sui generis relations" with Cuba and the "intimate responsibility" for the protection of life, property and liberty and concluded "that we may not . . . properly or safely ignore rumors as persistent as those which are rife regarding the situation in Cuba." He continued:

> Attention must be called to the fact that we have assumed such a *treaty relation* with Cuba as exists between us and no other Latin American country, that a corrupt national Executive of Cuba could find it possible, under that relationship, to impose such a rule upon Cuba as would not be possible except for the armed force of the United States which stands behind him as the representative of the duly constituted government and that very fact that our own military power could thus afford a facility for imposition of a corrupt and despotic rule in Cuba, imposes upon us a responsibility to see that our power is not used for any such purpose. If Machado is guilty of half the things with which he is charged, it is open to serious question whether the United States should continue longer its support of his administration. . . . A finding of corruption and despotism would bring us face to face with a problem as serious as has ever faced this Government in connection with Cuba. . . . But it seems to me we may not properly blink our responsibility of knowing what is actu-

ally happening there and of taking the steps necessary to correct any iniquitous conditions.[56]

This was a somewhat novel interpretation of the Platt Amendment, earnest but not especially effective. It suggested, too, that even at this early date Washington was not unaware of conditions in Cuba. But in the internal policy debate, nonintervention prevailed. In mid-April Ambassador Judah confirmed from Havana that Machado ruled with "a strong hand." "It can be said, with complete fairness," Judah conceded, "that President Machado is a dictator." But Machado had matters well under control.[57] Several weeks later, Judah reported that conditions had become "certainly better as far as the desire of Machado . . . to cooperate with us." Judah noted: "I have been getting the utmost cooperation from Machado on everything I have asked of him, and it is certainly his policy, not only expressed but acted upon, to play as close to our Government as possible."[58] In Washington, Frances White acknowledged to the new Secretary of State Henry L. Stimson that "President Machado's election is probably unconstitutional." White explained:

> At the time of the amendment to the Constitution and of the election, Secretary Kellogg did not want to go into this phase of the matter. . . . I do not advise reopening it as, unless we were to take the position that the election is illegal and that we would not permit Machado to take office, we should have to intervene in Cuba by force, which I think would be disastrous in our Latin-American relations. Short of that, we will have to work with Machado for the next six years and it would therefore be better to have him as friendly disposed as possible.[59]

X

Machado's unabashed assault on constitutional legality in 1927 and palpably specious mandate for a second term in 1928, to be sure, deepened opposition and focused dissent. But it was, finally, the depression after 1929 that accelerated political confrontation and intensified the social struggle. The worldwide depression wrought utter havoc to the already ailing Cuban economy. A second blow was not long in coming. In mid-1930, the United States passed the Hawley-Smoot Tariff Act which increased the duty on Cuban sugar. Domestic producers and island possessions gained an increasing share of the U.S. market at the expense of Cuban sugar. The Cuban share of the market declined from 49.4 percent in 1930 to 25.3 percent in 1933.[60] Early in 1931, Cuba joined six other sugar-producing countries in the Chadbourne Plan, a plan designed to raise floundering prices by restricting exports for five years. The cumulative effect of these developments was devastating. Sugar production, the fulcrum upon which the entire economy balanced, dropped 60 percent. Cuban exports declined by 80 percent, while the price of the island's principal export, sugar, fell over 80 percent. Sugar producers struggled to remain solvent by lowering wages and cutting production through labor layoffs. The *zafra* was reduced again, this time to a sixty-two day harvest—that is, only two months' work for tens of thousands of sugar workers.[61] The value of tobacco, the island's second largest export, declined from $43 million in 1929 to $13 million in 1933. Salaries and wages were reduced, workers laid off, and businesses and factories closed. Unemployment soared. Some 250,000 heads of families, representing approximately one million people out of a total population of 3.9 million, found themselves totally unemployed. Those fortunate enough to escape total unemployment found temporary work difficult to come by and wages depressed. Pay for agricultural workers fell by 75 percent. In the sugar zones, wages fell as low as twenty cents for a twelve-hour work day. On one large estate, workers received ten cents a day—five in cash and five in credit at the company store. In some districts, laborers received only food and lodging for their work. "Wages paid . . . in 1932," one wage survey indicated, "are reported to have been the lowest since the days of slavery."[62] Wages for the urban proletariat decreased by 50 percent. Wages for carpenters, mechanics, electricians, and painters declined from sixty cents an hour to thirty. Linotypists who formerly received $52 dollars a week earned $35. Cannery workers who in 1930 earned $12 a week, in 1932 earned eighty cents a day. Dock workers who earned $4 a day received $2.[63] And as wages fell in absolute terms, the value of the peso decreased in purchasing power. The peso was worth 28 centavos less in 1928 than in 1913.[64] Profits plummetted everywhere. Commerce came to a standstill. Local industry and manufacturing reduced production in response to reduced purchasing power of the population; this, in turn, sparked a new round of unemployment and wage cuts. The cycle seemed to have no end. Commercial, banking, and manufacturing failures reached record proportions. Business failures produced another spiral of unemployment and new rounds of shortages and price rises. Local business sectors called for government subsidies, relief programs, and economic supports.[65] Increasingly under Machado, during the worst moments of the depression, when national need was the greatest, government revenues that long had served as the major source of both the subsidy of the entrepreneurial bourgeoisie and the solvency of the political class went toward servicing the external debt. The result was that national enterprise declined, public servants were dismissed and political opposition increased. No longer could the political class accommodate the interests of both foreign capital and the local bourgeoisie. The Cuban state, through involvement in consumption and production, had subsidized the emergence of the entrepreneurial bourgeoisie and underwritten the solvency of the political class. The state apparatus that had taken such an active part in class formation before the late 1920s, however, could no longer continue at once to support both Cuban and foreign interests. "The burden, of course," wrote Crowder as early as 1927, "falls more heavily on the middle classes whose businesses, professions, and shops feel the curtailment of the flow of currency. . . . Even the Government employee, who formerly at least felt himself secure in the receipt of a modest salary, is worried by proposals for the cutting of wages and the laying off of personnel."[66]

The consequences were immediate. Many local manufacturers, industrialists, and landowners abandoned the government and transferred their hopes for a settlement of the crisis to the moderate dissident sector of the old political class, most notably the Unión Nacionalista.[67] They recognized, too, along the way, that as economic conditions worsened and political opposition intensified, Machado himself had become the issue. And between 1930 and 1931, there was a portentous development: the government inaugurated a policy of drastic salary cuts for all public employees except the armed forces. Reductions of as much as 60 percent were not uncommon. A year later, budget cuts resulted in the first of a series of sweeping layoffs of civil servants. Highway construction projects that had employed some 15,000 workers in 1928 were suspended, creating immediate hardships in thousands of households. In the second half of 1931 alone, the government closed 200 post offices, nine diplomatic legations, seven public hospitals, as well as several nurseries, schools, and agricultural stations. In desperation, civil servants turned on each other. As early as 1928, pressure mounted on Machado to enforce the constitutional requirement that only voters could occupy government positions, a move designed to expel women employees.[68] And for all who continued as public officials, government employment offered diminishing consolation as salaries fell hopelessly in arrears. By 1932, the salaries of the vast majority of civil servants had fallen six months behind. Thousands of government employees, traditionally secure in civil service and public administration, were among the newest arrivals to augment the swelling ranks of the unemployed.[69]

As the economic crisis deepened, political discontent spread. Repression increased. Arrests, torture, and assassination became commonplace. Government critics were routinely kidnapped, and most victims were never heard from again.[70] Censorship and harrassment of the opposition press served to curb public criticism of the government.

But rising repression did not reduce resistance. On the contrary, opposition increased. As the political crisis deepened and the economy deteriorated, the estrangement between Machado and the local bourgeoisie became all but complete and public. "The upper classes," the Cuban ambassador in Washington conceded, "are not only opposed to Machado but are very bitter against him and all the active opposition comes from the better elements in the Republic. This makes the situation of course very serious. The root of the whole matter is economic. Cuba has gone from great riches to poverty. It is not the fact of being poor that has affected the people so much as the change from affluence to poverty. A great many men who had been very wealthy before are now very poor."[71] And as a telling sign of the times, in late 1930 the government closed the Havana Yacht Club, perhaps the most pretigious social club in Havana, on the grounds that it served as a center of antigovernment activity.

Through the late 1920s and early 1930s the conflict deepened and confrontations intensified. Labor continued to organize, union membership expanded, and the frequency of strikes increased. In 1927 cigar workers organized the Federación Nacional de Torcedores, uniting some 30,000 · workers in all six provinces. In 1928, electrical workers organized nationally into the Unión de Obreros y Empleados de Plantas Electricas. In 1932, sugar workers established the first national union, the Sindicato Nacional de Obreros de la Industria Azucarera (SNOIA). By 1929 the PCC had established control over large sectors of organized labor. Mass demonstrations and hunger marches increased. Between 1929 and 1930, strikes halted production in a number of industries, including cigar manufacturing, metallurgy, construction, and textiles. In March 1930, the CNOC, now outlawed, organized a stunning general strike. Directed by Martínez Villena and involving some 200,000 workers, the strike paralyzed the island. It ended only after a wave of government violence and repression, but not without lasting effects. A month later, workers and soldiers clashed again. The occasion was the May 1 celebration in Regla, and in the ensuing confrontation scores of demonstrators were killed and injured. Several weeks later, railroad workers struck and paralyzed national rail transportation. Strike organizers were arrested and trains resumed operations under army direction. Encouraged by the events of mid-1930, the PCC and CNOC established provincial committees and expanded into the countryside to organize agricultural workers and peasants.[72]

Clashes increased, too, between the government and its political opponents. In May 1930, the Unión Nacionalista organized a political rally in Artemisa. Even before speakers addressed the assembled thousands, the army opened fire, and moved in to disperse by force the panic-stricken crowd. The attack resulted in eight deaths and hundreds of wounded, including children. Within twenty-four hours, virtually all ranking Unión Nacionalista leaders were either in jail or in exile. The following September, a student demonstration in Havana led to another armed confrontation that left one student dead and scores of others injured. In October Machado suspended constitutional guarantees in the province of Havana. Students outside Havana reacted immediately and demonstrations in Santiago de Cuba, Santa Clara, and Pinar del Río produced a new wave of clashes with the police. Classes were suspended and the university closed. Normal schools, too, one by one across the island, were closed.

At the same time, a kind of desultory warfare broke out in the countryside. The torching of cane fields became commonplace, and millions of *arrobas* of cane went up in smoke. Armed bands operated throughout the interior, ambushing trains, cutting telephone and telegraph wires, destroying rail bridges and tunnels, and attacking isolated Rural Guard posts. Military escorts became a permanent and necessary feature of railroad traffic between Havana and Santiago de Cuba. In November 1930, constitutional guarantees were lifted throughout the island and a state of siege proclaimed. Army units in full combat dress assumed police functions throughout provincial cities and towns. Military supervisors displaced civilian governors in Pinar del Río, Matanzas, Las Villas, Camagüey, and Oriente. Army tribunals superseded civilian courts. Constitutional guarantees were restored on December 1, but suspended again ten days later—portents of the protracted struggle in the offing. In January 1931, Machado invoked an old colonial law of public order, never before used in the republic, to suspend the publication of some fifteen newspapers and periodicals and order the arrest of the editors. Military censors supervised editorial boards of newspapers and magazines. Repression on such a scale summoned into existence an extensive police apparatus penetrating every aspect of Cuban social life, not only to arrest, torture, and execute, but also to maintain surveillance over Cubans not in prison and the countless thousands who were. A secret police was organized. The Sección de Expertos was formed, specialists—or, as they were known, "experts"—in the method of torture. The Partida de la Porra served as a government death squad. Cuba assumed the appearance of an armed camp, and terror became the principal means of government. The government physically eliminated critics in anticipation of opposition, and constantly struck at people willing to conform on the suspicion that they might eventually cease to be willing. Neutrality was suspect, criticism was subversive.

XI

The adoption of nonintervention signified a return to the Root interpretation of Article 3 of the Platt Amendment. But there was another aspect to nonintervention: Article 2. Now, too, the United States waived all authority over the supervision of Cuban finances, and Article 2 fell into disuse. As the Cuban economy deteriorated, as the national debt enlarged, U.S. loans and credits increased. And, eventually, so did the U.S. economic stake in the Machado government. Machado routinely contracted new loans and obtained additional credits with rare reference to Article 2 and even rarer reservations from Washington. During the bleakest moments of the late 1920s and early 1930s, as the national debt increased and government revenues declined loans were transacted with almost casual abandon: a $10 million credit from Chase Bank in 1926, a $9 million loan from J. P. Morgan and Company in 1927, a $50 million loan from Chase in 1928, a $20 million short-term note from Chase in 1930. And as dreadful conditions worsened, a new series of loans staved off default: an extension of a $20 million credit in 1931; in 1932 Chase advanced Machado another $1.6 million. When Ambassador Harry F. Guggenheim protested that these new advances violated Article 2, the State Department responded almost with insouciance that the plan was a private affair between independent business groups and the Cuban government.[73] Chase Bank had interests, too, in Machado's personal finances: a personal loan of $130,000, an unsecured loan of $45,000 to the president's construction company, and $89,000 to his shoe factory.[74]

Through the late 1920s and early 1930s, Washington remained committed to nonintervention. In October 1930, Secretary of State Stimson publicly acknowledged that conditions in Cuba had assumed some gravity, but again invoked the Root interpretation of the Platt Amendment. "A great many people," Stimson asserted in a press conference, "seem to think that the Platt Amendment gives us a protectorate over the internal affairs of Cuba and that we are to go in there any time the Cubans seem to be running their government in a little different way from what the Secretary or the President of the United States think they should run it. That view is entirely different from the attitude of this Government as it was officially stated at the time the Platt Amendment was made."[75]

But in Havana, Ambassador Guggenheim was indeed involved in Cuban internal affairs, if not formally and officially, then personally and privately. He attributed political disorders to deteriorating economic conditions. But he insisted, too, that an improvement of economic conditions was impossible without first a settlement of the political conflict. "Cuba's financial problem," Guggenheim wrote to Stimson, "is so bound up with its political problem that I hesitate to make any specific recommendations." He outlined a series of proposals as a way of easing the Cuban crisis that included a solution of the "fundamental economic problem," namely, the disposal of surplus sugar and the restoration of political liberties. Guggenheim also urged a reduction of the national budget and a readjustment of government finances. "Only one way to avert a financial collapse," he insisted, "and that was to settle the political agitation and to win [for Machado] the general support of the country so as to make possible the severe budget reductions." And lastly, and most important, if these proposals were to have any likelihood of success, "the immediate prevention of revolutionary sentiments which are particularly prevalent in this period."[76]

Guggenheim pursued these proposals in discussions with government representatives and opposition factions. To Machado he appealed for reform and concession; to the opposition he asked for restraint and compromise. Through late 1930 and early 1931, Guggenheim privately urged Machado to adopt new reforms, including the appointment of Unión Nacionalistas to his cabinet, the reduction of his term by two years, and the convocation of special presidential elections.[77] On occasion he adopted stern tones. In October 1930 Guggenheim warned Machado that a "financial collapse was imminent," and added:

> I pointed out to the President that . . . his finances had reached a point where we must face the situation as it exists. I told him that he was facing two serious problems; one, financial; that in my opinion it might be possible to make the necessary drastic cuts in his budget, but that it seemed extremely unlikely as long as he was faced with his second problem—a political one. He would have to contend with poverty, political opposition, a new discontent in the Government after the cuts in the budget and proposed reorganization of the Cabinet, probably Government weakness after the political reforms unless his political forces could be consolidated in some manner. . . . I told him that, in my opinion, there was only one way to avert a collapse and that was to remove the political agitation and get the country behind him, in which case it would be possible to make drastic budget reductions.[78]

Guggenheim met also with representatives of the moderate opposition, urging them to negotiate a compromise directly with Machado. Guggenheim offered the good offices of the embassy, albeit in unofficial terms, to facilitate a settlement.[79]

These efforts failed to produce either concession from the government or compromise from the moderate opposition. Mendieta declined to accept anything less than a commitment in advance of resignation from Machado. These were no doubt anxious moments for Machado, for it was not clear if Guggenheim's proposals reflected a shift in U.S. policy and constituted a veiled demand of resignation. Once assured that the Guggenheim recommendations carried no official weight, Machado could casually ignore the embassy.

Guggenheim, too, knew that he acted without authority. And without authorization from Washington and authority in Havana, the value of his role and the utility of his service would be determined entirely by the government to which he was accredited. Even his effort to arrange a meeting between the president and the opposition drew a reprimand from Stimson. Wrote the secretary of state:

> While I fully appreciate your desire to be helpful in the present difficult political situation in Cuba, yet I am somewhat troubled at the implications involved in your taking any initiative in extending good offices between President Machado and the Opposition leaders, particular in your saying anything to the Opposition which they might take as encouragement at this critical time. If President Machado asks your informal cooperation and help, the matter would have a somewhat different aspect.

I think you should be very careful not to originate any more which might be interpreted as interfering either by the Government of the United States or by you personally in Cuban internal political affairs.[80]

In the end, nonintervention in Cuba was tantamount to intervention. Intent was not as important as effect, and if effect was not disclaimed, then intent was assumed. Most Cubans assumed that the United States remained entirely committed to Machado. As early as 1930, Guggenheim informed Washington that the "policy of non-intervention is interpreted as definite support of Machado."[81] And indeed it was. The slightest suggestion of official displeasure with the Machado government would have immediately encouraged opponents and disheartened supporters. The most efficacious support Washington could offer Machado was nonintervention, universally interpreted in Cuba as support.[82] The United States could not disclaim nonintervention without impairing Machado's political authority and weakening the prestige of a government very much in distress and under siege. Nor could the United States withdraw support for Machado without fear of creating the very conditions the Platt Amendment was designed to prevent. Nonintervention was now the means to prevent the necessity of intervention.

Machado also represented the best safeguard for U.S. interest. Both Washington and Machado knew this. Machado reminded the State Department that he was not only maintaining order, but he was "the only man who could do it. There was certainly no other man capable of maintaining order."[83] When Ambassador Guggenheim advocated reforms a bit too vigorously, Machado smarted and threatened the United States with resignation.[84] "If Machado resigned now," the Cuban ambassador Orestes Ferrara warned Guggenheim, "there would be chaos."[85]

As conditions in Cuba deteriorated, Machado remained steadfastly devoted to U.S. interests. Even as government receipts declined, as the administration discharged thousands of public employees, as the clamor of local industry for state subsidies increased, Machado steadfastly serviced the foreign debt. In December 1931, Cuba met its scheduled payment of $2.2 million to Chase—two weeks early.[86] A staggering indebtedness to U.S. banks had piled up on Cuba. But this development had an internal logic and carried its own set of policy imperatives. Machado may have been under heavy economic pressure from New York banks, but Washington was under no less political pressure to support his government as a means of protecting U.S. loans. Both sides recognized the importance of maintaining a government in Cuba capable of meeting its financial obligations, defending foreign property, and containing social tensions.

The complexities of the Cuban crisis, as well the implications of policy, were set in sharp relief during negotiations for a new loan in 1929. A previous Chase Bank loan fell short of the funds necessary to complete various public works projects, including the Central Highway. Machado promptly applied for a new loan. Between July and October, Chargé d'Affaires C. B. Curtis prepared a number of reports detailing political and economic conditions in Cuba. "The Government of Cuba is today a dictatorship," Curtis asserted bluntly, "not a very bad one but nevertheless a dictatorship." It was also a government in difficulty. Much of the support for the president rested traditionally on political support secured through the distribution of sinecures and patronage and popular support obtained by the disbursement of government revenues in the form of public office and public works. In a system where the social overhead of dependency was traditionally underwritten by public spending, the contraction of government revenues and expenditures bode ill for the political class. "There is already much grumbling against President Machado by the working classes, the small farmers and small shopkeepers, as is inevitable during a period of severe economic depression," Curtis reported, "and this dissatisfaction cannot but increase by reducing public offices and employment on public works and by ignoring the demands for local benefits in the way of roads, buildings, etc. . . . The people must be kept satisfied by a proper expenditure of money for Government purposes and the money must be found." Public expenditure had exceeded revenues, and the deterioriating economy required a reduction of the government spending. "Economically, all kinds of expenses must be reduced but, politically, this is almost impossible."[87] The necessity for a new loan, Curtis wrote as early as 1929, was "almost desperate," and the prospects of new loan negotiations offered the United States an opportunity to demand reforms vital to the amelioration of economic and political conditions. But, Curtis hastened to add, the United States could not reasonably reject the Cuban application without exacerbating economic and social conditions, which in turn would lead to political disorders, and possibly revolution. He described the dilemma with precision, and pessimism:

> I feel that the economic situation of Cuba is such that our refusal to consent to the issuance of a loan would so greatly increase the economic distress of the country that it would be impossible for us to justify the refusal. There is widespread discontent among merchants and also

> throughout the agricultural population due to economic conditions, for which the Government is, as usual, subjected to much criticism. While there seems to be no organized opposition and while it seems at present unlikely that the discontent will coalesce into any organized effort to embarrass or overthrow the Government, the failure of the latter to obtain a loan which would tend to tide the country over the period of depression would certainly enhance the possibilities of disorder taking place.

Reforms were necessary, Curtis acknowledged, but, without direct U.S. supervision, they enjoyed little prospect of realization. But neither could the United States supervise Cuban finances without delivering a body blow to the power and prestige of Machado. To intervene, either to deny the loan or oversee the administration of the loan, threatened to weaken the Cuban government and create the conditions that nonintervention was designed to prevent.[88]

XII

Reform became something of a moot issue after mid-1931, however. An armed uprising in August 1931 involving the principal moderate political leaders, sputtered ingloriously to an end, resulting in the arrest of scores of Machado opponents, including Mendieta and Menocal.[89] The ill-starred revolt of 1931 had far-reaching consequences. Most immediately, it announced the political bankruptcy of the nineteenth-century political class. The *cooperativista* consensus had thoroughly discredited the traditional political parties; the depression revealed the traditional power holders unable to respond to the economic crisis. The 1931 debacle similarly showed the old political leadership incapable of resolving the national crisis. The arrests of Mendieta and Menocal eliminated the leading dissident members of the political class who, for all their differences with Machado, still shared the basic assumptions and attitudes that had given decisive shape to three decades of republican politics.

Old-line incumbents and old-line opposition alike revealed a singular incapacity to resolve the deepening contradictions of Cuban society. The failure of the dissidents to overthrow the government in 1931 summoned new political forces to front lines in the struggle against Machado. The new republican generation that rejected traditional politics as unacceptable also repudiated traditional methods of opposition as unworkable.

New opposition organizations emerged after 1931. The ABC Revolutionary Society consisted of intellectuals, professionals, and students, organized around clandestine cells. The ABC embraced armed struggle and responded to government violence with reprisals, committing itself to creating conditions of revolution through systematic use of terror against the government.[90] The Organización Celular Radical Revolucionaria also adopted a cellular structure and adapted armed struggle and sabotage as the means to overthrow Machado. Other new antigovernment groups joined the swelling ranks of the opposition. Women's resistance groups, university professors, and normal school teachers and students became part of a vast underground network dedicated to armed struggle against Machado. These were, in good part, representatives of the vast body of new professionals, mainly lawyers, teachers, engineers, and accountants, as well as many of those discharged from public service, who now emerged to challenge the old political class for control of the state. This was first republican generation who faced problems not dissimilar to the last colonial generation: finding a place in Cuba. To the ordinary urgency normally associated with politics was added a new immediacy, for if there was little economic opportunity for Cubans outside government before 1929, there was less afterward. Old-line politicians who opposed Machado experienced distress and destitution as they were banished from the public rolls. Guggenheim perceived the implications of this development: "The Machadistas had been in power for five years; all the politicians without power and without jobs were in desperate financial situation, and the Liberal Party was giving them no hope of returning to power for many years to come."[91] And for the republican-born generation, conditions were especially desperate, as the nineteenth-century political class clung tenaciously to key positions in public administration. Jorge Domínguez's examination of the pattern of reelection in the Cuban House of Representatives underscores the drift toward monopolization of office during the *machadato*. Between 1910 and 1924, an average of 38 percent of House members obtained reelection, suggesting an open and apparently unobstructed circulation of elective office. After 1924, however, during the Machado years, the reelection rate increased suddenly to 53 percent, evidence, Domínguez posits, "that the incumbents had changed the rules of the political game in order to freeze others out of power indefinitely."[92] They could not have chosen a worse time to change the rules. In the preceding years, government had continued to expand its activities and seemed infinitely able to absorb and accommodate the needs of trained Cubans. Education was the obvious preparation for such a career, and the preponderance of graduating lawyers, teachers, and engineers suggested that Cubans in vast numbers had early committed themselves to the pursuit of careers in public office. Government was the most rewarding outlet for the talents of the republican generation. That was before the collapse of the economy, and by the early 1930s conditions prevented most of the educated and talented young Cubans from achieving full gratification of their aspirations. They were not slow to hold the old political class responsible. "Many of Cuba's ills," the ABC proclaimed in 1931, "derive from the fact that the generation of '95 has kept for itself the governmental posts, systematically excluding those Cubans who came of age under the republic."[93]

The failure of the 1931 revolt, and the subsequent imprisonment of the political leaders, had one other effect. By eliminating the moderate opposition leadership, Machado also removed the most prominent dissidents from the political class, those with the greatest likelihood of appealing to the United States. Their threat to Machado was less from the possibility of winning support from within than it was from the prospect of receiving support from without. They posed the threat Machado feared most, the possibility that one of them would obtain U.S. backing as a reform candidate of compromise. These were opponents that Machado could not take lightly, for they possessed access to U.S. policy circles. As long as they offered alternatives to his government, Machado could not reject outright counsel for conciliation. It was a tactic that Machado employed effectively, always attentive to advice from the embassy, but always artfully evading compliance.

That was before August 1931. After the imprisonment of the leadership of the moderate opposition, Machado no longer felt obliged to feign interest in counsel from the embassy. Only weeks after the government triumph, Guggenheim reported that Machado was increasingly intractable and "in a very aggressive mood."[94] In January 1932, the ambassador reported that Machado had become "progressively less amenable to suggestions . . . after he became convinced that the United States would not interfere in the internal affairs of Cuba and after the opposition was defeated in the revolution of August, 1931."[95] At about the same time, and independently, the U.S. military attache concluded:

> It now appears that all the work and money involved in trying to bring about the Constitutional Reforms have been for naught. Apparently President Machado is determined to revert to the methods employed by him during the first years of his present term to keep himself in office for

the next two and a half years. With the press censored, the Army loyal, and the principal leaders of the Opposition in jail, he should have very little difficulty in continuing for sometime in this manner.[96]

XIII

Open warfare broke out in Cuba after 1931. With the elimination of the old-guard opposition, Machado turned his attention to those sectors of the opposition without the benefit of patronage and protection in the United States—workers, students, communists, peasants. Repression increased, but so did reprisals. Government opponents were murdered and the murderers were assassinated. Captain Miguel Calvo, head of the Sección de Expertos, and several aides fell dead in a burst of machine gunfire. Lieutenant Francisco Echenique, military supervisor of Marianao, and Captain Estanislao Mansip, chief of police, were assassinated. Clemente Vázquez Bello, president of the senate, was killed. Every member of the Machado government was a potential target. Assassinations, bombings, and sabotage became the principal expression of opposition. But the price for success was dear. The government responded with mounting fury and indiscriminate violence. Jails filled with government opponents, and they were the fortunate ones. More often, suspects were executed summarily at the site of capture. Since the failure of the August revolt, Guggenheim reported in January 1932, "the Cuban political situation has been characterized by a policy of terrorism."[97] And these developments, Guggenheim wrote five days later, had serious policy implications.

> The conditions outlined . . . would seem to indicate a new problem to which our policy must adapt itself. At present, we are no longer faced with the problem of an intransigent opposition unwilling to accept reforms and only intent on revolution, but we confront the consequences of a Government intent on perpetuating an unpopular grip on the country. Machado, by renouncing his policy of conciliation and reform . . . has clearly served notice that he is no longer seeking to return to normal constitutional government in the Latin American sense of the term, but to extend his dictatorship.[98]

And the economy continued to deteriorate. Sixty percent of the population lived at submarginal levels, with under $300 in annual real income; another 30 percent earned marginal wages of between $300 and $600. Discontent within the government inaugurated a new round of personnel cuts and additional reductions of expenditures on public services.[99] Salaries of the public employees were cut, and soon the reduced salaries themselves fell hopelessly behind. By mid-1933, the total salary arrears for government personnel approached $19 million. Almost all government agencies moved to a half-day at half-pay work schedule.[100] The salaries of teachers dropped to one-third of that of the police.[101] Outlays destined for productive investments, particularly highway construction, were cut. And while salaries were reduced and employees discharged, the armed forces remained fully funded and intact. Once the state lost the capacity to finance itself and to underwrite the precarious social order, contradictions long muted appeared in sharp relief. Labor militancy continued; strikes increased. In 1932, sugar workers halted production in Oriente, Camagüey, and Havana. Streetcar operators in Havana remained on strike for forty-five days.[102]

After 1931, too, the moderate opposition despaired of a political settlement to the crisis. The failure of the revolt, and the subsequent imprisonment of moderate opponents—some 400 arrests in all—polarized the crisis further.[103] The elimination of the moderate center set the stage for confrontation between the embattled extremities of the Cuban polity. As economic conditions deteriorated and social unrest spread, the struggle against Machado was transforming daily into a movement seeking more to overturn a system than a president. The elimination of the moderate opposition, particularly the Unión Nacionalista, lastly, left the Cuban bourgeoisie without political representation in the conflict. After 1931, local manufacturers, industrialists, merchants, and landowners, as well as members of the moderate old-line opposition, found themselves economically insolvent and politically impotent, facing repression from above and revolution from below. After 1931, their only hope was relief from outside Cuba. While a political settlement was impossible, at the same time, the struggle against Machado assumed fully the character of revolutionary upheaval. As the prospects of a moderate settlement decreased, the possibilities of a radical solution increased.

After 1931, the beleaguered bourgeoisie concluded, only U.S. intervention offered redemption from Machado and rescue from revolution. Even as the United States held to the narrower Root interpretation of the Platt Amendment, Cubans were arguing for a wider meaning of Article 3. As early as 1927, soon after congressional passage of the constitutional amendments, Fernando Ortiz, the leader of the Junta de Renovación in 1923, appealed to the State Department for "moral intervention." Ortiz insisted upon the "obligation" of the United States to guarantee "good government," based on the right of intervention and a right that could not "exist without a corresponding obligation."[104] Two years later, Octavio Seigle, a founder of the Unión Nacionalista, struck a similar tone: "The United States is duty bound to see that Cuba does not continue in the hands of a dictator. Under the Platt Amendment, which is the law in such matters, the United States is obliged to see to it that a government is maintained . . . 'capable of protecting life, property and individual liberty.' . . . There is a direct obligation to protect the Cubans' right to vote for a government of their own choosing and under which their lives and liberties will be safe."[105]

In the years that followed, appeals for intervention increased. The United States had a responsibility for ending the Cuban crisis, anti-government representatives insisted. The opposition also invoked the Root interpretation, insisting that Article 3 committed the United States to the maintenance of a government that, in Root's words, observed "the limitations and safeguards which the experience of constitutional government has shown to be necessary for the preservation of individual rights."[106] Cosme de la Torriente, a member of the Unión Nacionalista, declared that the Machado government could not comply with the terms imposed by the Platt Amendment, namely, protect life, property, and liberty, and called for the United States to mediate the dispute.[107] As the regime demonstrated unexpected resilience against the opposition, the belief grew that only U.S. intervention could resolve the crisis. In 1930, several ranking leaders of the moderate opposition visited the embassy to urge privately the adoption of a "preventive intervention policy" to unseat Machado. "This policy is," Guggenheim speculated, "for the moment, the opposition's best and possibly only, chance of success."[108] A year later, Mendieta urged the United States to pressure Machado to resign and call new elections.[109] Francisco Peraza, another founder of the Unión Nacionalista, exhorted the United States to intervene to stop the bloodshed.[110] In fact, so frequent were opposition calls for U.S. intervention that the pro-Machado congress proposed amending the penal code to provide a penalty of long-term or life imprisonment for "any Cuban who seeks the intervention or interference of a foreign power in the internal or external development of national life."[111]

These were frustrating times for members of the moderate opposition. The Unión Nacionalista seemed doomed to dissolution. Most moderate opposition leaders were in prison, in exile, or dead. Machado seemed stronger, not weaker. Government confidence increased, as well as repression. In the early 1930s, the struggle against Machado entered a new phase, and in this one the United States was the object of opposition ire—specifically, the destruction of foreign property. The attack on the United States was a calculated strategy designed to secure through force what could not be obtained through reason. As before, by destroying foreign property and threatening the lives of foreigners, antigovernment forces set out deliberately to provoke intervention. The regime would be shown incapable of complying with Article 3, specifically unable to protect foreign lives and property—up to 1931, Machado's strongest claim to U.S. support. The attack against property served notice on foreign interests that they would no longer be free to operate in Cuba insulated from the crisis that gripped the island. As long as Machado remained in power, foreign interests would share the fate of all Cubans. It was believed, too, that these conditions would encourage foreign capital to pressure Washington to intervene either to protect property or arrange a political settlement. Even as the opposition faltered in 1931, Guggenheim warned of impending "attacks on American and other foreign property in Cuba with the hope of forcing the United States to intervene."[112] A year later, Guggenheim wrote of a "deliberate assault on foreign properties and persons," with threats made directly against his own life.[113] Once again the Platt Amendment contributed to creating the very conditions it was designed to prevent.

XIV

Developments after 1931 had a sobering impact on Guggenheim. The collapse of the moderate opposition and new government intransigence ended any reasonable hope for a negotiated political settlement. It was now a contest of arms, and the spectre of revolution loomed large. After 1931, Guggenheim concluded that the United States could no longer remain aloof from the deteriorating Cuban crisis. Only months after the 1931 revolt, he returned to Washington to urge personally for a change of policy: "Pressure had to be brought to bear not on the opposition now but Machado." The government would fall, Guggenheim predicted with certainty, and urged that the State Department "get out from under the present charges that we are backing Machado." The policy of nonintervention had been interpreted in Cuba as support of the government, and no amount of disclaimers could disabuse the opposition of this view. "If he falls," Guggenheim warned, "then it will come back on us that while we did bolster him and keep him in office for some time, we backed the wrong horse." He urged the State Department to deny that nonintervention was synonymous with support, thereby distancing itself from the unpopular government. This would also add pressure on Machado to compromise with the opposition. Such a disclaimer, lastly, would condemn the "willful misrepresentation" of U.S. policy and indicate that the responsibility for Cuban "political development and for the building up of sound, orderly, political institutions rests and must rest with the Cuban people." [114]

But Stimson did not yield. Such a disclaimer, the secretary countered, "would cause speculation in this country and people would wonder whether conditions were such that we were close to an intervention, and this would have effects that could not well be foreseen." If the statement were in response to specific development, it would conceivably have some merit, "but a blast in the open, not directed at anything in particular usually does not prove effective, and it would certainly weaken the Ambassador's position vis-à-vis Machado because he would have set off a bomb which was a dud." Stimson concluded with one last consideration: "The bankers, who have a big stake in Cuba, are working hard on a scheme which they hope will work out satisfactorily." He feared that a policy statement at that moment would jeopardize the bankers' plans. "It [was] better not to make any statement until the situation develops more clearly." [115]

Guggenheim returned to Havana discouraged but undeterred. Conditions in Cuba had deteriorated in his absence, and in early 1932, now with a new urgency, Guggenheim urged reappraisal of U.S. policy. "The faith of the Cuban in the ability and disposition of the President to restore moral peace has been wholly lost," he cabled. Machado had skillfully parlayed the policy of nonintervention into a political asset, and the "widespread belief that Machado has our support" had placed the United States in "an extremely and unnecessarily difficult position." Once again, Guggenheim pressed for the adoption of an "attitude which avoids any appearance of supporting Machado or of sympathizing with his policies." Even if this new policy did not contribute immediately to the amelioration of Cuban conditions, Guggenheim suggested, it had the virtue of relieving the U.S. "Government from responsibility for the inevitable consequences of Machado's persistence in his present course." [116]

Two months passed before Stimson responded, and when he did, it was with a categorical policy formulation. In a measured reproof, an impatient Stimson reviewed the precedents of nonintervention. Cuba was a sovereign and independent nation, he insisted, and in the interest of self-government Cuba should find a solution to its own problems without U.S. interference:

> It is my considered opinion that this Government should continue its policy of refraining from any semblance of intermeddling or interference with Cuban internal affairs. In spite of great pressure during the past two years from opponents of the Cuban Government and their sympathizers in this country, this Government has maintained . . . this policy of non-interference. The fact that this policy has not always been understood would not appear to affect the propriety or advisability of its continuance. I feel that any indication, such as you suggest, of lack of sympathy with President Machado either by the Department of State or by the Embassy, would constitute a marked departure from that policy. It would be tantamount to taking sides on a purely internal political question, a step to be avoided whether on behalf of the 'Opposition' or on behalf of President Machado, and one which this Government has hitherto so scrupulously endeavored to avoid. It would further appear to be a step of doubtful efficacy which might be justly resented by the established Government of a State with which this Government enjoys friendly relations. . . . While this Government does, of course, earnestly desire the reestablishment of what you characterize as "moral peace" (which you appear to feel can only be accomplished through President Machado's early retirement), the question of the President's continuance in office until the expiration of his term. . . . is not one upon which this Government can appropriately take any position. . . . In view of the foregoing I trust that you refrain from taking any attitude or position which could be fairly interpreted as a departure from our policy of complete non-interference in Cuba's internal affairs.

Stimson's admonition concluded with one last rebuke. Refuting Guggenheim's suggestion that the United States bore responsibility for developments in Cuba, Stimson advised: "The Department cannot acquiesce in the view that the continuance of its policy of non-interference in Cuba's internal affairs involves out Government in any responsibility for any consequences of the policies of the Cuban Executive." [117]

XV

The policy debate was over, and Guggenheim was duly reprimanded. Rebuked, he passed his last year in Havana as a witness to the unfolding tragedy. Conditions in Cuba weighed heavy upon him, and these closing months in Havana were given to searching reflections on the Cuban crisis. Again and again his thoughts turned to the Platt Amendment, particularly the policy sources of the Cuban crisis. Guggenheim remained convinced that the United States did indeed bear some responsibility for developments under Machado, and that the Platt Amendment in particular, in its past application and prevailing interpretation, served as much to impede U.S. relations with Cuba as it imperiled U.S. interests. If the United States had, in fact, committed itself to nonintervention, the Platt Amendment no longer served any useful purpose. Rather than deter disorders, Guggenheim believed, the Platt Amendment discouraged order; instead of ensuring the security of property in Cuba, it endangered property:

> The existence of the Platt Amendment has . . . led to requests for intervention on the part of both thoughtful and thoughtless leaders in Cuba. More than that, despite our present policy of strict non-interference, the existence of Article III of the Permanent Treaty increases the possibility of the ever present threat of an intervention deliberately provoked. It is a traditional method of a despairing opposition in Cuba to provoke intervention by causing violence to foreigners. For example, in the existing situation, the opposition, recognizing the power which President wields with the Army and Police, believes that his Government can only be changed by assassinating him or other government leaders, or by forcing a foreign intervention.[118]

Enforcement of Article 2 also created as many problems as it solved. The United States, Guggenheim wrote, has assumed a "moral obligation" that could not be adequately met without a thorough supervision of Cuban fiscal affairs: "The is impracticable and undesirable." And as long as Article 2 remained in force, the assumption of any public debt by Cuba would be perceived as conforming with treaty requirements. "The inference will thus be drawn that the United States has given its tacit endorsement of all Cuban loans."[119] Guggenheim complained, too, of the inconsistent application of the Platt Amendment. The United States had discouraged insurrection, curtailed expenditures, revised government contracts, and protested legislation, on one hand, and, on the other, adopted a policy of strict noninterference. These shifts in policy had created uncertainty in Cuba, allowing political factions in Cuba the opportunity to manipulate the purpose of the United States for any number of ends.[120]

Conditions required a review of policy, Guggenheim counseled, with a view toward renegotiating the Permanent Treaty. He argued:

> If in practice we are to avoid invoking Article III . . . as a basis for exercising special supervision over Cuban affairs—if we are to intervene in Cuba only when such intervention would be justified and pursued under similar circumstances in other countries—we might well secure the benefits which would derive from its formal modification and avoid the evils resulting from our present ambiguous position. We should consider whether the United States should not voluntarily offer to negotiate with Cuba a new Permanent Treaty, from which should be omitted the terms of the present Article III, which is obnoxious to the Cuban people and which, in effect, impedes their political growth. This would mean that we treat Cuba as we treat the republics of South America, for example, permitting the people to work out their own institutions over a period of years regardless of which mistakes are made, and retaining only the right of the United States under international law to use its own forces to protect the lives and property of American citizens, if necessary. I believe that such a gesture would enhance the prestige of the United States throughout Latin America, and increase the friendliness of Latin American Governments toward the United States.[121]

But the negotiation of a new treaty would not be entirely unconditional. The occasion to end treaty-sanctioned intervention would be used to intervene one last time. Guggenheim hoped to parlay the abrogation of the Platt Amendment into political concessions from Machado, specifically to obtain "certain constitutional reforms and the reestablishment of truly representative government in Cuba." The United States, he predicted, "would have the satisfaction of again starting Cuba on the road to democratic government, as it has twice done before, but this time only after disposing of an obligation that is both irksome to Cuba and useless, if not actually harmful, to the United States."[122] There was advantage, too, in negotiating a new treaty in economic hard times:

> The present economic crisis, with its extreme deflation of market values, offers from the investors' viewpoint the least objectionable time for modification of the Permanent Treaty. Normally, such a modification might be harmful to market values in Cuba, since the immediate reaction might be a feeling that Cuban investments were less secure. The

deflated values that prevail today, however, could hardly be further re-duced by Treaty modification.[123]

Guggenheim added: "I have no doubt that some American citizens having large investments in Cuba would vigorously oppose any modifications of Article III of the Permanent Treaty. They would probably assert that their investments in Cuba had been made in reliance upon the Treaty and in the belief that in Cuba would receive from their own government a special protection which would not be extended to them in other countries. This theory, however, seems to rest upon a mistaken interpretation of the terms of the treaty which, although supported by certain past precedents, is not, I believe, reflected in the present view of the Department or in the original Root interpretation."[124]

11.

Echoes of
Contradictions

I

In early 1933, Washington had come to recognize the gravity of
conditions in Cuba. The new Roosevelt administration also understood
the sources of the crisis, and recognized it faced in Cuba nothing less
than a crisis of hegemony. The United States' grip over Cuba was slipping. Between 1923 and 1933, Cuban imports from the United States
had declined from $191 million to $22 million while Cuban exports to the
United States decreased from $362 million to $57 million. U.S. participation in Cuban import trade diminished from 74.3 percent during World
War I, to 66.7 percent in 1922, 61.7 percent in 1927, and 57.4 percent in
1931. Cuba dropped from sixth to sixteenth place as customer of U.S. exports. The Department of Agriculture estimated that the loss of Cuban
markets for foodstuffs alone meant the withdrawal of some 817,267 acres
from agricultural production in the United States. Exports to Cuba of raw
materials and manufactured products other than foodstuffs dropped from
$133 million in 1924 to $18 million in 1933.[1]
Certainly the collapse of the Cuban economy contributed in great part
to the loosening of commercial ties between Cuba and the United States.
But other factors were at work. The Customs Tariff Law of 1927, and the
subsequent impetus given to the diversification of the economy, served to
increase Cuban self-sufficiency. Due to expanded local production, commodity imports formerly supplied by foreign producers, including eggs,
butter, and lard, had ended entirely or, as in the case of shoes, furniture,

and hosiery, diminished markedly.[2] The decline of U.S. participation in Cuban import trade resulted too from increased foreign competition. The depression and the drop of Cuban purchasing power combined to make the island a price market and opened the door to the importation of cheap commodities from Europe and Japan previously supplied by the United States on a quality basis. Mounting tariffs and increased taxes, lastly, contributed to making U.S. imports uncompetitive.[3]

These developments concerned the new administration in Washington very much. Certainly they were also relevant to domestic planning, for hopes of economic revival in the United States depended on renewed economic expansion abroad. "Foreign markets," Roosevelt exhorted, "must be regained if America's producers are to rebuild a full and enduring domestic prosperity for our people. There is no other way if we would avoid painful economic dislocation, social readjustments, and unemployment."[4] New conditions required new reciprocal trade arrangements with Cuba designed to restore advantage to U.S. producers. "At a time when national recovery was the salient objective of the Government in Washington," Sumner Welles, the new ambassador to Cuba, later wrote, "it was clear that the immense market for American agriculture and industrial exports should be restored to us."[5]

But it was also clear that economic revival could not commence under conditions of political uncertainty. The Roosevelt administration early concluded that Machado's continued presence could not but frustrate any attempt to revive the Cuban economy, and hence hinder efforts for the recovery of the U.S. economy. Welles recalled:

> So long as the political situation remained what it was in the spring of 1933, it was apparent to any observer that economic improvement in Cuba could not be looked for. So long as the vital energy of a large proportion of the Cuban people was solely directed toward the overthrow of the Machado dictatorship either by revolution or by terroristic methods, no one could envisage the possibility of a solution of the financial and commercial problems, which had to be found before Cuba could again rise to her feet.[6]

The fate of the Machado government affected policy considerations in still one other way. The president's diversified property interests would inevitably influence negotiations for a new tariff schedule, for it was highly improbable that Machado would permit the entry of imports to compete with his investments. In a very real sense, U.S. economic interests would be best served if Machado were not party to negotiations for a new commercial treaty. This was the purport of a confidential memorandum prepared by Philip Jessup. Hired by several U.S. corporations to investigate Cuban conditions with a view to making suggestions for a new reciprocity treaty, Jessup stressed the policy implications of Cuban attempts at diversification. "Cuba has been endeavoring to get away from being practically a one crop country," he wrote. "She has built up a number of industries which may or may not be suitable for permanent development. Some of these infant industries are owned or controlled by President Machado; Cuban interests in their maintenance might well therefore depend somewhat upon whether or not Machado remains in power."[7]

These considerations affected more than the president. Indeed, many ranking members of the Machado administration, as well as officeholders at all levels of government, had acquired interests in many enterprises protected by tariff regulations that competed directly with U.S. manufactures. Rogelio Zayas Bazan, secretary of *Gobernación,* had investment in food processing plants, including cheese and *tasajo*. Orestes Ferrara was involved in paint manufacturing. Several senior legislators held interests in beer, paper, and textiles.[8] Concern in Washington, hence, was not only that the continued presence of the government would obstruct a political settlement, but also that it would also present an obstacle to U.S. efforts to reclaim Cuban markets.[9]

Bankers, too, were growing restless with deteriorating political conditions in Cuba. As early as 1931, Assistant Secretary of State Francis White reported a rising impatience among bankers with the failure of the Cuban government to restore order. "Unless adequate reforms are put through that will satisfy the opposition so that peace can be restored," White predicted, "permitting a reduction in the armed forces which will help toward balancing the budget, I do not see how a default can possibly be avoided. The bankers are very much alive to the situation and concerned about it and are in pretty constant communication with the Department."[10] In early 1933, default seemed one step closer when the Cuban congress proclaimed a partial moratorium on private debts and urged Machado to defer amortization payments on the foreign debt. By May, Machado appeared disposed to use his new authority.[11]

II

Sumner Welles arrived in Havana in May 1933. Only weeks earlier, representatives of the political opposition had united into a Revolutionary Junta and called for revolution against Machado. In Washington, the Cuban ambassador appealed for U.S. support of Machado, warning that "otherwise chaos would result, the sort of chaos that might easily require the United States to intervene in a military way."[12]

But Welles did not arrive in Havana to preside over either the collapse of government or the continuation of misgovernment. This was no ordinary diplomatic appointment. "You will point out to President Machado in the most forceful terms," Welles' instructions stipulated, "that in the opinion of your Government, there can be expected no general amelioration of conditions in Cuba until there is a definite cessation of that state of terrorism which has existed for so long." The United States wished to prevent the conditions "which would tend to render more likely the need of the Government of the United States to resort to that right of formal intervention." In view of the possibility of "open rebellion against a Cuban Government," it was necessary to take "measures intended to prevent the necessity of intervention." To this end, Welles was instructed to offer "the friendly mediation" of the United States government to Machado and the political opposition. Hull added:

> You will . . . regard as your chief objective the negotiation of a definite, detailed, and binding understanding between the present Cuban Government and the responsible leaders of the factions opposed to it, which will lead to a truce in the present dangerous political agitation to continue until such time as national elections can be held in Cuba and the responsible officials of a new constitutional government can be elected under reasonable guarantees of popular suffrage without fraud, without intimidation, and without violence.[13]

Welles arrived in Havana with a specific charge: to mediate "in any form most suitable" an end to the Cuban crisis. This involved two interrelated objectives. "First," Welles later recalled, "to assist the Cuban people themselves to solve the political crisis which had developed and, second, to provide, by cooperation between our two Governments, a means for the rehabilitation of Cuba's national economy, and thereby likewise to reestablish, to the advantage of American agriculture and industry, the market which our own exports had previously enjoyed."[14] And the latter was as important as the former. Welles wrote after only days in Havana:

> The negotiation at this time of a reciprocal trade agreement with Cuba. . . will not only revivify Cuba but will give us practical control of a market we have been steadily losing for the past ten years not only for our manufactured products but for our agricultural exports as well notably in such categories as wheat, animal fats, meat products, rice and potatoes.[15]

Washington initially hoped that Machado could serve through the end of his term in May 1935, thereby preserve constitutional legitimacy and political continuity. The success of this strategy, however, depended upon the willingness of the president to compromise with and offer concessions to the opposition. Welles proposed to secure Machado's cooperation in this endeavor by alternatively applying political pressure and economic compensation. The mediation project was to serve as the forum through which the government would extend concessions and antigovernment groups would suspend opposition. The president would complete his term, and during which time the opposition could prepare for elections in November 1934 while the United States and Cuba negotiated a new commercial treaty.

In his first formal meeting with Machado on May 13, Welles reminded the president of U.S. responsibilities under the Platt Amendment, stressing that essential to "the permanent welfare of Cuba was the maintenance of constitutional government." He urged Machado to implement a "program of conciliation" leading toward fair and uncontrolled elections in 1934. The United States was disposed to negotiate a new commercial treaty that would not only relieve economic conditions in Cuba but also, Welles was confident, turn the "attention of the general public from political agitation to economic interest [and] have a marked beneficial psychological effect." But reforms were necessary, Welles stressed, reminding Machado that the Cuban government could not long survive if U.S. support were withdrawn. The United States would provide economic concessions to Cuba if the Cuban government would offer political compromise to the opposition.[16] Welles linked commercial concession to political conciliation, insisting that "no accommodations or concessions, financial or economic" would be forthcoming until Machado reached a political settlement with the opposition.[17] "The granting by the United States of this [commercial] advantage," Cordell Hull informed Roosevelt, "is to be dependent . . . upon the taking by the Cuban Government of certain measures to settle the distressing political situation. In other words, the prospect of increased economic advantages is a plum which will not be granted until the Cuban Government has taken positive and satisfactory steps to conclude the present unrest."[18]

Welles was confident that the Cuban government would participate in the negotiations. Machado was hardly in a position to spurn mediations proposed by the ambassador, not certainly without jeopardizing continued U.S. support. Nor did Machado have reason to doubt U.S. motives or distrust U.S. maneuvers. On the contrary, he had much to gain—or so he believed. A negotiated settlement offered the depressed economy and the politically embattled president promise of relief. The official emphasis on constitutionality, moreover, could not have been interpreted by Machado as anything less than a U.S. commitment to the completion of his term.

But Welles was not certain about the willingness of antigovernment groups to negotiate with the regime. Their participation could be obtained only by the promise of Machado's removal. As early as May 13, after only five days in Cuba, Welles could already envision the necessity of having to force Machado into early retirement as the central condition to any settlement. "If the present acute bitterness of feeling against the President and the members of his Government persists or becomes intensified during the coming year," Welles reported, "it would in all probability be highly desirable that the present chief executive be replaced at least during the electoral period by some impartial citizen in whom all factions have confidence."[19]

Within five days, Welles's worst fears were confirmed. On May 18, Welles described deteriorating conditions in Cuba to Hull: "Frankly, I am worried. I think the situation is very precarious, much more so than I anticipated."[20] On the same day, Welles proposed directly to Roosevelt a four-point plan that included the use of new treaty negotiations to distract Cuban public opinion away from politics, congressional reform of the Cuban constitution, the convocation of a new constituent assembly, and continued cooperation with the Machado government "until such time as the electoral law can be properly revised." Welles was now more explicit about the fate of Machado than five days earlier: "The feeling is so bitter and the state of agitation so general that I feel it may be necessary to suggest a change in the Presidency, through constitutional procedure, some time before the electoral period commences. But I am confident that in any event General Machado should be replaced, at least during the electoral period, by some individual in whom all parties have confidence."[21]

III

This was the unannounced agenda of the proposed negotiations. The mediations offered the means through which to obtain Machado's early retirement, creating the constitutional basis for presidential succession. It was essential to end the revolutionary threat to continued rule of the political class, through which the United States exercised hegemony. The salvation of the political class required the sacrifice of Machado. In no other fashion could the crisis be brought to an end with the structures of hegemony intact. Machado had outlived his usefulness. The order and stability that he had so deftly provided during his first term, the basis upon which he had received U.S. support for reelection, had disintegrated in his second term. Neither repression nor attempts at reconciliation seemed capable of diminishing the intransigence of the opposition. After five years of sustained political strife and unrelieved economic stress, it had become apparent that Machado could not end disorder. His continued presence was now the central issue for the political opposition, and was easily the greatest single obstacle to the restoration of political stability. The impossibility of attaining political reform increased the improbability of averting social revolution.

The mediations also provided the forum through which to retrieve opposition groups, specifically, the "responsible leaders," in Hull's words, from the fringes of illegality. This meant a repudiation of revolution, and a way to relieve mounting revolutionary pressure by diverting the opposition away from a conspiratorial solution to a constitutional settlement. The mediations provided, too, the means through which opposition groups obtained their objectives and joined the political process in an orderly fashion. Just as important as easing Machado out was the necessity of easing the new opposition in. The mediations conferred on sectors of the outlawed opposition a measure of political legitimacy, providing them with a vested interest in a settlement sanctioned by the United States. This served as a recruitment process, a method by which the United States selected the participants of the mediations, determining in the process which groups were "legitimate" and which were not, which groups were compatible with U.S. interests, and who would participate in the subsequent government. Through U.S. intervention, in the form of the mediations, select opposition groups would be linked to the United States by ties of gratitude. U.S. influence over the new government would be preserved, and the United States' position as a power broker among political contenders would be preserved. This was a renewal of hegemony built into the planned changing of the guard in Havana, a method by which the United States established a political lien on a new generation of power holders.

Symbolically, certainly—but substantively, too: the opposition's acceptance of the mediations signified endorsement of the assumptions of U.S. hegemony, indication that these sectors of the opposition were disposed to accommodate themselves to continued subordination to the United States. This was a U.S. solution to the Cuban problem, and collaboration with this solution promised the opposition political mobility. The Unión Nacionalista agreed to join the mediations. So did the ABC, the OCRR, reform Liberals led by Mariano Gómez, university professors, women's opposition groups, and normal school teachers.

But not all opponents of the regime were invited, and not all participated. The ABC split over the mediations, and the dissenting wing reorganized as the ABC Radical. The DEU declined. Those opposing mediations denounced foreign intermeddling in Cuban internal affairs, and vowed to seek a Cuban solution independent of the United States. The Ala Izquierda, the PCC, and labor organizations were excluded from negotiations. The government representatives included leaders of the Liberal, Conservative, and Popular parties, and Secretary of War General Alberto Herrera representing the administration.

IV

The mediations began on July 1, and pressure on the government for reform began immediately. But reforms were only the beginning. The end was the removal of Machado himself. Methodically, and patiently, Welles edged the unsuspecting Machado closer to his expulsion. Successively the president acquiesced to pressure for constitutional reform, restoration of the vice-presidency, freedom of the press, release of political prisoners, and revision of the electoral code. In mid-July, Welles prepared to deliver the final blow. He explained to Roosevelt:

> At some time within the next two or three weeks, the suggestion will be made that after a Vice President satisfactory to all parties has been

selected and has taken office, the President resign and make it thus possible for the Vice President to remain in entire control of the Government until a new Constitutional Government has been elected in November 1934. The reason for this suggestion, which to my mind must necessarily be acceded by President Machado, is that no opposition party will go to the national elections in November 1934 if President Machado remains in control of the Government. They are confident that fair elections cannot be held so long as he remains in the Presidency.[22]

Two weeks later, Welles informed Machado that a satisfactory solution to the crisis required him to shorten his term by one year.[23] Machado responded first with incredulity, and then rage. He convened a special session of congress to repudiate publicly the proposal, vowing to remain in power through his full term of office.

In the days that followed, Welles worked to isolate the president and encourage his supporters to defect. The recommendation calling for Machado to shorten his term by a year all but ended the mediations. Government party leaders viewed Machado's defiance with foreboding, sensing uneasily that this was a contest the president could not win. And what, then, would become of them? Once again the political class faced the prospects of being displaced by the United States. Leaders of the Liberal, Conservative, and Popular parties, determined to preserve their positions, recognized the necessity of participating in the solution proposed by the United States. If the Machado government fell solely through U.S. pressure, the traditional parties, discredited for their part in *cooperativismo,* faced the prospect of drastic reorganization, under the best of circumstances, or complete dissolution—as many opposition factions demanded. Alternatively, the success of revolution against Machado also threatened the old parties with extinction and party leaders with reprisals at the hands of their foes. Endorsement of the U.S. proposal, however, and a timely defection from a president facing an uncertain future, had the virtue of aligning the old parties with the new politics, thereby assuring their survival in post-Machado Cuba. If the new opposition factions could obtain legitimacy by participation in the mediations, the old political parties would guarantee longevity by supporting the mediator. As early as August 5, Welles reported with some satisfaction that the Liberal party had "summoned up sufficient courage to dictate to the President and was not being dictated [to] by him."[24] Two days later, leaders of the Liberal, Conservative, and Popular parties endorsed the proposed early retirement of Machado and turned to the task of framing the legislation necessary to expedite the president's departure.[25] The Conservative party exhorted Machado to retire as an "act of the highest nobility."[26] The Popular party, Welles reported, endorsed the recommendation as a way "to reestablish moral peace among the Cubans."[27]

But Machado continued to resist. On August 5, he protested to Welles that the mediations had undermined the authority of his government. Machado reiterated his commitment to "any fair solution proposed" but, he added, he would not be "thrown into the street."[28] In Washington, Cuban ambassador Oscar Cintas warned that the "improper course" pursued by Welles would lead to certain disaster: "One or two alternatives would result—either President Machado would be shot or American marines would be landed."[29]

In late July Welles and Machado faced a new problem. On July 25, bus drivers in Havana organized a strike to protest a new government tax. Within a week, a clash between the protesting drivers and police resulted in sympathy strikes among taxi drivers, streetcar operators, and truck drivers. Under the direction of the PCC and the CNOC, the strike quickly spread to other sectors and within days all movement of people and goods came to a halt. The strike had become general, and Havana was paralyzed.[30] On August 7, a clash between demonstrators and police resulted in scores of deaths and injuries. The crisis deepened. By the end of the first week of August, the general strike had acquired the full proportions of a revolutionary offensive.

The general strike changed everything. No longer was the dispute confined to a struggle between the U.S. ambassador and the Cuban president. In the August strike Welles and Machado had acquired a much more formidable adversary, one that threatened to sweep aside both the regime of Machado and the regimen of U.S. hegemony. The strike announced the imminence of revolution.

Machado and Welles recognized the gravity of the strike and turned immediately to defuse the deepening revolutionary situation. Each responded in a manner designed at once to end the strike and establish advantage over the other. Machado conferred with the leadership of the PCC and CNOC, and offered the party legality and the union recognition in exchange for their support to end the strike.

Welles, too, took extraordinary measures. On August 6, he presented Machado with "the only possible solution to prevent a state of utter chaos." Welles warned the president that the situation would "very rapidly degenerate into a condition of absolute anarchy which would result in the loss of innumerable lives and destruction of property," and proposed a settlement that included congressional reorganization, cabinet changes preparing for presidential succession, and a leave of absence for Machado. "I reminded him," Welles wrote to Cordell Hull, "of the obligations of the United States under the permanent treaty but I told him that the whole purpose of my mission here was to avoid the United States Government having to consider the carrying out of such obligations." Machado expressed a willingness to reorganize the cabinet and appoint a vice president, but on the issue of early retirement, he remained unmoved: he vowed to serve his full term.[31]

In early August the tenor of negotiations underwent a marked change. Welles assumed increasingly a preemptory posture. All pretense of mediation ended. By the end of the first week in August, the request for Machado's early retirement was transformed into an official ultimatum. After August 7, Welles later recalled, "it was clearly apparent that there could be no hope of political peace in Cuba so long as President Machado retained office."[32]

The source of the new urgency was self-evident. If Machado could not be persuaded to relinquish the presidency, then the general strike would sweep aside the whole government, an eventuality, Welles predicted grimly, with catastrophic consequences and inevitability requiring U.S. armed intervention. Only the most "forceful and positive action" by the United States, he insisted, could bring rapidly deteriorating conditions to a satisfactory end. Only the direct threat of armed intervention, a prospect with calamitous implications for the political class, could undermine Machado's internal position. But Welles needed authorization to invoke military intervention, and to obtain this permission he used the prospects of intervention against Washington. Welles now predicted to the State Department the inevitability of armed intervention if Machado remained in power. This prospect had a chilling effect in Washington, for Roosevelt and Hull were loath to inaugurate the "Good Neighbor" policy on the debacle of an armed intervention in Cuba. But to obtain authorization to threaten Machado with armed intervention as a means of forcing his retirement, Welles was obliged also to threaten Washington: armed intervention would be inevitable if he were denied the use of its threat. He warned the State Department in terms calculated to emphasize U.S. treaty responsibilities:

If President Machado remains in power, he can only continue through the exercise of the most brutal methods of repression. . . . It will be impossible for him to govern without a continuance of martial law and the suspension of all constitutional guarantees, which condition makes it possible, of course, for the President and military authorities to assassinate, to throw into prison, and to deprive of "life, property and individual liberty," any citizen of the Republic. The Government of the United States has clearly demonstrated its intention to use every possible means at its disposal to further and to support a peaceful and constitutional adjustment by the Cuban people of their problem. The realization of that end is made impossible solely by the unwillingness of one man, President Machado, to retire from the office which he holds through a reelection which in its genesis is unquestionably unconstitutional. Throughout the course of my mission here, I have exerted every possible effort to avoid the creation of a situation which might result in an intervention by the United States. If the present condition is permitted to continue much longer, I am positive that a state of complete anarchy will result which might force the Government of the United States, against its will, to intervene in compliance with its obligations under the Permanent Treaty.[33]

And this, Welles reminded Washington, was a responsibility the United States could not evade. "The permanent treaty imposes upon us," he stressed with artful purposefulness, "responsibilities as regards the Cuban people. I do not see how the Government of the United States can, in view of its treaty obligations, continue its formal support of a Cuban Government which has consistently deprived the Cuban people of their constitutional rights, which has been guilty of atrocities which have shocked the entire continent, and which refused to consider the acceptance of a fair and Cuban solution of this disastrous situation."[34] Welles recommended that "if at the end of a reasonable period" Machado remained in power, that he be informed of the intention of the United States to withdraw its recognition of his government. And after the expiration of this time if Machado still refused to resign, Welles proposed meeting with the government parties and opposition groups to prepare for the installation of a new government.[35]

Welles was certain that withdrawal of recognition, together with the threat of armed intervention, would prevent the necessity of intervention. But this threat was not directed as much to Machado as it was to his supporters, including the traditional political parties, the congress, the cabinet, and the armed forces. Indeed, as early as July 25, Welles had alluded to military intervention if Machado did not restore constitutional guarantees in Havana province.[36] The proposal to withdraw recognition, Welles assured the State Department, would not "in all probability force us to intervene." Welles added:

> I think if the President himself was advised that we would withdraw recognition unless he accepted a fair solution of the problem, he would be obliged to accept such solution by most of the members of his Cabinet, the army, and by the great majority of Congress. If, however, he persists in refusing to accept any compromise after notification that recognition would be withdrawn, in such event, I do not believe that his Government would be able to maintain itself for more than an exceedingly brief period and should steps be taken by me in advance in accordance with the leaders of the political parties and with the important leaders of the opposition to provide for a stable government immediately upon Machado's forced resignation, I have every reason to believe that the situation here would continue sufficiently within control to make it unnecessary for the United States Government to undertake even a brief armed intervention.[37]

To the horror of the State Department, however, Machado defied the United States to intervene. "Inform the President of the United States," Machado taunted Welles, "that [I] would prefer armed intervention to the acceptance of any such proposal."[38] Worse still for Washington, Machado seized the threat of intervention to appeal for national support for his government. He denounced U.S. meddling in Cuban internal affairs, vowing to defend national sovereignty and exhorting Cubans to defend the homeland against armed aggression from the United States.[39] Privately he informed Welles that he would repel with arms the landing of foreign troops on national territory.[40] And as a last resort, Machado appealed to the court of Latin American public opinion, asking the Western Hemisphere republics to condemn U.S. intervention in Cuba.[41]

On August 9, Welles concluded bluntly:

> 1. There is absolutely no hope of a return to normal conditions in Cuba as long as President Machado remains in office. No one other than the small clique of officeholders surrounding him has any trust or confidence in him and he represents in his person to every other Cuban the cause of economic distress and personal suffering which has existed during the past 3 years.

2. So long as this condition continues there is no possible chance of improving economic conditions in Cuba, and there will be immense loss to the Cuban people themselves and as a natural corollary to all the American interests doing business in or with Cuba.[42]

And tensions mounted. The general strike deepened the crisis, raising for many, including Welles, the spectre of a far-reaching social upheaval. The *New York Times* correspondent described conditions as "a race between mediation by the United States Ambassador and open revolution."[43] Machado had publicly repudiated the ultimatum threatening intervention. For more than two decades, the United States had obtained the acquiescence of the political class by threatening to displace officeholders through armed intervention. In 1933, the threat no longer worked.

Welles appealed to Washington for help. He was certain that Machado's actions were based on advice received from Cuban ambassador Oscar Cintas in Washington who believed Welles had exceeded his authority and that the Roosevelt administration would not intervene in Cuba. Welles urged the State Department to disabuse Cintas of both these views:

> If Machado is permitted to believe as he apparently does that the United States will under no conditions and under no circumstances comply with its treaty obligations, I have every reason to believe that he will not give in until the very last possible moment. If on the other hand it is emphatically made clear to him that while the whole object of my mission has been to avoid intervention and that the United States will only consider intervention if it is forced to do so by the clear requirements of its treaty obligations as contained in article three of the permanent treaty it is much more probable that he will finally agree to the solution proposed. I cannot help but feel that it is an infinitely wiser policy on our part to state very clearly at this juncture that we will not evade our treaty obligations if we are obliged to comply with them rather than to evade the issue and let matters slide into a state of affairs where we will have to take the only action which we desire to avoid. The President himself and those around him are confident that because of the prejudice to our own interests the United States Government will not intervene now under any conditions whatsoever. If they can be dissuaded from that belief a peaceful solution will be far more probable.[44]

Washington complied, but nothing changed in Havana.[45] The moment was critical, and Welles was desperate. "The ominous signs provided by a paralyzing general strike," he later wrote, "wholly political in character, made it doubly clear that only some radical solution could forestall the cataclysm which otherwise was inevitable."[46]

Almost two weeks after Welles had submitted his original proposal he devised a "new solution"—what he later called the "radical solution." On August 11 he reported holding a "confidential talk" with Secretary of War General Alberto Herrera in which Herrera pledged to support a new proposal. The new plan allowed Machado to present a counterproposal, thereby saving face by ostensibly accepting a plan of his own making. The counterproposal contained all the substantive elements of the original recommendation: the president was to request a leave of absence, accepting the resignation of all cabinet members with the exception of Herrera, who thereupon became acting president.[47]

By offering Herrera the presidency, Welles deliberately invited the armed forces to impose the political settlement continuing to elude his mediation efforts. He no doubt realized that Herrera's only contribution to the "new solution"—certainly an adequate contribution to warrant appointing him president—lay entirely in leading the army against Machado. Herrera's participation in his plan, Welles predicted confidently, insured "the loyal support of the Cuban Army," which was unanimously devoted to the general.[48]

But the army was already predisposed to act. As the balance of power tipped against the government, the armed forces found their vulnerability increasing in the changing political conditions. The mediations had not inspired confidence in the army command. Rising antimilitarism among opposition groups added to growing army uneasiness. Antigovernment factions denounced the military, pledging to reduce the size of the armed forces, restrict military authority, and cut the army budget.[49] Business groups, too, weary of excessive budget allocation to support the military, advocated reductions in the armed forces.[50] Throughout the summer, the army leadership had viewed the mediations with mounting misgiving. Participation in the mediation had conferred legitimacy on the formerly outlawed opposition groups, guaranteeing the sectors which the armed forces had persecuted in the preceding years positions of political authority in post-Machado Cuba. It was essential for the army command to participate at some point in the settlement, if only as a means to protect its interests. For the army to have remained aloof from a political settlement would have inevitably placed it at the mercy of a vastly reorganized government composed of former army foes.[51] Indeed, army intervention was not entirely unconditional. The army command acted only after having secured assurances from opposition leaders, to which Welles subscribed, that the subsequent government would respect the integrity of the armed forces. A "strictly confidential" memorandum, couched in Machado's counterproposal, stipulated that the armed forces would be maintained without reorganization until May 20, 1935, the scheduled expiration date of Machado's second term. Members of the armed forces could neither be retired nor punished in any fashion inconsistent with existing laws.[52]

But it was the growing fear of U.S. intervention that finally moved the army to act. Welles had calculated correctly. Army leaders shrank in horror at the spectacle of Machado defying U.S. authorities, seeking to arouse the population to the defense of the island against the threatened armed intervention, and appealing to Latin American public opinion to condemn the United States. The "sole purpose" of the military coup, one army representative later explained, "was the avoidance of American intervention."[53] No less than the political class, the army also feared displacement by an armed intervention. U.S. intervention would certainly have resulted in a sweeping reorganization of the armed forces, leading ultimately to drastic reductions.[54] During the mediations, one Havana local newspaper carried a front-page story asserting that the U.S. military attache had urged reducing the Cuban army from 12,000 to 3,000.[55] Because of the army's susceptibility to the threat of intervention, Welles was not reluctant to use it. As early as July, Welles informed Herrera that he had obtained authority to land marines.[56] Similarly, the U.S. military attache informed senior military chiefs that the State Department was prepared to intervene unless Machado retired from office.[57] The army originally organized by the United States in 1908 to support the Cuban government against political disorders, and thereby obviate the necessity of armed intervention, was used by the United States in 1933 to overthrow the Cuban government as a means to end disorders, and thereby obviate the necessity of armed intervention.

U.S. support of constituted government had traditionally underwritten stability and political consensus in Havana. In 1933 the United States effectively undermined government with the demand that Machado shorten his term by one year. Indeed, this public announcement must be viewed as nothing less than a calculated maneuver to force Machado out of office. Welles possessed sufficient insight into the subtleties of Cuban politics to anticipate the consequences of making this demand public. In

June 1933 Welles the mediator, committed to personal diplomacy as a means to persuade Machado to accept early retirement, guarded his proposal carefully, fearing that a premature disclosure would "weaken" the president's control over congress and the armed forces.[58] Subsequently frustrated by his inability to convince Machado to resign, Welles publicly revealed the withdrawal of U.S. support and precipitated a realignment of the political balance of power, thereby releasing Machado's supporters to seek new arrangements to guarantee their survial in post-Machado Cuba.

The army intervention saved the beleaguered political class from the folly of its own excesses. The real threat in August 1933, as Welles readily understood, was contained in the deepening social struggle on the island and expressed most dramatically in the August general strike. Once again the United States rescued the social system threatened with revolution and prevented the displacement of its local political allies, thereby preserving intact the classes and structures essential for continued U.S. hegemony.

Plans to have Herrera assume the presidency encountered strong opposition from the army, and instead Carlos Manuel de Céspedes was appointed. Under the new regime, the political class hoped to renew its lease over the state. Machado was removed and the cabinet replaced, but congress remained virtually unchanged, the bureaucracy untouched, and the army unaffected.[59]

V

Carlos Manuel de Céspedes emerged from political obscurity. Apart from his family name, his principal virtue consisted in his lack of affiliation with any political party or political tendency. He was the U.S. ambassador's choice, and no one would deny the ambassador his choice. Céspedes was something of a political nonentity—a "statesman," he described himself loftily, above partisan passions, lacking a public personality—and as such he represented an inoffensive compromise candidate to the embattled extremes of the Cuban polity. He was without popularity, without a party, and without a program, and all at once he inherited a cabinet, a constituency, and a country in collapse.

The Céspedes government set in sharp relief the contradictions accumulating during the *machadato*. The mediations had served to legitimize the new political groups and guarantee their inclusion in the new government. The timely desertion of Machado by the government parties, moreover, assured the old-line groups a place in the new administration. Participation in the mediations had created the conditions whereby diverse and ideologically irreconcilable groups obtained legitimacy in post-Machado Cuba, and on August 12, these groups combined into an anomalous association that constituted itself into the Céspedes government. The distribution of the cabinet portfolios to representatives of such diverse groups as the ABC, the Liberal party, the Unión Nacionalista, the Conservative party, the OCRR, and the Popular party served to give institutional form to the unresolved ambiguities and persisting contradictions of the *machadato*.

The difficulties confronting the new government were not confined to internal contradictions, however. To be sure, the departure of Machado brought to an end the most repressive features of government. Certainly, too, the change of governments reduced political tension and armed conflict. But Cuba remained in the throes of depression, and the economic stagnation and social unrest that had plunged the *machadato* into crisis continued unrelieved after August 12. Strikes continued. The labor militancy that precipitated the fall of Machado continued unabated. Unions in Santiago threatened a general strike. Tobacco workers in Pinar del Río, stevedores in Havana, railroad workers in Camagüey, and coffee workers in Oriente remained on strike. Sugar production came to a virtual halt. Workers seized sugar mills, organized soviets, and called for revolution. Those opposition groups that earlier had boycotted the mediations, principally those sectors of the opposition that aspired to something more than simply a change of presidents, found the Céspedes succession wholly unsatisfactory. Many of these groups, including labor organizations, the DEU, the Ala Izquierda, and the PCC, had toiled too long in the pursuit of revolution to settle for a palace coup as the denouement of their political labor.

There were other problems for Céspedes. Beset by contradictions from within and besieged by opposition from without, the authority of the new government deteriorated. Old-line political parties maneuvered to recover lost prestige and authority, while new political groups intrigued to expand power and influence. Reports that former *machadista* officials had returned to their old jobs weakened the moral authority of the Céspedes government.[60] That the government had permitted the flight of large numbers of officials responsible for atrocities offended public sensibilities. Legislators could not meet for fear of precipitating a mob attack against congress. Many provincial governors and municipal mayors and their staffs had gone into hiding, leaving local government unattended. Public order had collapsed. The rioting produced by Machado's flight continued intermittently through August. Angry mobs stalked Havana streets and outlying suburbs bent on dispensing revolutionary justice to suspected *machadista* officials. Government offices were gutted, stores looted, and homes sacked.[61] Suspected Machado supporters were lynched. Army and police authorities moved to restrain civilian excesses tentatively, when at all. Too many officers feared that strict enforcement of public order would serve to revive antimilitary sentiment among their former opponents now in power. The "inability of the Government as yet to enforce the maintenance of public order," Welles reported a week after the coup, had created "an almost anarchic condition."[62] Within a week Welles struck a note of new urgency, predicting that "a general state of chaos [was] inevitable" and describing "a general process of disintegration."[63]

The Céspedes government was an administration without a mandate. It formed largely to facilitate Machado's succession and accommodate debts incurred to the groups participating in the mediations. It was a government made up of discredited political parties that had functioned under the pall of unconstitutionality and dissident clandestine factions that had operated on the fringes of illegality. It neither possessed popularity nor promised a program. On the contrary, under pressure from the United States to preserve constitutionality, the Céspedes administration continued to govern under the 1928 amendments—even though they were unconstitutional. This was a government summoned into existence in response to U.S. needs. And because it was so patently artificial in origins and palpably superfluous in function, and because it recognized the sources of its origins and the constituency it served, the government proceeded haltingly and indecisively, and this only after approval from Welles. "My personal situation is becoming increasingly difficult," Welles complained a week after the fall of Machado. "Owing to my intimate personal friendship with President Céspedes and the very close relationship which I have formed during these past months with all the members of this Cabinet I am now daily being requested for decisions on all matters affecting the Government of Cuba. These decisions range from questions of domestic policy and matters affecting the discipline of the Army to questions involving appointments in all branches of Government."[64]

Welles tried mightily to breathe life into the moribund government. Very early he appealed to Washington for government assistance. Facing the necessity of proclaiming a moratorium on the Cuban debt, threatened with a civil service strike to protest salary arrears, Welles urged the State Department to provide the Céspedes government with a loan. "If steps are not taken immediately to make the Cuban people confident that their distress will in some measure be relieved in the not distant future," he warned, "a condition of chaos will unquestionably ensue which will . . . make stable and constitutional government in Cuba impossible."[65]

But, in fact, the appearance of constitutional succession was becoming increasingly impossible to preserve. More and more, it was becoming a choice between stability or constitutionality. The national mood rejected the continued incumbency of public officials holding office under the auspices of the 1928 amendments. Welles wrote on August 24, "I am rapidly coming to the conclusion that my original hope that the present Government of Cuba could govern as a constitutional government for the remainder of the term for which General Machado had himself elected must be abandoned."[66] It was now necessary for the Céspedes government to repudiate its constitutional base, proclaim itself a de facto provisional government, and quickly prepare for new elections. "I do not believe that the present Government can maintain itself in power for an indefinite period," Welles conceded, "and I think that nothing would be more likely to prevent a further attempt at revolution than the prospect of elections in the near future."[67]

VI

The end of the Céspedes government came from the most improbable and wholly unexpected sources. On the evening of September 3, sergeants, corporals, and enlisted men of Camp Columbia in Havana met to discuss a backlog of grievances. Deliberations concluded late into the night with the preparation of a list of demands to be submitted to the army command. The officers on duty, however, declined to discuss the demands of the aroused soldiery and, instead, retired from regimental headquarters. Suddenly, and unexpectedly, the troops found themselves in control of Camp Columbia—and in mutiny. The army protestors, under the leadership of Sergeant Fulgencio Batista, exhorted the troops to hold the post until the officer agreed to negotiate their demand.

Antigovernment groups immediately rallied around the mutinous troops. In the early morning hours of September 4, leaders of the DEU arrived at Camp Columbia and persuaded the sergeants to expand the objectives of their movement.[68] The intervention of civilians changed radically the nature of the army protest, transforming a mutiny into a putsch. The "Sergeants' Revolt," as the mutiny later became known, originally had modest objectives. The sergeants planned a demonstration to protest deteriorating conditions in the army, specifically poor pay, inadequate housing facilities, and rumored cuts in enlisted ranks—not overthrow Céspedes or oust the officer corps. Civilian participation, however, conferred on the mutiny political dimensions that transcended its original limited goals. Having unexpectedly found themselves in a state of mutiny, and thereby effectively in rebellion against the Céspedes government, the sergeant leaders now faced the certain prospect of severe disciplinary action, including court martial and imprisonment. For many there was no going back, although through some anxious moments on the morning of September 4, they were not quite certain how to proceed.

The antigovernment opposition provided the means. Civilians transformed an act of insubordination into a full-fledged military coup and used the mutiny as an instrument of political change. It was a coalition of convenience, to be sure, an improvisation not without flaws, but one that offered rebellious soldiers pardon and dissident civilians power. Out of this tentative civil-military arrangement emerged a revolutionary junta organized around a pentarchy of Ramón Grau San Martín, Porfirio Franca, Guillermo Portela, José Miguel Irisarri, and Sergio Carbó. On September 5, a political manifesto announced the establishment of a new provisional revolutionary government and proclaimed national sovereignty, the establishment of a modern democracy, and the "march toward the creation of a new Cuba."[69] Within a week, the pentarchy dissolved in favor of an executive form of government under Grau San Martín.

VII

The new government was fulfillment of the reformist movement that began fully a decade earlier. Fernando Ortiz never wavered in his public support of the new government. Many members of the provisional government in 1933 had been active in the reformist projects of 1923. Out of the pentarchy, Professor Grau San Martín, banker Porfirio Franca, and attorney José Miguel Irisarri had participated in the Veterans and Patriots movement. The members of the subsequent cabinet included physicians, attorneys, academics, an engineer, all representatives of the liberal professions. The new cabinet included Carlos Finlay (Health), Manuel

Costales Latatu (Education), Julio Aguado (Defense), Antonio Guiteras (Gobernación), Gustavo Moreno (Public Works), Ramiro Capablanca (Presidency), Joaquín del Río Balmaseda (Justice), and Manuel Márquez Sterling (State). Coming out of retirement to assume the portfolio of treasury was Manual Despaigne, the position he held as a member of the "honest cabinet."

For one hundred days the provisional government devoted itself to the task of transforming Cuba with exalted purposefulness. The demands of 1923 became the decrees of 1933. This was the first government of the republic formed without the sanction and support of the United States. Under the injunction of "Cuba for Cubans," the new government proceeded to enact reform laws at a dizzying pace. Organizing its program along the "lines of modern democracy and . . . upon the pure principles of national sovereignty," the provisional government committed itself to economic reconstruction, social reform, and political reorganization. On the day of his inauguration as president, Grau unilaterally proclaimed the abrogation of the Platt Amendment. Reforms followed rapidly. The traditional political parties were dissolved. The government lowered utility rates by 40 percent and reduced interest rates. Women received the vote and the University secured autonomy. In labor matters, government reforms included minimum wages for sugar cane cutters, compulsory labor arbitration, an eight-hour day, workers' compensation, the establishment of a Ministry of Labor, a Nationalization of Labor decree requiring Cuban nationality for 50 percent of all employees in industry, commerce, and agriculture, and the cancellation of existing contract labor arrangements with Haiti and Jamaica. In agricultural matters, the government sponsored the creation of a *colono* association, guaranteed farmers permanent right over the land under cultivation, and inaugurated a program of land reform.[70]

The rhetoric of revolution notwithstanding, this was preeminently a reformist regime. It chose regulation over expropriation, the distribution of public lands over the redistribution of private property, the defense of trade union objectives over workers' party objectives. This was not a government without opposition, however. The forces of old Cuba responded to the September usurpation with unrestrained indignation. This was the ouster of the old political class, and it came at a singularly inopportune moment. The *cooperativista* parties that had deserted Machado as a means to survive the discredited regime once again faced persecution and extinction. So, too, did the ousted army officers who, for all their efforts to secure immunity from post-Machado reprisals, now found themselves vulnerable to prosecution and imprisonment. Foreign capital recoiled in horror at the new laws that regulated and restricted the freedom it had traditionally enjoyed under previous governments.[71]

Nor was it only old Cuba that opposed the provisional government. New political groups, including the ABC, OCRR, and the Unión Nacionalista, organizations that earlier had paid dearly to acquire political legitimacy in post-Machado Cuba, were not reconciled to this abrupt and inglorious end to their debut in national politics.

If the faction that made up the Céspedes government denounced the Grau regime as too radical, the PPC and CNOC condemned the new government as too moderate. The Communist party and labor continued to apply pressure on the Grau government throughout the autumn. Under ordinary circumstances, labor reforms might have met long-standing worker demands. But these were not ordinary circumstances. Neither minimum wages and maximum hours nor compulsory arbitration and workers' compensation addressed the immediate and fundamental issue: there was no work for workers. Labor demonstrations continued. By the end of September, workers had seized control of thirty-six sugar mills, representing some 30 percent of the national sugar production. Workers' militias organized, and in several instances, engaged army units.[72]

But the most implaccable opposition came from the United States. More than constitutionality had perished. The overthrow of the pro-U.S. government, the suppression of the traditional political parties, and the removal of the officer corps represented the dismantling of the internal structures that had underwritten and institutionalized U.S. hegemony. And in repudiating the Platt Amendment, the new government abolished the external source of Cuban dependency. The long-term implications of the policies of the new government were not lost on Washington. The defense of Cuban interests jeopardized U.S. interests. Labor legislation affected North American employers. Agrarian reform concerned U.S. landowners. The reduction of utility rates affected the Electric Bond and Share Company. In fact, so thoroughly had the United States penetrated Cuba that it was hardly possible for any social and economic legislation not to affect U.S. capital adversely. The tempo and tenor of the reform measures persuaded Welles that the provisional government aspired to nothing less than the elimination of U.S. influence in Cuba. "It is . . . within the bounds of possibility," Welles wrote with alarm two weeks after the coup, "that the social revolution which is under way cannot be checked. American properties and interests are being gravely prejudiced and the material damage to such properties will in all probability be very great."[73] Many of the government decrees were outright "confiscatory" in nature and enormously prejudicial to United States property interests.[74] "Our own commercial and export interests in Cuba," he asserted flatly, "cannot be revived under this government."[75] When the government announced in October an agreement with Mexico to train Cuban army officers, Welles drew immediate conclusions: "In view of the existing situation here and particularly in view of the fact that since the independence of the Republic of Cuba the training of Cuban officers had been undertaken solely in the United States or under the direction of American officers this step can only be construed as a deliberate effort by the present Government to show its intention of minimizing any form of American influence in Cuba."[76]

In unequivocal terms, Welles deliberately characterized the new government in terms calculated to promote suspicion and provoke opposition. The army had fallen under "ultra-radical control," Welles charged, and the new government was "frankly communistic."[77] He described Irisarri as a "radical of the extreme type" and Grau and Portela as "extreme radicals." Welles conceded that Franca was a "conservative business-man of good reputation," but insisted that he served merely as "window dressing."[78]

For the remainder of his stay in Havana, Welles pursued a policy designed to isolate the government diplomatically abroad and weaken the government at home. He turned immediately to unifying the opposition. Welles was mindful to the necessity to bolster the resolve of the ousted political groups and the dispossessed army officers to prevent either a diminution of antigovernment activity or, worse still, defections to the provisional regime. He accomplished this in several ways. The dispossessed groups looked immediately to Welles for help, and he did not disappoint them. He assured civilian and military groups that Washington would respond decisively. With the traditional political parties barred from government councils and the old officers removed from the army, the United States had lost direct access to and influence over local government. Armed intervention offered one means to recover lost authority. On the day of the formation of the pentarchy, Welles summoned the ousted political groups and army commanders to plot the restoration of the Céspedes government. Welles urged Washington to land "a certain number of troups," ostensibly to guard the U.S. embassy and protect foreign lives and property. In fact, he acknowledged, Céspedes could not be restored without the "aid of an American guard."[79] Welles was certain that the enlisted men would submit to the officers "if they could be freed from the control of the non-commissioned officers." And the only way to underwrite the Céspedes government "until a new Army could be organized under Cuban Army officers," Welles suggested, was "for the maintenance of order in Habana and Santiago de Cuba and perhaps one or two other points in the island by American Marines."[80] Two days later, he made his most ambitious proposal, recommending a "strictly limited intervention" entailing "the landing of a considerable force at Habana and lesser forces in certain of the most important ports of the Republic." This "strictly limited intervention" would provide the "police force to the legitimate Government of Cuba for a comparatively brief period," thereby enabling the Céspedes government to function as it had prior to its fall. Welles added:

> It is obvious, of course, that with a great portion of the Army in mutiny [the Céspedes government] could not maintain itself in power in any satisfactory manner unless the United States Government were willing, should it so request, to lend its assistance in the maintenance of public order until the Cuban Government had been afforded the time sufficient, through utilizing the services of the loyal officers of the Cuban Army, to form a new Army for which it would possess a nucleus in the troops which are still loyal and detachments of the rural guards, most of whom have not come out in support of the present regime.[81]

But requests for intervention received no support in Washington. On the contrary, Roosevelt moved immediately to prohibit intervention for the purpose of protecting property alone.[82] Secretary of State Hull also shrank from intervention. "Despite the legal right we possessed," Hull later recalled, "such an act would further embitter our relations with all Latin America." Armed intervention in Cuba, Hull feared, would have undone "all our protestations of nonintervention and noninterference."[83]

But the disinclination in Washington to act militarily did not suggest an inclination to acquiesce politically. If the United States would not overthrow the government from without, it would seek to undermine it from within by promoting continued instability. Three decades of policy imperatives fell suddenly into desuetude—stability and order were now inimical to U.S. interests in Cuba.

Destabilization required first the denial of U.S. recognition. Welles had earlier threatened to withdraw recognition to force Machado out of office. The withholding of recognition from the Grau government had a similar end, if the means differed somewhat. Optimally, nonrecognition would produce the collapse of the government. But failing that, it would force the government into moderation, a way of exacting concessions from Havana in exchange for normalization of relations. "If our Government recognized the existing Cuban government before it has undergone radical modification," Welles argued, "such action would imply our lending official support to a regime which is opposed by all business and financial interests in Cuba; by all the powerful political groups and in general . . . all the elements that hold out any promise of being able to govern Cuba. . . . Such action on our part would undoubtedly help to keep the present government in power."[84] Nonrecognition would contribute to overthrowing a government antagonistic toward U.S. interests in Cuba, Welles noted, without damaging "our continental interests."[85]

Nonrecognition was also indispensable to encourage continued turbulence in Cuba. This was deliberate orchestration of chaos, designed to maintain pressure on both the government and the opposition. Nonrecognition obstructed government efforts to reach reconciliation with the opponents precisely because it offered the opposition incentive to resist the government. Those who otherwise might have supported the government were deterred; those who opposed the government were encouraged to participate in active conspiracy and armed resistance.

With the government thus thrown on the defensive, the United States was free to pursue internal subversion. To the deposed political groups, Welles urged continued resistance. To the displaced officers, he counseled a continued boycott of the army. Nowhere, in fact, did U.S. policy have as telling results as with the army officers. Throughout early September the new government urgently sought to reunite the officers with the army. The sergeants' mutiny had separated the officers from their commands, resulting in a deterioraion of morale and discipline. The dispossessed commanders, moreover, quickly developed into the axis of conspiracy and antigovernment intrigue, a continual source of problems to the new government. The officers' return would restore the technical and professional skills necessary to morale and military discipline. The officers' resumption of command, further, would also relieve the noncommissioned officers of the odiom of mutiny while strengthening the government internally, validating the September 4 movement in much the same fashion that the officer's participation on August 12 had lent support ot the Céspedes government.

On September 7 the government summond an officers' delegation to the presidential palace to discuss the means through which to reunite the armed forces. The government proposed organizing a junta of five officers and Sergeant Batista to supervise a reorganization of the armed forces and oversee the reintegration of the military. The officers declined the government offer, refusing to sanction in any form the legitimacy of the sergeants' mutiny.[86] In late September, the Grau government ordered the officers to return to their command, an order rejected by the army chiefs.

The unwillingness of the officers to rejoin the army was a decision inspired in large part by U.S. policy. The officers' boycott contributed to conditions of instability and uncertainty. In mid-September, some 400 army officers assembled at the Hotel Nacional in Havana. The army commanders sustained their boycott through September, maintaining an attitude of watchful waiting, certain that, even as they remained idle, larger if as yet unrevealed forces were at work to oust the Grau government and return them to their positions of command. Certainly these were impressions encouraged by U.S. authorities. As early as September 11, Horacio Ferrer, secretary of war under Céspedes, conferred with Welles and learned that the new government would "continue unrecognized by the United States."[87] Nonrecognition exercised a powerful restraint on the officers, encouraging army leaders to remain away from their command in the belief that the new government could not long survive without U.S. support. On September 9 Welles reported that the officers had entered into a "definite compact" not to support "any government except a legitimate government."[88] Several days later, Ferrer asserted flatly that the officers would never serve under any government not recognized in Washington.[89] Stated in different terms, as the U.S. military attache learned, many officers were prepared to "pledge allegiance to any government in the United States recognizes."[90]

Certainly, in case of the officers, the policy of nonrecognition encouraged the military leadership to distance itself from the government, which was precisely what it was designed to achieve. Had the United States recognized the government and allowed it to constitute itself under conditions of normal diplomatic relations, a continuation of the officers' boycott would have been unlikely. Such a turn of events would have made their position untenable, transforming the officers into mutineers against duly recognized authority. As long as the new government remained un-recognized, however, as long as the United States claimed to uphold the authority of the "legitimate government" of Céspedes, the officers too could also righteously claim to defend legitimacy.

The prospect of armed intervention further encouraged the officers to remain away from their commands. Indeed, in the days immediately fol-lowing the coup, military intervention seemed imminent. An estimated 1,000 marines were mobilized in Quantico, Virginia, and prepared for de-ployment to Cuba. The Atlantic Fleet, a flotilla of some thirty warships, formed a cordon around the island.[91] One Cuban officer later recalled that Welles had dissuaded the army commanders "from returning to their commands, which would have strengthened the position of the student government and might have tipped the scales in their favor both with the Cuban public and the American government." The U.S. military attache also advised the officers "under no circumstances to return to their com-mands, stating that the American government would never tolerate a re-volt of the enlisted men, such as had taken place, or a change of govern-ment by them, and that American intervention was undoubtedly the next step."[92]

The signs were unmistakable—armed intervention was imminent. These were compelling circumstances, certainly sufficient to persuade the officers of the logic of their decision and the legitimacy of their deed. Few army leaders were disposed to jeopardize their careers by breaking ranks to join a government expected momentarily to fall to U.S. military intervention. The continued boycott was essential, for it corroborated the charge that the new government lacked support and authority. The offi-cers who only three weeks earlier had led the army against Machado to prevent intervention now refused to lead the army under Grau to provoke intervention.

In late September, the government abandoned all hopes of reconcilia-tion with the officers. The separated officers were proclaimed deserters and ordered arrested. After a brief siege of the Hotel Nacional in early October, the army leaders surrendered to government authorities.[93]

A second blow to antigovernment forces was not long in coming. In early November, a combined force of the ABC and Unión Nacionalista joined a rebellion of dissident army elements. After several days of fight-ing in Havana, government forces overcame resistance and ended the revolt.

The arrest of the officers and the defeat of the ABC and Unión Nacionalista had several immediate effects. Both reversals signaled the collapse of organized opposition to the new government. Resistance continued, to be sure, consisting of sporadic acts of sabotage an desultory deeds of terrorism. But the principal opposition groups that had formed the previous government, and around which Welles had hoped to reconstitute the "legitimate government," had been dispersed and demoralized. The displacement of the former officer corps also paved the way for a sweeping reorganization of the armed forces. Some four hundred sergeants, corporals, and enlisted men received commissions and filled the newly created vacancies in the army command. Batista was formally promoted to the rank of colonel and ratified in his position as chief of the army.[94]

VIII

The arrest of the former officers, to be sure, strengthened the position of the provisional government. But more than the prestige and power of the government increased. The defeat of the ABC and the Unión Nacionalista and, in particular, the purge of the old officer corps were political triumphs for the army and a personal victory for Fulgencio Batista. Certainly government successes eased political pressure, but in so doing also served to set in sharp relief the contradictions within the ruling coalition. In a very real sense, the civilians and the soldiers had gone separate ways shortly after September 4. This was not so much the result of new disagreements as it was the product of old differences. To be sure, both remained inextricably joined by a common transgression against duly constituted authority. They shared a mutual concern in the success of the provisional government, if only because they shared a common fate if it failed. Mishap to one meant misfortune for the other.

Nevertheless, the gap between the civilians and the soldiers continued to widen through the early fall. The civilians had carried Cuba deep into the uncertain realm of experimental government. As the civilians continued to advance on their "march to create a new Cuba," the army became an increasingly reluctant escort. Military support of the provisional government was always more practical than political, more a form of self-interest than a function of solidarity. This was the government that had sanctioned the sedition and validated 400 new commissions. This was the government, in short, from which the new army command derived legitimacy and to which it was inexorably linked. But the military leaders were anxious for a political settlement, if for no other reason than to legitimize their recent promotions. The army command saw little to be gained by social experimentation, except a prolongation of the political crisis. Indeed, many commanders feared the government policies would result inevitably in visiting grief on the new officers corps. It had been from the start only a coalition of convenience, and nothing had changed except that by mid-autumn the soldiers found themselves increasingly inconvenienced by civilian policies. The new army command perceived the reform projects as hazardous ventures, ill-conceived programs by a government upon whose continued solvency they depended to underwrite their ill-gotten commissions.

But alternatives were scarce. Who else would have sanctioned 400 new commissions in the aftermath of an army mutiny? Only another source of authority, capable of constituting itself into a legitimate government willing to underwrite the new order in the army, or evidence that the provisional government no longer possessed the will or means to uphold the new commissions, could persuade Batista to abandon the government that had originally infused political life into military sedition.

These were the fateful flaws, stress points discerned perceptively by Welles. By mid-fall, the emphasis of U.S. policy shifted away from promoting unity among government opponents to encouraging disunity among its supporters. Welles early perceived the inherent cross-purposes that separated the civilian reformers from the army officers. He quickly devoted himself to exploiting these internal contradictions. The September army mutiny, he reminded Washington only days after the arrests of the old officers, did "not take place in order to place Grau San Martín in power." He noted, correctly, that the "divergence between the Army and civilian elements in the government is fast becoming daily more marked" as Batista's authority and influence increased. The surrender of the former officers did not "indicate consolidation of the position of the government but solely a decidedly increased prestige for the Army as distinguished from the government."[95] Two weeks later Welles reiterated his contention: "The mutiny was not directed against Céspedes or his cabinet; it was not political in its origin and it was not . . . in any sense responsive to a social movement."[96]

These conditions had important implications for the shaping of U.S. policy, for they suggested the absence of unanimity within the provisional government and the presence of mutual suspicions to play upon. These were insights, too, into the character of the ruling coalition and, with the fall of the old officer corps, gave direction to U.S. policy. For the second time in as many months, the United States appealed directly to the army to overturn a government that had fallen into disfavor in Washington. Throughout the autumn Welles maintained a close and increasingly cordial contact with Batista. "The situation as regards my relations with Batista is," Welles conceded in early October, "of course, anomalous. I feel it necessary to make plain, however, that there does not exist at the present time in Cuba any authority whatever except himself and that in the event of further disturbances which may endanger the lives and properties of Americans or foreigners in the Republic it seems to be essential that this relationship be maintained."[97]

But Welles had more on his mind than protection for foreign property. On October 4, only days after the arrest of the former officers, Welles held a "protracted and very frank discussion" with Batista in which he informed the army chief that he was the "only individual in Cuba today who represented authority." He explained that his leadership of the army had earned him the support of "the very great majority of the commercial and financial interests in Cuba who are looking for protection and who could only find such protection in himself." Political factions that only weeks earlier had openly opposed him were now "in accord that his control of the Army as Chief of Staff should be continued as the only possible solution and were willing to support him in that capacity." However, the only obstacle to an equitable political settlement, and presumably recognition and a return to conditions of normality, the ambassador suggested, "was the unpatriotic and futile obstinancy of a small groups of young men who should be studying in the university instead of playing politics and of a few individuals who had joined with them for selfish motives." In a thinly veiled warning, Welles reminded Batista of the tenuous position in which his continued affiliation with the government placed him: "Should the present government go down in disaster, that disaster would necessarily inextricably involve not only himself but the safety of the Republic, which he has publicly pledged himself to maintain."[98]

They met again several days later, this time at Batista's request. Since their last conversation, Batista indicated to Welles, he had been "deeply impressed by the fact that delegates of all the important business and financial groups in Cuba" had visited him to insist upon the creation of a government in which the public could have confidence." Batista was now persuaded that the provisional government was a "complete failure" and that a new coalition government, one in which moderate political groups and commercial interests of the country could have confidence, was "an absolute necessity." Batista had also come to appreciate the necessity of U.S. recognition "before any improvement in conditions" on the island could be expected."[99]

Welles's comments could not have been interpreted by Batista in any other fashion than an invitation to create a new government. By the end of October, Batista had arrived at the conclusion that "a change in government is imperative."[100] Welles had forged a coalition consisting of the new political groups, the traditional political parties, foreign capital, and the State Department to which Batista could find an alternative authority that would at once ratify the new army command and organize a government consistent with U.S. policy needs.

Welles's tacit invitation to Batista to create a new government and providing the army chief with necessary political base created the conditions that allowed Batista to disassociate himself from the government. By early December, Welles reported that Batista was "actively seeking a change in government" owing to apprehansion of army intrigue against him, the constant and "inevitable" attempts at revolution, and fear of U.S. military intervention.[101]

In early December, too, Welles was replaced in Havana by Jefferson Caffery, appointed "personal representative of the president." Not a change of policy, only a change of personnel. Several weeks later, Batista asked Caffery bluntly what the United States "wanted done for recognition." Reiterating Washington's determination to withhold recognition, Caffery urged the creation of a new government capable of inspiring confidence at home and abroad.[102] In mid-January, Batista transferred army support from Grau to Unión Nacionalista leader Carlos Mendieta. Within five days, the United States recognized the new government.

12.

Cuba, 1902–1934:
A Retrospect

I

The inauguration of Carlos Mendieta seemed to signify a return to the established political conventions. A veteran officer of the war for independence, he had reached the rank of colonel. Mendieta was somewhat younger than the generals who had dominated republican politics, but youth proved to be no obstacle to his advancement in the Liberal party. He received the Liberal nomination for vice-president in 1916. In 1923 he joined the reformist cause and served as one of the directors of the Veterans and Patriots movement. He late broke with Machado over the issue of reelection and led a reformist contingent out of the Liberal party to form the new Unión Nacionalista.

For all the differences that may have existed between Mendieta and his predecessors, however, he was still a representative of the old politics, a member of the political class that had governed Cuba since the establishment of the republic in 1902. So it seemed that his inauguration in January 1934 heralded the return of old times and the restoration of old leaders. The political class, it appeared, had reclaimed its dominant position over the polity and now politics as usual would return to the ways of the past.

But Cuba was different after 1933, and would never be the same. The brief Mendieta presidency (1934–1935) did not, in fact, signify the restoration of the political class; Mendieta presided helplessly over the final dissolution of the old state bourgeoisie. The traditional political parties emerged from the *machadato* disorganized and discredited, their leaders in disgrace, and their programs in disarray.

The new political groups had not fared much better. By the end of 1933 the rank and file had dispersed, some in exile, others in prison. The ABC, for example, was already in decline by early 1934. The reformist sector of the provisional government regrouped in exile under Grau San Martín and subsequently organized into the Partido Revolucionario Cubano (Auténtico). Another group organized in Cuba another Antonio Guiteras into Joven Cuba and returned to armed struggle.

Fragmented political organizations were symptomatic of a fractured polity. Old parties were without leaders, new leaders were with parties. But social tensions continued, indeed, they intensified. Labor militancy increased and the influence of the PCC expanded. Only two months after the installation of the Mendieta administration, Caffery wrote that the new government was "fighting for its life against the communistic element."[1] Cuba again appeared at the threshold of open class warfare. In March 1935 a general strike once more raised the spectre of revolution.[2]

The old political class may have expired, but the United States was not left without local allies. New political leadership emerged to fill the vacuum created by the demise of the traditional parties, this in the form of the new army command. The military had long been the armed extension of the state bourgeoisie. It had served the civilian officeholders well, principally as the bulwark of status-quo politics. In fact, so well had the military performed its assigned task that by the early 1930s it had been singled out for extinction by the new generation of political opposition. After 1933, the military acquired interests of its own and effectively transformed political groups—old and new—into instruments for the defense of those interests. Under Fulgencio Batista, the army established its autonomy from a formerly autonomous political class. The articulation of social structures created new pressures on the old officeholders, pressures they were ill prepared to meet. Indeed, these developments challenged the fundamental assumptions of republican politics. After 1933, only the army retained unity and cohesion, the basis upon which it advanced its claim to rule. It possessed the means to contain class conflict. The army dislodged the old political groups and displaced the new ones, becoming in the process itself transformed into an autonomous sector of the political class, allied to and in defense of foreign interests. After the 1935 general strike, Batista emerged as a Bonapartist personality.[3] The military leadership replaced the old civilian officeholders, controlling the state as a means of expanding its political power and personal fortune. Graft and corruption prevailed. From the senior levels of the new army command to remote Rural Guard posts, the members of the armed forces actively pursued personal wealth. Control of the army, the U.S. military attache reported in 1938, "is similar to that practiced by American gang-leaders; that as long as the chief of Staff can obtain certain emoluments, financial, political and military, for his Lieutenant Colonels, and guarantee their immunity to punishment, he can command their loyalty and obedience as a body."[4]

II

Social tensions continued into the 1930s, but old forms of intervention could no longer adequately protect U.S. interests. Nor were they perhaps even relevant to the new social reality in Cuba. This was the meaning of the abrogation of the Platt Amendment in May 1934. A new commercial treaty later in August revised tariff schedules and opened the way for restored U.S. dominance over the Cuban economy.[5]

Intervention in both its military form and political function had served two distinct but interrelated purposes. Immediately, it was designed to protect and promote U.S. interests. Secondarily, it defended local elites, whose survival was vital to the success of the hegemonial system. But the rescue of the local bourgeoisie was not entirely unqualified. Both in 1898 and 1933 U.S. intervention served to contain revolutionary movements. On both occasions, representatives of bourgeois interests had unsuccessfully advanced claims of leadership over the polity; first in the form of the Autonomist party and later in the Veterans and Patriots movement, they organized for political power, and failed. But more than this, they contributed to conditions that soon threatened them with extinction. And quickly, on both occasions, they abandoned aspirations of political leadership to preserve positions of privilege and property. And each time they appealed for U.S. intervention.

But intervention, when it did come, was not an unmixed blessing. In the end it facilitated the total eclipse of the remnants of a nationally based dominant class. In the aftermath of the military occupation of 1899–1902, the Cuban planter class had all but ceased to function. These developments were repeated during the late 1920s and early 1930s, and institutionalized in the new Reciprocity Treaty of 1934. In both cases the indigenous threat to local bourgeois interests was contained by U.S. intervention. But in the aftermath so were local bourgeois interests, as the United States expanded its control over Cuban property and production. During the early 1900s, foreign capital expanded at the expense of the old landed elite, principally in agriculture, mining, and transportation. During the 1930s, foreign capital expanded again, this time at the expense of the new entrepreneurial bourgeoisie, principally in industry and manufacturing. In a curious and fateful fashion, the Customs-Tariff Law of 1927, designed originally to promote national industry, ultimately encouraged foreign manufacture at the expense of Cuban capital. Almost immediately U.S. capital expanded directly into those sectors of the economy that Cubans had previously opened for themselves. One effective method of eluding the Cuban tariff regulations was for foreign manufacturers to establish subsidiary firms on the island. Cuban manufacturers producing commodities originally protected by Cuban tariff regulations received new competition. The depression dealt another blow to the nascent entrepreneurial bourgeoisie. That many entrepreneurs had been also ranking political leaders, many of whom were forced into exile during the 1933 crisis and required to liquidate their property, also weakened the ranks of the Cuban property owners. Many foreign-owned subsidiaries in Cuba secured the participation of local capital, many did not. Some local operations were absorbed totally by the new foreign firms, others simply failed. The effects were not dissimilar to the displacement of the planter class earlier in the century, whereby Cuban landowners were integrated directly into North American capitalist structures. As early as 1928, only a year after the passage of the Customs-Tariff Law, new foreign factories were established in Cuba to produce the precise commodities protected by law, specifically processed foods, soaps, perfumes, and textiles. The U.S. companies included Mennen, Armour, Proctor and Gamble, Colgate, Pabst, and Fleischmann. The Swiss Nestlé Company established a factory in Bayamo to produce condensed milk and butter.[6]

III

For more than three decades the Platt Amendment served as the means to establish and expand U.S. hegemony in Cuba. It was not an indispensable means of hegemony, just a convenient one—it was always available and altogether adaptable. Hegemony was a system affecting all of Cuban society. It could not be exercised on this scale without affecting profoundly the structure and substance of Cuban society. The result was debased political institutions, deformed social formations, and dependent economic relationships.

Intervention seemed to have no limits. It was a self-perpetuating process. More intervention required more intervention. Thus, the demand for political order led to the call for honest elections as a means to avert armed rebellion. To guarantee honest elections, the United States established appropriate governmental agencies, prepared electoral codes, and ordered new censuses. To make certain that the agencies operated efficiently, the codes were enforced impartially, and the census was taken correctly required, in turn, the United States to oversee their operation. To guarantee the integrity of the ballotting procedure, the United States placed election supervisors in the field. And once in the field, these agents were called upon to mediate even the slightest dispute between a voter and the local election agency.

In the end, the United States came to distrust Cuban politics altogether, fearful that political dabate would lead to political disorder. For almost thirty years, the United States moved toward replacing politics from within by administration from without. And because almost every issue in Cuba involved at least two sides, hence debate, and—in the judgment of the State Department—potential disorder, nothing escaped U.S. attention. Under the auspices of the Platt Amendment, Washington claimed open and unlimited authority over all aspects of all levels of public administration. On occasion it reached preposterous extremes. Between 1914 and 1915, the Cuban congress debated the liberalizing of divorce laws and repealing religious marriage. The State Department opposed both. Secretary of State William Jennings Bryan instructed the U.S. minister in Havana:

> I write to suggest that you unofficially and confidentially confer with the President and *advise against any change in the marriage law*. Marriage should be allowed before religious and civil authorities. To deny either kind of marriage would be a backward step. . . . Earnestly advise against any change of the law in this respect. In the matter of divorce consideration should be given to the fact that Cuba is a Catholic country, and causes should be as few as public opinion will permit. While insisting on religious freedom in every respect the Cuban government should be

careful not to undermine that respect for religion which is essential for moral progress.[7]

The Platt Amendment as an instrument of hegemony had long outlived its usefulness at the time of its abrogation. Defenders and detractors alike agreed that it contributed to creating more problems than it solved. It was a visible symbol and provocative manifestation of U.S. tutelage, always palpable reminder of stunted sovereignty. Nothing served to arouse national indignation more than the Platt Amendment.[8] In 1934, no one less than Sumner Welles ccould proclaim: "No greater impediment to the free exercise by the Cuban people of their inherent right to sovereignty could have been devised. It has operated as a means of deterring the Cubans from exercising the muscles of self-reliance essential for self-government."[9]

As armed intervention diminished as a plausible policy option, it became essential to abrogate the Platt Amendment. Over the course of three decades, political contenders in Cuba learned to manipulate U.S. treaty requirements, and the treaty requirement of intervention became a source of instability that created precisely the conditions requiring the intervention the Platt Amendment was designed to prevent. Rather than forestalling disorder, the Platt Amendment provided on incentive. Cuban political contenders early displayed considerable talent and ingenuity in exploiting U.S. interests as a means to promote local partisan needs. Having imposed the Platt Amendment on Cuba to meet U.S. needs, Washington could not prevent its manipulation to meet Cuban needs. By requiring a government adequate for the protection of life, liberty, and property, the Platt Amendment placed foreign property precisely in the jeopardy it desired to avoid.

These realizations developed slowly in Washington. Shifting interpretations of the purview and purpose of intervention reflected accurately recurring attempts to come to terms with new realities as they affected the changing nature of North American interests in Cuba. Needs defined by Washington as strategic between 1898 and 1906 were met with the treaty guaranteeing the right of intervention and the armed intervention of 1906. Direct investment in Cuba in the form of industrial capital and commercial needs between 1909 and 1919 inspired political intervention designed to influence diplomatically the course of public administration in Cuba. The increase of finance capital to Cuba and the increasing concentration of monopoly capital after 1919 prompted direct supervision over national government. Each policy shift, in turn, required reinterpretation of the scope of intervention sanctioned by the Platt Amendment.

But shifts in the exercise of hegemony also corresponded to the political and social changes overtaking Cuban society. Cuba between 1923 and 1933 was considerably different from the Cuba of between 1902 and 1912. The social system had become more complicated, class structures were more clearly defined, and social confict more distinctly articulated. New social groups emerged to rival the incumbent officeholders for power. They were in a position to make—and they made—new demands on the state. The net effect was the creation of new constituencies to which the political class was increasingly obliged to respond. No longer could the powerholders remain wholly and unabashedly subservient to foreign interests—not without serious repercussions. No longer could control of the state serve solely the interests of the incumbent officeholders.

These developments had far-reaching implications for the exercise of U.S. hegemony. The United States faced new political and economic rivals in Cuba. No longer could it make unlimited demands on power holders without impairing their ability to rule. Pressure from without could be disastrous within, effectively incapacitating the ability of the state bourgeoisie to govern and serve foreign interests. Hegemonial demands were placing local allies in an untenable position. Too many competing constituencies with too many conflicting demands created impossible contradictions, all of which were exposed during the early 1930s. The revolutionary crisis developed when the regime failed to meet the challenge of international conditions and was caught between the conflicting pressures of internal class structures on one hand, and international pressures on the other.

The usefulness of the Platt Amendment was over. As the struggle against Machado revealed, it was the political opposition to a government supported by the United States that found the Platt Amendment of any political value—an anomaly that did not pass undetected in Washington. Antigovernment forces resorted to the destruction of property as a means of embarrassing the government and precipitate armed intervention to overthrow an unpopular regime. By 1934, the defense of U.S. interests in Cuba required the abrogation of the Platt Amendment. It served to remove an irritant in U.S.-Cuban relations. It also provided a powerful boost to the Mendieta-Batista government. Even the final act of abrogation was not without some political utility.

An era came to a close, but the effects lasted through another. The Platt Amendment would be something that Cubans would neither forgive nor forget. The new generation that emerged from the *machadato* made its political debut in a national system dominated by the Platt Amendment, and would long continue to display behavior conditioned by that experience. Long after the Platt Amendment ceased to govern U.S. relations with Cuba, it continued to influence Cuban relationships with the United States. Its impact on Cuban political culture survived one more generation.

Notes

Bibliography

Index

Notes

Chapter 1.   Everything in Transition

1. Cabrera to Rodríguez, September 18, 1896, José Ignacio Rodríguez Papers.

2. José R. Alvarez Díaz, et al., *A Study on Cuba* (Coral Gables: University of Miami Press, 1965), pp. 91–92; Ramiro Guerra y Sánchez, *Sugar and Society in the Caribbean* (New Haven, Conn.: Yale University Press, 1964), p. 63; Ramiro Guerra y Sánchez, et al., *Historia de la nación cubana* (Havana: Editorial Historia de la Nación Cubana, 1952), 7:153; H. E. Friedlander, *Historia económica de Cuba* (Havana: Jesús Montero, 1944), p. 432.

3. Alvarez Díaz, *A Study on Cuba*, p. 93.

4. Hugh Thomas, *Cuba, the Pursuit of Freedom* (New York: Harper and Row, 1971), p. 272.

5. Badeau, "Report on the Present Condition of Cuba," February 7, 1884, Despatches from U.S. Consuls in Havana, 1783–1906, General Records of the Department of State, RG 59, U.S. National Archives (hereinafter cited as Despatches/Havana).

6. Vickers to Assistant Secretary of State Davis, October 24, 1883, Despatches from U.S. Consuls in Matanzas, 1820–1899, General Records of the Department of State, RG 59, U.S. National Archives (hereinafter cited as Despatches/Matanzas).

7. Pierce to Assistant Secretary of State Davis, August 10, 1883, Despatches from U.S. Consuls in Cienfuegos, 1876–1906, General Records of the Department of State, RG 59, National Archives (hereinafter cited as Despatches/Cienfuegos).

8. Badeau to Secretary of State, March 6, 1884, Despatches/Havana.

9. Gaston Descamps, *La crisis azucarera y la Isla de Cuba* (Havana: La Propaganda Literaria, 1885), p. 143.

10. Badeau, "Report on the Present Condition of Cuba," February 7, 1884, Despatches/Havana.

11. *New York Times,* July 17, 1884.

12. *El País,* November 26, 1889.

13. *Diario de Matanzas,* January 18, 1885.

14. Vickers to Davis, July 2, 1884, Despatches/Matanzas.

15. Vickers to Davis, August 27, 1884, ibid.

16. See Williams to Porter, January 12, 1887, Despatches/Havana; Francisco Moreno, *Cuba y su gente (apuntes para la historia)* (Madrid: Establecimiento Tipográfico de Enrique Teodora, 1887), pp. 158−59.

17. Vickers to Davis, August 27, 1884, Despatches/Matanzas.

18. *La Lucha*, March 18, 1889.

19. Victor S. Clark, "Labor Conditions in Cuba," *Bulletin of the Department of Labor* 7 (July 1902), 675.

20. Ibid.

21. *Diario de la Marina*, August 16, 1892; Rafael María Merchán, *Cuba, justificación de sus guerras de independencia*, 2d ed. (Havana: Imprenta Nacional de Cuba, 1961), p. 140.

22. *Diario de la Marina*, August 16, 1892.

23. See *El País*, August 24, 1892; Merchán, *Cuba*, p. 376.

24. See Benjamín de Céspedes, *La prostitución en la ciudad de La Habana* (Havana: Establecimiento Tipográfico O'Reilly, 1888); Ignacio D. Ituarte, *Crímenes y criminals en La Habana* (Havana: n.p., 1893).

25. *Boletín Comercial*, April 10, 1890.

26. Massimo Livi-Bacci, "Fertility and Population Growth in Spain in the Eighteenth and Nineteenth Centuries," *Daedulus* 97 (Spring 1968), 525.

27. Raimundo Cabrera, *Cuba and the Cubans*, trans. Laura Guiteras (Philadelphia: Levytype, 1896), p. 41; Francisco Moreno, *El país chocolate (la inmoralidad en Cuba)* (Madrid: Imprenta de F. García Herrero, 1887), pp. 21−26; Rafael G. Eslava, *Juicio crítico de Cuba en 1887* (Havana: Establecimiento Tipográfico, 1887), pp. 27−28, 69.

28. For biographical annotations on the key Spanish property owners, see Francisco Camacho, *Peninsulares y cubanos* (Havana: Imprenta Mercantil, 1891).

29. *El País* reported on March 8, 1892, that several Spanish commercial firms had agreed among themselves to hire only *peninsulares*. See Luis Estévez Romero, *Desde el Zanjón hasta Baire*, 2d ed. (Havana: Editorial de Ciencias Sociales, 1974), 1 : 310.

30. Tesifonte Gallego García, *Cuba por fuera* (Havana: La Propaganda Literaria, 1890), p. 160.

31. Merchán, *Cuba*, pp. 38−39; Duvon C. Corbitt, "Immigration in Cuba," *Hispanic American Historical Review* 22 (May 1942), 302−08; Carlos Martí, *Los catalanes en América: Cuba*, 2d ed. (Havana: Imprenta J. Hernández Lapido, 1921), pp. 275−327.

32. Merchán, *Cuba*, p. 49. See also Juan Luis Martín, "El combatiente cubano en función de pueblo," *Cuadernos de Historia Habanera* 30 (1945), 49−50, 57.

33. Fernando Portuondo del Prado, *Historia de Cuba*, 6th ed. (Havana: Instituto Cubano del Libro, 1965), p. 434.

34. See Calixto C. Masó, *Historia de Cuba* (Miami: Ediciones Universal, 1976), p. 299; Portuondo del Prado, *Historia de Cuba*, pp. 437, 484.

35. José Antonio Ramos, *Manual del perfecto fulanista. Apuntes para el estudio de nuestra dinámica política-social* (Havana: Jesús Montero, 1916), pp. 166−67; Dennis B. Wood, "The Long Revolution: Class Relations and Political Conflict in Cuba, 1868−1968," *Science and Society* 24 (Spring 1970), 4−5; Robin Blackburn, "Prologue to the Cuban Revolution," *New Left Review* 21 (October 1963), 56.

36. James W. Steele, *Cuban Sketches* (New York: G. P. Putnam's Son, 1811), p. 124. See also Fernando Ortiz, *Cuban Counterpoint: Tobacco and Sugar*, trans. Harriet de Onis (New York: Random House, 1970), p. 63.

37. Edwin F. Atkins, *Sixty Years in Cuba* (Cambridge, Mass.: Riverside Press, 1926), pp. 30−121; Thomas, *Cuba, the Pursuit of Freedom*, p. 290.

38. By the early 1890s, ranking members of the planter bourgeoisie had acquired U.S. citizenship and included: Juan Pedro Baró, Perfecto Lacosta, Andrés Terry, Arturo Averhoff,

Francisco J. Cazares, Francisco D. Duque, Carlos Manuel García y Ruiz, Alberto V. de Goicuría, José González, Domingo González y Alfonso, Cristobal N. Madán, Antonio Martínez, Federico P. Montes, Luis Felipe Morejón y Márquez, Joaquín Pérez Cruz, Manuel A. Recio, José Rafael de los Reyes y García, Juan Rosell, Francisco Soria y Díaz, Manuel de la Torre, José Ignacio Toscano, Manuel de la Vega, and José Antonio Yznaga.

39. Williams to Assistant Secretary of State Porter, December 28, 1886, Despatches/ Havana.

40. For the Autonomist program, see *Diario de la Marina*, August 2, 1878. See also Ramón Infiesta, *El autonomismo cubano: su razón y manera* (Havana: Jesús Montero, 1939); F. A. Conte, *Las aspiraciones del Partido Liberal de Cuba* (Havana: Imprenta de A. Alvarez y Compañía, 1892); Eliseo Giberga, "Las ideas políticas en Cuba en el siglo XIX," *Cuba Contemporánia* 10 (April 1916), 347–81. For one of the most thorough studies of the Autonomist party, see Rafael Montoro, *El ideal autonomista* (Havana: Editorial Cuba, 1936).

41. See José Martí, "El Partido Revolucionario Cubano," April 3, 1892, in José Martí, *Obras Completas*, ed. Jorge Quintana (Caracas: n.p., 1964), vol. 1, pt. 2, pp. 307–13. Some of the better accounts of the origins and organization of the PRC include José Antonio Portuondo, "Ideología del Partido Revolucionario Cubano," *Cuadernos de Historia Habanera* 22 (1942), 63–70; Jorge Ibarra, "Hacia la organización revolucionaria." *Bohemia* 71 (January 26, 1979); Jorge Román Hernández, "Consideración sobre la obra unificadora de Martí y el Partido Revolucionario Cubano," *Anuario Martiano* 7 (1977), 241–51; Mario Mencia, "Martí: la unidad revolucionaria," *Bohemia* 68 (January 30, 1976), 88–93.

42. Portuondo del Prado, *Historia de Cuba*, p. 501. See also "Estadística electoral," in Estévez Romero, *Desde el Zanjón hasta Baire* 2:303–04.

43. Merchán, *Cuba*, pp. 46–47, 73, 111, 121; Cabrera, *Cuba and the Cubans*, 172–73; Estévez Romero, *Desde el Zanjón hasta Baire* 1:313, 2:54–57, 68–69.

44. In Merchán, *Cuba*, p. 172.

45. *El País*, January 7, 1891.

46. *Diario de la Marina*, April 5, 1895. See also Enrique José Varona, *De la colonia a la república* (Havana: Sociedad Editorial Cuba Contemporánea, 1916), p. 78.

47. See María de Labra to María Gálvez, June 18, 1895, *Boletín del Archivo Nacional* 26 (January–December 1927), 240–43. See also "Exposición dirigida al gobierno de S.M. por la Junta Central del Partido Liberal," September 18, 1895, enclosure in Williams to Uhl, October 18, 1895, Despatches/Havana.

48. In Juan Ortega Rubio, *Historia de la regencia de María Cristina Habsbourg Lorena* (Madrid: Imprenta, Litografía y Casa Editorial Felipe González Rojas, 1905–1906), 3:11; F. de León y Castillo, *Mis tiempos* (Madrid: Librería de los Sucesores de Hernando, 1972), 2:82.

49. Perhaps General Weyler himself provides the most detailed account of the Weyler command: see Valeriano Weyler, *Mi mando en Cuba* (Madrid: Imprenta de Felipe González Rojas, 1910–1911).

50. See Eliseo Giberga, *Obras de Eliseo Giberga* (Havana: Imprenta y Papelería de Rambla, Bouza y Cía., 1930–1931), 3:241–43; Lorenzo G. del Portillo, *La guerra de Cuba (el primer año)* (Key West: Imprenta "La Propaganda," 1896), p. 203; Emilio Roig de Leuchsenring, *Weyler en Cuba* (Havana: Editorial Páginas, 1947), p. 54; Emilio Reverter, *Cuba española*. *Reseña histórica de la insurrección cubana en 1895* (Barcelona: Centro Editorial de Alberto Martín, 1897–1899), 3:454–60.

51. Lee to Rockwell, July 3, 1896, Despatches/Havana.

52. Francisco Pi y Margall and Francisco Pi y Arsuaga, *Historia de España en el siglo XIX* (Barcelona: Miguel Seguí, 1902), 7:362; José Conangla Fontanilles, *Cuba y Pi y Margall* (Havana: Editorial Lex, 1947), pp. 309–10. See also Emilio Valdés Ynfante, *Cubanos en*

Fernando Poo: horrores de la dominación española (Havana: Imprenta "El Fígaro," 1898).

53. Gilson Willets, *The Triumph of Yankee Doodle* (New York: F. Tennyson Neely, 1896), pp. 171–72.

54. The role of José Martí in the ideological transfiguration of Cuban separatism is central. See John Kirk, *José Martí, Mentor of the Cuban Nation* (Gainesville: University Presses of Florida, 1983), pp. 65–152; Pedro Pablo Rodríguez, "La idea de liberación nacional en José Martí," *Pensamiento Crítico* 49–50 (February–March 1971), 120–69; Manuel Navarro Luna, "Martí y la reforma agraria," *Hoy Domingo*, May 20, 1962, p. 2; Manuel Maldonado, "Martí y su concepto de la revolución," *Casa de las Américas* 20 (July–August 1971), 3–12; Leopoldo Horrego Estuch, "Martí: su ideología," *Bohemia* 57 (January 22, 1965), 99–101.

55. Máximo Gómez, "Carta al presidente del Club 'Obreros de Independencia,'" n.d., *Casa de las Américas* 9 (September–October, 1968), p. 123.

56. See Matías Duque, *Nuestra patria* (Havana: Imprenta Montalvo y Cía., 1923), p. 144; Juan F. Risquet, *Rectificaciones: la cuestión político-social en la isla de Cuba* (Havana: Tipografía "América," 1900), pp. 96–193; Kenneth F. Kiple, *Blacks in Colonial Cuba, 1774–1899* (Gainesville: University Presses of Florida, 1976), p. 81; Rafael Fermoselle, *Política y color en Cuba* (Montevideo: Ediciones Geminis, 1974), p. 26; Donna M. Wolf, "The Cuban 'Gente de Color' and the Independence Movement, 1879–1895," *Revista/Review Interamericana* 5 (Fall 1975), 403–21; Thomas T. Orum, "The Politics of Color: The Racial Dimension of Cuban Politics During the Early Republican Years, 1900–1912," Ph.D. diss., New York University, 1975, pp. 17–35. A compilation of biographies of insurgent officers killed during the war indicated that many were workers and Afro-Cubans. See Alejandro del Pozo y Arjana, *Páginas de sangre, o el libro del cubano. Relación de los caudillos cubanos muertos en la actual campaña (1895 a 1898)* (Havana: Imprenta "La Juventud," 1898).

57. Fermín Valdés Domínguez, *Diario de soldado* (Havana: Universidad de La Habana, 1972–1974), 1:197. See also Avelino Sanjenís, *Mis cartas. Memorias de la revolución de 1895 por la independencia de Cuba* (Sagua la Grande: Imprenta "El Comercio," 1900), p. 123.

58. Máximo Gómez, "A los señores hacendados y dueños de fincas ganaderas," 1 de julio de 1895, Fondo de Donativos y Remisiones, Legajo 257, no. 14, Cuban National Archives, Havana. See also "Manuscrito del acuerdo del Consejo de Gobierno en sesión 13 de julio de 1896 in relación a la prohibición de la zafra de 1896 a 1897," July 30, 1896. Fondo de Donativos y Remisiones, Legajo 624, no. 34, Cuban National Archives. See also Máximo Gómez, "Circular," November 6, 1895, in Máximo Gómez, *Algunos documentos políticos de Máximo Gómez*, ed. Amalia Rodríguez Rodríguez (Havana: Biblioteca Nacional "José Martí," 1962), p. 16; Leopoldo Horrego Estuch, *Máximo Gómez, libertador y ciudadano* (Havana: Imprenta de P. Fernández y Cía., 1948), pp. 158–59; Benigno Souza y Rodríguez, *Ensayo histórico sobre la invasión* (Havana: Imprenta del Ejército, 1948), pp. 75–76.

59. "If any one had told us four months ago," wrote one planter in early 1896, "that [Gómez] would be able to stop the crushing of cane in the Province of Havana, or even in Matanzas, we would have laughed in his face. Today not a planter disobeys his orders." See "Extract From a Letter Received February 22, 1896, Dated at Havana," Philip Phillips Family Papers.

60. See José Martí, "Guatemala," in José Martí, *Obras completas* 3:220; José Martí,. "El Partido Revolucionaria a Cuba," May 27, 1893, in ibid., 1:345. See also Manuel Navarro Luna, "Martí y la reforma agraria," p. 2; Pedro Pablo Rodríguez, "La idea de liberación nacional en José Martí," pp. 160–65; Emilio Roig de Leuchsenring, *Máximo Gómez: el libertador de Cuba y el primer ciudadano de la república* (Havana: Oficina del Historiador de la Ciudad de La Habana, 1959), p. 30; Horrego Estuch, *Máximo Gómez, libertador y*

ciudadano, 167–95; Jorge Castellanos, "El pensamiento social de Máximo Gómez," *América* (Havana), February–March, 1946) pp. 22–28.

61. Headquarters of the Army of Liberation, "Proclamation," July 4, 1896, in *Correspondencia diplomático de la delegación cubana en Nueva York durante la guerra de 1895 a 1898* ed. Joaquín Llaverías y Martínez (Havana: Imprenta del Archivo Nacional, 1943–1946), 5:176–77.

62. "To the President of the United States of America," enclosure in Lee to Olney, June 24, 1896, Richard Olney Papers.

63. *New York Herald,* December 14, 1897.

64. Hyatt to Day, March 28, 1898, U.S. Congress, Senate, *Consular Correspondence Respecting the Conditions of the Reconcentrados in Cuba, the State of War in the Island, and the Prospects of the Projected Autonomy,* 55th Cong., 2d sess. S. Doc. 230 (Washington, D.C.: GPO, 1898), p. 44.

Chapter 2.   The Imperial Transfer

1. James D. Richardson, ed., *A Compilation of Messages and Papers of the Presidents, 1789–1902* (Washington, D.C.: Library of Congress, 1896–1902), 10:63–64.

2. Ibid.

3. *Congressional Record* 31 (April 16, 1898), pp. 3988–89. For the best single account of the details of the congressional debate, see Paul S. Holbo, "Presidential Leadership in Foreign Affairs: William McKinley and the Turpie-Foraker Amendment," *American Historical Review* 72 (July, 1967), 1321–35.

4. Burr McIntosh, *The Little I Saw of Cuba* (New York: F. Tennyson Neely, 1899), p. 74.

5. *New York Times,* July 29, 1898. See also *The State,* July 20, 1898; and Charles Morris, *The War With Spain* (Philadelphia: J. B. Lippincott, 1899), p. 312.

6. *New York Times,* July 29, 1898.

7. Ibid., December 24, 1898.

8. *The State,* December 19, 1898; *New York Times,* December 19, 1898.

9. In Walter Millis, *The Martial Spirit. A Study of Our War With Spain* (Boston: Houghton Mifflin, 1931), p. 362.

10. *New York Times,* July 22, 1898.

11. In George Kennan, "Cuban Character," *Outlook* 63 (December 23, 1899), 1021–22.

12. *New York Evening Post,* November 17, 1899.

13. Brooke to Carter, October 21, 1899, John R. Brooke Papers.

14. *Washington Daily Star,* June 20, 1899.

15. Wood to McKinley, April 12, 1900, Wood Papers. Secretary of War Elihu Root summarized official thinking in late 1899. "That probably two-thirds of the people of the island are unable to read and write, that the people in general have had no experience in any real self-government, but have been for centuries under the dominion of arbitrary power; that the blood conflicts which enraged so long have necessarily left behind bitter factional feeling, make it necessary to proceed somewhat more slowly in the formation of a government which is to command universal respect and allegiance that would be necessary in a country accustomed to the discussion of public questions, familiar with the problems presented, and trained to the acceptance of the decisions reached by the ballot." See Elihu Root, *Military and Colonial Policy of the United States,* ed. Robert Bacon and James Brown Scott (Cambridge, Mass.: Harvard University Press, 1916), p. 172.

16. Wood to McKinley, February 6, 1900, Special Correspondence, Elihu Root Papers.

17. Herbert Pelham Williams, "The Outlook in Cuba," *Atlantic Monthly* 83 (June 1899), 835–36.

18. Brooke to Adjutant General, June 2, 1899, File 248666, Records of the Adjutant General's Office, 1780s–1917, RG 94, U.S. National Archives (hereinafter cited as AGO/RG 94).

19. Berry to Adjutant General, June 2, 1899, file 248666, AGO/RG 94.

20. Shafter to Corbin, July 29, 1898, U.S. War Department, Adjutant General's Office, *Correspondence Relating to the War With Spain* (Washington, D.C.: GPO, 1902), p. 186. See also *New York Times,* July 31 and August 5, 1898.

21. *New York Tribune,* August 9, 1898.

22. *Washington Post,* October 8, 1898.

23. "Cosas de Cuba," n.d., File 294/24, Records of the Bureau of Insular Affairs, RG 350, U.S. National Archives (hereinafter cited as BIA/RG 350).

24. "Statement of Marquis de Apezteguía," September 9, 1898, in U.S. Department of Treasury, *Appendix to the Report on the Commercial and Industrial Condition of the Island of Cuba* (Washington, D.C.: GPO, 1899), pp. 332–33.

25. Atkins to McKinley, March 7, 1899, in Edwin F. Atkins, *Sixty Years in Cuba* (Cambridge, Mass.: Riverside Press, 1926), p. 306.

26. See William Ludlow, "The Transition in Havana," *Independent* 52 (April 12, 1900), 868; J. D. Whelpley, "Cuba of To-Day and To-Morrow," *Atlantic Monthly* 85 (July 1900), 46.

27. Wood to McKinley, September 26, 1899, William McKinley Papers.

28. Williams, "The Outlook in Cuba," pp. 835–36.

29. Brooke to Castle, September 6, 1899, Brooke Papers.

30. Wood to Root, February 23, 1900, Special Correspondence, Root Papers.

31. Wood to Root, February 23, 1900, Wood Papers. Leonard Wood also warned of economic implications: "I believe that if it were known to be a fact that we were going to give universal suffrage it would stop investments and advancement in the island to an extent which would be disastrous in its results" (ibid.).

32. *New York Evening Post,* November 17, 1899, p. 7.

33. *New York Times,* December 19, 1898, p. 2.

34. Root to Dana, January 15, 1900, Personal Correspondence, Root Papers.

35. Wood to Root, January 13, 1900, Wood Papers.

36. Wood to Root, February 23, 1900, ibid.

37. Ibid.

38. See "Order of the Military Government Relative to the Municipal Elections to be Held Throughout the Island of Cuba on June 1900," May 12, 1900, File 1305, Letters Received, Records of the Military Government of Cuba, RG 140, U.S. National Archives (hereinafter cited as MGC/RG 140). See also U.S. Congress, Senate, *Qualification of Voters at Coming Elections in Cuba,* 56th Cong., 2d sess., S. Doc. 243, ser. 3867 (Washington, D.C.: GPO, 1900), p. 2.

39. Matthews to Peabody, January 17, 1902, File 102, Letters Received, MGC/RG 140.

40. Rodriguez to McKinley, June 21, 1900, McKinley Papers.

41. Wood to Root, February 6, 1900, Wood Papers.

42. See Wood to McKinley, February 6, 1900, Special Correspondence, Root Papers. See also Francisco Figueras, *La intervención y su política* (Havana: Imprenta Avisador Comercial, 1906), pp. 6–8.

43. Wood to Root, January 1900, in Hermann Hagedorn, *Leonard Wood, A Biography* (New York: Harper and Brothers, 1931), 1:267.

44. Wood to Root, August 13, 1900, Wood Papers.

45. *New York Times,* August 27, 1900. See also Washburn to Cortelyou, September 10, 1900, File 331-24, BIA/RG 350.

46. Charles Warren Currier, "Why Cuba Should Be Independent," *Forum* 30 (October 1900), 145–46.

47. Wood to Adjutant General, September 1, 1900, file 340125/B, AGO/RG 94.

48. Wood to McKinley, August 31, 1900, Wood Papers.

49. Wood to Root, September 8, 1900, Special Correspondence, Root Papers.

50. Wood to Platt, December 6, 1900, Wood Papers.

51. Wood to Root, March 4, 1901, in Hagedorn, *Leonard Wood* 1:359.

52. Wood to Root, September 26, 1900, Wood Papers.

53. Wood to Root, January 12, 1901, ibid.

54. Wood to Root, December 23, 1900, Special Correspondence, Root Papers.

55. Wood to Root, February 27, 1901, File 331-71, BIA/RG 350.

56. Wood to Root, March 4, 1901, Special Correspondence, Root Papers.

57. *New York Times*, July 23, 1898.

58. Leonard Wood, "The Future of Cuba," *Independent* 54 (January 23, 1902), 193.

59. Richardson, ed., *A Compilation of the Messages and Papers of the Presidents, 1789–1902* 10:152.

60. In Louis A. Coolidge, *An Old-Fashioned Senator: Orville H. Platt of Connecticut* (New York: C. P. Putnam's Sons, 1910), p. 331.

61. Orville H. Platt, "The Pacification of Cuba," *Independent* 53 (June 27, 1901), 1466.

62. *New York Journal*, February 27, 1899.

63. U.S. Congress, Senate, Committee on Relations With Cuba, *Conditions in Cuba* (Washington, D.C.: GPO, 1900), pp. 17–18. Senator Mark Hanna was a bit more vague, but no less explicit: "We propose to establish a stable government on that island, but what constitutes a stable government, has not yet been defined. I think, however, Cuba will be an evolution, and in about twenty years it will be so thoroughly Americanized that there will be no question as to what a stable government means." See *New York Tribune*, August 26, 1898.

64. Brooke to Adjutant General, October 1, 1899, in John R. Brooke, *Civil Report of Major-General John R. Brooke, U.S. Army, Military Governor Island of Cuba, 1899* (Washington, D.C.: GPO, 1900), p. 14.

65. Wood to Root, January 13, 1900, Wood Papers.

66. Wood to McKinley, February 6, 1900, Special Correspondence, Root Papers.

67. Root to Wood, January 9, 1901, ibid.

68. The decision to link relations with Cuba to the Monroe Doctrine, Root later insisted, was necessary as an "international basis for stepping in to protect Cuba without appearing to be the state which was butting in." See Philip Jessup, "Conversation With Mr. Root," October 28, 1935, Philip Jessup Papers.

69. Root to Wood, January 9, 1901, Root Papers.

70. Root to Hay, January 11, 1901, ibid.

71. Ibid.

72. Root, *Military and Colonial Policy of the United States*, pp. 172–73.

73. Ibid.

74. Root to Shaw, February 23, 1901, Root Papers.

75. Orville H. Platt, "The Solution of the Cuban Problem," *The World's Work* 2 (May 1901), 730–31.

76. William Eaton Chandler, "Senator Platt and the Platt Amendment," April 21, 1906, William Eaton Chandler Papers. See also *Washington Evening Star*, January 29, 1901.

77. Wood to Root, January 19, 1901, Wood Papers.

78. Ibid.

79. Wood to Foraker, January 11, 1901, ibid.

80. Wood to Root, February 8, 1901, ibid. See also *Washington Evening Star*, February 11, 1901.

81. Root later recalled, "At the time of the Platt Amendment's being framed Germany was

nosing around all over trying to get a foothold and we didn't propose to have her secure such a position in Cuba. . . . All the small Central American and Caribbean island governments had been borrowing large sums at enormous rates of interest. . . . The ultimate result of borrowing money from a predatory government like Germany is that the lending government takes possession as a mortgagee and there is no power of ouster" (Philip Jessup, "Root Interview," January 11, 1930, Jessup Papers). And at another point: "The real substance of the Platt Amendment," Root insisted, "is that we did give the island of Cuba on condition that they should not give it up or sell it to anyone else, and that they would lease naval stations to us so that we could see that no one took it by force" (Philip C. Jessup, "Root Interview," November 11, 1930, Jessup Papers).

82. *Washington Evening Star,* June 1, 1901.

83. Albert J. Beveridge, "Cuba and Congress," *North American Review* 172 (April 1901), 545.

84. Platt, "The Solution of the Cuban Problem," pp. 732–33.

85. Orville H. Platt, "Our Relation to the People of Cuba and Puerto Rico," *Annals of the American Acadmy of Political and Social Science* 18 (July 1901), 158.

86. Root to Wood, February 9, 1901, Root Papers.

87. Platt, "The Solution of the Cuban Problem," pp. 729–30.

88. Platt, "Our Relation to the People of Cuba and Puerto Rico," p. 147.

89. Orville H. Platt, "Cuba's Claim Upon the United States," *North American Review* 175 (August 1902), 146.

90. Root to Wood, March 2, 1901, Root Papers. See also Philip C. Jessup, *Elihu Root* (New York: Dodd, Mead, 1938), 1:316.

91. Platt, "The Pacification of Cuba," *Independent* 53 (June 27, 1901), 1466–67. See also Joseph Benson Foraker, *Notes of a Busy Life,* 3d ed. (Cincinnati: Steward and Kidd, 1917), 2:51–52.

92. Wood to Root, March 20, 1901, Special Correspondence, Root Papers.

93. Wood to Root, March 4, 1901, in Hagedorn, *Leonard Wood, A Biography* 1:359.

94. Root to Wood, March 29, 1901, Root Papers.

95. Wood to Root, April 2, 1901, Wood Papers.

96. Root to Wood, April 3, 1901, Root Papers.

97. "Purpose of this visit is in reality to accept Platt Amendment," Wood cabled Root, "but this must not be even intimated. That such is the fact I know from the men themselves. Everything depends upon this being unknown. . . . Apparent purpose here will be to obtain information on certain of the articles of the amendment which they do not quite understand. Information received will remove doubt and the Amendment will be passed. This is Latin method but we are after results" (Wood to Root, April 15, 1901, Wood Papers).

98. "Report of the Committee Appointed to Confer With the Government of the United States, Giving an Account of the Result of its Labor," May 6, 1901, Subject File: Cuba, Root Papers.

99. Platt to Root, April 26, 1901, General Correspondence, Root Papers. See also Platt to Quilez, n.d., in Rafael Martínez Ortiz, *Cuba: los primeros años de independencia,* 3d ed. (Paris: Le Livre Libre, 1929), 1:301.

100. "Report of the Committee Appointed to Confer with the Government of the United States," Root Papers. For further discussions of the Root interpretation of the Platt Amendment, see James Brown Scott, "The Origin and Purpose of the Platt Amendment," *American Journal of International Law* 3 (July 1914), 590–91, and *The Recommendations of Habana Concerning International Organization* (New York: Oxford University Press, 1917), p. 12.

Chapter 3.   Heroes Without Homes

1. See *La Lucha*, April 11, 1899, and *La Discusión*, September 23, 1900. See also "Confidential Report: Province of Santiago de Cuba," Records of the Post Office Department, RG 28, U.S. National Archives (hereinafter cited as POD/RG 28).

2. See Francisco López Segrera, *Raíces históricas de la revolución cubana (1868–1959)* (Havana: Unión de Escritores y Artistas, 1981), p. 257.

3. For excellent accounts of the expulsion of Spaniards in Mexico, see Harold D. Sims, *La expulsión de los españoles de México (1821–1828)* (Mexico City: Fondo de Cultura Económica, 1974), and *Descolonización en México. El conflicto entre mexicanos y españoles (1821–1831)* (México: Fondo de Cultura Económica, 1982). See also Victor Alba, *Nationalists Without Nations* (New York: Praeger, 1968), pp. 23–26; John Lynch, *The Spanish-American Revolutions, 1808–1826* (New York: Norton, 1973), pp. 222–23.

4. International Bank for Reconstruction and Development, *Report on Cuba* (Washington, D.C.: International Bank for Reconstruction and Development, 1951), p. 1046.

5. U.S. War Department, *Informe sobre el censo de Cuba, 1899* (Washington, D.C.: GPO, 1900), p. 228.

6. Ibid., pp. 448–49.

7. José M. Alvarez Acevedo, *La colonia española en la economía cubana* (Havana: Ucar, García y Cía., 1936), pp. 223–24. See also Edwin F. Atkins, "The Spaniards of the Island of Cuba," *Economic Bulletin of Cuba* 1 (March 1922), 133–34; *New York Times*, December 6, 1931.

8. U.S. War Department, *Censo de la república de Cuba, 1907* (Washington, D.C.: GPO, 1908), pp. 572–73.

9. Alvarez Acevedo, *La colonia española en la economía cubana*, p. 238.

10. Irene A. Wright, *Cuba* (New York: Macmillan, 1910), pp. 134–35.

11. U.S. War Department, *Censo de la república de Cuba, 1907*, p. 574; Cuba, Office of the Census, *Census of the Republic of Cuba, 1919* (Havana: Maza, Arroyo y Caso, 1919), p. 735. See also José Sixto de Sola, "Los extranjeros en Cuba," *Cuba Contemporánea* 8 (June 1915), 109–11.

12. U.S. War Department, *Informe sobre el censo, 1899*, pp. 104, 481–83. See also Duvon Clough Corbitt, *A Study of the Chinese in Cuba, 1847–1947* (Wilmore, Ky.: Asbury College, 1971), pp. 87–94.

13. U.S. War Department, *Censo de la república, 1907*, pp. 60, 572–73; and Corbitt, *A Study of the Chinese in Cuba, 1847–1947*, pp. 94–95; Raymond Leslie Buell et al., *Problems of the New Cuba* (New York: Foreign Policy Association, 1935), pp. 35–36.

14. U.S. War Department, *Censo de la república, 1907*, p. 60; Calixto C. Masó, *Historia de Cuba* (Miami: Ediciones Universal, 1976), p. 414.

15. Havana declined from some 238,000 acres to 105,000, while Matanzas dropped from 365,838 to 161,766. The total figures for 1895 are approximate, since no information was available for Camagüey province. See U.S. War Department, *Informe sobre el censo de Cuba, 1899*, p. 564.

16. U.S. War Department, *Informe sobre el censo de Cuba, 1899*, pp. 551, 563–64; José P. Alvarez Díaz et al., *A Study on Cuba* (Coral Gables, Fla.: University of Miami Press, 1965), pp. 96–97; Julio E. LeRiverend Brusone, *La Habana (biografía de una provincia)* (Havana: Imprenta "El Siglo XX," 1960), pp. 458–59; George Bronson Rea, "The Destruction of Sugar Estates in Cuba," *Harper's Weekly* 41 (October 16, 1897), 10–34; L. V. de Abad, "The Cuban Problem," *Gunton's Magazine* 21 (December, 1901), pp. 515–25; Richard J. Hinton, "Cuban Reconstruction," *North American Review* 164 (January 1899), 92–102; Franklin Matthews, "The Reconstruction of Cuba," *Harper's Weekly* 42 (July 14, 1899), 700–01;

Jorge Quintana, "Lo que costó a Cuba la guerra de 1895," *Bohemia* 52 (September 11, 1960), 4–6, 107–08.

17. U.S. War Department, *Informe sobre el censo de Cuba, 1899*, pp. 44–45. See also Felipe Pazos, "La economía cubana en el siglo XIX," *Revista Bimestre Cubana* 47 (January–February, 1941), pp. 105–06; Abad, "The Cuban Problem," p. 521.

18. See L. V. de Abad, *Azúcar y caña de azúcar. Ensayo de orientación cubana* (Havana: Editora Mercantil Cubana, 1945), pp. 244–45.

19. Bliss to Wilson, January 12, 1902, General Correspondence, James Harrison Wilson Papers.

20. In Edwin F. Atkins, *Sixty Years in Cuba* (Cambridge, Mass.: Riverside Press, 1926), p. 287.

21. Atkins to Wood, April 11, 1901/109, Records of the Military Government of Cuba, RG 140, U.S. National Archives, Washington, D.C. (hereinafter cited as MGC/RG 140).

22. Military Order No. 46, April 24, 1899, in John R. Brooke, *Civil Report of Major-General John R. Brooke, U.S. Army, Military Governor, Island of Cuba, 1899* (Washington, D.C.: GPO, 1900), p. 40.

23. U.S. Congress, Senate, Committee on Relations with Cuba, *Hearings Before the Committee on Relations with Cuba: Statement of Major General John R. Brooke* (Washington, D.C.: GPO, 1900), p. 6. Copy located in John R. Brooke Papers.

24. Brooke to Adjutant General, October 1, 1899, in Brooke, *Civil Report of Major-General John R. Brooke*, p. 13.

25. Ibid., pp. 13, 14.

26. Porter to Gage, November 15, 1898, in U.S. Treasury Department, *Report on the Commercial and Industrial Condition of the Island of Cuba* (Washington, D.C.: GPO, 1899), p. 9.

27. See "Statement of Pedro Rodríguez of Caibarién," September 20, 1898, in ibid., pp. 193–94.

28. Muñoz to Porter, April 4, 1900, William McKinley Papers. See also Arroyo to Porter, September 28, 1898, in U.S. Treasury Department, *Report on the Commercial and Industrial Condition of the Island of Cuba*, p. 245.

29. Madán to Wood, May 22, 1901, File 1901/109, MGC/RG 140.

30. Seigle to Root, October 3, 1900, File 1900/3589, MGC/RG 140.

31. Perfecto Lacosta, "Report of the Department of Agriculture, Commerce, and Industry," March 15, 1901, U.S. War Department, *Annual Reports of the War Department for the Fiscal Year Ended June 30, 1900* (Washington, D.C.: GPO, 1900), vol. 1, pt. 2, sec. 4, p. 9. Lacosta himself may have had compelling personal motives to advocate public assistances to landowners. As owner of several estates and ranches, Lacosta had earlier filed a claim of war damages totalling some $653,000. See Lacosta to Williams, January 26, 1896, Despatches from U.S. Consuls in Havana, 1783–1906, General Records of the Department of State, RG 59, U.S. National Archives (hereinafter cited as DS/RG 59).

32. Lacosta, "Report of the Department of Agriculture, Commerce, and Industry," p. 6.

33. Leonard Wood, "Report of Brigadier General Leonard Wood," July 5, 1902, U.S. War Department, *Civil Report of Brigadier General Leonard Wood, Military Governor of Cuba, for the Period from January 1 to May 20, 1902* (Washington, D.C.: GPO, 1902), 1:13.

34. Bliss to Wilson, January 12, 1902, General Correspondence, Wilson Papers.

35. Wood to Root, May 18, 1901, Wood Papers.

36. Wood to Adjutant General, October 31, 1899, File 1899/2594, MGC/RG 140. For a detailed discussion of the general economic policy of the military government during the occupation, see Philip S. Foner, *The Spanish-Cuban-American War and the Birth of American Imperialism* (New York: Monthly Review Press, 1972), 2:466–83.

37. Wood to Root, May 18, 1901, Wood Papers.

38. Military Order No. 139, May 27, 1901, File 1901/109, MGC/RG 140.

39. Wood to Root, May 30, 1901, Wood Papers.

40. Rousseau to Wood, May 29, 1901, File 1901/109, MGC/RG 140.

41. Círculo de Hacendados to Root, May 27, 1901, File 1901/109, MGC/RG 140.

42. Wood to Root, May 30, 1901, Wood Papers.

43. In Brooke, *Civil Report of Major-General John R. Brooke,* p. 149.

44. Manuel Hidalgo, "Informe," November 15, 1900, File 1900/3589, MGC/RG 140.

45. In Brooke, *Civil Report of Major-General John R. Brooke,* p. 150.

46. José Rodríguez, "Informe," November 22, 1900, File 1900/3589, MGC/RG 140.

47. James L. Hitchman, "U.S. Control Over Cuban Sugar Production, 1898–1902," *Journal of Inter-American Studies and World Affairs* 12 (January, 1970), 90–106; Atkins, *Sixty Years in Cuba,* p. 112; Atherton Brownell, "The Commercial Annexation of Cuba," *Appleton's Magazine* 8 (October, 1906), 409; Leland H. Jenks, *Our Cuban Colony* (New York: Vanguard Press, 1928), pp. 128–32; Zona Fiscal de Manzanillo, "Relación de las fincas que han adquirido en compra los no residentes en la isla de Cuba desde la fecha de la ocupación americana," March 25, 1902, File LMC 1902/31, MGC/RG 140.

48. Jenks, *Our Cuban Colony,* p. 130; Hugh Thomas, *Cuba, the Pursuit of Freedom* (New York: Harper and Row, 1971), p. 467; Alejandro García and Oscar Zanetti, eds., *United Fruit Company: un caso del dominio imperialista en Cuba* (Havana: Editorial de Ciencias Sociales, 1976), pp. 56–66.

49. "Synopsis of Reports by Different Land Companies Respecting their Properties in Cuba," *Cuba Review* 5 (December, 1906), 78.

50. Frank G. Carpenter, "Cuba in 1905," *Cuba Review* 3 (November 1905), 11; Jenks, *Our Cuban Colony,* pp. 143–44. Other acquisitions by foreign enterprises included: The Cuba Colonial Company, incorporated in Chicago, which acquired 40,000 acres in Camagüey. The Canada Land and Fruit Company purchased some 23,000 acres in Las Villas and on the Isle of Pines. The Cuban Development Company, based in Detroit, purchased the 12,500-acre "Vista Alegre" estate in Oriente. The Havana Land and Mortgage Company of New York secured the "Saratoga" estate in Santa Clara. The Paso Real Plantation Company of Chicago purchased the "Paso Real" estate in Pinar del Río. The Cuba Land, Loan, and Title Guarantee Company from Chicago, acquired title to tracts of land in Camagüey and Oriente. The Cuban Agricultural and Development Company, incorporated in Pittsburgh, purchased over 135,000 acres around the region of Guantánamo. The Cuban Realty Company from New Jersey purchased 25,000 acres in western Oriente. The San Claudio Land Company of New York acquired title to property on Cabañas Bay near Havana. The Holguín Fruit Company, based in Ontario, purchased the "Pedernales" estate in Oriente. The Development Company of Cuba from New York acquired the "Ceballos" estate in Camagüey. The Eastern Cuba Development Company purchased 1,000 acres near Victoria de Las Tunas. The Swedish Land and Colonization of Minneapolis acquired the 6,000-acre estate of "Palmarito" in the Cauto Valley. The Cuba Polish Land Company of Toledo purchased 1,000 acres of land near Victoria de Las Tunas.

51. Squiers to Hay, September 17, 1904, Despatches from U.S. Ministers to Cuba, 1902–1906, DS/RG 59.

52. Brownell, "The Commercial Annexation of Cuba," p. 411.

53. Alvarez Acevedo, *La colonia española en la economía cubana,* p. 239.

54. Rionda to Czarnikow, MacDougal, and Company, February 20, 1909, Cuban Letters, November 1908–April 1909, Braga Brothers Collection.

55. Jenks, *Our Cuban Colony,* 157; Brownell, "The Commercial Annexation of Cuba," p. 410; Teresita Yglesia Martínez, *Cuba: primera república, segunda intervención* (Havana:

Editorial de Ciencias Sociales, 1976), pp. 68–69; Enrique Barbarrosa, *El proceso de la república* (Havana: Imprenta Militar de Antonio Pérez Sierra, 1911), pp. 59–61.

56. See Lisandro Pérez, "Iron Mining and Socio-Demographic Change in Eastern Cuba, 1884–1940," *Journal of Latin American Studies* 14 (November 1982), 390–95; Pulaski F. Hyatt and John T. Hyatt, *Cuba: Its Resources and Opportunities* (New York: J. S. Ogilvie, 1898), pp. 77–84; and William J. Clark, *Commercial Cuba* (New York: Charles Scribner's Sons, 1898), pp. 402–19; Thomas, *Cuba, the Pursuit of Freedom*, p. 466.

57. See Jules R. Benjamin, *The United States and Cuba: Hegemony and Dependent Development, 1880–1934* (Pittsburgh, Pa.: University of Pittsburgh Press, 1974), p. 19.

58. Jenks, *Our Cuban Colony*, pp. 150–54, 166–74; Brownell "The Commercial Annexation of Cuba," pp. 408–10; Clark, *Commercial Cuba*, pp. 77–125, 277.

59. Jenks, *Our Cuban Colony*, p. 164; Edwin Morgan, "British Interests in Cuba," June 30, 1906, Despatches from U.S. Ministers to Cuba, 1902–1906, DS/RG 59.

60. Francisco Figueres, *La intervención y su política* (Havana: Imprenta Avisador Comercial, 1906), p. 23; Jenks, *Our Cuban Colony*, pp. 164–65; Oscar Pino Santos, *El asalto a Cuba por la oligarquía yanqui* (Havana: Casa de las Américas, 1973), pp. 33–69; Harold S. Sloan, "Los effectos de las inversiones norteamericanas en Cuba," *Cuba Contemporánea* 44 (June–July–August 1927), 150–55; Buell, *Problems of the New Cuba*, pp. 44–45.

61. Squiers to Hay, September 17, 1904, Despatches from U.S. Ministers to Cuba, 1902–1906, DS/RG 59.

62. Harry F. Guggenheim, *The United States and Cuba* (New York: Macmillan, 1934), pp. 116–18.

63. Clark, "Labor Conditions in Cuba," p. 775.

64. Barbarrosa, *El proceso de la república*, p. 35.

65. López Segrera, *Raíces históricas de la revolución cubana*, pp. 50, 55–56, 72–73.

66. Clark, "Labor Conditions in Cuba," p. 670.

67. Ibid., p. 685.

68. U.S. War Department, *Censo de la república de Cuba, 1907*, p. 59; Cuba, Office of the Census, *Census of the Republic of Cuba, 1919*, p. 181. See also José A. Duarte Oropesa, *Historiología cubana* (n.p., n.p., 1969–1970), 3:24, 164; and Miguel de Carrión, "El desenvolvimiento social de Cuba en los ultimos veinte años," *Cuba Contemporánea* 27 (September 1921), 21–22.

69. Data derived from U.S. War Department, *Censo de la república de Cuba, 1907*, p. 60 and Cuba, Secretaria de Hacienda, Sección de Estadística, *Inmigración y movimiento de pasajeros en el año ... 1912–1918* (Havana: Imprenta "La Propagandista," 1913–1919).

70. Clark, "Labor Conditions in Cuba," p. 686.

71. Ibid., p. 779.

72. Ibid.

73. Clark, *Commercial Cuba*, p. 39.

74. Van Horne to Quesada, July 16, 1901, in Gonzalo de Quesada, *Archivo de Gonzalo de Quesada*, ed. Gonzalo de Quesada y Miranda (Havana: Imprenta "El Siglo XX," 1948–1951), 2:329.

75. Clark, "Labor Conditions in Cuba," pp. 693, 711–12, 726, 739.

76. Samuel M. Whitside, *Annual Report of Colonel Samuel M. Whitside, 10th U.S. Cavalry, Commanding Department of Santiago and Puerto Principe, 1900* (Santiago de Cuba: Adjutant General's Office, 1900), pp. 152–53.

77. The Spanish-American Iron Company, Cuban Steel Ore Company, and the Juraguá Iron Company to Whitside, January 15, 1901, File 1901/372, MGC/RG 140.

78. U.S. Department of War, *Censo de la república de Cuba, 1907*, pp. 572–74. See also Alvarez Acevedo, *La colonia española en la economía cubana*, pp. 218–22.

79. Cuba, Secretaria de Hacienda, Sección de Estadística, *Inmigración y movimiento de pasajeros en el año . . . 1915–1919* (Havana: Imprenta "La Propagandista," 1916–1920)

80. Clark, "Labor Conditions in Cuba," pp. 774–75.

81. *Cuba Review* 10 (October 1912), 16. See also Clark, "Labor Conditions in Cuba," p. 750.

82. Squiers to Hay, August 16, 1902, Despatches from U.S. Ministers to Cuba, 1902–1906, DS/RG 59. See also Fernando Berenguer, *La riqueza de Cuba* (Havana: Imprenta "El Arte," 1917), pp. 83–89.

83. Hanna to Squiers, February 12, 1903, Despatches from U.S. Ministers to Cuba, 1902–1906, DS/RG 59.

84. See Buell, *The Problems of the New Cuba*, p. 45.

85. See Juan Pérez de la Riva, "Cuba y la migración antillana, 1900–1931," in Juan Pérez de la Riva et al., *La república neocolonial* (Havana: Editorial de Ciencias Sociales, 1975–1978), 2:5–73.

86. Rionda to Czarnikow-Rionda Company, February 21, 1921, Cuban Matters, Letterbook, September 1909–March, 1912, Braga Brothers Collection.

87. Roloff to Quesada, April 10, 1899, in Quesada, *Archivo* 2:205.

88. Rodríguez to Quesada, June 13, 1899, in ibid., p. 180.

89. Bates to Adjutant General, Division of Cuba, January 28, 1899, File 196, LS/Santa Clara, Records of U.S. Army Overseas Operations and Commands, 1898–1942, RG 395, U.S. National Archives (hereinafter cited as AOOC/RG 395).

90. Logan to Adjutant General Department of Santa Clara, February 3, 1899, File 294/11, Records of the Bureau of Insular Affairs, RG 350, U.S. National Archives (hereinafter cited as BIA/RG 350).

91. Davis to Chaffee, January 15, 1899, File 297, MGC/RG 140.

92. Leonard Wood, "Dictates System of Government Desired by Cubans," January 1899, File 331, BIA/RG 350.

93. See Mario Averhoff Purón, *Los primeros partidos políticos* (Havana: Instituto Cubano del Libro, 1971), pp. 17–18. See also José María Céspedes, "Empleo-manía," *Cuba y América* 3 (April 1899), pp. 6–7.

94. Munoz to Wood, May 17, 1900, File 2870, MGC/RG 140.

95. "Confidential Report: Province of Santiago de Cuba," n.d., POD/RG 28.

96. See "A List of Municipal Employees Who Have Served in the Cuban Army," April 1899, File 2020, Segregated Correspondence and Related Documents, MGC/RG 140. See also *New York Times*, January 6, 1899.

97. Wood to Assistant Secretary of War, May 6, 1899, File 84, Santiago de Cuba, AOOC/RG 395.

Chapter 4.   The Republic Inaugurated

1. See José Antonio Ramos, *Manual del perfecto fulanista. Apuntes para el estudio de nuestra dinámica político-social* (Havana: Jesús Montero, 1916), pp. 93–103; Orestes Ferrara, *Una mirada sobre tres siglos: memorias* (Madrid: Playor, S.A. 1975), p. 147; Enrique Meitín, "De los partidos en la primera etapa de la Cuba neocolonial," *Bohemia* 67 (January 24, 1975), pp. 88–92.

2. See Estrada Palma to Benigno and Placido Gener, January 13, 1978, in Tomás Estrada Palma, *Desde el Castillo de Figueras. Cartas de Estrada Palma (1877–1878)*, ed. Carlos de Velasco (Havana: Sociedad Editorial Cuba Contemporánea, 1918), pp. 72–75.

3. See Squiers to Hay, August 16, 1902, Despatches from U.S. Ministers to Cuba, 1902–

1906, General Records of the Department of State, RG 59, U.S. National Archives (hereinafter cited as Despatches/Cuba).

4. Susan Schroeder, *Cuba: A Handbook of Historical Statistics* (Boston: G. K. Hall, 1982), p. 224; José Alvarez Díaz et al., *Cuba: geopolítica y pensamiento económico* (Miami: Duplex, 1964), p. 73.

5. Enrique Barbarrosa, *El proceso de la república* (Havana: Imprenta Militar de Antonio Pérez, 1911), p. 35.

6. Hanna to Squiers, February 12, 1903, Despatches/Cuba.

7. Victor S. Clark, "Labor Conditions in Cuba," *Bulletin of the Department of Labor* 7 (July 1902), 737.

8. Rionda to Czarnikow, MacDougal, and Company, March 17, 1909, Cuban Letters, November 1908–April 1909, Braga Brothers Collection.

9. Barbarrosa, *El proceso de la república*, pp. 32, 26. See also Vicente Mestre Amabile, *Cuba, un año de república: hechos y notas* (Paris: Imprenta Charaire, 1903); J. Buttari Gaunaurd, *Boceto crítico histórico* (Havana: Editorial Lex, 1954), pp. 131–34.

10. For a discussion of political developments, see Teresita Yglesia Martínez, *Cuba: primera república, segunda intervención* (Havana: Editorial Ciencias Sociales, 1976), pp. 146–54.

11. As early as 1904, the U.S. minister wrote of Estrada's growing political isolation. "In Congress he has no supporting party in either house, that is, a party giving loyal support to measures he recommends" (Squiers to Hay, July 28, 1904, Despatches/Cuba).

12. Jorge Ibarra, "Agosto de 1906: una intervención amañada," in Jorge Ibarra, *Aproximaciones a Clio* (Havana: Editorial de Ciencias Sociales, 1979), p. 121.

13. Eduardo Varela Zequeira, *La política en 1905, o episodios de una lucha electoral* (Havana: Imprenta y Papelería de Rambla Bouza, 1905), pp. 5–60; Duarte Oropesa, *Historiología Cubana* 3:28–29; Yglesia Martínez, *Cuba: primera república segunda intervención*, pp. 203–04, 208; Mario Guiral Moreno, "El problema de la burocracia en Cuba," *Cuba Contemporánea* 2 (August 1913), 260; Luis de Juan Puñal, *Tirando de la manta* (Havana: Arroyo, Fernández y Cía., n.d.), pp. 18–20; Rafael Martínez Ortiz, *Cuba, los primeros años de independencia*, 2d ed. (Paris: Le Livre Libre, 1921), 2:529–42. Charles E. Chapman, *A History of the Cuban Republic* (New York: Macmillan, 1927), p. 167. The municipal purges affected Guane, San Juan y Martínez, San Luis, Consolación del Sur, Artemisa, Guanajay, Cabañas, and Vivales in the province of Pinar del Río; Havana, Marianao, Güines, Batabanó, Aguacate, Alquizar, and Guanabacoa in Havana province; and Camajuaní, Vueltas, Placetas, Yaguajay, Calabazar, Trinidad, Cienfuegos, Rodas, Lojas, Ranchuelo, Sagua la Grande, Santo Domingo, Cruces, Caibarién, Rancho Veloz, Santa Clara, and Sancti-Spíritus in Las Villas.

14. Squiers to Hay, April 28, 1905, Despatches/Cuba.

15. Baehr to Squiers, November 22, 1905, ibid.

16. Anderson to Squiers, August 13, 1905, ibid.

17. Mario Riera Hernández, *Cuba política, 1899–1955* (Havana: Impresora Modelo, 1955), pp. 83–106.

18. See "Record of Sessions of the Constitutional Convention of the Island of Cuba" (Bureau of Insular Affairs Library, U.S. National Archives, 1901), 3:n.p.; Julio Villoldo, "Las reelecciones," *Cuba Contemporánea* 10 (March 1916), 237–52.

19. Sleeper to Root, August 25, 1906, U.S. Department of State, *Foreign Relations of the United States: 1906* (Washington, D.C.: GPO, 1909), p. 456 (hereinafter cited as FRUS: 1906).

20. Ibarra, "Agosto de 1906: una intervención amañada," p. 130.

21. Sleeper to Root, September 4, 1906, *FRUS: 1906*, p. 467.

22. Steinhart to Loeb, Jr., September 8, 1906, Theodore Roosevelt Papers. A similar message was cabled to the Department of State. See Steinhart to Root, September 8, 1906, *FRUS: 1906*, p. 473.

23. Steinhart to Bacon, September 12, 1906, Roosevelt Papers.

24. Steinhart to Bacon, September 13, 1906, ibid; Sleeper to Root, September 13, 1906, *FRUS: 1906*, p. 478.

25. Steinhart to Root, September 14, 1906, Roosevelt Papers.

26. Roosevelt to White, September 13, 1906, ibid.

27. Roosevelt to Bacon, September 10, 1906, ibid. See also Martínez Ortiz, *Cuba, los primeros años de independencia* 2:613–55.

28. Bacon to Steinhart, September 10, 1906, Roosevelt Papers.

29. Roosevelt to Bacon, September 10, 1906, ibid.

30. Bacon to Steinhart, September 10, 1906, ibid.

31. Roosevelt to Trevelyn, September 9, 1906, ibid.

32. Roosevelt to Eliot, September 13, 1906, ibid.

33. Roosevelt to Bacon, September 14, 1906, *FRUS: 1906*, p. 480.

34. Dana G. Munro, *Intervention and Dollar Diplomacy in the Caribbean, 1900–1921* (Princeton, N.J.: Princeton University Press, 1964), p. 130. See also Allan Reed Millett, *The Politics of Intervention: The Military Occupation of Cuba, 1906–1909* (Columbus; Ohio State University Press, 1968), pp. 89–102.

35. Taft to Roosevelt, September 20, 1906, in William Howard Taft and Robert Bacon, "Cuban Pacification: Report of William H. Taft, Secretary of War, and Robert Bacon, Assistant Secretary of State, of What Was Done Under the Instruction of the President in Restoring Peace in Cuba," in U.S. Department of War, *Report of the Secretary of War, 1906*, Appendix E, U.S. Congress, House, 59th Cong. 2d sess. H. Doc. no. 2, ser. 1505 (Washington, D.C.: GPO, 1906), p. 459 (hereinafter cited as *Taft/Bacon Report*).

36. Ibid., p. 450.

37. Taft to Roosevelt, September 21, 1906, Roosevelt Papers. See also *Taft/Bacon Report*, p. 456.

38. W. H. Taft to Helen Taft, September 20, 1906, William Howard Taft Papers.

39. *Taft/Bacon Report*, p. 456.

40. Taft to Roosevelt, September 20, 1906, Roosevelt Papers; *Taft/Bacon Report*, pp. 469, 470.

41. *Taft/Bacon Report*, p. 456.

42. Taft to Roosevelt, September 20, 1906, Roosevelt Papers.

43. Taft to Roosevelt, September 21, 1906, ibid.

44. Taft to Root, September 15, 1906, Taft Papers.

45. Taft to Roosevelt, September 22, 1906, Roosevelt Papers.

46. See *Taft/Bacon Report*, p. 460.

47. W. H. Taft to Helen Taft, September 21, 1906, Taft Papers.

48. *Taft/Bacon Report*, pp. 461–462.

49. Ibid., p. 462.

50. William Ingles, "The Collapse of the Cuban House of Cards," *Harper's Weekly* 50 (October 13, 1906), 1490.

51. See Taft and Bacon to Estrada Palma, September 24, 1906, *Taft/Bacon Report*, p. 462.

52. W. H. Taft to Helen Taft, September 23, 1906, Taft Papers.

53. Taft to Roosevelt, September 24, 1906, Roosevelt Papers.

54. Taft to Roosevelt, September 26, 1906, ibid.

55. Hanna to Squiers, February 12, 1903, Despatches/Cuba.

56. See Buttari Gaunaurd, *Boceto critico historico*, p. 137.

57. Enrique Collazo, *La revolucion de agosto de 1906* (Havana: Casa Editorial C. Martinez y Cia., 1907), pp. 7–11.

58. Elihu Root, *Military and Colonial Policy of the United States*, ed. Robert Bacon and James Brown Scott (Cambridge, Mass.: Harvard University Press, 1916), p. 100.

59. W. H. Taft to Charles Taft, October 9, 1906, Taft Papers.

60. W. H. Taft to Helen Taft, September 20, 1906, ibid. A day later, Taft wrote of his hope for a settlement that would "avoid great disaster to business and property interests of the Island" (W. H. Taft to Helen Taft, September 21, 1906, ibid.).

61. See W. H. Taft to Helen Taft, September 21, 1906, ibid.

62. Roosevelt to Foraker, September 28, 1906, Roosevelt Papers. Estrada admitted to the United States, Roosevelt wrote, that he was "utterly powerless to make any headway against the insurgents" (Roosevelt to Eliot, September 28, 1906, ibid.).

63. *Taft/Bacon Report*, pp. 456, 457. See also Estrada Palma's address to the Cuban congress on September 14, 1906, in Cuba, Congreso, Cámara de Representantes, *Mensajes presidenciales remitidos al congreso, transcurridos desde el veinte de mayo de mil novecientos dos, hasta el primero de abril de mil novecientos diez y siete* (Havana: n.p., n.d.), p. 176.

64. Magoon to Roosevelt, April 16, 1908, Roosevelt Papers.

65. See Louis A. Pérez, Jr., *Army Politics in Cuba, 1898–1958* (Pittsburgh, Pa.: University of Pittsburgh Press, 1976), pp. 22–23; Millett, *The Politics of Intervention*, pp. 221–27.

66. Taft to Magoon, October 31, 1906, File 866/16, Records of the Bureau of Insular Affairs, RG 350, U.S. National Archives.

67. Taft to Magoon, January 23, 1907, Taft Papers.

68. Magoon to Roosevelt, April 16, 1908, Roosevelt Papers.

69. Charles E. Magoon, *Report of Provisional Administration from December 1st, 1907 to December 1st, 1908* (Havana: n.p., 1908), p. 108.

Chapter 5. The Republic Restored

1. W. H. Taft to Helen Taft, September 20, 1906, William Howard Taft Papers.

2. W. H. Taft to Helen Taft, September 27, 1906, ibid.

3. See Eugene P. Lyle, Jr., "The Control of the Caribbean," *The World's Work* 10 (September 1905), pp. 6666–68; Lester D. Langley, *The United States and the Caribbean in the Twentieth Century* (Athens: University of Georgia Press, 1982), pp. 13–52.

4. Roosevelt to Root, May 20, 1904, Theodore Roosevelt Papers.

5. *Congressional Record*, 58th Cong., 2d sess., pp. 9–10.

6. Francis B. Loomis, "The Attitude of the United States Toward Other American Powers," *Annals of the American Academy of Political and Social Science* 26 (1905), 22, 24.

7. Philander C. Knox, "Latin America," October 6, 1909, Philander C. Knox Papers.

8. Dana G. Munro, *Dollar Diplomacy and Intervention in the Caribbean, 1900–1921* (Princeton, N.J.: Princeton University Press, 1964), pp. 533, 537; Albert K. Weinbert, *Manifest Destiny* (Baltimore: Johns Hopkins Press, 1935), p. 432.

9. *Congressional Record*, 62nd Cong., 3d sess., December 3, 1912, p. 9.

10. "Secretary Knox's Speech at the University of Pennsylvania," June 15, 1910, Knox Papers. See also Philander C. Knox, *The Spirit and Purpose of American Diplomacy* (New York: n.p., 1910), p. 46.

11. "Address of the Honorable Philander C. Knox Before the New York Bar Association," January 19, 1912, in *Papers Relating to the Foreign Relations of the United States: 1912* (Washington, D.C.: GPO, 1919), p. 1092.

12. F. M. Huntington Wilson, "Huntington Wilson's Address at Baltimore," May 4, 1911, Knox Papers.

13. *Congressional Record,* 62nd Cong., 3d sess., December 3, 1912, p. 9.

14. William H. Taft, "The President's Speech at the American Club," May 2, 1910, Knox Papers.

15. Ibid.

16. L. W. Strayer, "Secretary Knox Inaugurated Strenuous Policy Toward the Expansion of American Trade," *Pittsburgh Dispatch Magazine* (November 14, 1909), p. 1.

17. F. M. Huntington Wilson, "The Relation of Government to Foreign Investment," *Annals of the American Academy of Political and Social Science* 68 (November 1916), p. 304.

18. Knox, *The Spirit and Purpose of American Diplomacy,* pp. 51–52.

19. Philander C. Knox, "Latin America," October 6, 1909, Knox Papers.

20. Ibid.

21. Philander C. Knox, "Rough Notes on Honduras Loan," February 1911, Knox Papers.

22. See Philander C. Knox, "The Policy of the U.S. in Central America," n.d. [ca. 1911], Knox Papers.

23. Wilson to President, March 9, 1912, 837.00/777a, March 9, 1912, General Records of the Department of State, RG 59, U.S. National Archives (hereinafter cited as DS/RG 59). See also Leland H. Jenks, *Our Cuban Colony* (New York: Vanguard Press, 1928), pp. 104–06; Munro, *Dollar Diplomacy and Intervention in the Caribbean,* p. 480. To wait until conditions of disorder actually led to the destruction of property before undertaking armed intervention, U.S. officials reasoned, would subject foreign capital to unnecessary risks. Insurgents possessed the capacity, the United States consul reported in 1912, to "destroy in an hour property representing millions of dollars in value and that has taken years to construct." See Haladay to Beaupré, June 13, 1912, 837.00/763, DS/RG 59. And at another point: during the "considerable time required for the arrival of an expedition from the United States," the U.S. military attaché in Havana acknowledged, "insurrectionists would have an opportunity to inflict tremendous damages on very valuable properties" (Hobson to Chief of Staff, G-2, December 13, 1921, File 2012-86, Records of the War Department, General and Special Staffs, RG 165, U.S. National Archives).

24. Knox, *The Spirit and Purpose of American Diplomacy,* p. 46.

25. Office of the Solicitor, Department of State, "The Platt Amendment," July 5, 1912, 711.37/39½, DS/RG 59.

26. Office of the Solicitor, Department of State, "Intervention in Cuba," July 12, 1912, 711.37/33½, DS/RG 59, emphasis in original.

27. Ibid., emphasis in original.

28. Ibid., emphasis in original. See also Clark to Doyle, July 12, 1912, 711.37/38½, DS/RG 59.

29. Office of the Solicitor, Department of State, "Intervention in Cuba," July 12, 1912, 711.37/33½, DS/RG 59, emphasis in original.

30. Ibid.

31. Clark to Doyle, July 12, 1912, 711.37/38½, DS/RG 59.

32. Office of the Solicitor, Department of State, "Intervention in Cuba," July 12, 1912, 711.37/33½, DS/RG 59.

33. Clark to Doyle, July 12, 1912, 711.37/38½, DS/RG 59.

34. Knox to Beaupré, August 9, 1912, 837.6112/2, DS/RG 59.

35. Knox to Jackson, May 6, 1911, 837.00/473, DS/RG 59. An earlier internal memorandum phrased these instructions in slightly different terms: "It should be made clear to Mr. Jackson that it is our policy, apart from the direct protection of American interests, to endeavor by friendly representation or advice to keep Cuba from enacting legislation of any kind which appears to us to be of an undesirable character purely from the Cuban standpoint and consequently that, though he should not undertake to supervise Cuba in these

matters without previous instructions, he should continue carefully to report them and exert proper influences in cases of emergency so that suitable opportunity may be afforded to this Government to offer such friendly representation and advice, should it feel disposed to do so" (Division of Latin American Affairs to Doyle, May 1, 1911, ibid).

36. Many of these had been suppressed earlier during U.S. occupations on the ground that they lacked the economic base to support local administration and government service. These included Abreus, Banes, Encrucijada, Zulueta, Perico, Manguito, San José de los Ramos, Agramonte, Sabanilla del Encomendador, Victoria de las Tunas, Corralillo, San Fernando de Camarones, San Antonio de Cabezas, Guamacaro, San Juan de las Yeras, Caimito del Guayabal, Los Palacios, Candelaría, Mariel, Carlos Rojas, Santa Ana, Cifuentes, Regla, La Salud, San Nicolás, Campechuela and San Diego del Valle. See Emetrio S. Santovenia and Raúl M. Shelton, *Cuba y su historia,* 2d ed. (Miami: Cuba Corporation, 1966), 3:36.

37. Emeterio S. Santovenia, *José Miguel Gómez* (Havana: Imprenta "El Siglo XX," 1958), pp. 21–22, Rodolfo A. Carballal, *Estudio sobre la administración de José Miguel Gómez, 1909–1913* (Havana: Imprenta y Papelería de Rambla, Bouza y Cía., 1915), pp. 17–18, 29–39; Enrique Barbarrosa, *El proceso de la república* (Havana: Imprenta Militar de Antonio Pérez, 1911), pp. 46–50; *Cuba bajo la administración presidencial del mayor General José Miguel Gómez* (Havana: Imprenta and Papelería de Rambla y Bouza, 1911).

38. Jackson to Secretary of State, April 15, 1910, 837.00/1, DS/RG 59.

39. See Burlingham to Stimson, September 13, 1911, 836.857/2, DS/RG 59; and Burlingham to Clark, September 20, 1911, 837.857/3, DS/RG 59.

40. Jackson to Secretary of State, April 20, 1911, 837.6113/10, DS/RG 59.

41. Rodgers to Secretary of State, June 26, 1911, 837.77/36, DS/RG 59.

42. Rodgers to Secretary of State, July 3, 1911, 837.77/44, DS/RG 59.

43. Jackson to Secretary of State, June 22, 1911, 837.77/40, DS/RG 59.

44. See Fowler to Beaupré, March 12, 1912, 837.77/63, DS/RG 59.

45. Beaupré to Secretary of State, March 13, 1912, 837.77/63, DS/RG 59, and February 17, 1913, 837.77/98, DS/RG 59, emphasis in original.

46. See Beaupré to Secretary of State, June 9, 1912, 837.77/75, DS/RG 59.

47. Beaupré to Secretary of State, January 3, 1913, 837.77/91, DS/RG 59.

48. Wilson to Beaupré, December 23, 1912, 837.77/89, DS/RG 59.

49. Beaupré to Secretary of State, January 3, 1913, 837.77/91, DS/RG 59.

50. Knox to Jackson, April 19, 1911, 837.6113/6, DS/RG 59.

51. Wilson to Jackson, April 67, 1911, 837.6113/10, DS/RG 59.

52. Jackson to Secretary of State, April 28, 1911, 837.6113/14, DS/RG 59.

53. Beaupré to Secretary of State, July 23, 1912, 837.51/167, DS/RG 59.

54. Beaupré to Secretary of State, July 5, 1912, 837.6112/—, DS/RG 59.

55. Knox to Beaupré, July 17, 1912, 837/6112/1, DS/RG 59. This note was formally delivered to Gómez a day later. See Beaupré to Gómez, July 18, 1912, 837.6112/4, DS/RG 59.

56. Knox to Beaupré, July 26, 1912, 837.6112/—, DS/RG 59.

57. Knox to Beaupré, July 26, 1912, ibid.

58. Ibid.

59. Knox to Gibson, August 15, 1912, 837.6112/2, DS/RG 59.

60. E. H. Harrison, "Memorandum," June 5, 1911, 837.51/138, DS/RG 59.

61. J. Reuben Clark, "The Construction of Article 2 of the Treaty of Relations with Cuba, with Reference to Proposed Grants of Financial Assistance to Railroad Enterprises," July 20, 1911, Francis White Papers.

62. Ibid. See also J. Reuben Clark, "Memorandum," July 20, 1911, 837.77/54, DS/RG 59.

63. Harrison to Clark, May 1912, 837.77/71, DS/RG 59.

64. Beaupré to Gómez, March 6, 1912, 837.77/61, DS/RG 59. For letter of instruction, see Wilson to Legation, Havana, Cuba, March 5, 1912, 837.77/58a, DS/RG 59.

65. Knox to Beaupré, June 22, 1912 837.77/73, DS/RG 59.

66. Knox to Jackson, May 31, 1911, 837.00/475, DS/RG 59.

67. Knox to Beaupré, August 9, 1912, 837.6112/2, DS/RG 59.

68. Acting Secretary of Commerce to Secretary of State, September 28, 1911, 837.857/4, DS/RG 59.

69. Harrison to Legation, Havana, Cuba, October 18, 1911, 837.857/4, DS/RG 59.

70. Knox to Legation, Havana, Cuba, January 10, 1912, 837.57/14, DS/RG 59.

71. Chapin to Knox, March 29, 1910, 4197/67, DS/RG 59.

72. Chapin to Knox, June 16, 1910, 837.152H11/72, DS/RG 59.

73. Wilson to Jackson, February 10, 1911, 337.115 M 17/78, DS/RG 59.

74. See Green to Crane, May 2, 1911, 837.602/4, DS/RG 59 and June 6, 1911, 837.602/5, DS/RG 59.

75. See Jackson to Knox, May 10, 1911, 837.602/3, DS/RG 59; and Division of Latin American Affairs, "Memorandum," August 22, 1911, 837.602/6, DS/RG 59. See also José Antonio Ramos, *Manual del perfecto fulanista. Apuntes para el estudio de nuestra dinámica político-social* (Havana: Jesús Montero, 1916), pp. 123–27.

76. Knox to Legation, Havana, Cuba, May 9, 1911, 837.602/1A, DS/RG 59.

77. Wilson to Gibson, August 26, 1911, 837.602/7, DS/RG 59.

78. Adee to Beaupré, November 1, 1912, 837.602/24, DS/RG 59.

79. Beaupré to Knox, June 28, 1912, 637.003/187, DS/RG 59.

Chapter 6. The Pursuit of Politics

1. See Alberto Lamar Schweyer, *La crisis del patriotismo*, 2d ed. (Havana: Editorial Martí, 1929), pp. 173–75.

2. Irene A. Wright, *Cuba* (New York: Macmillan, 1910), pp. 164–66.

3. Ruby Hart Phillips, *Cuban Sideshow* (Havana: Cuban Press, 1935), p. 130.

4. See José Antonio Ramos, *Manual del perfecto fulanista. Apuntes para el estudio de nuestra dinámica político-social* (Havana: Jesús Montero, 1916), pp. 200–04.

5. Miguel de Carrión, "El desenvolvimiento social de Cuba en los últimos veinte años," *Cuba Contemporánea* 9 (September 1921), 19–20. See also Raimundo Menocal, *Tres ensayos sobre la realidad cubana* (Havana: Imprenta O'Reilly, 1935), p. 33; and Rogelio de Armas, "Los partidos políticos y los problemas sociales," *Cuba Contemporánea* 2 (July 1913), 225–29.

6. Ramos, *Manual del perfecto fulanista. Apuntes para el estudio de nuestra dinámica político-social*, pp. 83–87, 133–36; Fernando Ortiz, *La crisis política cubana (sus causas y remedios)* (Havana: Imprenta y Papelería "La Universal," 1919), p. 9.

7. James L. Rodgers, "Memorandum," May 24, 1911, 837.00/476. The U.S. minister had written earlier: "Everyone in politics seems anxious to get and to be kept upon the Government's pay-roll. Already about half of Cuba's revenue goes to 'personnel,' and new offices are constantly being created. . . . On every change in the Cabinet (and even in minor offices) an addition is made to the already large number of incompetents—or others who do merely nominal work—who are protected from removal from office upon subsequent changes." See Jackson to SS, May 10, 1911, 837.00/474, General Records of the Department of State, RG 59, U.S., Washington, D.C. (hereinafter cited as DS/RG 59).

8. See Ramos, *Manual del perfecto fulanista. Apuntes para el estudio de nuestra dinámica político-social*, pp. 40–43, 62, 67; Carlos de Velasco, *Aspectos nacionales* (Havana:

Jesús Montero, 1915), p. 48; Carlos M. Raggi Ageo, *Condiciones económicas y sociales de la república de Cuba* (Havana: Editorial Lex, 1944), p. 117.

9. Long to Secretary of State, May 28, 1921, 837.154/8, DS/RG 59.

10. Rionda to Czarnikow-Rionda, January 5, 1911, Cuban Matters, Letterbook September 1909–March 1912, Braga Brothers Collection.

11. Avelino Sanjenís, *Tiburón* (Havana: Librería Hispanoamericana, 1915), pp. 155–67; Charles E. Chapman, *A History of the Cuban Republic* (New York: Macmillan, 1927), p. 289.

12. See Orestes Ferrara, *Una mirada sobre tres siglos: memorias* (Madrid: Playor, S.A., 1975), pp. 241, 415–16.

13. See Walter Fletcher Johnson, *The History of Cuba* (New York: B. F. Buck, 1920), 5:192.

14. José A. Duarte Oropesa, *Historiología cubana* (n.p., n.p.), 3:169–70.

15. See Carlos Márquez Sterling, *Historia de Cuba* (New York: Las Américas, 1963), p. 276; Calixto C. Masó, *Historia de Cuba* (Miami: Ediciones Universal, 1976), p. 485; Carlos M. Trelles, *El progreso (1902 a 1905) y el retroceso (1906 a 1922) de la república de Cuba* (Matanzas: Imprenta de Tomás González, 1923), p. 9.

16. Hugh Thomas, *Cuba, the Pursuit of Freedom* (New York: Harper and Row, 1971), pp. 505–06; Chapman, *A History of the Cuban Republic*, p. 430.

17. See Jackson to Knox, April 28, 1911, 837.6113/14, DS/RG 59.

18. "Los veteranos de la independencia, al pueblo de Cuba," October 28, 1911, in Manuel Secades y Japón. *La justicia en Cuba. Patriotas y traidores* (2 vols., Havana: Imprenta P. Fernández y Cía., 1912–1914), 1:57–62. On the veterans' protest, see Luis de Juan Puñal, *Tirando de la manta* (Havana: Arroyo, Fernández, y Cía., n.d.), pp. 147–51 and Gerardo Castellanos Garcia, *Panorama histórico* (Havana: Ucar, García y Cía., 1934), pp. 1368–69; Masó, *Historia de Cuba*, p. 486.

19. "Los veteranos de la independencia, al pueblo de Cuba," in Secades y Japón, *La justicia en Cuba* 1:62.

20. In Secades y Japón, *La justicia in Cuba* 1:254.

21. Philander C. Knox to Legation, Havana, Cuba, January 16, 1912, 837.00/541, DS/RG 59. See Dana G. Munro, *Dollar Diplomacy and Intervention in the Caribbean, 1900–1921* (Princeton, N.J.: Princeton University Press, 1964), pp. 475–76; Chapman, *A History of the Cuban Republic*, pp. 306–07.

22. In Secades y Japón, *La justicia in Cuba* 1:172–73, 2:171–72; see also Teresita Yglesia Martínez, *El segundo ensayo de república* (Havana: Editorial de Ciencias Sociales, 1980), pp. 206–10.

23. See Antonio Maceo, "A los cubanos de la raza negra," n.d., Fondo de Donativos y Remisiones, Legajo 525, no. 13, Cuban National Archives.

24. Rafael María Merchán, *Cuba, justificación de sus guerras de independencia*, 2d ed. (Havana: Imprenta Nacional de Cuba, 1961), p. 41.

25. Dwight Aultman, "Project for Combining the Cuerpo de Artilleria with the Rural Guard," enclosure in Dwight Aultman to Adjutant General, January 25, 1902, File (1902) 2, Records of the Military Government of Cuba, RG 140, U.S. National Archives. See also Thomas T. Orum, "The Politics of Color: The Racial Dimension of Cuban Politics During the Early Republican Years, 1900–1912," Ph.D. diss., New York University, 1975, pp. 57–92.

26. Esteban Montejo, *The Autobiography of a Runaway Slave*, trans. Jocasta Innes, ed. Miguel Barnet (New York: Random House, 1973), p. 216.

27. Serafín Portuondo Linares, *Los independientes de color. Historia del Partido Independiente de Color* (Havana: Ministerio de Educación, 1950), pp. 13–14; Masó, *Historia de Cuba*, p. 487.

28. *La Lucha,* June 9, 1901.

29. U.S. War Department, *Censo de la república de Cuba, 1907* (Washington, D.C.: GPO, 1908), p. 546.

30. A. A. Schomburg, "General Evaristo Estenoz," *Crisis* 4 (July 1912), 143–44.

31. See Orum, "The Politics of Color," pp. 93–119; and Alberto Arredondo, *El negro en Cuba* (Havana: Editorial "Alfa," 1939), pp. 58–63.

32. See Orum, "The Politics of Color," pp. 115–34.

33. See Portuondo Linares, *Los independientes de color,* pp. 62–80.

34. Arangurén et al., to Beaupré, March 22, 1912, 837.00/578, DS/RG 59. See also Alejandro Lima Boyez, *et al.,* to William Howard Taft, March 23, 1912, 837.00/579, DS/RG 59.

35. Portuondo Linares, *Los independientes de color,* pp. 244–68; Chapman, *A History of the Cuban Republic,* pp. 312–13. For a progovernment account, see Rafael Conte and José M. Capmany, *Guerra de razas (negros contra blancos en Cuba)* (Havana: Imprenta Militar de Antonio Pérez, 1912).

36. See Duarte Oropesa, *Historiología Cubana* 3:6; Rafael Martínez Ortiz, *Cuba, los primeros años de independencia,* 2d ed. 2 (Paris: Le Livre Libre, 1921), 2:414–16; Pedro Luis Padrón, "Inició Estrada Palma en 1902 la política de reprimir con violencia a los trabajadores," *Granma,* May 13, 1969, p. 2, "Policías y guardias rurales agredieron brutalmente a trabajadores en huelga en 1902," *Granma,* May 15, 1969, p. 2.

37. José Rivero Muñiz, *El movimiento laboral cubano durante el período 1909–1911* (Santa Clara: Universidad de Las Villas, 1962), pp. 82–99.

38. See Victor S. Clark, "Labor Conditions in Cuba," *Bulletin of the Department of Labor* 7 (July 1902), 765.

39. See Carlos Toro González, "La fundación de la primera sindical nacional de los trabajadores cubanos (los congresos obreros de 1892 a 1934)," in Juan Pérez de la Riva et al., *La república neocolonial* (Havana: Editorial de Ciencias Sociales, 1975–1979), 2:93–98; Mario Riera Hernández, *Historial obrero Cubano, 1574–1965* (Miami: Rema Press, 1965), p. 44.

40. See León Primelles, *Crónica cubana, 1919–1922* (Havana: Editorial Lex, 1957), pp. 86–90.

41. Beaupré to Secretary of State, May 4, 1912, 837.5041/22, DS/RG 59.

42. Bingham to Secretary of State, January 19, 1919, 837.504/90, DS/RG 59.

43. Stephenson to Crowder, December 8, 1920, Correspondence, File 276, Enoch H. Crowder Papers.

44. Davis to Enoch H. Crowder, March 3, 1922, 837.504/235, DS/RG 59.

45. Orestes Ferrara, *Mis relaciones con Máximo Gómez,* 2d ed. (Havana: Molina y Compañía, 1942), p. 266.

46. Crowder to Secretary of State, March 3, 1922, 837.504/235, DS/RG 59.

47. Squiers to Hay, December 2, 1902, Despatches, DS/RG 59. See also Pedro Luis Padrón, "La huelga de los apréndices de 1902 y la enmienda Platt," *Granma* (December 23, 1966), p. 2.

48. Wilson to Legation, Havana, Cuba, May 9, 1912, 837.5041/24, DS/RG 59.

49. Clark, "Labor Conditions in Cuba," p. 767.

50. Marson to Maslen, December 19, 1918, 837.504/94, DS/RG 59.

51. Marson to Maslen, December 29, 1918, 836.504/94, DS/RG 59.

52. Gonzales to Secretary of State, March 9, 1919, 837.504/118, DS/RG 59.

53. See Sánchez Agramonte to Director of Military Intelligence, March 29, 1919, File 2046-171, Records of the War Department, General and Special Staff, U.S. National Ar-

chives (hereinafter cited as WD/RG 165). See also Olga Cabrera, *El movimiento obrero cubano en 1920*, pp. 51–59.

54. Welles to Department of State, December 30, 1918, File 20969-5, Subject File, 1911–1927, Box 629, RG 45, U.S. National Archives.

55. Winans to Scholle, October 20, 1917, 837.504/26, DS/RG 59. See also John Dumoulin, *Azúcar y lucha de clases, 1917* (Havana: Editorial de Ciencias Sociales, 1980), pp. 106–74.

56. Gonzales to Secretary of State, March 9, 1919, 837.504/118, DS/RG 59.

57. Beaupré to Secretary of State, May 8, 1912, 837.5041/23, DS/RG 59.

58. Clum to Secretary of State, December 3, 1918, 837.504/57, DS/RG 59.

59. Henry H. Morgan, "Memorandum Regarding the Political, Economic and Labor Situation in Cuba," January 3, 1919, 837.00/1526, DS/RG 59.

60. See Van Natta to Director of Military Intelligence, November 6, 1918, File 2056-39, WD/RG 165. See also Gallatin to Military Staff, December 4, 1918, File 2056-52, WD/RG 165; Primelles, *Crónica cubana*, p. 89.

61. Gallatin to Director of Military Intelligence, January 27, 1919, 837.00/1524, DS/RG 59. For an excellent study of the impact of the Russian Revolution on Cuban labor, see Angel García and Piotr Mironchuk, *La revolución de octubre y su influencia en Cuba* (Havana: Academia de Ciencias, 1977), pp. 99–154.

62. Morgan to Carr, November 22, 1918, 837.504/62, DS/RG 59.

63. George M. Rolph, "Labor Situation—Cuba," October 22, 1917, 837.504/25, DS/RG 59.

64. See Gonzales to Secretary of State, September 29, 1917, 837.504/22, DS/RG 59 and Scholle to Secretary of State, October 31, 1917, 837.504/32, DS/RG 59.

65. See Wilson to Legation, Havana, Cuba, May 9, 1912, 837.5041/24, DS/RG 59.

66. Williamson to Hernández, June 24, 1920, 837.504/181, DS/RG 59. See also Primelles, *Crónica cubana*, p. 257.

67. See Brown to Van Natta, January 28, 1918, File 7299-36, DW/RG 165.

68. Martínez and Domenech to Gompers, October 21, 1917, 837.504/35, DS/RG 59.

69. Daniels to Secretary of State, January 4, 1919, 837.504/82, DS/RG 59.

70. Daniels to Secretary of War, February 2, 1920, 837.504/167, DS/RG 59; Frank Polk to Legation, Havana, Cuba, January 10, 1919, 837.504/85, DS/RG 59.

71. Primelles, *Crónica cubana*, p. 89; Paul W. Beck, "Report on Cuban Strikes Since January 1, 1919," April 14, 1919, 837.504/147, DS/RG 59.

72. Consular District of Santiago de Cuba, "Monthly Report on Economic and Political Conditions," January 31, 1919, File (1919) 850, Miscellaneous Correspondence, U.S. Consulate, Santiago de Cuba, Records of the Foreign Service Posts of the Department of State, RG 84, U.S. National Archives.

73. Colonel M. J. Shaw, Seventh Regiment to Major General Commandant, "Report of Operations, 7th Regiment," December 15, 1917, File 2082-111:14, Secretary of Navy, General Correspondence, 1916–1926, General Records of the Department of the Navy, RG 80, U.S. National Archives.

74. Shaw to Major General Commandant, October 23, 1917, 837.00/1437, DS/RG 59.

75. Major Albert Gallatin to Director, Military Intelligence, January 11, 1919, File 10546-204(90), DW/RG 165. See also Primelles, *Crónica cubana*, p. 87.

76. See "Huelga de los apréndices," in *Documentos para la historia de Cuba*, ed. Hortensia Pichardo Viñals (Havana: Editorial de Ciencias Sociales, 1969), 2:210–11.

77. Jackson to Secretary of State, November 21, 1910, 837.5041/9, DS/RG 59. For British and German protest, see Jackson to Secretary of State, November 18, 1910, 837.5041/8, DS/RG 59.

78. Knox to Jackson, December 3, 1910, 837.5041/8, DS/RG 59. For the formal U.S. diplomatic protest, see Jackson to Sanguily, May 23, 1911, 837.5041/15, DS/RG 59.

79. Crowder to Secretary of State, November 13, 1925, 837.504/275, DS/RG 59.

80. See Kellogg to American Embassy, November 14, 1925, 837.504/275, DS/RG 59.

81. Crowder to Secretary of State, November 13, 1925, 837.504/275, DS/RG 59.

82. Kellogg to Embassy, Havana, Cuba, November 14, 1925, 837.504/275, DS/RG 59.

83. Crowder to White, November 16, 1925, 837.504/307, DS/RG 59.

84. See "Memorandum on Proposed Legislation Fixing a Minimum Wage for Labor, as Affecting Contracts of American Concerns," July 14, 1910, 837.5041/2, DS/RG 59.

85. Wilson to Jackson, July 21, 1910, 837.5041/—, DS/RG 59.

86. "Conversation Between Leland Harrison, Assistant Secretary of State, and John H. Edwards, Consolidated Railroads of Cuba," March 24, 1927, 837.504/308, DS/RG 59.

87. Mendoza to Babst, May 28, 1925, ser. 1, RG 2, Braga Brothers Collection.

88. *The Visit of the President-Elect of Cuba General Gerardo Machado to the United States in April 1925* (Washington, D.C.: Capitol Press, 1925), p. 572.

89. Raymond Leslie Buell, "Cuba and the Platt Amendment," *Foreign Policy Association Information Service* 5 (April 17, 1929), 42. See also Luis E. Aguilar, *Cuba 1933: Prologue to Revolution* (Ithaca, N.Y.: Cornell University Press, 1972), pp. 82–83.

Chapter 7. Free and Honest Elections

1. See Horacio Ferrer, *Con el rifle al hombro* (Havana: Imprenta "El Siglo XX," 1950), p. 246; Herminio Portell Vilá, "La Chambelona en Oriente," *Bohemia* 52 (April 24, 1960), 12–13, 124; "La Chambelona en Camagüey," ibid. (May 8, 1960), 12–13, 119; and "La Chambelona en Las Villas," ibid. (May 15, 1960), 36–37, 98; Bernardo Merino and F. de Ibarzabal, *La revolución de febrero. Datos para la historia*, 2d. ed. (Havana: Librería Cervantes, 1918), pp. 223–26; Wilfredo Ibrahim Consuegra, *Hechos y comentarios. La revolución de febrero en Las Villas* (Havana: La Comercial, 1920), pp. 19–30; José Navas, *La convulsión de febrero* (Matanzas: Imprenta y Monotypo "El Escritorio," 1917), pp. 10–11.

2. Gonzales to Lansing, February 15, 1917, 83700/1090, DS/RG 59. See also Rodgers to Secretary of State, February 13, 1917, 837.00/1073, General Records of the Department of State, RG 59, U.S. National Archives (hereinafter cited as DS/RG 59).

3. Lansing to Gonzales, February 13, 1917, in U.S. Department of State, *Foreign Relations of the United States, 1917* (Washington, D.C.: GPO, 1923), p. 356 (hereinafter cited as *FRUS: 1917*).

4. Lansing to Gonzales, February 18, 1917, *FRUS: 1917*, p. 363.

5. Desvernine to Céspedes, February 23, 1917, 837.00/1211, DS/RG 59.

6. *Diario de la Marina*, February 20, 1917; "La guerrita de febrero de 1917," *Boletín del Archivo Nacional* 62 (1962), 232.

7. Gonzales to Lansing, February 15, 1917, 837.00/1085, DS/RG 59.

8. Gerardo Rodríguez Morejón, *Menocal* (Havana: Cárdenas y Cía., 1941); Raúl de Cárdenas, *Como funcionó la cláusula intervencionista de la enmienda Platt* (Havana: L. Ruiz, 1948), p. 13; Ferrer, *Con el rifle al hombro*, p. 232.

9. Gonzales to Lansing, February 14, 1917, 837.00/1083, DS/RG 59.

10. Desvernine to Céspedes, February 14, 1917, 837.00/1093, DS/RG 59; *New York Times*, February 16, 1917. See also Emilio Roig de Leuchsenring, "La ingerencia norteamericana en los asuntos interiores de Cuba," *Cuba Contemporánea* 30 (September 1922), 36–51.

11. Colonel E. B. Babbitt, Ordinance Department, "Memorandum for the Chief of Staff," February 28, 1917, File 25458417, Records of the Adjutant General's Office, RG 94, U.S.

National Archives; Gonzales to Secretary of State, February 12, 1917, 837.24/26, DS/RG 59; *New York Times,* February 21, 1917.

12. Scott to Barnes, March 13, 1917, General Correspondence, Hugh L. Scott Papers.

13. Frank L. Polk, confidential diary, January 1, 1917–February 15, 1919, Drawer 88, Frank L. Polk Papers.

14. Polk to Legation, Havana, Cuba, January 15, 1919, 837.00/1504a, DS/RG 59.

15. Crowder had gained considerable prestige in Cuba and Washington for his legal work during the second intervention, resulting in the electoral code of 1908. See David A. Lockmiller, *Enoch H. Crowder: Soldier, Lawyer and Statesman* (Columbia: University of Missouri Press, 1955), p. 219.

16. Gonzales to Secretary of State, February 12, 1919, 837.00/1514, DS/RG 59; Lockmiller, *Enoch H. Crowder: Soldier, Lawyer and Statesman,* p. 219.

17. Desvernine to Bingham, January 20, 1919, 837.00/1510, DS/RG 59.

18. Gonzales to Polk, February 4, 1919, File 243, Drawer 77, Polk Papers.

19. Ibid.

20. Frank L. Polk, confidential diary, February 16, 1919–March 31, 1919, Drawer 88, Polk Papers.

21. Ibid.

22. For the full report of Crowder's findings, see Enoch H. Crowder, "Report of Major General E. H. Crowder on Investigation of Electoral Laws in Cuba," Material on Cuba, File 1240–47, Crowder Papers.

23. *Gaceta Oficial de la República (edición extraordinaria),* August 12, 1919. See also Fernando Ortiz, "La reforma electoral de Crowder en Cuba," *La Reforma Social* 20 (July 1921), 214–25; and Crowder to Secretary of State, January 17, 1921, William M. Connor Papers.

24. Major Harold E. Stephenson, "Report on Political Conditions," n.d., Material on Cuba, File 1207, Crowder Papers.

25. See Cuba, Office of the Census, *Census of the Republic, 1919* (Havana: Maza, Arroyo y Caso, 1919).

26. Orestes Ferrara, "La lucha presidencial en Cuba," *La Reforma Social* 17 (August 1920), 349.

27. Carlos Mendieta, "Adios dictadura," in Miguel de Marcos Suárez, *Carlos Mendieta* (Havana: Talleres Tipográficos de "El Magazine de la Raza," 1923), pp. 129–33; Ferrara to Secretary of State, October 26, 1920, 837.00/1823, DS/RG 59; Orestes Ferrara, "Supervisión electoral o intervención permanente," *La Reforma Social* 13 (March 1919), 201–10.

28. Gómez to Márquez Sterling, December 21, 1918, 837.00/1505, DS/RG 59. This letter was intercepted by postal censors in Key West.

29. *Diario de la Marina,* February 1 and 3, 1919. See also Leon Primelles, *Crónica cubana, 1919–1922* (Havana: Editorial Lex, 1957), p. 8.

30. See Crowder to Baker, July 19, 1919, Box 9, Newton D. Baker Papers.

31. Phillips to Legation, Havana, Cuba, October 23, 1919, 837.00/1581a, DS/RG 59.

32. Ibid.

33. Gonzales to Secretary of State, November 5, 1919, 837.00/1583, DS/RG 59; Primelles, *Crónica cubana,* p. 32.

34. Desvernine to Crowder, November 17, 1919, File 186, Correspondence, Crowder Papers.

35. Enoch H. Crowder, "Memorandum For Dr. Rowe," December 12, 1919, File 187, Correspondence, Crowder Papers.

36. Gonzales to Secretary of State, November 7, 1919, 837.00/1590, DS/RG 59.

37. Crowder to Steinhart, November 25, 1919, File 188, Correspondence, Crowder Papers.

38. Mario Riera Hernández, *Cuba política, 1899–1955* (Havana: Empresora Modelo, 1955), pp. 265, 273.

39. Colby to Legation, Havana, Cuba, March 25, 1920, 837.00/1626 (Supplemental), DS/RG 59; Daniel M. Smith, "Bainbridge Colby and the Good Neighbor Policy, 1920–1921," *Mississippi Valley Historical Review* 50 (June 1963), 67.

40. Long to Secretary of State, March 27, 1920, 837.00/1641,DS/RG 59.

41. In "Memorandum on Platt Amendment," n.d., Box 35, Frances White Papers.

42. Colby to Legation, Havana, Cuba, March 30, 1920, 837.00/1629, DS/RG 59.

43. Crowder to Steinhart, April 28, 1920, File 227, Correspondence, Crowder Papers. See also Jacinto López, "El fracaso del General Crowder en Cuba," *La Reforma Social* 20 (June 1921), 99–112.

44. Long to Polk, March 19, 1920, 837.00/1636, DS/RG 59.

45. Colby to Legation, Havana, Cuba, March 25, 1920, 837.00/1626 (Supplemental), DS/RG 59; Smith, "Bainbridge Colby and the Good Neighbor Policy, 1920–1921," p. 67.

46. Long to Secretary of State, March 23, 1920, 837.00/1653, DS/RG 59.

47. Colby to Legation, Havana, Cuba, March 29, 1920, 837.00/1641, DS/RG 59.

48. Long to Secretary of State, April 5, 1920, 837.00/1652, DS/RG 59.

49. The *Havana Post*, September 3, 1920, reported learning that if the Conservatives failed to block Gómez at the polls, Menocal "would not hand over to him the reins of power on May 20 and would go to the extent of provoking a revolution and hand over the Republic to the Americans." See also Clum to Long, October 1, 1920, 837.00/1808, DS/RG 59.

50. "Minutes of Conference Held in Dr. Rowe's Office," March 12, 1920, 837.00/1649, DS/RG 59.

51. Charles E. Seijo, "Memorandum for Major Stephenson: Political Situation in Camagüey and Santa Clara," October 27, 1920, File 266, Correspondence, Crowder Papers.

52. Buck to Clum, June 28, 1920, File (1920) 800, Miscellaneous Correspondence, American Consulate, Santiago de Cuba, Records of the Foreign Service Posts of the Department of State, RG 84, U.S. National Archives. See also Jacinto López, "El problema del sufragio en Cuba," *La Reforma Social* 14 (May 1919), 53.

53. "Brief Synopsis of Cuba's Present Internal Politics," October 1919, Material on Cuba, File 1249, Crowder Papers. See also Louis A. Pérez, Jr., "The Military and Electoral Politics: The Cuban Election of 1920." *Military Affairs* 37 (February 1973), 5–8.

54. Rowe to Latin American Affairs Division, June 24, 1920, 837.00/1680, DS/RG 59.

55. Boaz W. Long, "Memorandum of Interview with President Menocal and Dr. Desvernine," March 27, 1920, 837.00/1646, DS/RG 59.

56. Colby to Legation, Havana, Cuba, July 30, 1920, 837.00/1710, DS/RG 59.

57. Division of Latin American Affairs to Under Secretary of State, August 27, 1920, 837.00/1764, DS/RG 59.

58. Davis to Wilson, October 16, 1920, Box 198, ser. 2, Woodrow Wilson Papers.

59. White to Secretary of State, August 24, 1920, 837.00/1746, DS/RG 59.

60. Colby to White, August 25, 1920, 836.00/1737, DS/RG 59.

61. Charles Evans Hughes, "Memorandum," April 14, 1921, Box 174, File 65, Charles Evans Hughes Papers.

62. See Carlos Manuel de Céspedes, Legación de Cuba, Washington, "Memorándum de mi conversación con el señor Secretario de Estado," October 5, 1920, 837.00/1822d, DS/RG 59.

63. Davis to Long, October 20, 1920, 837.00/1822d, DS/RG 59.

64. Colby to Legation, Havana, Cuba, October 22, 1920, 837.00/1822a, DS/RG 59.

65. Davis to Legation, Havana, Cuba, October 25, 1920, 837.00/1826a, DS/RG 59.

66. Colby to Long, October 27, 1920, 837.00/1826, DS/RG 59.

67. Davis to Legation, Havana, Cuba, October 28, 1920, 837.00/1826, DS/RG 59.

68. Stephenson to Crowder, October 15, 1920, File 263, Correspondence, Crowder Papers. For accounts of the election by one U.S. supervisor, see Herbert J. Spinden, "Shall the United States Intervene in Cuba?" *The World's Week* 41 (March 1921), 465–83; Herbert J. Spinden, "Elecciones espurias en Cuba," *La Reforma Social* 19 (April 1921), 353–67, and "America and Her Duty in Cuba," *Boston Evening Transcript*, August 6, 1923.

69. Davis to Crowder, December 21, 1920, 837.00/1952b, DS/RG 59.

70. Davis to Wilson, July 28, 1920, Colby Papers.

71. Colby to Wilson, 837.00/1860a, DS/RG 59.

72. Long to Davis, February 10, 1921, Box 40, Norman H. Davis Papers. For the details of the activities of Crowder in Cuba in 1921, see Dana G. Munro, *The United States and the Caribbean Republics, 1921–1933* (Princeton, N.J.: Princeton University Press, 1974), pp. 16–23; Lockmiller, *Enoch H. Crowder: Soldier, Lawyer and Statesman*, pp. 230–32.

Chapter 8.   Reason to Rule

1. National Bank of Commerce, *Commerce Monthly* 1 (August 1919), 21–22.

2. Special Committee on the National Foreign Trade Council, "Report on American Trade Policy," in National Foreign Trade Council, *Official Report of the Eleventh Foreign Trade Convention* (New York: National Foreign Trade Council, 1924), p. 181.

3. Ibid., pp. 185–86.

4. National Bank of Commerce, *Commerce Monthly* 1 (August 1919), 22.

5. Franklin Remington, "Foreign Loans as Trade Builder," in National Foreign Trade Council, *Official Reports of the Eleventh National Foreign Trade Convention* (New York: National Foreign Trade Council, 1924), p. 170.

6. Walter Parker, "The Trade of the New World," in National Foreign Trade Council, *Official Report of the Fifteenth National Foreign Trade Convention* (New York: National Foreign Trade Council, 1928), pp. 142–43.

7. E. H. Pennington, "The Square Deal in Business," *Pan American Magazine* 31 (July 1920), 170.

8. Charles Evans Hughes, *Some Aspects of the Department of State* (Washington, D.C.: GPO, 1922), p. 10.

9. Grew to Wright, January 18, 1920, in Joseph C. Grew, *Turbulent Era* (Boston: Houghton Mifflin, 1952), 1:410.

10. J. Butler Wright, "The Department of State and American Enterprises Abroad," National Foreign Trade Council, *Official Report of the Twelfth National Trade Convention* (New York: National Foreign Trade Council, 1925), p. 169.

11. W. R. Castle, Jr., "The Department of State and American Enterprise Abroad," in National Foreign Trade Council, *Official Report of the Fifteenth National Foreign Trade Convention* (New York: National Foreign Trade Council, 1928), p. 192.

12. Welles to Fletcher, March 6, 1922, 710.11/568, DS/RG 59.

13. Division of Latin American Affairs to Welles, September 29, 1921, 811.51/2981, General Records of the Department of State, RG 59, U.S. National Archives (hereinafter cited as DS/RG 59).

14. W. W. Cumberland, Office of the Foreign Trade Adviser, "Memorandum," September 27, 1921, 811.51/2981, DS/RG 59.

15. Welles to Dearing, October 6, 1921, 811. 51/ 2981, DS/RG 59.

16. See Cumberland, Office of the Foreign Trade Adviser, to Dearing, October 12, 1921, 811.51/2981, DS/RG 59.

17. Dearing to Welles, November 18, 1921, 811.51/2981, DS/RG 59.

18. See Henry Christopher Wallich, *Monetary Problems of an Export Economy* (Cambridge, Mass.: Harvard University Press, 1950), pp. 52–54; Oscar Pino-Santos, *El asalto a Cuba por la oligarquía financiera yanqui* (Havana: Casa de las Américas, 1973), pp. 73–135.

19. Leland H. Jenks, *Our Cuban Colony* (New York: Vanguard Press, 1926), 212–13; Hugh Thomas, *Cuba, the Pursuit of Freedom* (New York: Harper and Row, 1971), 545–46.

20. Wallich, *Monetary Problems of an Export Economy*, p. 53.

21. Jenks, *Our Cuban Colony*, p. 214. See, for example, Banco Mercantil Americano de Cuba, "Loans and Advances as of August 31, 1919 (Amounts in Excess of $10,000)," and "Loans Made by the Banco Mercantil Americano de Cuba to Colonos of the Cuba Cane Sugar Corporation," n.d., RG 2, ser. 10, Braga Brothers Collection.

22. Carlton Bailey Hurst, *The Arms Above the Door* (New York: Dodd, Mead, 1932), p. 278.

23. Robert F. Smith, *The United States and Cuba, Business and Diplomacy, 1917–1960* (New Haven, Conn.: College and University Press, 1960), p. 29.

24. Jenks, *Our Cuban Colony*, pp. 281–82; Smith, *The United States and Cuba*, p. 30.

25. Miguel Alonso Pujol, *Ensayo de sociología económica* (Havana: Imprenta Avisador Comercial, 1928), pp. 28–88; Jenks, *Our Cuban Colony*, p. 282.

26. Jenks, *Our Cuban Colony*, pp. 244–45. Foreign banks generally dominated Cuba, accounting for some 76.1 percent of total deposits in 1923 from the 20 percent in 1920. See Wallich, *Monetary Problems of an Export Economy*, p. 69.

27. Jenks, *Our Cuban Colony*, pp. 288–98; Smith, *The United States and Cuba*, pp. 30–32.

28. Long to Secretary of State, November 5, 1920, 837.00/1870, DS/RG 59.

29. Davis to American Legation, December 31, 1920, 837.00/1947a, DS/RG 59. See also David A. Lockmiller, *Enoch H. Crowder: Soldier, Lawyer and Statesman* (Columbia, Mo.: University of Missouri Press, 1955), pp. 228–29.

30. Davis to American Legation, January 4, 1920, 837.00/1959, DS/RG 59.

31. Long to Secretary of State, December 21, 1920, 837.51/399, DS/RG 59.

32. Hoover to Harding, December 13, 1921, 837.61351/314, RG 59.

33. Davis to Crowder, December 31, 1920, 837.00/1952b, DS/RG 59.

34. Long to Secretary of State, December 21, 1920, 837.51/339, DS/RG 59.

35. Long to Davis, February 10, 1921, Norman H. Davis Papers.

36. Davis to American Legation, January 4, 1921, 837.00/1949, DS/RG 59.

37. "American bankers," Davis added, "can naturally not be indifferent to the present disturbed conditions, particularly when there is no certainty who the successor to the Presidency will be and when the situation is such that the possibility of serious disturbances is by no means remote" (ibid.).

38. See Crowder to Knox, February 7, 1921, File 283. Enoch H. Crowder Papers.

39. Sumner Welles, "Memorandum," March 1, 1921, 837.00/2216, DS/RG 59.

40. Carr to Johnson, September 9, 1921, 837.6135/294, DS/RG 59.

41. Hoover to President, December 13, 1921, 837.61351/314, DS/RG 59.

42. Hughes to Crowder, April 3, 1923, 837.002/62, DS/RG 59.

43. See Russell H. Fitzgibbon, *Cuba and the United States, 1900–1935* (Menasha, Wis.: George Banta, 1935), p. 169; Charles E. Chapman, *A History of the Cuban Republic* (New York: Macmillan, 1927), pp. 407–08.

44. Hughes to Crowder, June 17, 1921, 837.00/2137, DS/RG 59.

45. Crowder to Welles, April 29, 1921, 837.00/2208, DS/RG 59, emphasis in original.

46. It was the anticipation of this default that inspired the Crowder appointment. See Chapman, *A History of the Cuban Republic*, pp. 424–25.

47. Crowder to Secretary of State, February 6, 1921, 837.51/447, DS/RG 59.

48. Colby to American Legation, February 11, 1921, 837.51/447, DS/RG 59.

49. Crowder to Secretary of State, February 6, 1921, 837.51/447, DS/RG 59.

50. Crowder to Secretary of State, June 25, 1921, 837.51/498, DS/RG 59.

51. Jenks, *Our Cuban Colony*, pp. 248–49.

52. Hoover to Harding, December 13, 1921, 837.61351/314, DS/RG 59.

53. Crowder to Secretary of State, June 25, 1921, 837.51/498, DS/RG 59.

54. Hughes to Crowder, July 15, 1921, 837.51/504, DS/RG 59.

55. Crowder to Secretary of State, July 3, 1921, 837.51/508, DS/RG 59.

56. Crowder to Secretary of State, November 12, 1925, 837.61351/391, DS/RG 59.

57. Crowder to Secretary of State, July 31, 1921, 837.51/541, DS/RG 59.

58. Crowder to Secretary of State, August 22, 1921, 837.00/2158, DS/RG 59.

59. Crowder to Secretary of State, September 11, 1921, 837.51/584, DS/RG 59.

60. Chapman, *A History of the Cuban Republic*, pp. 556–58.

61. Crowder to Secretary of State, July 1, 1922, 837.51/504, DS/RG 59.

62. Crowder to Secretary of State, September 7, 1921, 837.51/583, DS/RG 59.

63. Crowder to Secretary of State, June 25, 1921, 837.51/499, DS/RG 59.

64. Crowder to Secretary of State, August 22, 1921, 837.00/2158, DS/RG 59.

65. Ibid.

66. Crowder to Secretary of State, September 7, 1921, 837.51/583, DS/RG 59.

67. Hughes to Crowder, June 29, 1921, 837.51/498, DS/RG 59.

68. See Hughes to Morgan and Company, July 9, 1921, 837.51/515a, DS/RG 59.

69. Morgan and Company to Secretary of State, July 13, 1921, 837.51/515, DS/RG 59.

70. Davis and Morrow to Secretary of State, September 23, 1921, 837.51/607, DS/RG 59.

71. Hughes to Crowder, October 13, 1921, 837.51/610, DS/RG 59.

72. Hughes to Crowder, September 24, 1921, 837.51/594a, DS/RG 59.

73. Hughes to Crowder, September 29, 1921, 837.51/604a, DS/RG 59.

74. Morrow to Zayas, October 7, 1921, 837.51/625, DS/RG 59.

75. See Zayas to Crowder, October 16, 1921, 837.51/621, DS/RG 59.

76. Crowder to Secretary of State, October 17, 1921, 837.51/618, DS/RG 59.

77. Hughes to J. P. Morgan and Company, October 20, 1921, 837.51/624, DS/RG 59.

78. Hughes to Crowder, November 19, 1921, 837.51/643, DS/RG 59.

79. Munro to Secretary of State, December 17, 1921, 837.51/713, DS/RG 59.

80. Hughes added and later deleted an ominous warning that stalled negotiations threatened to produce a situation in which "the United States will be forced to take appropriate steps, under the Treaty, to save Cuba from open bankruptcy." See Hughes to Crowder, December 20, 1921, 837.51/664, DS/RG 59.

81. See Smith, *The United States and Cuba*, pp. 90–91.

82. Hughes to Cespedes, January 14, 1922, 837.51/680, DS/RG 59.

83. Hughes to Crowder, January 21, 1922, 837.51/696a, DS/RG 59.

84. Ibid.

85. See Crowder to Zayas, February 24, 1922, 837.51/711, DS/RG 59.

86. In Harry F. Guggenheim, *The United States and Cuba* (New York: Macmillan, 1934), pp. 214–15; Fitzgibbon, *Cuba and the United States*, p. 171.

87. Crowder to Secretary of State, March 25, 1922, 837.51/746, DS/RG 59.

88. Enoch H. Crowder, "Memorandum for the Secretary of State," July 10, 1922, 837.00/2318, DS/RG 59.

89. Crowder to Zayas, April 12, 1922, 837.51/758, DS/RG 59.

90. Crowder to Zayas, April 21, 1922, 837.51/764, DS/RG 59. See also Division of Latin-American Affairs, "Synopsis of General Crowder's 13 Memoranda," November 14, 1923, 123 c 8812/51, DS/RG 59 and León Primelles, *Crónica cubana, 1919–1922* (Havana: Editorial Lex, 1957), pp. 468–85; Lockmiller, *Enoch H. Crowder*, pp. 233–40.

91. Crowder to Secretary of State, June 9, 1922, 837.51/786, DS/RG 59.

92. Crowder to Zayas, June 10, 1922, 837.51/792, DS/RG 59.

93. Crowder to Secretary of State, June 12, 1922, 837.51/792, DS/RG 59.

94. Crowder to Secretary of State, June 19, 1922, 837.002/53, DS/RG 59.

95. Crowder's indictment was based on information provided directly by the secretary of the treasury for use against the president. See Crowder to Zayas, March 9, 1923, 837.512/48, DS/RG 59.

96. Phillips to Crowder, September 14, 1922, 837.51/842, DS/RG 59.

97. Crowder to Hughes, June 23, 1922, DS/RG 59.

98. Crowder to Pershing, January 30, 1923, AG 210.681 Cuba, Project Files 1917–1924, Records of the Adjutant General's, Office, 1917–   , RG 407, U.S. National Archives.

99. Morrow to Crowder, May 26, 1922, Dwight Morrow Papers.

100. Crowder to Zayas, July 21, 1922, 837.51/808, DS/RG 59. See also Division of Latin American Affairs, "Synopsis of General Crowder's 13 Memoranda," November 14, 1923, 123 C 8812/51, DS/RG 59 and Chapman, *A History of the Cuban Republic*, pp. 435–36.

101. White to Secretary of State, October 16, 1922, 837.51/866, DS/RG 59.

102. White to Secretary of State, December 21, 1922, 837.51/944, DS/RG 59.

103. *New York Times*, January 15, 1923.

104. Morrow to Hughes, December 27, 1922, Morrow Papers. For the general United States business support given to Crowder see Smith, *The United States and Cuba*, pp. 94–96.

Chapter 9.   For High Reasons of State

1. Charles E. Chapman, *A History of the Cuban Republic* (New York: Macmillan, 1927), pp. 441, 454.

2. These included Alfredo Zayas, Jr., son: director-general of the National Lottery; Francisco Zayas, brother: ambassador to France and secretary of public instruction; Willie Gómez Colón, stepson: majordomo of the palace; Andrés Pereira, son-in-law: comptroller general of the republic; Oscar Zayas, nephew: judge of the first instance; Celso Cuéllar, son-in-law: a palace notary public and later senator; José Mario Zayas, nephew: chief of Havana customs; Alfonso Echavarría, cousin: magistrate of the *audiencia* of Havana; Carlos Portela, cousin: undersecretary of the Department of Treasury; Alfredo Bosque Reyes, nephew: director of commerce in the Department of Agriculture, Commerce, and Labor; José Ars, son-in-law: director of prisons; Juan Manuel Alfonsón, nephew: attorney in the Department of Public Works.

3. In Chapman, *A History of the Cuban Republic*, p. 443.

4. Crowder to Secretary of State, May 4, 1922, 837.513/50, General Records of the Department of State, RG 59, U.S. National Archives (hereinafter cited as DS/RG 59). See also Chapman, *A History of the Cuban Republic*, pp. 556–57; León Primelles, *Crónica cubana, 1915–1918* (Havana: Editorial Lex, 1955), pp. 12–13; Ana Cairo Ballester, *El movimiento de Veteranos y Patriotas* (Havana: Instituto Cubano del Libro, 1976), p. 39; José M. Muzaurieta, *Manual del perfecto sinvergüenza* (Havana: Imprenta "El Siglo XX," 1922), pp. 37–38.

5. See Crowder to White, May 4, 1922, 837.513/57, DS/RG 59.

6. See *El Heraldo de Cuba*, 1922–1924, and *Diario de la Marina*, 1923–1924.

7. See "Consolidated Table of Indictments Brought Against Members of Congress," December 30, 1921, 837.71/65 DS/RG 59; Crowder to Secretary of State, July 17, 1923, 837.032/68, DS/RG 59.

8. Jorge I. Domínguez, *Cuba, Order and Revolution* (Cambridge, Mass.: Harvard University Press, 1978), p. 37; Fernando Ortiz, "La decadencia cubana," *Revista Bimestre Cubana* 19 (January–February, 1924), 27.

9. See Francisco Llaca y Argudín, ed., *Legislación sobre amnistía e indultos de la república de Cuba* (Havana: Cultural, S.A., 1933); Vicente Pardo Suárez, *Funerales y responso* (Havana: Imprenta de Rambla, Bouza y Cía., 1926), pp. 25–26. See also Chapman, *A History of the Cuban Republic*, pp. 526–46; Carlos M. Trelles, *El progreso (1902 a 1905) y el retroceso (1906 a 1922) de la república de Cuba* (Matanzas: Imprenta de Tomás González, 1923), p. 21. Crowder tried mightily to prod the Zayas administration into vigorous prosecution of official corruption, without success. Wrote a discouraged Crowder: "Thus, at the end of two years in some cases, and six months in others, the prosecution of guilty persons who have defrauded the public treasury of thousands of dollars apparently is no nearer accomplishment than when the frauds were discovered, and the further investment of what is known to be a fertile field for similar frauds has been left untouched." See Crowder to Secretary of State, July 12, 1923, 837.00/2318, DS/RG 59.

10. Trelles, *El progreso*, p. 22; Ortiz, "La decadencia cubana," p. 28.

11. Olga Cabrera, *El movimiento obrero cubano en 1920* (Havana: Instituto del Libro, 1970), p. 25.

12. Crowder to Secretary of State, July 17, 1923, 837.032/68, DS/RG 59. See also Trelles, *El progreso*, p. 17.

13. "List of Bills Passed by the House of Representatives at Its Session of December 16, 1925," 837.032/86, DS/RG 59.

14. Crowder to Secretary of State, July 17, 1923, 837.032/68, DS/RG 59.

15. Crowder to Secretary of State, May 4, 1922, 513/50, DS/RG 59.

16. *El Comercio*, May 17, 1911.

17. Ibid.

18. See Jackson to Secretary of State, April 15, 1910, 837.001.

19. José Antonio Ramos, *Manual del perfecto fulanista. Apuntes para el estudio de nuestra dinámica político-social* (Havana: Jesús Montero, 1916), pp. 197–99.

20. Lionel Soto, *La revolución del 33* (Havana: Editorial de Ciencias Sociales, 1977), 1:265–66.

21. *Havana Post*, November 23, 1926.

22. Mario Averhoff Purón, *Los primeros partidos políticos* (Havana: Instituto Cubano del Libro, 1971), pp. 29–31.

23. Rionda to Czarnikow, MacDougal and Company, February 8, 1909, Cuban Letters, November 1908–April 1909, Braga Brothers Collection.

24. Gerardo Machado, *Memorias: ocho años de lucha* (Miami: Ediciones Históricas Cubanas, 1982), p. 15.

25. See Salutio García to Orestes Ferrara, 15 de abril de 1916, Fondo de Donativos y Remisiones, Legajo 383, no. 10, Cuban National Archives.

26. See Herminio Portell Vilá, "La danza de los millones," *Bohemia* 52 (June 5, 1960), 44–45, 79; Calixto C. Masó, *Historia de Cuba* (Miami: Ediciones Universal, 1976), p. 560.

27. For data dealing with Cuban trade, see Susan Schroeder, *Cuba: A Handbook of Historical Statistics* (Boston: G. K. Hall, 1982), pp. 422–33.

28. See Adolfo Dollero, *Cultura cubana* (Havana: Imprenta "El Siglo XX," 1916), pp. 339–71; Cuba, Office of the Census, *Census of the Republic of Cuba, 1919* (Havana: Maza, Arroyo y Caso, 1920), pp. 918–19.

29. Cuba, Office of the Census, *Census of the Republic of Cuba, 1919*, pp. 632-34. See also José M. Alvarez Acevedo, *La colonia española en la economía cubana* (Havana: Ucar, Garcia y Cía., 1936), p. 232.

30. Ramiro Guerra y Sánchez, *Un cuarto de siglo de evolución cubana* (Havana: Librería "Cervantes," 1924), pp. 50-51.

31. See "El desarrollo industrial de Cuba," *Cuba Socialista* 56 (April 1966), 136.

32. See Chapman, *A History of the Cuban Republic*, pp. 428-31; Wyatt MacGaffey, "Social Structure and Mobility in Cuba," *Anthropological Quarterly* 34 (January 1961), 102.

33. Pardo Suárez, *Funerales y responso*, pp. 89-170.

34. President was Carlos Azugaray and membership included Andrés Terry, Porfirio Franca, Adolfo Delgado, Gabriel García Echarte, Ricardo Sarabassa, César Castella, Miguel A. Riva, Alfredo O. Ceberio, Juan Marinello, Enrique Berenguer, José Blanco Laredo, and Leonardo Sorzano Jorrín. See J. Buttari Gaunaurd, *Boceto crítico histórico* (Havana: Editorial Lex, 1954), pp. 440-43; José A. Duarte Oropesa, *Historiología cubana* (n.p.: n.p., 1969-1970), 3:257.

35. León Primelles, *Crónica cubana, 1919-1922* (Havana: Editorial Lex, 1957), pp. 465, 507-08, 515, 517. See also Buttari Gaunaurd, *Boceto crítico histórico*, pp. 449-50; and Duarte Oropesa, *Historiología cubana* 3:263.

36. Soto, *La revolución del 33* 1:137-41; Chapman, *A History of the Cuban Republic*, pp. 466-68.

37. Soto, *La revolución del 33* 3:106-28; Ladislao González Carbajal, *Mella y el movimiento estudiantil* (Havana: Editorial de Ciencias Sociales, 1977), pp. 12-21; Jaime Suchlicki, *University Students and Revolution in Cuba, 1920-1968* (Miami: University of Miami Press, 1969), pp. 19-23; Raúl Amaral Agramonte, *Al margen de la revolución (impresiones políticos-sociales)* (Havana: Cultural, S.A., 1935), pp. 16-23.

38. See "Protesta de los trece," in Mario Riera Hernández, *Historial obrero cubano, 1574-1965* (Miami: Rema Press, 1965), p. 276.

39. Soto, *La revolución del 33* 1:134. Cairo Ballester, *El movimiento de Veteranos y Patriotas*, p. 132.

40. For a thorough survey of the intellectual currents of the early 1920s, see Carlos Ripoll, *La generación del 23 en Cuba* (New York: Las Américas, 1968). For an excellent study of the Grupo Minorista, see Ana Cairo Ballester, *El Grupo Minorista y su tiempo* (Havana: Editorial de Ciencias Sociales, 1978).

41. Rutherford Bingham, "Economic Situation in Cuba," April 26, 1919, 837.50/26, DS/RG 59.

42. See Long to Secretary of State, October 13, 1920, 837.516/26, DS/RG 59.

43. Long to Secretary of State, October 15, 1920, 837.516/34, DS/RG 59.

44. See Cuba, Office of the Census, *Census of the Republic of Cuba, 1919*, pp. 666-67.

45. See Fabio Grobart, "The Cuban Working Class Movement from 1925 to 1933," *Science and Society* 39 (Spring 1975), 74-75.

46. Olga Cabrera, *El movimiento obrero cubano en 1920* (Havana: Instituto Cubano del Libro, 1970), pp. 75-90; Riera Hernández, *Historial obrero cubano*, p. 50; Carlos Toro González, "La fundación de la primera sindical nacional de los trabajadores cubanos (los congresos obreros de 1892 a 1934)," in *La república neo-colonial*, ed. Juan Pérez de la Riva, et al., (Havana: Editorial de Ciencias Sociales, 1975-1979), 2:98-103.

47. Grobart, "The Cuban Working Class Movement," pp. 76, 79; Toro González, "La fundación de la primera sindical nacional," pp. 105-10.

48. Primelles, *Crónica cubana*, pp. 261-62. See also "Estatutos del Partido Socialista Radical," in Cabrera, *El movimiento obrero Cubano in 1920*, pp. 122-26.

49. For discussions of the establishment of the PCC, see Pedro Serviat, *40 aniversario de*

la fundación del partido comunista (Havana: Editorial EIR, 1965); José Cantón Navarro, "La Agrupación Comunista de La Habana y nuestro primer partido marxista-leninista," *Verde Olivo* 16 (August 18, 1974), 36−38; Mario G. del Cueto, "El vívero ideológico: de Manzanillo hasta la fundación del primer partido comunista de Cuba," *Bohemia* 67 (August 15, 1975), 36−41; Fabio Grobart, "El cincuentenario de la fundación del primer partido marxista-leninista de Cuba," *Verde Olivo* 17 (August 17, 1975), 34−47; Blanca Melchor, "La Agrupación Comunista de La Habana," *Bohemia* 65 (September 14, 1973), 100−06; Pedro Serviat, "El primer partido marxista-leninista de Cuba," *Verde Olivo* 14 (August 20, 1972), 8−11.

50. Grobart, "The Cuban Working Class Movement," pp. 87−88.

51. "Exposición de los Veteranos y Patriotas," in Cairo Ballester, *El movimiento de Veteranos y Patriotas,* pp. 253−58; Buttari Gaunaurd, *Boceto crítico histórico,* pp. 476−89, 493−96.

52. See Veterans and Patriots Association, "Al país: por la regeneración de Cuba," October 14, 1923, in Buttari Gaunaurd, *Boceto crítico histórico,* pp. 515−21.

53. See Cairo Ballester, *El Grupo Minorista y su tiempo,* p. 54.

54. Cord Meyer, "Memorandum" January 24, 1922, 837.00/2196, DS/RG 59.

55. Ibid.

56. W. H. Shutan, "Attitude of Cuban Army Officers Toward President Zayas and the Present Administration," July 31, 1923, File 2657-Q-141 (8), Records of the War Department, General and Special Staffs, RG 165, U.S. National Archives (hereinafter cited as WD/RG 165).

57. Military Intelligence Division, War Department, "Survey of the Political Situation in Cuba (With Special Reference to the Veterans' Movement)," September 19, 1923, File 2657-Q-146 (1), WD/RG 165. See also J. M. Hobson, "Memorandum for General Crowder: Alleged Conspiracy Against Present Cuban Government," January 7, 1922, File 2657-Q-113, DW/RG 165.

58. W. H. Shutan, "The Cuban Political Situation," October 23, 1923, File 2657-Q-143 (26), WD/RG 165.

59. Howell to Secretary of State, September 4, 1923, 837.00/2342, DS/RG 59.

60. William Phillips, "Memorandum of Conversation with Dr. Padro, Cuban Charge d'Affaires," March 31, 1923, 837.002/92, DS/RG 59.

61. Hughes to Crowder, March 31, 1923, 837.002/60a, DS/RG 59.

62. Crowder to Zayas, April 4, 1923, 837.002/71, DS/RG 59.

63. See Crowder to Secretary of State, April 13, 1923, 837.002/74, DS/RG 59.

64. Padro to Hughes, April 5, 1923, 837.002/64a, DS/RG 59.

65. Crowder to Secretary of State, April 12, 1923, 837.002/73, DS/RG 59.

66. Phillips to Embassy, Havana, Cuba, August 28, 1923, 837.00/2327a, DS/RG 59.

67. Shutan to Adjutant General, October 18, 1923, File 2654-Q-143 (23), WD/RG 165.

68. Howell to Secretary of State, September 24, 1923, 837.00/2353, DS/RG 59.

69. This silence was not lost on Zayas. He concluded early that Washington had determined to allow conditions to deteriorate as a pretext for new intervention, and thereby remove him from office. See Howell to Secretary of State, October 26, 1923, 837.00/2400, DS/RG 59, and Office of the Secretary of State, "Memorandum of Interview with Cuban Chargé d'Affaires and Dr. Torriente," November 15, 1923, Charles Evans Hughes Papers.

70. White to Secretary of State, July 24, 1923, 837.00/2472, DS/RG 59.

71. Crowder to Secretary of State, January 24, 1924, 837.00/2476, DS/RG 59.

72. Crowder to Hughes, November 11, 1923, 123 C 8812/36, DS/RG 59.

73. White to Phillips, October 3, 1923, 837.00/2373, DS/RG 59.

74. Crowder to Secretary of State, January 25, 1924, 837.00/2476, DS/RG 59.

75. See Buttari Gaunaurd, *Boceto crítico histórico*, pp. 587–639; Chapman, *A History of the Cuban Republic*, pp. 476–80.

76. Howell to Secretary of State, September 27, 1923, 837.00/2361, DS/RG 59.

77. Crowder to Secretary of State, January 25, 1924, 837.00/2496, DS/RG 59.

78. Hughes to Crowder, April 4, 1923, 837.00/62 Supplement, DS/RG 59.

79. Ibid.

80. See Crowder to Secretary of State, July 14, 1923, 837.00/2319, DS/RG 59.

81. Hughes to Crowder, October 8, 1924, 837.00/2555, DS/RG 59.

82. See Ambrosio López Hidalgo, *Cuba y la enmienda Platt* (Havana: Imprenta "El Siglo XX," 1921); Luis Machado y Ortega, *La enmienda Platt, estudio de su alcance e interpretación y doctrina sobre su aplicación* (Havana: Imprenta "El Siglo XX," 1922); Manuel Sanguily, "Sobre la génesis de la enmienda Platt," *Cuba Contemporánea* 30 (October 1922), 117–25; Pedro Capo Rodríguez, "The Platt Amendment," *American Journal of International Law* 17 (October 1923), 761–65; Enrique Gay, "Génesis de la enmienda Platt," *Cuba Contemporánea* 60 (May–August 1926), 47–63; Cosme de la Torriente, "The Platt Amendment," *Foreign Affairs* 7 (April 1930), 364–78. For a full bibliographical review of the literature on the Platt Amendment, see James H. Hitchman, "The Platt Amendment Revisited: A Bibliographical Survey," *The Americas* 23 (April 1967), 343–69.

83. Crowder to Secretary of State, March 13, 1922, 711.37/65, DS/RG 59.

84. See Crowder to Secretary of State, August 5, 1924, 837.00/2533, DS/RG 59. For a discussion of Machado's views on the Platt Amendment, see "Cuba's Dislike of the Platt Amendment," *Literary Digest* 85 (June 6, 1925), pp. 21–22; Rafael Rodríguez Altunaga, "Cuba's Case for the Repeal of the Platt Amendment: The Views of President Machado," *Current History* 26 (September 1927), 925–27.

85. Machado y Ortega, *La enmienda Platt*, pp. 115–30.

86. See Crowder to Secretary of State, September 15, 1926, 711.37/86, DS/RG 59.

87. Crowder to Hughes, September 7, 121, 837.51/538, DS/RG 59.

88. Norman H. Davis, "Wanted: A Consistent Latin America Policy," *Foreign Affairs* 9 (July 1931), 556–63.

89. Sumner Welles, *Inter-American Relations* (Washington, D.C.: GPO, 1935), p. 9. See also Sumner Welles, "Is America Imperialistic?" *Atlantic Monthly* 134 (September 1924), 412–23.

90. Francis White to Jordan Herbert Stabler, May 15, 1926, Francis White Papers.

91. William O. Scroggs, "The American Investment in Latin America," *Foreign Affairs* 10 (April 1932), 502–03; Robert H. Patchin, "Latin-American Investments and Foreign Trade Revival," National Foreign Trade Council, *Official Report of the Eighteenth National Foreign Trade Convention* (New York: National Foreign Trade Council, 1931), pp. 203–07; Francis H. Sisson, "Our Latin-American Investment" *American Review of Reviews* 77 (January 1928), 45–48.

92. Lawrence A. Downs, "Our Commerce With the Other Americas," in National Foreign Trade Council, *Official Report of the Sixteenth National Foreign Trade Convention* (New York: National Foreign Trade Council, 1929), p. 119.

93. Palmer E. Pierce, "American Business and Latin-America," in National Foreign Trade Council, *Official Report of the Seventeenth National Foreign Trade Convention* (New York: National Foreign Trade Council, 1930), p. 76.

94. Francis R. Hart, "Changes in Our Relations with Spanish-America During the Last Quarter Century," *Harvard Business Review* 6 (July 1928), 391.

95. In William A. Williams, *Tragedy of American Diplomacy*, rev. ed. (New York: Dell, 1962), p. 152.

96. Dana G. Munro, "Our New Relation to Latin America," *Unpopular Review* 10 (October–December 1918), 308–10.

97. Henry L. Stimson and McGeorge Bundy, *On Active Service in Peace and War* (New York: Harper and Row, 1948), p. 183.

98. White to Grew, November 7, 1924, 711.13/65, DS/RG 59.

Chapter 10. Promise Without Proof

1. See Pedro González-Blanco, *El presidente Machado, o la autoridad rescatada* (Madrid: Imprenta San Martín y Cía., 1929), pp. 41–45; M. Franco Varona, *Machado, su vida y su obra* (Havana: Seonne y Fernández, 1927), pp. 35–59.

2. Leland H. Jenks, *Our Cuban Colony* (New York: Vantage, 1927), pp. 299–300; José R. Alvarez Díaz et al., *A Study on Cuba* (Coral Gables, Fla.: University of Miami Press, 1968), p. 267; Carlton Baily Hurst, "Extent and Ownership of Cuban Centrals," December 18, 1926, 837.61351/424, General Records of the Department of State, RG 59, U.S. National Archives (hereinafter cited as DS/RG 59).

3. Crowder to Secretary of State, August 26, 1924, 837.00/2544, DS/RG 59.

4. Crowder to Secretary of State, January 30, 1925, 711.37/78, DS/RG 59.

5. Crowder to Charles E. Chapman, March 25, 1925, Enoch H. Crowder Papers.

6. See White to Crowder, April 23, 1925, 033.3711/32a, DS/RG 59.

7. *The Visit of the President-Elect of Cuba General Gerardo Machado to the United States in April, 1925* (Washington, D.C.: National Capital Press, 1925), p. 36. Hugh Thomas, *Cuba, the Pursuit of Freedom* (New York: Harper and Row, 1968), p. 572.

8. Ibid.

9. Ibid., pp. 31, 36. See also Lionel Soto, *La revolución del 33* (Havana: Editorial de Ciencias Sociales, 1977), 1:210–12.

10. See Raúl Amaral Agramonte, *Al margen de la revolución (impresiones político-sociales)* (Havana: Cultural, S.A., 1935), pp. 57–61.

11. In *The Visit of the President-Elect of Cuba*, p. 10.

12. Machado also retained ties to foreign capital, holding power of attorney for U.S. interests totaling some $14 million. See Crowder to Secretary of State, August 26, 1924, 837.00/2544, DS/RG 59.

13. Gerardo Machado, *Por la patria libre* (Havana: Imprenta de F. Verdugo, 1926), pp. 14–16. See also Gerardo Machado, *Memorias: ocho años de lucha* (Miami: Ediciones Históricas Cubanas, 1982), p. 11.

14. González-Blanco, *El presidente Machado*, pp. 121–37; Division of Latin American Affairs, "Excerpts Regarding Government Finances and Kindred Matters from the Annual Report of the Consul General at Habana," April 12, 1929, 837.51/1342, DS/RG 59.

15. Alvarez Díaz, *A Study on Cuba*, pp. 222–74; Jenks, *Our Cuban Colony*, pp. 274–75; Aguilar, *Cuba, 1933: Prologue to Revolution* (Ithaca, N.Y.: Cornell University Press, 1972), pp. 56–58; Rafael Estenger, *Sincera historia de Cuba* (Medellín: Editorial Bedout, 1974), pp. 270–71; Emeterio S. Santovenia and Raúl M. Shelton, *Cuba y su historia*, 2d ed. (Miami: Cuba Corporation, 1966), 3:67–68; González-Blanco, *El presidente Machado*, pp. 219–24.

16. Ana Núñez Machín, *Rubén Martínez Villena: hombre y época* (Havana: Editorial de Ciencias Sociales, 1974), pp. 182–97.

17. In Raymond Leslie Buell, "Cuba and the Platt Amendment," *Foreign Policy Association Information Service* 5 (April 17, 1929), 42. See also Carlos G. Peraza, *Machado, crímenes y horrores de un régimen* (Havana: Cultural, S.A., 1933), p. 15. Cf. Pedro Luis Padrón, "Ordenaron los yanquis a Machado perseguir a la CNOC y al Partido Comunista,"

Granma, May 22, 1969, p. 2; "Machado anunció desde 1925 que emplearía mano fuerte contra los trabajadores," *Granma*, May 23, 1969, p. 2.

18. W. R. Valance, "Memorandum," July 15, 1925, 711.379/4, DS/RG 59.

19. Julio LeRiverend, *La república: dependencia y revolución*, 3d ed. (Havana: Editorial de Ciencias Sociales, 1971), pp. 251–52.

20. Susan Schroeder, *Cuba: A Handbook of Historical Statistics* (Boston: G. K. Hall, 1982), p. 413.

21. Machado to Charles Hayden, December 22, 1925, ser. 10, RG 2, Braga Brothers Collection. For a discussion of this dilemma, see Emilio del Real y Tejera, *La industria azucarera de Cuba* (Havana: A. Dorrbecker, 1928), pp. 63–91.

22. Stewart to Crowder, May 4, 1927, 837.00/2659, DS/RG 59.

23. Ibid.

24. Dickinson to Crowder, May 3, 1927, 837.00/2659, DS/RG 59.

25. Richards to Crowder, May 4, 1927, 837.00/2659, DS/RG 59.

26. Ostertag to Crowder, May 4, 1927, 837.00/2659, DS/RG 59.

27. William B. Murray, "Economic Conditions in the Interior Portion of the Habana Consular District," May 26, 1927, 837.00/2663, DS/RG 59.

28. C. B. Curtis, "Memorandum Concerning Political and Economic Conditions in Cuba," November 1927, 837.00/2687, DS/RG 59.

29. Crowder to Secretary of State, May 13, 1927, 837.00/2659, DS/RG 59.

30. Ibid.

31. Ibid.

32. Ibid.

33. Cuba, Congreso, *Acuerdos sobre reforma de la constitución y manifiesto del honorable señor Presidente General Gerardo Machado y Morales al país* (Havana: n.p., 1927).

34. See Crowder to Secretary of State, March 31, 1927, 837.00/2634, DS/RG 59; Crowder to Secretary of State, April 8, 1927, 837.00/2636, DS/RG 59.

35. Crowder to Kellogg, February 14, 1927, 837.00/2627, DS/RG 59.

36. Ibid.

37. See Crowder to Secretary of State, April 16, 1927, 837.00/2646, DS/RG 59.

38. See Crowder to Secretary of State, April 8, 1927, 837.00/2636, DS/RG 59; Scotten to Morgan, April 25, 1927, 837.00/2646, DS/RG 59.

39. Morgan to Secretary of State, April 11, 1927, 837.00/2681, DS/RG 59.

40. R. Morgan, "Memorandum of Conversations Between the President of Cuba and the Chief of the Division of Latin American Affairs," April 20–22, 1927, 837.00/2655, DS/RG 59.

41. "Conversation Between President Coolidge and President Machado," April 23, 1927, 033.3711/73, DS/RG 59.

42. Morgan, "Memorandum of Conversations," April 20–22, 1927, 837.00/2655, DS/RG 59.

43. Kellogg to Crowder, May 13, 1927, 837.00/2646, DS/RG 59.

44. Machado, *Memorias*, pp. 21–22, 31.

45. J. R. Baker, "Authority of the Constitutional Convention in Cuba Over Proposed Constitutional Amendments Passed by the Cuban Congress," May 12, 1928, 837.011/35, DS/RG 59.

46. See Curtis to Secretary of State, May 14, 1928, 837.011/23, DS/RG 59.

47. Judah to Secretary of State, May 31, 1928, 837.011/29, DS/RG 59.

48. Judah to White, May 31, 1928, Francis White Papers.

49. Judah to Secretary of State, May 31, 1928, 837.011/29, DS/RG 59.

50. Judah to White, May 31, 1928, White Papers.

51. White to Judah, June 9, 1928, White Papers.

52. Carlos G. Peraza, *Machado, crímenes y horrores de un régimen* (Havana: Cultural, S.A. 1933) p. 99.

53. Curtis to Secretary of State, October 28, 1928, 837.00/2714, DS/RG 59.

54. Briggs to Secretary of State, November 2, 1928, 837.00/2716, DS/RG 59.

55. In Curtis to Secretary of State, November 6, 1928, 837.00/2717, DS/RG 59.

56. Clark to Secretary of State, April 26, 1929, 837.00/2749, DS/RG 59, emphasis in original.

57. Judah to White, April 12, 1929, White Papers.

58. Judah to White, April 30, 1929, White Papers.

59. White to Stimson, April 25, 1929, White Papers.

60. During the same period the domestic share rose from 18.4 percent to 26.6 percent and the insular portion increased from 31.8 percent to 47.9. See Robert F. Smith, *The United States and Cuba: Business and Diplomacy, 1917–1961* (New Haven, Conn.: College and University Press, 1960), p. 70.

61. Sergio Aguirre, *Eco de caminos* (Havana: Editorial de Ciencias Sociales, 1974), p. 398.

62. "General Survey of Wages in Cuba, 1931 and 1932," *Monthly Labor Review* 35 (December, 1932), 1403–04.

63. Ibid., pp. 1409–11.

64. José Antonio Taboadela, *Cuestiones económicas cubanas de actualidad* (Havana: Imprenta de "El Fígaro," 1929), p. 54.

65. For a discussion of the depression in Cuba, see Gustavo Gutiérrez y Sánchez, *El problema económico de Cuba. Sus causas, sus posibles soluciones* (Havana: Molina y Cía., 1931); Raymond Leslie Buell, et al., *Problems of the New Cuba* (New York: Foreign Policy Association, 1935), pp. 52–54; Peraza, *Machado, crímenes y horrores de un régimen*, pp. 71–160.

66. Crowder to Secretary of State, May 13, 1927, 837.00/2659, DS/RG 59.

67. The case of Arturo del Pina is illustrative, who after the ruin of his clothing factory, joined the moderate opposition against Machado. He was killed by the police in 1931.

68. Curtis to Secretary of State, November 12, 1928, 837.00/General Conditions/11, DS/RG 59.

69. Tomás Montero, *Grandezas y miserias* (Havana: Editorial "Alfa," 1944), p. 188; Reed to White, October 3, 1931, White Papers; Francis White, "Memorandum," April 20, 1932, 837.51/1506, DS/RG 59; Fabio Grobart, "The Cuban Working Class Movement from 1925 to 1933," *Science and Society* 39 (Spring 1975), 91; Buell, *Problems of the New Cuba*, pp. 86–88.

70. Many political opponents were thrown into the shark-infested waters of Havana harbor. Local fishermen frequently caught sharks containing parts of the dismembered bodies of government foes. So common was this occurrence that in late 1930, a presidential decree banned shark fishing in Havana harbor to avoid, local opinion believed, the embarrassment of future catches. See James I. Mather, "Information as to Cuba," n.d., File 2056-240, Records of the War Department, General and Special Staffs, RG 165, U.S. National Archives (hereinafter cited as WD/RG 165).

71. Francis White, "Memorandum," April 10, 1931, U.S. Department of State, *Foreign Relations of the United States: 1931* (Washington, D.C.: GPO, 1946), 2:51 (hereinafter cited as *FRUS: 1931*).

72. Grobart, "The Cuban Working Class Movement," pp. 89–90.

73. Smith, *The United States and Cuba*, p. 131.

74. Ibid., pp. 124–32.

75. "Memorandum of the Conference by the Secretary of State with the Press," October 2, 1930, U.S. Department of State, *Foreign Relations of the United States: 1930* (Washington, D.C.: GPO, 1945), 2:662–63 (hereinafter cited as *FRUS: 1930*). See also Alexander DeConde, *Herbert Hoover's Latin American Policy* (Stanford, Calif.: Stanford University Press, 1951), p. 106.

76. Guggenheim to Secretary of State, November 24, 1930, *FRUS: 1930* 2:673–74.

77. See Harry F. Guggenheim, "Conference With President Machado," October 14, 1930, Harry F. Guggenheim Papers.

78. Harry F. Guggenheim, "Conference with the President of Cuba at his Finca," October 21, 1930, Guggenheim Papers.

79. See Guggenheim to Secretary of State, June 23, 1930, *FRUS: 1930* 2:649; Guggenheim to Secretary of State, November 14, 1930, ibid. 2:670; Harry F. Guggenheim, *The United States and Cuba* (New York: Macmillan, 1934), p. 170.

80. Stimson to Guggenheim, November 15, 1930, *FRUS: 1930* 2:671.

81. Guggenheim to Stimson, December 17, 1930, 711.37/146, DS/RG 59.

82. See Reed to White, September 10, 1930, White Papers.

83. Edward L. Reed, "Memorandum of Conversation with President Machado," October 22, 1931, 711.37/162, DS/RG 59.

84. Guggenheim to Secretary of State, May 29, 1931, *FRUS: 1931* 2:61.

85. Harry F. Guggenheim, "Conversation: Ambassador Ferrara and Ambassador Guggenheim at the American Embassy," January 10, 1931, Guggenheim Papers.

86. Smith, *The United States and Cuba*, p. 130.

87. Curtis to Secretary of State, July 9, 1929, 837.51/1352, DS/RG 59. The U.S. military attache struck a similar tone: "If money not received in the immediate future, it is possible that about 18,000 employees of the Public Works Department will be without employment." J. J. O'Hare, "Presidential Office," November 26, 1929, File 2657-Q-285, WD/RG 165.

88. Curtis to Secretary of State, October 25, 1929, 837.51/1360, DS/RG 59.

89. See Alfredo Lima, *La odisea de Río Verde* (Havana: Cultural, S.A., 1934), pp. 9–10; Julio Laurent y Dubet, "Datos esenciales de la expedición de Gibara," *Bohemia* 25 (August 20, 1935), 24–25, 72, 74–77; Machado, *Memorias*, pp. 40–43.

90. See José A. Tabares del Real, *Guiteras* (Havana: Instituto Cubano del Libro, 1973), p. 168; Francisco López Segrera, *Raíces históricas de la revolución cubana (1868–1959)* (Havana: Unión Nacional de Escritores y Artistas Cubanos, 1978), pp. 79–80.

91. Guggenheim to Secretary of State, January 20, 1931, *FRUS: 1931* 2:44.

92. Jorge I. Domínguez, *Cuba: Order and Revolution* (Cambridge, Mass.: Harvard University Press, 1978), pp. 4243.

93. In Grobart, "The Cuban Working Class Movement," pp. 93–94; ABC, *Doctrina del ABC* (Havana: Editorial Cenit, 1942), p. 20.

94. Guggenheim to Acting Secretary of State, September 2, 1931, *FRUS: 1931* 2:73.

95. "Conversation. Harry F. Guggenheim: General Discussion of Cuban Situation," November 13, 1931, 837.00/3207, DS/RG 59; Guggenheim to Stimson, January 20, 1932, 711.37/174, DS/RG 59.

96. Major J. J. O'Hare, "Important Problems and Issues Requiring Governmental Recognition and Action," December 29, 1931, File 2657-Q-330 (90), WD/RG 165.

97. Guggenheim to Stimson, January 20, 1932, 711.37/174, DS/RG 59. See also Machado, *Memorias*, pp. 48–49.

98. Guggenheim to Stimson, January 25, 1932, 837.00/3227, DS/RG 59. See also Guggenheim, *The United States and Cuba*, pp. 233–34.

99. See Carlos M. Raggi Ageo, *Condiciones económicas y sociales de la república de Cuba* (Havana: Editorial Lex, 1944), p. 77.

100. See Welles to Secretary of State, May 22, 1933, 837.51/1566, DS/RG 59.

101. Soto, *La revolución del 33* 2 : 105.

102. Grobart, "The Cuban Working Class Movement," pp. 96–97.

103. "The defeat of expeditionary force," Guggenheim predicted in August, "with its loss of war materials following inability of rebels to capture any towns or important positions, the incarceration of all oppression leaders . . . , and the loyalty of the army and naval personnel should greatly discourage further revolutionary activities." See Guggenheim to Secretary of State, August 20, 1931, 837.00 Revolutions/27, DS/RG 59.

104. R. Morgan, "Dr. Fernando Ortiz: Political Situation in Cuba," April 29, 1927, 837.00/2657, DS/RG 59.

105. *Washington Daily News*, April 6, 1929.

106. Guggenheim to Stimson, January 20, 1932, 711.37/174, DS/RG 59.

107. Soto, *La revolución del 33* 2 : 98–99.

108. Guggenheim to Secretary of State, November 24, 1930, *FRUS: 1930* 2 : 676.

109. Guggenheim to Secretary of State, March 30, 1931, *FRUS: 1931* 2 : 50.

110. Peraza and Adler to Judah, February 29, 1929, 837.00/2723, DS/RG 59. See also Soto, *La revolución del 33* 2 : 138.

111. While the State Department may have renounced the exercise of intervention, it refused to relinquish the right of intervention. In one of the few recorded instances of restraint on the Machado government, Stimson reacted with pique to the proposed amendment. The enactment of the proposed bill, he protested, would be perceived as an "affront by Cuba at the United States" and an attempt to repudiate U.S. treaty rights. Stimson stressed: "It must be obvious that to fulfill its duties in the premises, the Government of the United States must have free access to the sources of information and naturally citizens of Cuba constitute most important sources upon such questions as whether Cuban independence is threatened; whether the Government of Cuba, at a given time, is adequate for the protection of life, property and individual liberty, and whether the Government of Cuba is properly discharging the obligations imposed by the Treaty of Paris on the United States and thereafter assumed and undertaken by the Government of Cuba. In this relation it is not too much to say that the enactment of the proposed legislation would be strong evidence that that the existing government is not appropriately protecting individual liberty." See Stimson to Judah, April 23, 1929, 837.00/2730, DS/RG 59. See also Munro to White, March 29, 1929, 837.00/2735, DS/RG 59.

112. Guggenheim to Secretary of State, August 20, 1931, 837.00 Revolutions/27, DS/ RG 59.

113. Guggenheim to Stimson, January 20, 1932, 711.37/174, RG 59. See also Guggenheim to Secretary of State, November 24, 1930, *FRUS: 1930* 2 : 675–76; and Francis White, "Memorandum," November 22, 1932, 837.00/3411, DS/RG 59. For a discussion of these tactics, see Raúl Roa, *La revolución del 30 se fué a bolina* (Havana: Editorial de Ciencias Sociales, 1976), pp. 359–61.

114. "Conversation. Mr. Harry F. Guggenheim: General Discussion of Cuban Situation," November 13, 1931, 837.00/3207, DS/RG 59; "Memorandum Dictated by Ambassador Guggenheim," November 12, 1931, 837.00/3195½, DS/RG 59.

115. "Conversation. Mr. Harry F. Guggenheim: General Discussion of Cuban Situation," November 13, 1931, 837.00/3207, DS/RG 59. See also DeConde, *Herbert Hoover's Latin American Policy*, pp. 106–07; Smith, *The United States and Cuba*, p. 130.

116. Guggenheim to Stimson, January 25, 1932, 837.00/3227, DS/RG 59; Guggenheim, *The United States and Cuba*, pp. 235–36.

117. Stimson to Guggenheim, March 26, 1932, 837.00/3227, DS/RG 59.

118. Guggenheim to Stimson, January 20, 1932, 711.37/174, DS/RG 59.

119. Guggenheim, *The United States and Cuba*, p. 245; Guggenheim to Stimson, January 20, 1932, 711.37/174, DS/RG 59.

120. "Problems Confronting the American Embassy in Habana Since November 1929," March 29, 1933, 837.00/3481, DS/RG 59.

121. Guggenheim to Stimson, January 20, 1932, 711.37/174, DS/RG 59.

122. Ibid. See also Harry F. Guggenheim, "Amending the Platt Amendment," *Foreign Affairs* 12 (April 1934), 449–50, and *The United States and Cuba*, pp. 237–38.

123. Guggenheim to Secretary of State, January 20, 1933, 837.00/3442, DS/RG 59.

124. Ibid. For Machado's view of Guggenheim's conduct, see Machado, *Memorias*, pp. 45–46.

Chapter 11.   Echoes of Contradictions

1. See Charles William Taussig, "Cuba—and Reciprocal Trade Agreements," in National Foreign Trade Council, *Official Report of the Twenty-First National Foreign Trade Convention* (New York: National Foreign Trade Council, 1934), p. 554; Harry F. Guggenheim, "Changes in the Reciprocity Treaty Which Would Probably Benefit the United States Export Trade with Cuba," March 30, 1933, 611.3731/390, General Records of the Department of State, RG 59, U.S. National Archives (hereinafter cited as DS/RG 59); Sumner Welles, *Relations Between the United States and Cuba* (Washington, D.C.: GPO, 1934), pp. 14–15.

2. Guggenheim, "Changes in the Reciprocity Treaty."

3. Ibid. See also Charles M. Barnes, Department of Commerce, "Memorandum: Some Suggestions With Reference to the Pending Negotiations for the Revision of Cuban Reciprocity Treaty," September 12, 1933, 611.3731/466, DS/RG 59.

4. In William A. Williams, *The Tragedy of American Diplomacy*, 2d ed. (New York: Dell, 1962), p. 170.

5. Sumner Welles, *Two Years of the "Good Neighbor" Policy* (Washington, D.C.: GPO, 1935), pp. 5–6.

6. Ibid., p. 7.

7. Philip Jessup, "Confidential Memorandum on the Cuban Situation," n.d. [ca. early 1933], Philip Jessup Papers.

8. See *Havana Post*, October 28, 1927.

9. Machado later contended that U.S. opposition to his government began in earnest only after he had rejected the schedule proposed by Sumner Welles as the basis for a new reciprocity treaty. The United States plan, Machado protested, promised to undo Cuban progress in economic diversification and restore the island's dependency on North American imports. See Gerardo Machado, *Memorias: ocho años de lucha* (Miami: Ediciones Historicas Cubanas, 1982), pp. 58, 74–75.

10. White to Reed, September 22, 1931, Francis White Papers. See also Robert F. Smith, *The United States and Cuba: Business and Diplomacy, 1917–1960* (New Haven, Conn.: College and University Press, 1960), pp. 127–28.

11. Jules R. Benjamin, *The United States and Cuba: Hegemony and Dependent Development, 1880–1934* (Pittsburgh, Pa.: University of Pittsburgh Press, 1977), p. 122; Welles to Secretary of State, May 22, 1933, 837.51/1567, DS/RG 59.

12. William Phillips, "Memorandum of Conversation with Cuban Ambassador," May 4, 1933, 550. S I Washington/415, DS/RG 59.

13. Hull to Welles, May 1, 1933, 711.37/178a, DS/RG 59.

14. Welles, *Two Years of the "Good Neighbor" Policy*, p. 7.

15. Welles to Secretary of State, May 13, 1933, 837.00/3512, DS/RG 59.

16. Ibid. Cf. Machado, *Memorias*, pp. 70–78.

17. Welles to Hull, May 25, 1933, 837.00/3526, DS/RG 59.

18. Cordell Hull, "Memorandum for the President," May 27, 1933, Franklin D. Roosevelt Papers.

19. Welles to Secretary of State, May 13, 1933, 837.00/3512, DS/RG 59.

20. "Long Distance Telephone Conversation Between Secretary Hull and Ambassador Welles in Cuba," May 18, 1933, 611.3731/416½, DS/RG 59.

21. Welles to Roosevelt, May 18, 1933, Roosevelt Papers.

22. Welles to Roosevelt, July 17, 1933, 837.00/3579½, DS/RG 59.

23. Machado, *Memorias,* pp. 99–110.

24. Welles to Phillips, August 5, 1933, 837.00/3603, DS/RG 59.

25. Welles to Hull, August 7, 1933, 837.00/3606, DS/RG 59.

26. Welles to Hull, August 10, 1933, 837.00/3630, DS/RG 59.

27. Welles to Hull, August 9, 1933, 837.00/3626, DS/RG 59.

28. Welles to Secretary of State, August 5, 1933, 837.00/3603, DS/RG 59.

29. William Phillips, "Memorandum," August 8, 1933, 837.00/3629, DS/RG 59.

30. Fabio Grobart, "The Cuban Working Class Movement from 1925 to 1933," *Science and Society* 39 (Spring 1975), 98–100.

31. Welles to Hull, August 7, 1933, 837.00/3606, DS/RG 59.

32. Welles, *Two Years of the "Good Neighbor" Policy,* p. 8.

33. Welles to Hull, August 8, 1933, 837.00/3616, DS/RG 59.

34. Ibid.

35. Ibid.

36. William Phillips, "Memorandum of Conversation with Cuban Ambassador," July 25, 1933, 837.00/3582½, DS/RG 59. See also Enrique Lumen, *La revolución cubana, 1902–1934: Crónica de nuestro tiempo* (México: Ediciones Bota, 1934), p. 78.

37. Welles to Hull, August 8, 1933, 837.00/3616, DS/RG 59.

38. Ibid.

39. *New York Herald Tribune,* August 8, 1933.

40. Machado, *Memorias,* p. 125.

41. Welles to Hull, August 10, 1933, 837.00/3633, DS/RG 59.

42. Welles to Hull, August 9, 1933, 837.00/3622, DS/RG 59.

43. *New York Times,* August 7, 1933.

44. Welles to Hull, August 9, 1933, 837.00/3624, DS/RG 59. See also Welles to Hull, August 8, 1933, 837.00/3615, DS/RG 59.

45. See Hull to Welles, August 9, 1933, 837.00/3621, DS/RG 59 and Hull to Welles, August 10, 1933, 837.00/3623, DS/RG 59.

46. Welles, *Two Years of the "Good Neighbor" Policy,* pp. 8–9.

47. Welles to Hull, August 11, 1933, 837.00/3633, DS/RG 59.

48. Ibid.

49. ABC, *El ABC en la mediación* (Havana: Maza, Caso y Cía., 1934), pp. 46–48; Ricardo Adam y Silva, *La gran mentira. 4 de septiembre de 1933* (Havana: Editorial Lex, 1947), p. 67; Alberto Lamar Schweyer, *Como cayó el presidente Machado* (Madrid: Espasa-Calpe, S.A., 1941), pp. 179–80.

50. Lieutenant Colonel T. N. Gimperling, "Causes of Recent Revolt of Armed Forces Against Machado," G-2 Report, August 21, 1933, File 2012-133(7), Records of the War Department, General and Special Staffs, RG 165, U.S. National Archives (hereinafter cited as WD/RG 165).

51. Machado himself later attributed the military coup to fear of seeing enemies of the administration triumph, and thus intervened to offset anticipated reprisals against the

armed forces. See Machado to Roosevelt, September 4, 1933, Roosevelt Papers. See also Rafael Guas Inclán, *El general Gerardo Machado y Morales* (Havana: n.p., 1956), p. 23.

52. "Memorandum," August 11, 1933, in Orestes Ferrara to Sumner Welles, August 12, 1933, File (1933) 800, U.S. Embassy, Cuba, Correspondence, Records of the Foreign Service Posts of the Department of State, RG 84, U.S. National Archives, Washington D.C. See also Machado, *Memorias,* pp. 112–13.

53. *New York Times,* August 12, 1933.

54. Charles A. Thomson, "The Cuban Revolution: Fall of Machado," *Foreign Policy Reports* 11 (December 18, 1935), 257; *New York Times,* August 7, 1933; Lamar Schweyer, *Como cayó el presidente Machado,* p. 180.

55. Gimperling, "Causes of Recent Revolt."

56. William Phillips, "Memorandum of Conversation With Cuban Ambassador," July 25, 1933, 837.00/3582½, DS/RG 59.

57. Lamar Schweyer, *Como cayó el presidente Machado,* p. 180. See also Machado, *Memorias,* pp. 109–10.

58. Welles to Phillips, June 6, 1933, 837.00/3537, DS/RG 59.

59. Luis E. Aguilar, *Cuba, 1933: Prologue to Revolution* (Ithaca, N.Y.: Cornell University Press, 1972), pp. 155–56; Louis A. Pérez, Jr., *Army Politics in Cuba, 1898–1958* (Pittsburgh, Pa.: University of Pittsburgh Press, 1976), pp. 78–79.

60. R. Hart Phillips, *Cuba: Island of Paradox* (New York: McDowell, Obolensky, 1959), p. 55.

61. See Carlos G. Peraza, *Machado, crímenes y horrores de un régimen* (Havana: Cultural, S.A., 1933), pp. 320–21.

62. Welles to Hull, August 19, 1933, Department of State, *Foreign Relations of the United States: 1933* (Washington, D.C.: GPO, 1952), 5:367–68 (hereinafter cited as *FRUS: 1933*).

63. Welles to Hull, August 24, 1933, Roosevelt Papers.

64. Welles to Hull, August 19, 1933, *FRUS: 1933* 5:367–68.

65. Benjamin, *The United States and Cuba,* p. 123.

66. Welles to Hull, August 24, 1933, Roosevelt Papers.

67. Welles to Hull, August 24, 1933, 837.00/3706, DS/RG 59.

68. Rafael García Bárcena, "Razón y sinrazón del 4 de septiembre," *Bohemia* 44 (September 7, 1952), 60; Francisco Masiques Landeta, "Puntos sobresalientes del septembrismo," *Bohemia* 31 (September 11, 1949), 54; Ramón Grau San Martin, *La revolución cubana ante América* (Mexico City: Ediciones del Partido Revolucionario Cubano, 1936), p. 92.

69. A copy of the proclamation enclosed in Welles to Hull, September 5, 1933, 837.00/3753, DS/RG 59. See also Aguilar, *Cuba, 1933,* pp. 163–64.

70. See Lumen, *La revolución cubana,* pp. 149–54.

71. See Phillips, *Cuba: Island of Paradox,* pp. 69, 72.

72. The most notable confrontations occurred at the worker soviets established at Mabay, Jaronú, Nazabal, and Punta Alegre. See José A. Tabares del Real, *Guiteras* (Havana: Instituto Cubano del Libro, 1973), p. 263.

73. Welles to Hull, September 18, 1933, 837.00/3934, DS/RG 59.

74. Welles to Acting Secretary of State, December 7, 1933, 837.00/4480, DS/RG 59.

75. Welles to Hull, October 16, 1933, *FRUS: 1933,* 5:487.

76. Welles to Hull, October 13, 1933, 837.00/4193, DS/RG 59.

77. "Memorandum of Telephone Conversation Between Secretary of State Hull and Welles," September 5, 1933, 837.00/3800, DS/RG 59; E. David Cronon, "Interpreting the New Good Neighbor Policy: The Cuban Crisis of 1933," *Hispanic American Historical Review* 34 (November, 1959), 546.

78. Welles to Hull, September 5, 1933, 837.00/3757, DS/RG 59.

79. "Memorandum of Telephone Conversation Between Secretary of State Hull and Welles," September 5, 1933, 837.00/3757, DS/RG 59.

80. Welles to Hull, September 5, 1933, 837.00/3756, DS/RG 59.

81. Welles to Hull, September 7, 1933, 837.00/3778, DS/RG 59.

82. Harold L. Ickes, *The Secret Diaries of Harold L. Ickes* (New York: Simon and Schuster, 1953–1954), 1:87.

83. Cordell Hull, *The Memoirs of Cordell Hull* (New York: Macmillan, 1948), 1:313.

84. Welles to Hull, October 5, 1933, 837.00/4136, DS/RG 59.

85. Welles to Hull, September 18, 1933, 837.00/3934, DS/RG 59.

86. Rubén de León, "La verdad de lo ocurrido desde el cuatro de septiembre," *Bohemia* 25 (February 4, 1934), 39; Charles A. Thomson, "The Cuban Revolution: Reform and Reaction," *Foreign Policy Reports* 11 (January 1, 1936), 263.

87. Gimperling, "Army Officers Defy Present Regime."

88. "Memorandum of Conversation Between Secretary Hull at Washington and Ambassador Welles at Habana, by Telephone," September 9, 1933, 837.00/3939, DS/RG 59.

89. *New York Herald Tribune*, September 11, 1933.

90. Gimperling, "Army Officers Defy Present Regime."

91. *New York Times*, September 7, 1933; Cronon, "Interpreting the New Good Neighbor Policy," p. 550.

92. In Phillips, *Cuba: Island of Paradox*, pp. 90–92. Ruby Hart Phillips, the *New York Times* correspondent in Havana, also recalled hearing rumors that Welles had promised the officers intervention. See ibid., p. 71. See also Betancourt to Hull, November 5, 1933, Cordell Hull Papers.

93. See Lieutenant Colonel T. N. Gimperling, "Battle at National Hotel, on October 2," October 6, 1933, File 2012-193(19), DS/RG 59.

94. Pérez, *Army Politics in Cuba, 1898–1958*, pp. 92–93.

95. Welles to Hull, October 5, 1933, 837.00/4131, DS/RG 59.

96. Welles to Hull, October 16, 1933, 837.00/4206, DS/RG 59.

97. Welles to Hull, October 4, 1933, 837.00/4131, DS/RG 59.

98. Ibid.

99. Welles to Hull, October 7, 1933, 837.00/4146, DS/RG 59.

100. Welles to Hull, October 29, 1933, 837.00/4301, DS/RG 59.

101. Welles to Hull, December 5, 1933, 837.00/4475, DS/RG 59.

102. Caffery to Acting Secretary of State, January 13, 1934, 837.00/4605, DS/RG 59.

Chapter 12.   Cuba, 1902–1934: A Retrospect

1. Caffery to Secretary of State, March 14, 1934, 837.00/4929, General Records of the Department of State, RG 59, U.S. National Archives (hereinafter cited as DS/RG 59).

2. See José A. Tabares del Real, *La revolución del 30: sus dos últimos años* (Havana: Editorial de Ciencias Sociales, 1975), pp. 157–316.

3. This theme is examined in detail by Samuel Farber, *Revolution and Reaction in Cuba, 1933–1960* (Middletown, Conn.: Wesleyan University Press, 1976), pp. 20–22, 78–80.

4. Major E. W. Timberlake, "Restoration of Colonel Julio Velasco as Adjutant General of the Cuban Army," May 5, 1938, File 2012-133 (88), Records of the War Department, General and Special Staffs, RG 165, U.S. National Archives.

5. See Emilio Roig de Leuchsenring, "El Tratado Permanente de 1903 y su arbitraria modificación—no abrogación—por Norteamérica, en 1934," *Revista Bimestre Cubana* 39 (1937), 389–403.

6. See Jesús Chía, "El monopolio en la industria del jabón y del perfume," in *Monopolios norteamericanos en Cuba* (Havana: Editorial de Ciencias Sociales, 1973), pp. 1–52; Williamson to Secretary of State, July 9, 1978, 837.00/General Conditions/7, DS/RG 59; Jules Robert Benjamin, *The United States and Cuba: Hegemony and Dependent Development, 1880–1934* (Pittsburgh: University of Pittsburgh Press, 1977), pp. 19, 39, 40.

7. Bryan to Gonzales, May 18, 1914, William E. Gonzales Papers, emphasis in original. A year later Gonzales informed President Mario G. Menocal: "To change by statute this condition and to make illegal the sort of marriages that have always been recognized here as legal, and that are legal in the United States, is certain to deeply offend many Cubans and to create antagonisms which must inevitably be injurious to the country. See Gonzales to Menocal, April 28, 1915, 837.4054/1, DS/RG 59.

8. See Raúl Roa, *La revolución del 30 se fue a bolina* (Havana: Editorial de Ciencias Sociales, 1976), pp. 379–80.

9. Sumner Welles, *Relations Between the United States and Cuba* (Washington, D.C.: GPO, 1934), p. 3.

Bibliography

Archival Sources

U.S. NATIONAL ARCHIVES
General Records of the Department of State. Record Group 59.
General Records of the Navy. Record Group 80.
Records of the Adjutant General's Office, 1780s–1917. Record Group 94.
Records of the Bureau of Insular Affairs. Record Group 350.
Records of the Foreign Service Posts of the Department of State. Record Group 84.
Records of the Military Government of Cuba. Record Group 140.
Records of the Post Office Department. Record Group 28.
Records of the United States Overseas Operations and Commands, 1898–1942.
    Record Group 395.
Records of the War Department, General and Special Staffs. Record Group 165.

CUBAN NATIONAL ARCHIVES
Fondo de Donativos y Remisiones.

Manuscript Collections

LIBRARY OF CONGRESS, WASHINGTON, D.C.
Newton D. Baker Papers
Bainbridge Colby Papers
Norman H. Davis Papers
William Eaton Chandler Papers
Charles Evans Hughes Papers
Philip C. Jessup Papers

Philander C. Knox Papers
William McKinley Papers
Philip Phillips Family Papers
José Ignacio Rodríguez Papers
Theodore Roosevelt Papers
Elihu Root Papers
Hugh L. Scott Papers
James H. Wilson Papers
Woodrow Wilson Papers
Leonard Wood Papers

OTHER LOCATIONS
Braga Brothers Collection. Latin American Library, University of Florida.
John R. Brooke Papers. Historical Society of Pennsylvania, Philadelphia.
William M. Connor Papers. Alderman Library, University of Virginia.
Enoch H. Crowder Papers. Western Historical Manuscript Collection, University of Missouri.
William E. Gonzales Papers. South Caroliniana Library, University of South Carolina.
Dwight W. Morrow Papers. Robert Frost Library, Amherst College.
Frank L. Polk Papers. Sterling Memorial Library, Yale University.
Franklin D. Roosevelt Papers. Franklin D. Roosevelt Library, Hyde Park, N.Y.
Francis White Papers. U.S. National Archives, Washington, D.C.

Theses and Unpublished Manuscripts

Cuba. Constituent Assembly. "Record of Sessions of the Constitutional Convention of the Island of Cuba." 7 vols. Bureau of Insular Affairs Library. National Archives. Washington, D.C.
Orum, Thomas T. "The Politics of Color: The Racial Dimension of Cuban Politics During the Early Republican Years, 1900–1912." Ph.D. diss., New York University, 1975.

Documents

Brooke, John R. *Civil Report of Major-General John R. Brooke, U.S. Army, Military Governor, Island of Cuba, 1900.* Washington, D.C.: GPO, 1900.
Cuba. Congreso. *Acuerdos sobre reforma de la constitución y manifiesto del honorable señor Presidente General Gerardo Machado y Morales al país.* Havana: N. p., 1927.
———. Congreso. Cámara de Representantes. *Mensajes Presidenciales remitidos al congreso transcurridos desde el veinte de mayo de mil novecientos dos hasta el primero de abril de mil novecientos diez y siete.* Havana: N.p., n.d.
———. Convención Constituyente. *Opinión sobre las relaciones entre Cuba y los Estados Unidos.* Havana: Imprenta y Papelería "La Universal," 1901.

————. Secretaria de Hacienda. Sección de Estadística. *Inmigración y movimiento de pasajeros en el año . . . 1912–1918*. Havana: Imprenta "La Propagandista," 1913–1919.

Estrada Palma, Tomás. *Desde el Castillo de Figueras. Cartas de Estrada Palma (1877–1878)*. Ed. Carlos de Velasco. Havana: Sociedad Editorial Cuba Contemporánea, 1918.

Hughes, Charles Evans. *Some Aspects of the Department of State*. Washington, D.C.: GPO, 1922.

Llaverías, Joaquín. ed. *Correspondencia de la delegación cubana en Nueva York durante la guerra de 1895 a 1898*. 5 vols. Havana: Imprenta del Archivo Nacional, 1943–1946.

Magoon, Charles E. *Report of Provisional Administration from December 1st, 1907 to December 1st, 1908*. Havana: n.p., 1908.

Quesada, Gonzalo de. *Archivo de Gonzalo de Quesada*. ed. Gonzalo de Quesada y Miranda. 2 vols. Havana: Imprenta "El Siglo XX," 1948–1951.

Richardson, James D., ed. *A Compilation of Messages and Papers of the Presidents, 1789–1902*. Washington, D.C.: Library of Congress, 1896–1902.

Taft, William H., and Robert Bacon. "Report of William H. Taft, Secretary of War, and Robert Bacon, Assistant Secretary of State, of What was Done Under the Instructions of the President in Restoring Peace in Cuba," December 11, 1906, in Department of War, *Report of the Secretary of War, 1906*, appendix E, U.S. Congress, House, 59th Cong., 2d sess., 1906. H. Doc. 2, ser. 1505.

U.S. Congress. Senate. *Affairs in Cuba*. 56th Cong., 2d sess., 1901. ser. 4053.

————. Senate. Committee on Relations with Cuba. *Conditions in Cuba*. Washington, D.C.: GPO, 1900.

————. Senate. Committee on Relations with Cuba. *Hearings Before the Committee on Relations with Cuba: Statement of Major General John R. Brooke*. Washington, D.C.: GPO, 1900.

————. Senate. *Consular Correspondence Respecting the Condition of the Reconcentrados in Cuba, the State of the War in that Island, and the Prospects of the Projected Autonomy*. 55th Cong., 2d sess., 1898. S. Doc. 230.

————. Senate. *The Establishment of Free Government in Cuba*. 58th Cong., 2d sess., 1904. S. Doc. 312, ser. 4592.

————. Senate. *Qualifications of Voters at Coming Elections in Cuba*. 56th Cong., 2d sess., 1900. S. Doc. 243, ser. 3867.

————. Senate. *Report of the Commission Appointed by the President to Investigate the Conduct of the War Department in the War with Spain*. 56th Cong., 1st sess., 1900. ser. 3859–66.

————. Senate. *Report of the Committee on Foreign Relations: Affairs in Cuba*. 55th Cong., 2d sess., 1898. S. Rept. 885, Ser. 3624.

U.S. Department of State. *Papers Relating to the Foreign Relations of the United States: 1906–1934*. Washington, D.C.: GPO, 1909–1953.

U.S. Treasury Department. *Report on the Commercial and Industrial Condition of Cuba*. Washington, D.C.: GPO, 1899.

U.S. War Department. *Annual Report of the War Department for the Fiscal Year Ended June 30, 1900*. Washington, D.C.: GPO, 1900.

————. *Civil Report of Brigadier General Leonard Wood, Military Governor of Cuba, for Period from January 1 to May 20, 1902.* 6 vols. Washington, D.C.: GPO, 1902.

————. *Informe sobre el censo de Cuba, 1899.* Washington, D.C.: GPO, 1900.

————. *Censo de la república de Cuba, 1907.* Washington, D.C.: GPO, 1908.

————. Adjutant General's Office. *Correspondence Relating to the War with Spain.* Washington, D.C.: GPO, 1902.

Welles, Sumner. *Inter-American Relations.* Washington, D.C.: GPO, 1935.

————. *Relations Between the United States and Cuba.* Washington, D.C.: GPO, 1934.

————. *Two Years of the "Good Neighbor" Policy.* Washington, D.C.: GPO, 1935.

Newspapers

Boletín Comercial
Diario de la Marina
Diario de Matanzas
Gaceta Oficial de la República
La Lucha
New York Evening Post
New York Herald
New York Journal
New York Times
New York Tribune
El País
The State
Washington Evening Star
Washington Post

Memoirs, Autobiographies, and Reminiscences

Atkins, Edwin F. *Sixty Years in Cuba.* Cambridge, Mass.: Riverside Press, 1926.

Consuegra, Wilfredo Ibrahim. *Hechos y comentarios. La revolución de febrero en Las Villas.* Havana: La Comercial, 1920.

Ferrara, Orestes. *Memorias: una mirada sobre tres siglos.* Madrid: Colección Plaza Mayor, 1975.

————. *Mis relaciones con Máximo Gómez.* 2d ed. Havana: Molina y Compañía, 1942.

Ferrer, Horacio, *Con el rifle al hombro.* Havana: Imprenta "El Siglo XX," 1950.

Foraker, Joseph Benson. *Notes of a Busy Life.* 2 vols. 3d ed. Cincinnati: Stewart and Kidd, 1917.

Grew, Joseph C. *Turbulent Era.* 2 vols. Boston: Houghton Mifflin, 1952.

Hull, Cordell. *The Memoirs of Cordell Hull.* 2 vols. New York: Macmillan, 1948.

Hurst, Carlton Bailey. *The Arms Above the Door.* New York: Dodd, Mead, 1932.

Ickes, Harold L. *The Secret Diaries of Harold L. Ickes.* 3 vols. New York: Simon and Schuster, 1953–1954.

León y Castillo, F. de. *Mis tiempos*. 2 vols. Madrid: Librería de los Sucesores de Hernando, 1972.
Lima, Alfredo. *La odisea de Río Verde*. Havana: Cultural, S.A., 1934.
Machado, Gerardo. *Memorias: ocho años de lucha*. Miami: Ediciones Históricas Cubanas, 1982.
McIntosh, Burr. *The Little I Saw of Cuba*. New York: F. Tennyson Neely, 1899.
Montejo, Esteban. *The Autobiography of a Runaway Slave*. Trans. Jocasta Innes; ed. Miguel Barnet. New York: Random House, 1973.
Phillips, Ruby Hart. *Cuba: Island of Paradox*. New York: McDowell, Obolensky, 1959.
———. *Cuban Sideshow*. Havana: Cuban Press, 1935.
Steele, James W. *Cuban Sketches*. New York: G. P. Putnam's Sons, 1881.
Stimson, Henry L., and McGeorge Bundy. *On Active Service in Peace and War*. New York: Harper and Brothers, 1948.
Weyler, Valeriano. *Mi mando en Cuba*. 5 vols. Madrid: Imprenta de Felipe González Rojas, 1910–1911.

Books

Abad, L. V. de. *Azúcar y caña de azúcar. Ensayo de orientación cubana*. Havana: Editora Mercantil Cubana, 1945.
ABC. *El ABC en la mediación*. Havana: Maza, Caso y Cía., 1934.
Adam y Silva, Ricardo. *La gran mentira. 4 de septiembre de 1933*. Havana: Editorial Lex, 1947.
Aguilar, Luis E. *Cuba, 1933: Prologue to Revolution*. Ithaca, N.Y.: Cornell University Press, 1972.
Alba, Victor. *Nationalists Without Nations*. New York: Praeger, 1968.
Alvarez Acevedo, José M. *La colonia española en la economía cubana*. Havana: Ucar, García y Cía., 1936.
Alvarez Díaz, José R., et al. *Cuba: geopolítica y pensamiento económico*. Miami: Duplex, 1964.
———. *A Study on Cuba*. Coral Gables: University of Miami Press, 1965.
Amaral Agramonte, Raúl. *Al margen de la revolución (impresiones politícosociales)*. Havana: Cultural, S.A., 1935.
Arredondo, Alberto. *El negro en Cuba*. Havana: Editorial "Alfa," 1939.
Averhoff Purón, Mario. *Los primeros partidos políticos*. Havana: Instituto Cubano del Libro, 1971.
Barbarrosa, Enrique. *El proceso de la república*. Havana: Imprenta Militar de Antonio Pérez Sierra, 1911.
Benjamin, Jules R. *The United States and Cuba: Hegemony and Dependent Development, 1880–1934*. Pittsburgh, Pa.: University of Pittsburgh Press, 1977.
Berenguer, Fernando. *La riqueza de Cuba*. Havana: Imprenta "El Arte," 1917.
Brown Castillo, Gerardo. *Cuba colonial. Ensayo histórico social de la integración de la sociedad cubana*. Havana: Jesús Montero, 1952.
Buell, Raymond Leslie, et al. *Problems of the New Cuba*. New York: Foreign Policy Association, 1935.

Buttari Gaunaurd, J. *Boceto crítico histórico*. Havana: Editorial Lex, 1954.

Cabrera, Olga. *El movimiento obrero cubano en 1920*. Havana: Instituto Cubano del Libro, 1969.

Cabrera, Raimundo. *Cuba and the Cubans*. Trans. Laura Guiteras. Philadelphia: Levytype, 1896.

Cairo Ballester, Ana. *El Grupo Minorista y su tiempo*. Havana: Editorial de Ciencias Sociales, 1978.

——. *El Movimiento de Veteranos y Patriotas*. Havana: Instituto Cubano del Libro, 1976.

Callcott, Wilfrid Hardy. *The Caribbean Policy of the United States, 1890–1920*. Baltimore: Johns Hopkins Press, 1942.

Camacho, Francisco. *Peninsulares y cubanos*. Havana: Imprenta Mercantil, 1891.

Carballal, Rodolfo Z. *Estudio sobre la administración del General José Miguel Gómez, 1909–1913*. Havana: Imprenta y Papelería de Rambla, Bouza y Cía., 1915.

Cárdenas, Angel G. *Soga y sangre*. 2 vols. Havana: Jesús Montero, 1945.

Cárdenas, Raúl de. *Como funcionó la cláusula intervencionista de la enmienda Platt*. Havana: L. Ruiz, 1948.

Carreras, Julio A. *Historia del estado y el derecho en Cuba*. Havana: Ministerio de Educación Superior, 1981.

Carrera y Justiz, Francisco. *El municipio y los extranjeros. Los españoles en Cuba*. Havana: Librería y Imprenta "La Moderna Poesía," 1904.

Castellanos García, Gerardo. *Panorama histórico*. Havana: Ucar, García y Cía., 1934.

Céspedes, Benjamín. *La prostitución en la ciudad de La Habana*. Havana: Establecimiento Tipográfico, 1888.

Chapman, Charles E. *A History of the Cuban Republic*. New York: Macmillan, 1927.

Clark, William J. *Commercial Cuba*. New York: Charles Scribner's Sons, 1898.

Conangla Fontanilles, Jose. *Cuba y Pi y Margall*. Havana: Editorial Lex, 1947.

Conte, F. A. *Las aspiraciones del Partido Liberal de Cuba*. Havana: Imprenta de A. Alvarez y Cía., 1892.

Conte, Rafael, and José M. Capmany. *Guerra de razas (negros contra blancos en Cuba)*. Havana: Imprenta Militar de Antonio Pérez, 1912.

Coolidge, Louis A. *An Old-Fashioned Senator: Orville H. Platt of Connecticut*. New York: G. P. Putnam's Sons, 1910.

Corbitt, Duvon C. *A Study of the Chinese in Cuba, 1847–1947*. Wilmore, Ky.: Asbury College, 1971.

DeConde, Alexander. *Herbert Hoover's Latin-American Policy*. Stanford, Calif.: Stanford University Press, 1951.

Descamps, Gastón. *La crisis azucarera y la isla de Cuba*. Havana: La Propaganda Literaria, 1885.

Dollero, Adolfo. *Cultura cubana*. Havana: Imprenta "El Siglo XX," 1916.

Domínguez, Jorge I. *Cuba: Order and Revolution*. Cambridge, Mass.: Harvard University Press, 1978.

Duarte Oropesa, José A. *Historiología cubana*. 5 vols. N.p., 1969–1970.

Dumoulin, John. *Azúcar y lucha de clases, 1917.* Havana: Editorial de Ciencias Sociales, 1980.

Duque, Matías. *Nuestra patria.* Havana: Imprenta Montalvo, Cárdenas y Cía., 1923.

Eslava, Rafael. *Juicio crítico de Cuba en 1887.* Havana: Establecimiento Tipográfico, 1887.

Estenger, Rafael. *Sincera historia de Cuba.* Medellín: Editorial Bedout, 1974.

Estévez Romero, Luis. *Desde el Zanjón hasta Baire.* 2 vols. 2d ed. Havana: Editorial de Ciencias Sociales, 1974.

Fermoselle, Rafael. *Política y color en Cuba.* Montevideo: Ediciones Geminis, 1974.

Figueras, Francisco. *La intervención y su política.* Havana: Imprenta Avisador Comercial, 1906.

Fitzgibbon, Russell H. *Cuba and the United States, 1900–1935.* Menasha, Wis.: George Banta, 1935.

Foner, Philip S. *The Spanish-Cuban-American War and the Birth of American Imperialism.* New York: Monthly Review Press, 1972.

Franco Varona, M. *Machado, su vida y su obra.* Havana: Seonne y Fernández, 1927.

Friedlander, H. E. *Historia económica de Cuba.* Havana: Jesús Montero, 1944.

Gallego García, Tesifonte. *Cuba por fuera.* Havana: La Propaganda Literaria, 1890.

García, Alejandro, and Oscar Zanetti, eds. *United Fruit Company: un caso del dominio imperialista en Cuba.* Havana: Editorial de Ciencias Sociales, 1976.

García, Angel, and Piotr Mironchuk. *La revolución de octubre y su influencia en Cuba.* Havana: Academia de Ciencias, 1977.

Giberga, Eliseo. *Obras de Eliseo Giberga.* 4 vols. Havana: Imprenta y Papeleria de Rambla, Bouza y Cía., 1930–1931.

Gómez, Máximo. *Algunos documentos políticos de Máximo Gómez.* Ed. Amalia Rodríguez Rodríguez. Havana: Biblioteca Nacional "José Martí," 1962.

González Blanco, Pedro. *El presidente Machado, o la autoridad rescatada.* Madrid: Imprenta San Martín y Cía., 1929.

González Carbajal, Ladislao. *Mella y el movimiento estudiantil.* Havana: Editorial de Ciencias Sociales, 1977.

Grau San Martín, Ramón. *La revolución cubana ante América.* México: Ediciones del Partido Revolucionario Cubano, 1936.

Guas Inclán, Rafael. *El general Gerardo Machado y Morales.* Havana: n.p., 1956.

Guerra y Sánchez, Ramiro. *Un cuarto de siglo de evolución cubana.* Havana: Librería "Cervantes," 1924.

———. *et al. Historia de la nación cubana.* 10 vols. Havana: Editorial Historia de la Nación Cubana, S.A., 1952.

———. *Sugar and Society in the Caribbean.* New Haven, Conn.: Yale University Press, 1964.

Guggenheim, Harry F. *The United States and Cuba: A Study in International Relations.* New York: Macmillan, 1934.

Gutiérrez y Sánchez, Gustavo. *El problema económico de Cuba. Sus causas, sus posibles soluciones.* 2 vols. Havana: Molina y Cía., 1931.

Hagedorn, Hermann. *Leonard Wood; A Biography.* 2 vols. New York: Harper and Brothers, 1931.

Healy, David F. *The United States in Cuba, 1898–1902.* Madison: University of Wisconsin Press, 1963.

Hill, Howard C. *Roosevelt and the Caribbean.* Chicago: University of Chicago Press, 1927.

Horrego Estuch, Leopoldo. *Máximo Gómez, libertador y ciudadano.* Havana: Imprenta P. Fernández y Cía., 1948.

Hyatt, Pulaski F., and John T. Hyatt. *Cuba: Its Resources and Opportunities.* New York: J. S. Ogilvie, 1898.

Infiesta, Ramón. *El autonomismo cubano: su razón y manera.* Havana: Jesús Montero, 1939.

International Bank for Reconstruction and Development. *Report on Cuba.* Washington, D.C.: International Bank for Reconstruction and Development, 1951.

Ituarte, Ignacio D. *Crímenes y criminales en La Habana.* Havana: n.p., 1893.

Jenks, Leland H. *Our Cuban Colony.* New York: Vanguard, 1928.

Jessup, Philip C. *Elihu Root.* 2 vols. New York: Dodd, Mead, 1938.

Johnson, Walter Fletcher. *The History of Cuba.* 5 vols. New York: B. F. Buck, 1920.

Jones, Chester Lloyd. *Caribbean Interests of the United States.* New York: D. Appleton, 1916.

Juan Puñal, Luis de. *Tirando de la manta.* Havana: Arroyo, Fernández y Cía., n.d.

Kiple, Kenneth F. *Blacks in Colonial Cuba, 1774–1899.* Gainesville: University Presses of Florida, 1976.

Kirk, John. *José Martí, Mentor of the Cuban Nation.* Gainesville: University Presses of Florida, 1983.

Knox, Philander. *The Spirit and Purpose of American Diplomacy.* N.p., 1910.

Lamar Schweyer, Alberto. *Como cayó el presidente Machado.* Madrid: Espasa-Calpe, S.A., 1941.

———. *La crisis del patriotismo.* 2d ed. Havana: Editorial Martí, 1929.

LeRiverend Brussone, Julio E. *La Habana (biografía de una provincia).* Havana: Imprenta "El Siglo XX," 1960.

———. *La república: dependencia y revolución.* 3d ed. Havana: Editorial de Ciencias Sociales, 1971.

Llaca M. Argudín, Francisco, ed. *Legislación sobre amnistía e indultas de la república de Cuba.* Havana: Cultural, S.A., 1933.

Lockmiller, David A. *Enoch H. Crowder: Soldier, Lawyer and Statesman.* Columbia: University of Missouri Press, 1955.

López Hidalgo, Ambrosio. *Cuba y la enmienda Platt.* Havana: Imprenta "El Siglo XX," 1921.

López Segrera, Franciso. *Raíces históricas de la revolución cubana (1868–1959).* Havana: Unión de Escritores y Artistas, 1981.

Lumen, Enrique. *La revolución cubana, 1902–1934.* México: Ediciones Bota, 1934.

Machado, Gerardo. *Por la patria libre.* Havana: Imprenta de F. Verdugo, 1926.

Machado y Ortega, Luis. *La enmienda Platt, estudio de su alcance e interpretación y doctrina sobre su aplicación.* Havana: Imprenta "El Siglo XX," 1922.

Marcos Suárez, Miguel de. *Carlos Mendieta*. Havana: Talleres Tipográficos de "El Magazine de la Raza," 1923.

Márquez Sterling, Carlos. *Historia de Cuba*. New York: Las Américas, 1963.

Martí, José. *Obras completas*. Ed. Jorge Quintana. Caracas: n.p., 1964.

Martínez Ortiz, Rafael. *Cuba: los primeros años de independencia*. 2 vols. 2d ed. Paris: Editorial "Le Livre Libre," 1921.

Masó, Calixto C. *Historia de Cuba*. Miami: Ediciones Universal, 1976.

Menocal, Raimundo. *Tres ensayos sobre la realidad cubana*. Havana: Imprenta O'Reilly, 1935.

Merchán, Rafael María. *Cuba, justificación de sus guerras de independencia*. 2d ed. Havana: Imprenta Nacional de Cuba, 1961.

Merino, Bernardo, and F. de Ibarzabal. *La revolución de febrero. Datos para la historia*. 2d ed. Havana: Librería Cervantes, 1918.

Mestre Amabile, Vicente. *Cuba, un año de república: hechos y notas*. Paris: Imprenta Charaire, 1933.

Millett, Allan Reed. *The Politics of Intervention: The Military Occupation of Cuba, 1906–1909*. Columbus: Ohio State University Press, 1968.

Millis, Walter. *The Martial Spirit. A Study of Our War with Spain*. Boston: Houghton Mifflin, 1931.

Montero, Tomás. *Grandezas y miserias*. Havana: Editorial "Alfa," 1944.

Montoro, Rafael. *El ideal autonomista*. Havana: Editorial Cuba, 1936.

Moreno, Francisco. *Cuba y su gente (apuntes para la historia)*. Madrid: Establecimiento Tipográfico de Enrique Teodora, 1887.

———. *El país chocolate (la inmoralidad en Cuba)*. Madrid: Imprenta de F. García Herrero, 1887.

Morris, Charles. *The War with Spain*. Philadelphia: J. B. Lippincott, 1899.

Munro, Dana G. *Intervention and Dollar Diplomacy in the Caribbean, 1900–1921*. Princeton, N.J.: Princeton University Press, 1964.

———. *The United States and the Caribbean Republics, 1921–1933*. Princeton, N.J.: Princeton University Press, 1974.

Muzaurieta, José M. *Manual del perfecto sinvergüenza*. Havana: Imprenta "El Siglo XX," 1922.

Navas, José. *La convulsión de febrero*. Matanzas: Imprenta y Monotypo "El Escritorio," 1917.

Núñez Machín, Ana. *Rubén Martínez Villena: hombre y época*. Havana: Editorial de Ciencias Sociales, 1974.

Ortega Rubio, Juan. *Historia de la regencia de María Cristina Habsbourg-Lorena*. 5 vols. Madrid: Imprenta, Litografía y Casa Editorial de Felipe González Rojas, 1905–1906.

Ortiz, Fernando. *La crisis política cubana (sus causes y remedios)*. Havana: Imprenta y Papelería "La Universal," 1919.

———. *Cuban Counterpoint: Tobacco and Sugar*. Trans. Harriet de Onis. New York: Random House, 1970.

———. *Las responsabilidades de los Estados Unidos en los males de Cuba*. Washington, D.C.: Cuban Information Bureau, 1932.

Pardo Suárez, Vicente. *Funerales y responso*. Havana: Imprenta de Rambla, Bouza y Cía., 1926.

Peraza, Carlos G. *Machado, crímenes y horrores de un régimen*. Havana: Cultural, S.A., 1933.

Pérez, Louis A., Jr. *Army Politics in Cuba, 1898–1958*. Pittsburgh, Pa.: University of Pittsburgh Press, 1976.

Pérez de la Riva, Juan, et al. *La república neocolonial*. 2 vols. Havana: Editorial de Ciencias Sociales, 1975–1978.

Pi y Margall, Francisco, and Francisco Pi y Arsuaga. *Historia de España en el Siglo XIX*. 7 vols. Barcelona: Miguel Segui, 1902.

Pichardo, Hortensia. *Documentos para la historia de Cuba (época colonial)*. Havana: Editorial del Consejo Nacional de Universidades, 1965.

Pino Santos, Oscar. *El asalto a Cuba por la oligarquía yanqui*. Havana: Casa de las Américas. 1973.

Portillo, Lorenzo G. del. *La guerra de Cuba (el primer año). Apuntes*. Key West: Imprenta "La Propaganda," 1896.

Portuondo del Prado, Fernando. *Historia de Cuba*. 6th ed. Havana: Instituto Cubano del Libro, 1965.

Portuondo Linares, Serafín. *Los independientes de color. Historia del Partido Independiente de Color*. Havana: Ministerio de Educación, 1950.

Primelles, León. *Crónica cubana, 1919–1922*. Havana: Editorial Lex, 1957.

Pujol, Miguel Alonso. *Ensayo de sociología económica*. Havana: Imprenta Avisador Comercial, 1928.

Quesada, Gonzalo de. *Archivo de Gonzalo de Quesada. Epistolario*. Ed. Gonzalo de Quesada y Miranda. 2 vols. Havana: Imprenta "El Siglo XX," 1948–1951.

Raggi Ageo, Carlos M. *Condiciones económicas y sociales de la república de Cuba*. Havana: Editorial Lex, 1944.

Ramos, José Antonio. *Manual del perfecto fulanista. Apuntes para el estudio de nuestra dinámica político-social*. Havana: Jesús Montero, 1916.

Real y Tejera, Emilio del. *La industria azucarera*. Havana: A. Dorrbecker, 1928.

Reverter Delmas, Emilio. *Cuba española. Reseña histórica de la insurrección cubana en 1895*. 6 vols. Barcelona: Centro Editorial del Alberto Martín, 1897–1899.

Riera Hernández, Mario. *Cuba política, 1899–1955*. Havana: Impresora Modelo, 1955.

———. *Historial obrero cubano, 1574–1965*. Miami: Rema Press, 1965.

Ripoll, Carlos. *La generación del 23 en Cuba*. New York: Las Américas, 1968.

Rivero Muñiz, José. *El movimiento laboral cubano durante el período 1909–1911*. Santa Clara: Universidad de Las Villas, 1962.

Roa, Raúl. *La revolución del 30 se fué a bolina*. Havana: Editorial de Ciencias Sociales, 1976.

Rodríguez Morejón, Gerardo. *Menocal*. Havana: Cárdenas y Cía., 1941.

Roig de Leuchsenring, Emilio. *Análisis y consecuencias de la intervención norteamericana en los asuntos interiores de Cuba*. Havana: Imprenta "El Siglo XX," 1923.

————. *Máximo Gómez: el libertador de Cuba y el primer ciudadano de la república*. Havana: Oficina del Historiador de la Ciudad de La Habana, 1959.

Root, Elihu. *The Military and Colonial Policy of the United States*. Ed. Robert Bacon and James Brown Scott. Cambridge, Mass.: Harvard University Press, 1916.

————. *Miscellaneous Addresses*. Ed. Robert Bacon and James Brown Scott. Cambridge, Mass.: Harvard University Press, 1917.

Santovenia, Emeterio S., and Raúl M. Shelton. *Cuba y su historia*. 3 vols. 2d ed. Miami: Cuba Corporation, 1966.

Schroeder, Susan. *Cuba: A Handbook of Historical Statistics*. Boston: G. K. Hall, 1982.

Secades y Japón, Manuel. *La justicia en Cuba. Patriotas y traidores*. 2 vols. Havana: Imprenta P. Fernández y Cía., 1912–1914.

Serviat, Pedro. *40 aniversario de la fundación del partido comunista*. Havana: Editorial EIR, 1965.

Sims, Harold D. *Descolonización en México: el conflicto entre mexicanos y españoles (1821–1831)*. México: Fondo de Cultura Económica, 1982.

————. *La expulsión de los españoles de México (1821–1828)*. México: Fondo de Cultura Económica, 1974.

Smith, Robert J. *The United States and Cuba: Business and Diplomacy, 1917–1960*. New Haven, Conn.: College and University Press, 1960.

Soto, Lionel. *La revolución del 33*. 3 vols. Havana: Editorial de Ciencias Sociales, 1977.

Souza, B. *Ensayo histórico sobre la invasión*. Havana: Imprenta del Ejército, 1948.

Suchlicki, Jaime. *University Students and Revolution in Cuba, 1920–1968*. Miami: University of Miami Press, 1969.

Tabares del Real, José A. *Guiteras*. Havana: Instituto Cubano del Libro, 1973.

Taboadela, José Antonio. *Cuestiones económicas de actualidad*. Havana: Imprenta de "El Fígaro," 1929.

Thomas, Hugh. *Cuba, the Pursuit of Freedom*. New York: Harper and Row, 1971.

Varela Zequeira, Eduardo. *La política en 1905, o episodios de una lucha electoral*. Havana: Imprenta y Papelería de Rambla y Bouza, 1905.

Varona, Enrique José. *De la colonia a la república*. Havana: Sociedad Editorial Cuba Contemporánea, 1919.

Velasco, Carlos de. *Aspectos nacionales*. Havana: Jesús Montero, 1915.

The Visit of the President-Elect of Cuba General Gerardo Machado to the United States in April, 1925. Washington, D.C.: Capital Press, 1925.

Wallich, Henry Christopher. *Monetary Problems of an Export Economy*. Cambridge, Mass.: Harvard University Press, 1950.

Willets, Gilson. *The Triumph of Yankee Doodle*. New York: F. Tennyson Neely, 1898.

Williams, William Appleman. *The Tragedy of American Diplomacy*. 2d ed. New York: Dell, 1962.

Wright, Irene A. *Cuba*. New York: Macmillan, 1910.

Yglesia Martínez, Teresita. *Cuba: primera república, segunda intervención.* Havana: Editorial de Ciencias Sociales, 1976.
———. *El segundo ensayo de república.* Havana: Editorial de Ciencias Sociales, 1980.

Articles

Abad, L. V. de. "The Cuban Problem." *Gunton's Magazine* 21 (December 1901), 515–25.

Armas, Rogelio de. "Los partidos políticos y los problemas sociales." *Cuba Contemporánea* 2 (July 1913), 225–29.

Atkins, Edwin F. "The Spaniards of the Island of Cuba." *Economic Bulletin of Cuba* 1 (March 1922), 133–34.

Beveridge, Albert J. "Cuba and Congress." *North American Review* 172 (April 1901), 535–50.

Brownell, Atherton. "The Commercial Annexation of Cuba." *Appleton's Magazine* 8 (October 1906), 406–11.

Buell, Raymond Leslie. "Cuba and the Platt Amendment." *Foreign Policy Association Information Service* 5 (April 17, 1929), 37–62.

Capo-Rodríguez, Pedro. "The Platt Amendment." *American Journal of International Law* 17 (October 1923), 761–65.

Carpenter, Frank G. "Cuba in 1905." *Cuba Review* 3 (November 1905), 11.

Carrión, Miguel de. "El desenvolvimiento social de Cuba en los últimos veinte años." *Cuba Contemporánea* 27 (September 1921), 5–27.

Castellanos, Jorge. "El pensamiento social de Máximo Gómez." *América* (Havana), February–March 1946, 22–28.

Céspedes, José María. "Empleo-manía." *Cuba y America* 3 (April 1899), 6–8.

Clark, Victor S. "Labor Conditions in Cuba." *Bulletin of the Department of Labor* 7 (July 1902), 663–793.

Corbitt, Duvon C. "Immigration in Cuba." *Hispanic American Historical Review* 22 (May, 1942), 302–08.

Cronon, E. David. "Interpreting the New Good Neighbor Policy: The Cuban Crisis of 1933." *Hispanic American Historical Review* 39 (November 1959), 538–67.

Cummins, Lejeune. "The Formulation of the 'Platt Amendment.'" *The Americas* (April 1967), 370–89.

Currier, Charles Warren. "Why Cuba Should Be Independent." *Forum* 30 (October, 1900), 139–46.

Davis, Norman H. "Wanted: A Consistent Latin American Policy." *Foreign Affairs* 4 (July, 1931), 547–68.

"El desarrollo industrial de Cuba." *Cuba Socialista*, no. 56 (April 1966), 128–83.

Estrade, Paul. "Cuba en 1895: las tres vías de la burguesía insular." *Casa de las Américas* 13 (September–October 1972), 55–65.

Ferrara, Orestes. "La lucha presidencial en Cuba." *La Reforma Social* 17 (August 1920), 357–60.

———. "Supervisión electoral o intervención permanente." *La Reforma Social* 13 (March 1919), 201–10.

García Bárcena, Rafael. "Razón y sinrazón del 4 de septiembre." *Bohemia* 44 (September 7, 1952), 60–61.

Gay, Enrique. "Génesis de la enmienda Platt." *Cuba Contemporánea* 60 (May–August 1926), 47–63.

"General Survey of Wages in Cuba, 1931 and 1932." *Monthly Labor Review* (December 1932), 1403–11.

Giberga, Eliseo. "Las ideas políticas en Cuba en el siglo XIX." *Cuba Contemporánea* 10 (April 1916), 347–81.

Grobart, Fabio. "The Cuban Working Class Movement from 1925 to 1933." *Science and Society* 39 (Spring 1975), 75–103.

"La guerrita de febrero de 1917." *Boletín del Archivo Nacional* 61 (1962), 207–56.

Guggenheim, Harry F. "Amending the Platt Amendment." *Foreign Affairs* 12 (April 1934), 448–57.

Guiral Moreno, Mario. "Nuestro problemas políticos, económicos y sociales." *Cuba Contemporánea* 5 (August 1914), 401–24.

———. "El problema de la burocracia en Cuba," *Cuba Contemporánea* II (August, 1913), 252–67.

Hart, Francis R. "Changes in Our Relations with Spanish-America During the Last Quarter Century." *Harvard Business Review* 6 (July 1928), 385–93.

Hitchman, James H. "The Platt Amendment Revisited: A Bibliographical Survey." *The Americas* 23 (April 1967), 343–69.

———. "U.S. Control Over Cuban Sugar Production, 1898–1902." *Journal of Inter-American Studies and World Affairs* 12 (January 1970), 90–106.

Hinton, Richard J. "Cuban Reconstruction." *North American Review* 164 (January 1899), 92–102.

Holbo, Paul S. "Presidential Leadership in Foreign Affairs: William McKinley and the Turpie Foraker Amendment." *American Historical Review* 72 (July 1967), 1321–35.

Horrego Estuch, Leopoldo. "Martí: su ideología." *Bohemia* 57 (January 22, 1965), 99–101.

Ibarra, Jorge. "Agosto de 1906: una intervencion amañada." In Jorge Ibarra, *Approximaciones a Clio*. Havana: Editorial de Ciencias Sociales, 1979.

Ingles, William. "The Collapse of the Cuban House of Cards." *Harper's Weekly* 1 (October 20, 1906), 1488–91, 1505.

Ireland, Gordon. "Observations Upon the Status of Corporations in Cuba Since 1898." *University of Pennsylvania Law Review* 76 (November 1927), 43–73.

Laurent y Dubet, Julio. "Datos esenciales de la expedición de Gibara." *Bohemia* 25 (August 20, 1935), 24–25, 72.

León, Rubén de. "La verdad de lo ocurrido desde el cuatro de septiembre." *Bohemia* 25 (February 4, 1934), 30–31, 44–45, 48.

LeReverend Brussone, Julio. "La penetración económica extranjera en Cuba." *Revista de la Biblioteca Nacional "José Martí"* 3 (January–March 1966), 5–20.

Livi-Bacci, Massimo. "Fertility and Population Growth in Spain in the Eighteenth and Nineteenth Centuries." *Dædulus* 97 (Spring 1968), 523–35.

López, Jacinto. "El fracaso del General Crowder en Cuba." *La Reforma Social* 20 (June 1921), 99–121.

———. "El problema del sufragio en Cuba." *La Reforma Social* 14 (May 1919), 53–56.

Lyle, Eugene P. Jr. "The Control of the Caribbean." *The World's Work* 10 (September 1905), 6664–69.

Masiques Landeta, Francisco. "Puntos sobresalientes del septembrismo." *Bohemia* 31 (September 11, 1949), 54–57, 83.

Matthews, Franklin. "The Reconstruction of Cuba." *Harper's Weekly* 42 (July 14, 1899).

Munro, Dana G. "Our New Relation to Latin America." *Unpopular Review* 10 (October–December, 1918), 307–18.

Ortiz, Fernando. "La decadencia cubana." *Revista Bimestre Cubana* 19 (January–February 1924), 17–44.

———. "La reforma electoral de Crowder en Cuba." *La Reforma Social* 20 (July 1921), 214–25.

Parker, John H. "How the Cuban Problem Might be Solved." *American Reviews of Reviews* 37 (January 1908), 65–70.

Pazos, Felipe. "La economía cubana en el siglo XIX." *Revista Bimestre Cubana* 47 (January–February 1941), 83–106.

Pennington, E. H. "The Square Deal in Business." *Pan American Magazine* 31 (July 1920), 169–72.

Pérez, Lisandro. "Iron Mining and Socio-Demographic Change in Eastern Cuba, 1884–1940." *Journal of Latin American Studies* 14 (November 1982), 381–405.

Pérez, Louis A., Jr. "The Military and Electoral Politics: The Cuban Election of 1920." *Military Affairs* 37 (February 1973), 5–8.

Platt, Orville H. "Cuba's Claim Upon the United States." *North American Review* 175 (August 1902), 145–51.

———. "The Pacification of Cuba." *Independent* 53 (June 27, 1901), 1464–68.

———. "Our Relations to the People of Cuba and Porto Rico." *Annals of the American Academy of Political and Social Science* 18 (July 1901), 145–59.

———. "The Solution of the Cuban Problem." *The World's Work* 2 (May 1901), 729–35.

Portell Vilá, Herminio. "La Chambelona en Camagüey." *Bohemia* 52 (May 8, 1960), 12–13, 119.

———. "La Chambelona en Las Villas." *Bohemia* 52 (May 15, 1960), 36–37, 98.

———. "La Chambelona en Oriente." *Bohemia* 52 (April 24, 1960), 12–13, 124.

———. "La danza de los millones." *Bohemia* 52 (June 5, 1960), 44–45, 79.

Quintana, Jorge. "Lo que costó a Cuba la guerra de 1895." *Bohemia* 52 (September 11, 1960), 4–6, 107–108.

Rea, George Bronson. "The Destruction of Sugar Estates in Cuba." *Harper's Weekly* 41 (October 16, 1897), 10–34.

Rodríguez Altunaga, Rafael. "Cuba's Case for the Repeal of the Platt Amendment: The Views of President Machado." *Current History* 26 (September 1927), 925–27.

Roig de Leuchsenring, Emilio. "La colonia superviva: Cuba a los veintidos años de república." *Cuba Contemporánea* 36 (December 1924), 249–61.

———. "La ingerencia norteamericana en los asuntos interiores de Cuba." *Cuba Contemporánea* 30 (September 1922), 36–61.

———. "El Tratado Permanente de 1903 y su arbitraria modificación—no abrogación—por Norteamérica, en 1934." *Revista Bimestre Cubana* 39 (Primero Semestre, 1937), 389–403.

Rowe, Leo S. "The Extension of American Influence in the West Indies." *North American Review* 175 (August 1902), 254–62.

———. "Our Trade Relations with South America." *North American Review* 184 (March 1907), 513–19.

Sanguily, Manuel. "Sobre la génesis de la enmienda Platt." *Cuba Contemporánea* 30 (October 1922), 117–25.

Scott, James B. "The Origin and Purpose of the Platt Amendment." *American Journal of International Law* 3 (July 1914), 585–91.

Scroggs, William O. "The American Investment in Latin America." *Foreign Affairs* 10 (April 1932), 502–04.

Smith, Daniel M. "Bainbridge Colby and the Good Neighbor Policy, 1920–1921." *Mississippi Valley Historical Review* 50 (June 1963), 56–78.

Smith, Osgood. "Foreign Corporations in Cuba." *Corporation Trust Company Journal* 12 (September–October 1909), supplement.

Sola, José Sixto de. "Los extranjeros en Cuba." *Cuba Contemporánea* 8 (June 1915), 105–28.

Spinden, Herbert. "Elecciones espurias en Cuba." *La Reforma Social* 19 (April 1921), 353–67.

———. "Shall the United States Intervene in Cuba?" *The World's Week* 41 (March 1921), 465–83.

Stimson, Henry L. "Bases of American Foreign Policy During the Past Four Years." *Foreign Affairs* 11 (April 1933), 383–96.

"Synopsis of Reports by Different Land Companies Respecting their Properties Cuba." *The Cuba Review* 5 (December 1906), 75–79.

Thomson, Charles A. "The Cuban Revolution: Fall of Machado." *Foreign Policy Reports* 11 (December 18, 1935), 251–60.

———. "The Cuban Revolution: Reform and Reaction." *Foreign Policy Reports* 11 (January 1, 1936), 262–76.

Torriente, Cosme de la. "The Platt Amendment." *Foreign Affairs* 8 (April 1930), 364–78.

Villoldo, Julio. "Las reelecciones." *Cuba Contemporánea* 10 (March 1916), 237–52.

Welles, Sumner. "Is America Imperialistic?" *Atlantic Monthly* 134 (September 1924), 412–23.

Whelpley, J. D. "Cuba of To-Day and To-Morrow." *Atlantic Monthly* 86 (July 1900), 45–52.

Williams, Herbert Pelham. "The Outlook in Cuba." *Atlantic Monthly* 83 (June 1899), 827–36.

Williams, William Applemen. "Latin America: Laboratory of American Foreign Policy." *Inter-American Economic Affairs* 11 (Autumn 1957), 3–40.

Wilson, F. M. Huntington. "The Relation of Government to Foreign Investment." *The Annals of the American Academy of Political and Social Science* 68 (November 1916), 298–311.

Wolf, Donna M. "The Cuban 'Gente de Color' and the Independence Movement, 1879–1895." *Revista/Review Interamericana* 5 (Fall 1975), 403–21.

Wood, Leonard. "The Future of Cuba." *Independent* 54 (January 23, 1902), 193–94.

Index

Pitt Latin American Series

COLE BLASIER, EDITOR

Argentina

Argentina in the Twentieth Century
David Rock, Editor

Discreet Partners: Argentina and the USSR Since 1917
Aldo César Vacs

Juan Perón and the Reshaping of Argentina
Frederick C. Turner and José Enrique Miguens, Editors

The Life, Music, and Times of Carlos Gardel
Simon Collier

Brazil

The Politics of Social Security in Brazil
James M. Malloy

Urban Politics in Brazil: The Rise of Populism, 1925–1945
Michael L. Conniff

Colombia

Gaitán of Colombia: A Political Biography
Richard E. Sharpless

Roads to Reason: Transportation, Administration, and Rationality in Colombia
Richard E. Hartwig

Cuba

Army Politics in Cuba, 1898–1958
Louis A. Pérez, Jr.

Cuba Under the Platt Amendment
Louis A. Pérez, Jr.

Cuba Between Empires, 1878–1902
Louis A. Pérez, Jr.

Cuba, Castro, and the United States
Philip W. Bonsal

Cuba in the World
Cole Blasier and Carmelo Mesa-Lago, Editors

Cuban Studies, Volume 16
Carmelo Mesa-Lago, Editor

Intervention, Revolution, and Politics in Cuba, 1913–1921
Louis A. Pérez, Jr.

Revolutionary Change in Cuba
Carmelo Mesa-Lago, Editor

The United States and Cuba: Hegemony and Dependent Development, 1880–1934
Jules Robert Benjamin

Mexico

Essays on Mexican Kinship
Hugo G. Nutini, Pedro Carrasco, and James M. Taggart, Editors

The Mexican Republic: The First Decade, 1823–1832
Stanley C. Green

The Politics of Mexican Oil
George W. Grayson

Voices, Visions, and a New Reality: Mexican Fiction Since 1970
J. Ann Duncan

US Policies

Cuba, Castro, and the United States
Philip W. Bonsal

The Hovering Giant: U.S. Responses to Revolutionary Change in Latin America
Cole Blasier

Illusions of Conflict: Anglo-American Diplomacy Toward Latin America
Joseph Smith

Puerto Rico and the United States, 1917–1933
Truman R. Clark

The United States and Cuba: Hegemony and Dependent Development, 1880–1934
Jules Robert Benjamin

The United States and Latin America in the 1980s: Contending Perspectives on a Decade of Crisis
Kevin J. Middlebrook and Carlos Rico, Editors

USSR Policies

Discreet Partners: Argentina and the USSR Since 1917
Aldo César Vacs

The Giant's Rival: The USSR and Latin America
Cole Blasier

Other National Studies

Barrios in Arms: Revolution in Santo Domingo
José A. Moreno

Beyond the Revolution: Bolivia Since 1952
James M. Malloy and Richard S. Thorn, Editors

Black Labor on a White Canal: Panama, 1904–1981
Michael L. Conniff

The Origins of the Peruvian Labor Movement, 1883–1919
Peter Blanchard

The Overthrow of Allende and the Politics of Chile, 1964–1976
Paul E. Sigmund

Panajachel: A Guatemalan Town in Thirty-Year Perspective
Robert E. Hinshaw

Peru and the International Monetary Fund
Thomas Scheetz

Rebirth of the Paraguayan Republic: The First Colorado Era,
1878–1904
Harris G. Warren

Social Security
The Politics of Social Security in Brazil
James M. Malloy

Social Security in Latin America: Pressure Groups, Stratification, and
Inequality
Carmelo Mesa-Lago

Other Studies
Adventurers and Proletarians: The Story of Migrants in Latin America
Magnus Morner, with the collaboration of Harold Sims

Authoritarianism and Corporatism in Latin America
James M. Malloy, Editor

Constructive Change in Latin America
Cole Blasier, Editor

Female and Male in Latin America: Essays
Ann Pescatello, Editor

Public Policy in Latin America: A Comparative Survey
John W. Sloan

Selected Latin American One-Act Plays
Francesca Collecchia and Julio Matas, Editors and Translators

The State and Capital Accumulation in Latin America: Brazil, Chile,
Mexico
Christian Anglade and Carlos Fortin, Editors

Transnational Corporations and the Latin American Automobile
Industry
Rhys Jenkins